Charles Bernard Gibson

The History of the County and City of Cork

Charles Bernard Gibson

The History of the County and City of Cork

ISBN/EAN: 9783337326128

Printed in Europe, USA, Canada, Australia, Japan

Cover: Foto ©ninafisch / pixelio.de

More available books at **www.hansebooks.com**

THE

HISTORY OF THE COUNTY

AND

CITY OF CORK.

BY

REV. C. B. GIBSON, M.R.I.A.

"The spreading Lee, that like an island fayre,
Encloseth Corke with his divided flood."—*Spenser.*

"The Mayor of the town, with his brethren, received him in ther skarlet gowns, and ther typetts of velvett, after the English fashion, and made us the beste chere that ever we had in ower lyves."—*State Paper.*

IN TWO VOLUMES.

VOL. I.

LONDON:
THOMAS C. NEWBY, 30, WELBECK STREET.
1861.

CORK:
PRINTED BY GUY BROTHERS,
ACADEMY STREET.

DEDICATED

TO

EDMUND BURKE ROCHE,

BARON FERMOY, M.P.

LIEUTENANT AND CUSTOS ROTULORUM,

OF THE

COUNTY AND CITY OF CORK.

Dedication.

TO

THE RIGHT HONORABLE LORD FERMOY.

My Dear Lord,

I have much pleasure in dedicating this History of the County and City of Cork to you. It is not all that I could desire, but it is as good as I can make it.

I have the honor to remain,

My Dear Lord,

Yours very sincerely,

CHARLES B. GIBSON.

Monkstown, Cork,
Feb. 1, 1861.

CONTENTS.

Chapter.   Page.

I.—The Mac Carthys and O'Briens, -   -   -   -   1

II.—The Conquest of Cork—The Distribution of the Kingdom among the Anglo-Norman Knights, -   -   -   -   13

III.—The Earls of Desmond—Irish Literature and Laws, -   -   44

IV.—Thomas of Drogheda—Irish Poets and Poor Scholars,   -   74

V.—State of Society—Lambert Simnel and Perkin Warbeck—City Charters.   -   -   -   -   -   84

VI.—The Normans—The Commoners—The Army—The Church,   -   99

VII.—The Earls of Desmond, Ormond and Kildare,   -   -   113

VIII.—The Old Countess of Desmond—The Court Page, -   -   124

IX.—Sir John of Desmond—The Court Page—James Fitz-John, the Pretended Earl, -   -   -   -   -   130

X.—The Pretended Earl—The Court Page—Lord Leonard Gray—Sir Anthony St. Leger,   -   -   -   -   151

XI.—Edward VI.—Mary and Philip—The Earl of Desmond,   -   163

XII.—Garrett styled the Great Earl of Desmond,   -   -   182

XIII.—Irish Rulers—Lord President of Munster—Lord Deputy—Manners and Customs—Dress,   -   -   -   211

XIV.—The Landing at Smerwick—Lord Grey—Spenser—Raleigh—
  Lord Roche—The Death of the Earl of Desmond,   - 234

XV.—A Parliament—The Undertakers—Florence Mac Carthy—
  O'Neill and O'Donnell,   -   -   -   - 269

XVI.—The Poet Spenser,   -   -   -   -   - 296

XVII.—The Earl of Essex—Death of Sir Thomas Norris—Warham
  St. Leger and Hugh Maguire Slain—Sir George Carew and
  James Fitz-Thomas,   -   -   -   - 316

XVIII.—Florence Mac Carthy—John Annias—Sir George Carew, - 337

XIX.—The Spaniards at Kinsale,   -   -   -   - 354

XX.—Don Juan in Cork,   -   -   -   -   - 375

XXI.—The Siege of Dunboy Castle,   -   -   -   - 384

XXII.—Blarney Castle and Cormac Mac Dermot Mac Carthy,   - 403

THE HISTORY OF CORK.

CHAPTER I.

THE MAC CARTHYS AND O'BRIENS.

A.D. 976—1170.

THE province of Munster had been, from an early period, possessed by the Eugenians, or Mac Carthys of Cork, and the Dalcassians, or O'Briens of Limerick. The king of the whole of Munster*—for this province had a king paramount—was chosen alternately from these two great families. This arrangement was finally interrupted on the accession of Brian Boru to the throne of Limerick, or Thomond, whose brother, Mahon, had been treacherously and barbarously murdered by Molloy, the ancestor of the O'Mahonys of Cork, and Donovan, or O'Donovan, who lived at Bruree,† *now*

---

* *Munster*, from Mumho, a king of Munster, about 800 years before Christ. Munster, in old time, was divided into five Munsters, viz :—Ormond, Thomond, Desmond, Middle Munster, and West Munster.

† *Who lived at Brurec.*—The O'Donovans were the original princes of Carbery, on the south-western coast of the county of Cork, of which territory they were dispossessed by the ancestors of the famous Florence Mac Carthy, of Kilbrittan castle.

in the county Limerick, then in the kingdom of Cork. The murder is thus recorded in the Dublin copy of the Annals of Innisfallen :—

A.D. 976. " Donovan, son of Cathal, Prince of Cairbre Ardhbha, treacherously seized upon Mahon, son of Kennedy, in his own house, at Brugh-righ, where he was under the protection of Colum, son of Ciaragan, Bishop of Cork, (successor of Barra,) who guaranteed his safety, to make peace with Maolmhuadh, son of Bran, to whom, and to whose brothers, Teige and Brian Donovan treacherously delivered Mahon, who was murdered by them, without respect to the saint [recte, holy man] who had ensured his safety."

We have a more circumstantial account of this murder and its consequences, in a curious Irish work, called *Cogadh Gaeidheal re Gallaibh*, that is, " War of the Gaels [or Irish] with the Danes." We give an abstract from Doctor O'Donovan's translation :—

Donovan and Molloy, chiefs of Desmond, perceiving the increasing power of the O'Briens, and fearing that if it were not checked, the crown of Munster would remain in the family for ever, united with Ivor, king of the Danes of Limerick, to destroy Mahon, who was then king of Thomond and Ormond. Ivor suggested that Donovan should invite Mahon to a banquet at his house at Bruree. Although Mahon suspected the loyalty of his host, he accepted the invitation, for "his safety had been guaranteed by Columb Mac Kiergan, successor of St. Barry, bishop of Cork, and other of the clergy of Munster," in other words, by solemn oaths, in which the names of these pious men were invoked. He therefore attended the feast, where he was seized and delivered into the hands of his ruthless foes, Molloy and Ivor, who were waiting for him in a neighbouring wood, with a body of Irish and Danish troops. Molloy ordered his people instantly to despatch him. His order was obeyed. "A bright and sharp sword" was plunged into his heart, and his blood stained St. Barry's Gospel,* which he held in his hand, to protect him by its sanctity. Two of the clergy of St. Barry witnessed the transaction from a hillock. It is said that when Mahon received the stroke, he cast the gospel from his hand, with so much force, that it struck the breast of one of the priests of Cork. "What hast thou done?" demanded the priest, of Molloy. "Cure that man if he come to thee," was the sneering reply. The priest, in his wrath, cursed Molloy bitterly, predicting that his grave would be dug near the side of the hill where they stood, and that the sun would never shine upon it. The story goes that Molloy lost his eye-sight, was slain in a hut, constructed of alder trees, and buried on the north side of a hill, in a spot where the sun never shines. We learn from the Dublin copy of the Annals of Innisfallen, that Molloy was slain by Morough, son of Brian Boru:

"A.D. 978. Brian, son of Kennedy, and his son Moragh, at the head of the Dal-glais, fought the battle of Bealach-leachta, against *Maolmuaidh* [Molloy] son of Bran, at the head of the Eugenians, with the additional forces of the Danes of Munster. In this battle, Maolmuaidh was slain by the hand of Moragh, son of Brian; two hundred of the Danes were also slain, together with a great number of the Irish" Some think this battle was fought at Bearna-dhearg, (Red-Chair) on Sliabh-Caoin. An ancient manuscript says at Cnoc-ramhra, south of Mallow, on the road to Cork; another ancient manuscript, at Magh Cromtha (Macroom), near Muisire-na-mona-moire, or Mushera mountain."

* "*St. Barry's Gospel.*"—There is no such manuscript or book now in existence. Doctors Todd and O'Donovan, of Trinity College, agree with me in thinking it must have been a copy of the Four Gospels, written by the priests of Saint Finn Barr's of Cork.

Brian Boru is said to have given expression to his sorrowful revenge for his brother's death, in an elegy, which we have taken the liberty of paraphrasing, with something *more* than a poet's license.

> My heart within this breast had burst,
> If vengeance I had longer nursed:
> A king and brother! deed accursed!
> Oh! Mahon, generous and brave,
> I little thought this early grave,
> Would hide thy manly frame;
> Would thou hadst fallen behind thy shield,
> A victor in some bloody field,
> And poets sang thy fame.
> Mahon, confiding in a knave,
> Saw foeman's face in the clear wave,
> That gave his own.
> The church her safety pledged in vain;
> What power divine could bind a Dane,
> With breast of stone.
> The blood that warmed thy tender heart,
> Of Barry's Gospel stained a part—
> Ochone! Ochone!
> *Their* blood shall flow for this vile deed;
> I'll crush these vipers and their seed!
> Now, Ivor, you or I shall bleed.

There is an old harp in the museum of Trinity College, Dublin, called "Brian Boru's harp." Doctor Petrie says it belongs to a later period; but I believe there can be no doubt that this Irish monarch, like Richard Cœur de Lion, used the harp, or ceannaircruit, as well as the sword and battle-axe. The tradition of the harp is that it was sent to Rome after the death of Brian, who fell at Clontarf, where it remained more than five centuries, and was then presented by one of the Popes to Henry VIII., by whom it was returned to Ireland, "to be figured on his coins, in compliment to the musical taste of the Irish." The harp, when perfect, had thirty strings.

Brian Boru, who became king of Thomond, on his brother Mahon's death, directed his first efforts against Donovan's allies, the Danes of Limerick,* and slew Ivor, (who first suggested the murder,) and two of his sons. Upon their death, Donovan sent for Harold, another of Ivor's sons, whom Brian also slew, plundering Limerick, which was in their hands. He then assumed the chief kingship of Munster, and left no stone unturned to bring the whole province under his iron heel, and that of his successors.

The murder of Mahon was fearfully avenged, more than a century after, by the murder of Cormac, the bishop king of Desmond, one of the progenitors of the noble house of Mac Carthy. The Mac Carthy's are the descendants of Aenghus, the first christian king of Munster. He flourished in the fifth century. He received the rite of baptism from the hands of the great Irish Apostle, Saint Patrick, on the Rock of Cashel. An interesting circumstance, well calculated to put the faith of the new convert to the test, occurred on that occasion. Saint Patrick's crosier was so placed as to pierce the king's foot to the bone. He supposing it to be part of the ceremony of initiation, bore it like a christian soldier, without wincing. Aenghus fell in battle at Cell-Osnadha.† There is a story that his

---

* *Donovan's allies, the Danes of Limerick* :—"A battle was gained by Brian, son of Ceinneidigh, over the foreigners of Luimneach, and Donnabhan, son of Cathal, Lord of Ui-Fidhgeinte, wherein the foreigners of Luimneach were defeated and slaughtered."—*Four Masters, A.D.* 976.

† *Cell-Osnadha* :—"This place is now called Kelliston, and is situated in the barony of Forth, in the county of Carlow, and there exists among the old natives of the place, a most curious and remarkably vivid tradition of this battle, which explains the Irish name of the place as denoting '*Church of the groans*,' and which it received, according to this tradition, from the lamentations of the Munster women after the loss of their husbands and brothers in the battle."—*Four Masters, Dr. O'Donovan's edition, A D.* 487.

death, and that of his queen, Eithne,* had been predicted by St. Kieran, in consequence of some horrid crimes imputed to her. An Irish poet thus records his fall :—

> Died the branch, the spreading tree of gold,
> Aenghus the laudable son of Nadfraech,
> His prosperity was cut off by Illann,
> In the battle of Cell-Osnadha the foul.

"This Aenghus," (writes Doctor O'Donovan,) "is the common ancestor of the families of Mac Carthy, O'Keeffe, O'Sullivan, and O'Callaghan, now so widely spread in Ireland, England, and America, and even on the continent of Europe, where some of them bear coronets. If the saplings of this 'spreading tree of gold,' Aenghus Mac Nadfraech, could now be reckoned in the different countries in which they have pullulated, it would appear that they are vastly numerous, and that, as the multiplication of a race is a blessing, king Aenghus has reaped the full benefit of that 'alma benedictio' imparted by St. Patrick, when he baptized him at Cashel, and, by a singular mistake, put his faith to the trial, by piercing his foot with the top of his crosier." There is nothing very remarkable in this pullulation, for the descendants of the blood-royal in England, may now be reckoned by tens of thousands.— *Vide* Sir Bernard Burke on the " Vicissitudes of Noble Families."

The Mac Carthys, the kings of Desmond, or Cork, derived their name from Carthach. The son of Carthach was the first of the family who was called Mac Carthaigh

---

* *Eithne:*—There is a story told of her having being fed by her fosterers, with the flesh of children, in order to fit her for early marriage. Keating's Ireland, preface xxi. Tu enim, filia, et Dominus noster Rex, uno die, occidemini ab inimicis vestris : sed det Dominus vobis misericordiam.—*Acta Sanctorum. p.* 460.

or *Mac Carthy.* Cormac, son of Muireadhach,* and grandson of Mac Carthy, was the bishop-king of Desmond, perhaps the most distinguished member of this noble family. Doctors O'Brien and Lanigan, think he was merely honored with the title of bishop for his piety and liberality to the church, but they were mistaken, for we find his death thus recorded in the Annals of Kilronan, which were compiled in the fifteenth century:—

A.D. 1138.—"Cormac, grandson of Carthach, chief king of Desmond, and bishop-king of Ireland, in his time, for piety and the bestowal of jewels and wealth to the clergy and their churches, and for ecclesiastical wealth to God, in books and implements, fell treacherously by Thomond, and a blessing on his soul."

It is also recorded in the Four Masters, thus:—

A.D. 1138.—"Cormac, son of Muireadhach, son of Carthach, lord of Desmond, and bishop-king of Ireland, in his time, for his bestowal of jewels and wealth to the clergy and to the churches, the improver of territories and churches, was treacherously slain in his own house, by Toirdhealbhach, the son of Diarmaid O'Brien, and by the two sons of O'Connor Kerry."

The antiquarian may see, at the present day, the stone-roofed church on the rock of Cashel, called Cormac's Chapel, which Doctor Petrie styles "one of the most curious and perfect churches, in the Norman style, in the British Empire." Here we are pointed to king Cormac's tomb, in which was discovered a crosier of "exceedingly beautiful workmanship." It

---

* *Cormac, son of Muireadhach.*—Some are in the habit of confounding Cormac the bishop-king of Desmond, with Cormac, son of Cuileannan, king of Cashel, who was "a king, a bishop, an anchorite, and a scribe, profoundly learned in the Scotia tongue." This Cormac was slain in 927, at the battle at Bealach-Mughna, or rather was beheaded after the battle. The site of this battle is still pointed out, and the stone on which the king's head was cut off by a common kearn This Cormac was the author of an ancient Irish Glossary, called Sanason Chormaic, and is also said to have compiled the Psalter of Cashel.

is now in the possession of Doctor Petrie, from whom we have the following description :—

"The head is formed of copper, and measures twelve inches in length, and five in the diameter of the crook or circular. The crook, or upper portion of the crosier, represents a serpent terminated by a double-faced head. Its surface is covered with a sunk lozenge carving, filled with a vitreous enamel of a blue colour, and the intervening elevations of which are gilt—a design obviously intended to represent the scales of the reptile. Within the curve is a human figure, standing with one leg placed on the neck of the serpent, and the other on the back of a double-faced wingless dragon, which he has pierced in the back with a spear, which the dragon bites. This human figure is dressed in a simple tunic, tied round the waist, and the feet are covered with buskins, which extend above the ankles. This figure had wings fastened to the shoulders, and to the central bar, which connects the figure with the circle, but these wings have been detached and lost. Both the figures were gilt, and their eyes, as well as those of the serpent, are formed of small gems, and the sides of the dragon are ornamented with a line of turquoises, placed at equal intervals from each other. The bowl, or middle portion, which is hollow, is encircled by a central belt, ornamented with nine turquoises and nine sapphires, placed alternately, and at equal distances from each other, the intervening spaces being filled with sculptured beads. Above and below this belt there are figures of four dragons, gilt, and with eyes formed of gems. The tail of each of these animals is brought round the head of the other, so as to form a very symmetrical ornament, and the surrounding ground is filled with a blue enamel. Immediately above the bowl, and encircling the upper portion of the staff, is an ornament resembling the Irish crown, consisting of eight radii, ornamented above the fillet with the same number of gems. The lower portion of the head, or cylindrical socket, is ornamented with a very graceful pattern, composed of leaves, or flowers, in three vertical ranges. The ground in these ornaments is also of a blue enamel, but the stems are gilt, and the flowers are filled with an enamel of white and red, now a good deal decayed. These ranges are separated from each other by three figures of a fish, the well known mystical symbol of the early christians, and these figures are each ornamented with a range of seven gems—torquoises and sapphires alternately— placed at equal distances along the back."

We agree with Doctor Petrie, that this crosier is of the highest interest, as a specimen of the jewellery art in Ireland, before the arrival of the English.

The bishop-king was succeeded by his son Diarmaid. It was not till the year 1151, that an opportunity was afforded Diarmaid Mac Carthy of throwing off the yoke of the man who had murdered his pious father. Thorlough O'Conor, king of Connaught, led an army into Munster, and established Diarmaid in the sovereignty of Desmond. But O'Conor had not long withdrawn his forces, before O'Brien set out upon another of his predatory excursions. On his return he met O'Conor, king of Connaught, and Diarmaid Mac Murrough, king of Leinster, who, with their united forces, gave battle to this redoubtable descendant of Brian Boru. The Dalcassian, or O'Brien troops, were defeated with tremendous slaughter. Seven thousand of their carcases were left to blacken in the waters of Moin-mor,* or great bog. Among the slain was Muircheartach, son of Conor O'Brien,† lord of Thomond, and royal heir of Munster, " the second best man among the Dalcassians." There escaped but one shattered battalion out of three which came to the ground in all the pride and panoply of war. Turlough O'Brien was banished, and the supremacy of Munster assumed by the conqueror, Thorlough O'Conor, king

---

* *Moin-mor*, *i.e.* the "Large Bog."—There are many places of this name in Munster, but the place where this terrible battle was fought, would seem to be Moanmore, in the parish of Emly, barony of Clanwilliam, and county of Tipperary. —*O'Donovan's Edition Four Masters*, vol. i. p. 1098.

† *Son of Conor O'Brein :*—I conclude that Conor O'Brien, lord of Thomond, was the king's brother, and that the young man who fell was the king's nephew.

of Connaught. And thus was Diarmaid and his father, Cormac, revenged by the hand of a stranger.

The condition of Thorlough O'Brien, after the battle, appears to have been truly miserable and contemptible, that of an outcast and a wanderer. Take the following entry:—"Thorlough O'Brien went to Limerick, but he did not get shelter in Munster, and he took many jewels with him, *i.e.* ten score ounces of gold and sixty beautiful jewels, beside the drinking-horn of Brian Borumha, and he divided them among the chiefs of Sil-Muireadhaigh, (the O'Conors of Connaught,) Ui-Briuin, (the O'Rourkes of Brefney,) and Commhaicne, (the O'Farrells,) but his presents to the Connaught chieftains were of no avail ; two years after this (1153,) he was banished to the north of Ireland, and Munster was divided between Fadhg O'Brien and Diarmaid Mac Carthy.

Fadhg O'Brien's reign was of short duration; he was taken prisoner the next year by Finn O'Brien, blinded, and thus rendered, according to the Brehon law, incapable of reigning.

O'Neill of Ulster then rose, and united his forces with those of Leinster, to place Conor O'Brien on the throne of Thomond. The old king appeals to Roderick O'Conor, king of Connaught, who has just succeeded his father; Roderick responds to the appeal, enters Munster at the head of a large army, and not only replaces Thorlough on the throne of Thomond, but compels Diarmaid Mac Carthy to give him (Roderick O'Conor,) hostages of subjection as supreme monarch, although Mac Carthy had but a few months before given the same pledges of allegiance to O'Loughlin

O'Neill, king of Ulster. What could Diarmaid, or any one similarly circumstanced do, when placed between two such consuming fires. He gave tokens of allegiance to both.

Turlough O'Brien, the hoary king of Limerick or Thomond, who has managed once more to clamber to his old throne, now seeks his revenge, and in order to incapacitate Conor O'Brien from ever again assuming the government, or his son from succeeding him, he has them both seized and blinded.

Four years after his restoration (1162,) we find him at war, and winning. In the first battle, the grandson of Carthach, and other men of distinction were slain. In a second battle, he was also victorious, slaying Na-Caeimh, lord of Feara-muighe, (Hugh O'Keeffe, lord of Fermoy,) and two other chieftains. These two battles were only the commencement of a more general war between Thomond and Desmond, during which there was fearful slaughter and devastation on both sides.

The old man was soon after this deposed by his own son, and driven into Leinster. He made no further effort to regain his throne. It is probable that the unnatural conduct of his son shortened his life. We have the following entry in the annals under A.D. 1167 :—"Thorlough, son of Diarmaid O'Brien, king of Munster and Leath-Mhoga, a man who had aimed at the sovereignty of all Ireland, the best man that came in his time for bestowing jewels and wealth upon the poor and the indigent of God, died."

His son Murtagh, by whom he was dethroned, did not long survive him. He was murdered two years after, by the grandson of Conor O'Brien, and Morough M.'Carthy, the son of Diarmaid, king of Desmond. This murder brought Roderick O'Conor to Munster, which he again divided between Diarmaid Mac Carthy, and Donnell, the brother of the late king of Thomond, compelling the Mac Carthys to pay an eric (or fine) of three times twelve score cows, (720 cows) "for the killing of Murtagh O'Brien."

Diarmaid Mac Carthy, was king of Desmond, or Cork, and Donnell O'Brien, king of Thomond, or Limerick, when Robert Fitzstephen, and Richard, son of Gilbert, (Earl Strongbow,) came to Ireland, with a numerous force of knights and archers, in the pay of Diarmaid Mac Murrough, "to contest Leinster for him, and to disturb the Irish of Ireland in general."

CHAPTER II.

THE CONQUEST OF CORK—THE DISTRIBUTION OF THE KINGDOM
AMONG THE ANGLO-NORMAN KNIGHTS.

A.D. 1170—1295.

THE Norman Conquest of Ireland, under Henry II., did not take place till a hundred years after the conquest of England, by William I. Whether it was that *our* iniquities were not then full—England is a century before us in everything—or that we were unworthy of a Norman king till 1170, will depend altogether on the view taken of the conquest.

Camden, in his Itinerary, describes the English Conqueror William I. as standing on the high cliffs of Wales, which command the Wicklow mountains in Ireland, and saying, with something of the profane boasting of Artaxerxes, "I will have the ships of my kingdom brought hither, wherewith I will make a bridge to invade this land."

When Murchardt, king of Leinster, heard this boast, he asked, "Hath the king, in his great threatening, inserted the words, *if it please God?*" "No," was the reply. "Then," said Murchardt, "seeing this king putteth his trust only in man, and not in God, I fear not his coming." When this was told to William, he frowned, and bit his thumb.

Those who believe in an over-ruling Providence— that the God, who made the world, continues to govern it—may acknowledge a needs-be for the migration of those conquering hordes, who rushed, like destroying floods, from the North and East, to the West and South of Europe; that their course was directed by Him, who "hath determined the times before appointed, and the bounds of their habitation."

William of Malmsbury seems to view the English conquest as the work of a mightier arm than that of the Conqueror; to esteem it "an extraordinary work of Providence, that the English should have given up all for lost, after the battle of Hastings, where only a small, though brave army, had perished." "It was indeed," says the wise and judicious Hallam, "an event not easily paralleled, where the vanquished were little, if at all, less courageous than their enemies; and where no domestic factions exposed the country to an invader."

Henry of Huntington speaks even more emphatically: "In the year of Grace, 1060, the Divine Ruler accomplished what he had before purposed, respecting the English nation. He gave them up to the Normans, a cruel and wise people, to be exterminated."*

This is strong language — *ad exterminandum* — but it would not seem to be too strong for the occasion: "God sees the wretched people," says the Saxon Chronicler, "most unjustly oppressed; first, they are despoiled of their possessions, and then butchered. Whoever had any property lost it by heavy taxes and unjust decrees. "It is not easy to relate," says another writer, "the miseries sustained, at this time,

* "Millesimo et sexagesimo sexto anno gratiæ, perfecit dominator Deus de gente Anglorum quod diu cogitaverat. Genti namque Normanorum asperæ et callidæ tradidit eos ad exterminandum."

by England, from royal exactions."* "The nobles and bishops built castles, and filled them with devilish and wicked men, and oppressed the people cruelly, torturing men for their money. They imposed taxes on towns, and when they had exhausted them of everything, set them on fire. You might travel a day, and not find one man living in a town, nor any land in cultivation. Never did the country suffer greater evils. If two or three men [Normans] were seen riding up to a town, all its inhabitants left it, taking them for plunderers. And this lasted, growing worse and worse, throughout Stephen's reign. Men said openly that Christ and his saints were asleep." [See Chro. Saxon p. 239.]

"A more general proof of the ruinous oppression of William the Conqueror may be deduced," says Mr. Hallam, "from the comparative condition of the English towns in the reign of Edward the Confessor, and at the compilation of Doomsday. At the former epoch there were, in York, 1607 inhabited houses, at the latter 967; at the former there were in Oxford 721, at the latter 243; of 172 houses in Dorchester, 100 were destroyed; of 243 in Derby, 103; of 487 in Chester, 205. Some other towns had suffered less, but scarcely any one fails to exhibit marks of a decayed population."

But the same eminent writer, who records these devastating examples of the Norman sway, confesses that "good as well as evil resulted from the conquest, even in the time of the Conqueror, who was more despotic and ruthless than any of his descendants."

* "Non facile protest narrari miseria quam sustinit illo tempore terra Anglorum propter regius exactiones."—*Chro. Saxon, p. 228.*

"The first and more immediate advantage, was that of deterring a wild and unruly people from the evil of anarchy and rebellion, to which they were addicted, and all their risings were without concert and desperate. The tyranny of William displayed less of passion or insolence than of that indifference about human suffering, which distinguishes a cold and far-sighted statesman. Impressed by the frequent rising of the English at the commencement of his reign, and by the recollection, as one historian observes, that the mild government of Canute had only ended in the expulsion of the Danish line, he formed the scheme of rivetting such fetters upon the conquered nation, that all resistance should become impracticable."

But the weight and severity of the Norman yoke was greatly relieved after the death of the Conqueror. Henry II., during whose reign Ireland was conquered, and annexed to the English crown, is called by Mr. Hallam, "the best of these monarchs."*

And the reign of his son John, who was perhaps the worst, was distinguished by the granting of the *Magna Charta*. It is worthy of remark, that the same noble knights, who conquered Ireland, wrested the sword of oppression from the hands of this cowardly prince, and taught him to respect the liberties of the people. If the unsettled state of England in 1064, demanded the strong and stern rule of a conqueror, like William of Normandy, the necessity was even greater in Ireland in 1170, after a lapse of a century.

"Since the death of Malachy II." observes O'Conor,

* We say nothing here of the *private* character of Henry II., which Lingar and Macgeoghegan paint in the darkest colours.

"this nation was falling into a state of *political reprobation;* each province set up for itself, the monarchy grew indifferent, and the monarch hateful to the majority of the chieftains. *When Roderick mounted the throne, their measure of iniquity was full.*"

The first fleet of foreigners that came to Ireland with Diarmaid, king of Leinster, in 1169, are called "*Flemings*" by the Four Masters. With these Flemings were seventy heroes, in coats of mail. The men of Munster "set nothing by the Fleming," thought them unworthy of their steel. But those that followed Strongbow, Fitzstephen, Raymond Le Gros, and Milo de Cogan, were men of weightier metal. They took Wexford, and entered Waterford at the point of the sword, slaying about seven thousand of the Danish and Celtic inhabitants, and making prisoners of Gillemaire, the officer of the fortress, and O'Faclain, lord of Deisi, and his son.

Diarmaid Mac Carthy, king of Desmond, or Cork, acted a curious and dubious part during the progress of the Norman Invasion. His conduct appears brave, noble, and patriotic, at first; vacillating and suicidal in the end. The Annals of Ireland, for the year 1170, contain this entry :—" A victory was gained by the son of Cormac, (grandson of Carthach,) and the people of Desmond, over the knights who were left to protect Port Lairge," or Waterford. But the victory was not followed up by either Mac Carthy or O'Conor. The latter confined his revenge to the murder of one of the sons of the king of Leinster, whom he held as a hostage for his father's good conduct. Donnell O'Brien, king of Thomond, and his Dalcassians, in order, it would seem, still further to weaken the hands of the Irish party, turned against Roderick, and as if this were not enough, Diarmaid Mac Carthy attacked the Danes of Limerick, and burned their fortress and market-house. This onslaught upon the Danes was bad policy. The English met a more manly opposition from the Danes than from the native Irish. We find the Danes of Cork, in 1174, equipping thirty-five vessels to attack an English fleet. It is true, they lost the battle, through the valor of an Englishman named Philip Walsh, who leaped on board the Admiral's ship, sword in hand, and killed Gilbert, who commanded the Danes, but the Danes fought bravely.

But the Irish hated the Danes (who had taken possession of all their best ports) with a most sincere hatred. They were old enemies. "A.D. 820.—The city of Cork, and the adjacent country, were ransacked by a Danish fleet. A.D. 833.—The city was devastated by the Danes. A.D. 837.—This county was miserably harrassed by the Danes. Among other devastations, Inis Dambly, [Cape Clear] and Cork were plundered and burned"

"A.D. 913.—Cork was this year burned and plundered by the Danes, who, in the year 915, also laid waste the greatest part of Munster. The following year they were defeated by the Munster men, in a pitched battle; but in Leinster, the Danes, on their side, vanquished the Irish. A.D. 918.—The Danes of Munster, being then in peaceable possession of this province, joined a party of their countrymen from Scandinavia, and sailed to Albania, [Scotland,] where they committed great ravages. A.D. 960.—The

Danes being at war with the Irish, burned and plundered Cork, which was also wasted by them in the years 978 and 995. A.D. 1012.—The Danes wasted the country in this year also, and in the following year, a large Danish fleet sailed into the harbour, and burned the city. Its inhabitants, however, avenged the outrage. A.D. 1089.—The Danes of Dublin, Waterford, and Wicklow, united their forces to attack Cork, but they were overthrown in battle by the Irish of Oneachach, a part of South Carbery."

In 1172, two years after the arrival of Strongbow, we find Cork, which was then styled "the Great City of Munster," and the adjacent country, "*quietly possessed by the Danes or Ostmen.*"

We cannot, under these circumstances, accuse Mac Carthy of handing over, or delivering up the city, to the Normans. All we can say is that he allowed them to take what was in the possession of another. It would seem, from his subsequent attempts to seize the city, that he intended to use the Normans as a cat's-paw; but this was giving his walnut to the bear.

The Danes were not only in possession of the city, but of the "adjacent country." We find from Henry's grant to Fitzstephen and De Cogan, (which we shall quote by-and-bye,) that the Danes possessed the city, and a cantred of the adjoining territory. We learn from Cowel, that a cantred* is a hundred manors, or villages, but we must know the size of the manor or village, in order to decide on the extent of the cantred. There is another mode of doing it. Let us turn to

---

* *Cantred*, "the same in Wales as a hundred in England, for *cantre* in the British language, signifieth an hundred."—*Cowel.*

the Charter of Henry II., which is worthy the perusal of those who wish to define the boundaries of the ancient kingdom of Cork.

"HENRY, BY THE GRACE OF GOD, KING OF ENGLAND, AND DUKE OF NORMANDY AND AQUATAIN, EARL OF ANJOU,

"*To all Archbishops, Abbots,* Earls, Barons, Justices, and all Ministers, and Faithful Subjects, French, English, and Irish,† greeting.*

"Know ye, that I have granted, and by this my charter, confirmed to Robert Fitzstephen and Milo De Cogan, the government of the city of Cork, with the cantred which belonged to the Ostmen of the said city,—which I retain in my own hands—to have and to hold them together, during my pleasure, and as long as they shall serve me faithfully. I, moreover, by this my charter, give, grant, and confirm to them and their heirs, *all the Kingdom* of Cork, except the said city, and the before-mentioned cantred, which I retain in my own hands; to hold to them and their heirs, of me and of my son John, and our heirs, by an exact division, towards the Cape of Saint Brandon, on the sea-coast, and towards Limerick and other parts, and as far as the Water near Lismore, which runs between Lismore and Cork, and falls into the sea; by the service of sixty knights, to be performed thereout, to me and my son John, and our heirs; the service of thirty knights to be performed by the said Robert, and his heirs, and the service of thirty knights, by the said Milo, and his heirs. Wherefore, I will, and strictly command, that the said Robert and Milo, shall have and hold the government of the said city and cantred, in manner as it is before mentioned, and that they and their heirs, shall have and hold all the kingdom aforesaid, except the said city and cantred, (which I

---

* *Abbots* here rank after Archbishops, and before Earls. Coke says there used to be twenty-six Abbots in England, (Fuller says "twenty-seven,") and two Priors, who were Lords of Parliament, and sat in the House of Peers." William de Rose, Lord Chief Justice of Ireland, in 1355, was Prior of the Hospital of St. John of Jerusalem.

† *French, English, and Irish.* Henry here gives the precedence to his *French* subjects. He had large possessions in France, in right of his wife Eleanor, as well as of his grandfather, William the Conqueror.

retain in my own hands,) from me and my son John, and our heirs, by an exact division, as above described, well and peaceably, freely and quietly, entirely, fully, and honourably, in wood and in plain, in meadows and pastures, in waters and mills, in warrens, ponds, and fishings, in ways and paths, and in all other places and things belonging thereto, with all their liberties and free customs, so that from the aforesaid river that runs between Lismore and Cork, the whole land, as far as Waterford, together with the city of Lismore, shall remain in my hands, for the government of Waterford,

"Witnesses present:—John, Bishop of Norwich; Adam, Bishop of St. Asaph, and Augustine, Bishop of Waterford; Richard De Lucy, William Fitz-Adelm, my Sewer, Hugh de Lacy, Hugh de Burid, Roger Fitz-Remsey, Maurice de Prendergast, Robert Dene, Robert Fitz-Eliodore, Jeoffrey Poer, and Harvy de Monte Marisco. At Oxford."

The "Water near Lismore,"* can be none other than the Blackwater, which discharges itself into the sea at Youghal. This river, which now runs through a part of the present county of Waterford, then formed a portion of the north-eastern boundary of the kingdom of Cork. The line stretched thence into the county Limerick, running north of Kilmallock and Bruree, and then took a south-westerly course along the Shannon, to Brandon Head, in Kerry, sweeping thence round the coasts of Kerry and Cork, and terminating where it began, at the town of Youghal. This, at a rough estimate, gives an area of *over* three million two hundred thousand acres. We shall say three million two hundred thousand. Now, as this three million two hundred thousand, was divided by the charter into thirty-two cantreds, each cantred must have contained a hundred thousand acres; and as there were one hundred

* *The Water near Lismore* is said to run "between Lismore and Cork." By Cork, we must understand the *kingdom*, and not the city of Cork. The Blackwater falls into the sea at Youghal, on the borders of the ancient kingdom, and present county of Cork.

manors, or villages, in each cantred, we conclude, that each manor, or village, contained one thousand acres. This would be about the size of our largest baronies, as Fermoy, or Imokilly.

In the charter granted by John, while viceroy, "all the fields held of my city of Cork," as well as the ground on which the city stood, is granted to the citizens. By the charter of the 15th Edward IV., the franchise of the city extended "as far as the shore-point, or strand, called Rewrawne, on the western part of the said port, and as far as to the shore-point, or strand, called Benowdran, on the eastern part of the same port, and so far as the castle of Carrigrohan, on the western side of the said city, and in all towns, pills, creeks, burgs, and strands, in and to which the sea ebbs and flows, in length and breadth, within the aforesaid two points, called Rewrawne, and Benowdran."

We have neither of these "aforesaid two points" marked on any ancient or modern map of Cork, which we have met with, but conclude it is between those two points, outside the harbour's mouth, where the Mayor of Cork *throws the dart.*

We have no doubt that it was in this threatening and warlike way, those corsair Danes, of our city, marked out the sea-line of their cantred. We copy the following account of this time-honored ceremony, from one of our local papers. It reminds us of the marriage of the Adriatic, which was celebrated by the Doge, or chief magistrate of Venice, who cast a *ring* from his vessel, or gondola, into the waters.

"THROWING THE DART.—The ancient and important civic ceremony of *Throwing the Dart*, took place yesterday. It is performed every three years, and is in accordance with a clause in the city charter, which provides, that for the purpose of showing their jurisdiction over the port and harbour, the Mayor, accompanied by the officers of the Corporation of Cork, and such members of that body as may choose, shall go out to the mouth of the harbour, and, at a point as near to a straight line drawn from Poor Head to Cork Head, as can be determined on with the eye, shall throw a dart into the water. Having reached the necessary point at the Harbour's mouth, the Mayor put on his official robes, and the collar of S.S., took the arrow, which was about a yard and a-half in length, with a heavy iron barded head, and proceeding to the bow of the vessel, accompanied by the entire of the party, threw it into the water amid a loud cheer."

We can reckon, in the present day, at least twelve towns and villages, great and small, (not to speak of pills,* creeks, burghs, and strands,) to which the sea ebbs and flows, and over which the charter of Edward IV. gave our magistrates jurisdiction: Whitegate, Aghada, Cove, Glanmire, Cork, Douglas, Blackrock, Passage, Monkstown, Rinnaskiddy, Carrigaline, and Crosshaven. There is very little doubt, that these small towns, as well as the larger city, were included in the cantred, or territory, possessed by the Danes.

Henry's grant of "*all the kingdom of Cork,*" except the city and the before-mentioned cantred, to Fitzstephen and De Cogan, does not seem to have interfered with Mac Carthy's grant of a *part* of the kingdom to Raymond Le Gros. The circumstance is worthy of record. Cormac, eldest son of Dermot, king of Cork, rose in rebellion against his father, seized, imprisoned, and attempted to dethrone him. The old man, in his emergency, sought the aid of Raymond Le Gros, who

---

* *Pills, i.e.* castles or strongholds. It is likely that the verbs to pillage and pilfer, are derived from pill, a castle.

was then besieging Limerick. Raymond did not hesitate a moment, but marched, with a strong force, against Cormac, whom he arrested, and delivered into the hands of his infuriated parent, who had him beheaded. The Annals of Ireland say he was "treacherously slain by his own people." The father expressed his gratitude to the Norman knight, by bestowing on him a princely inheritance in Kerry, which then formed part of the kingdom of Cork. Raymond made over the inheritance on his eldest son, Maurice, the descendents of whom became powerful chieftains, under the name of Fitzmaurice, and barons of Lixnaw.*

It was two years after the signing of the charter, before Fitzstephen and De Cogan took possession of seven of the thirty-two cantreds, into which the kingdom of Cork was divided. The arrangement is thus recorded by Giraldus Cambrensis:—

"Therefore, Dermoth of Desmond being brought to terms, and other powerful men of those parts, Fitzstephen and Milo divided seven cantreds between them, which were contiguous to the city, and which they then possessed in great security, three of which, eastward, fell to Fitzstephen's lot, and four westward to Milo's. The one had the fewer in his division, because they were the best, and the other had the larger number, because they were of worse quality. The government of the city remained in common to them both, and the tribute of the other twenty-four cantreds, which remained undivided, was to be equally distributed between them, when they should be brought under subjection."

Cambrensis has left us a very imperfect account of the distribution of property made by Fitzstephen and De Cogan. But the confirmation charters of king John,

* *Barons of Lixnaw.*—Edmond Fitzmaurice, was created Baron of Odorney, and Viscount Kilmoule, in 1537.

granted in the 8th year of his reign, throw some light on the affair. He confirmed to William de Barry, the donation made by Robert Fitzstephen to Philip de Barry, his sister's son, namely the land of Olethain, with all its appurtenances, and the cantreds of Muscherie-Dunegan, and the cantred of Killede, by the service of ten knights.

Philip de Broase, to whom king John had granted the kingdom of Limerick, came to Cork in 1179, and was kindly received by Richard de Londres, an English gentleman, who was deputy there under Fitz-aldeline. Here he met De Cogan and Fitzstephen. The next year, 1180, we read of the death of Meredith, or Amere, Fitzstephen's eldest son, "a lusty young gentleman, and a towardlie." His death was cause of great grief to his father and friends.

Two years after this, 1182, we find Mac Carthy renouncing his allegiance to the English government, and marching upon Cork, which fills Fitzstephen with consternation and despair. Raymond Le Gros, who is in Waterford, marches to his relief, and obliges Mac Carthy to raise the seige.

Milo de Cogan and young Fitzstephen were slain in 1185, at Lismore, to which they were invited, by one Mac Tirid, "who stealing suddenly and unawares upon them, treacherously murdered them, and five of their servants. This left Fitzstephen without a son. Whether or not these murders had been previously arranged by Mac Carthy, we cannot say, but he at once took advantage of them to attack Fitzstephen, who was shut up in Cork. The Norman knight once more applied to his trusty friend, Raymond, who was at Wexford. He set sail with a hundred archers and twenty knights. With this reinforcement, Fitzstephen made a sally, and routed the Irish at the first onset. But this was one of his last acts. "Broken with age and misfortune, he first lost his senses, and not long afterwards his life." This was the end of a man whose inheritance, by royal charter, was a million and a-half acres. MacCarthy made a last attempt, in 1185, on the "Beautiful citie," and was encountered by Theobald Fitz-Walter, the founder of the house of Ormond. He came upon the old Irish prince, while engaged in conference with his men, and slew him and his whole party. Thus died one of the greatest and bravest of the kings of Cork. "There happened," says Friar Clin, "a great eclipse of the sun this year, which continued for some time, of a *bloody colour.*"

Diarmaid MacCarthy was succeeded by his son Donnell, who slew his own brother, Cathal Odhor. He then turned his sword against Donnell More O'Brien, who had aided the English in the erection of castles, "for the purpose of distressing the MacCarthy." This Donnell O'Brien is styled in the Dublin copy of the Annals of Innisfallen, "a beaming lamp in peace and war, and a brilliant star of the hospitality and valor of the Momonians." He was succeeded by Murtough, who commenced his reign by uniting his forces with those of O'Conor of Connaught, in aiding Mac Carthy to drive the English out of Cork, without permitting them to fire the city, which they attempted. MacCarthy at this time destroyed the castle of Kilfeakle, and slew many of the English, taking two of their chiefs prisoners. He also plundered the territory of Imokilly, destroying a castle, with many of the enemy. Four years after this, the old feud between these two families broke out again, like a smouldering fire, with renewed fury; but was suppressed by the Pope's legate, Mahon O'Heney, Archbishop of Cashel. After making peace with O'Brien, Mac Carthy buckled on his armour to attack the English, and gained a victory over them, slaying a hundred and sixty, or more. We are not informed when this battle was fought.

Every attentive reader of Irish Annals will observe the recurrence of internal feuds much less frequent, after the end of the twelfth century. Irish chieftains at length began to see the policy of uniting against the common foe, and the impolicy of burning, blinding, and slaying each other; but this wisdom came too late, for the Normans were not only in possession, but in security within the walls of their strong castles. A Norman knight, on his war-horse, with lance in rest, in all the panoply of coat-of-mail, helmet, greaves and gauntlet, was a formidable opponent in the field, and difficult to bring down. But Norman knights could not always keep the field or saddle, armed cap-a-pie. Without their armour, they were as vulnerable as the crab without his shell, and therefore adopted the crab's policy, and sought the protection of some rock or stronghold. These strongholds, or castles, were essential to their existence, when they came to spread themselves over the broad lands of which they had received royal grants. The number of such castles, built through the length and breadth of the country during the thirteenth century, is very great.

In the kingdom of Cork alone, we have the castle of Muinter Bhaire, in Kilcrohane, erected by Mac Cuddihy. The castles of Dun-na-mbare, or Dunnamarc, and Aird Tuilighthe, the castle of Dunloe, the castle of Kilforgla, or Killorglin, the castle of the Mang, or Castlemaine, (in Kerry,) the castles of Moylahiff, of Callanafersy, of Cloonmealane, and of Curreens, now Currans, by Fitzmaurice Fitzgerald. The castle of Airlioch, by Roche. The castles of Dunnagall and Dunna-sead, (Baltimore,) by Sleviny. The castle of Traigh-Chaile, near the harbour of Cuan-Dor, (Glandore,) by Barrett. This castle was afterwards called Cloghatradbally, and belonged to Donell na Carton O'Donovan, chief of Clan-loughlin, who died in 1580. The castles of Timoleague and Dundeady, by Nicholas Boy de Barry. The castle of Carrigaline, by De Cogan, and of Ahamartha, by the Fitzgeralds, both on the Carrigaline river, and Lohart castle, near Cecilstown, in the possession of the Earl of Egmont, which, although in a state of great preservation, is thought, by Smith and others, to have been built in the reign of king John. It is generally supposed, that the castle of Barry's court, near Carrigtwohill, was built during the same century. We suspect it is of a more modern date, although there is a tradition that Giraldus Cambrensis, who was a Barry, composed a portion of his work on the Irish conquest within its walls. It is a large quadrangular structure, with three towers, communicating at each story with the principal apartments of the quadrangle. The arches are beautifully turned, and the marks of the chisel on the cut-stone round the doors and windows, look as fresh as if executed a few years ago.

Philip de Barry (Fitzstephen's sister's son) succeeded to his uncle's large inheritance. Giraldus says that Philip's father, Robert de Barry, was the first man that was wounded in the conquest of Ireland,—he had some hard fighting with Donald, prince of Ossory—" he was the first that ever manned a hawk in this island," which afterwards became so celebrated for its hawks. " He was a man rather ambitious *to be* eminent, than to seem so."

Philip de Barry was succeeded by his son William, to whom king John gave a confirmatory charter. This charter " confirmed to William de Barry, the donation made by Robert Fitzstephen to his father, of " three cantreds of his lands in Cork, *i.e.* Olethian, with its appurtenances, and of the other two cantreds, *i.e.* Muscheric Dunegan, and the cantred of Killede."

This cantred of O'Lethan, or O'Leahan, was situated in the barony of Barrymore. It was possessed originally by the Mac Carthys, the O'Noonans, the O'Dalys, the Galweys, the O'Lynchs, the O'Kellehers, the O'Regans, and the O'Leahans, now Anglicised *Lyons*, from whom the whole district took its name. Here we have Castle-Lyons. This family derived its name from Eochaidh Leathonach, the second son of Daire Cearba.

We discover, by an inquisition taken in Cork, before William de Rose, Chief Justice of Ireland, that the great island on which Queenstown stands, was included in this cantred, and was in the possession of the Barrys in 1355. " The extent of Hy-Liathain appears," says Doctor O'Donovan, "from various ancient Irish and Anglo-Irish authorities, the present village of Castle-Lyons, or Caislean Ui Liathain, and the island of Oilean-Mor-Arda-Neimhedh, now the Great Island, near Cork, are mentioned in it."

By the cantred of Killede or Killeagh, we understand the present barony of Imokilly,* which was originally in the possession of the O'Ronaynes, O'Lomascys, and O'Brigans. The De Rupes, or Roches, got possession, at an early period, of the south-western part of the peninsula—we still have Roche's tower, and Trabolgan, the principal residence of Edmund Burke Roche, now Baron Fermoy—and the Fitzgeralds, the Earls of Desmond, of the north-eastern portion.

The cantred of Muscherie-Dunegan† constituted the present baronies of Orrery and Kilmore, with Buttevant as the principal town. The O'Donegans, the O'Cullanans, and the MacClancys, or MacClanchys, were the original inhabitants of this district, before the Anglo-Norman invasion. We learn from O'Brien, the author of an Irish Dictionary, that "O'Donegan was chief lord, or petty king," of Muscherie-Dunegan, in the end of the tenth century. He refers it to "the judicious reader, if it be a likely story, that one *Cairbre Musc*, supposed son of a king of Meath, in the beginning of the third century, should have given the name of Muscry, [Muskerry] to every one of those territories,

---

* *Imokilly* may be from *Ibh-a-cill-liath*, "the country of the grey church," i.e. the old church of Cloyne? Mr. Hackett derives Imokilly from *Ibh-muc-Olla*, the "country of the great pig." There is a tradition, that a great boar which kept the country in a state of alarm, was killed in this district. There were wild boars in Ireland at an early period.

† *Muscherie-Dunegan.*—Smith speaks of a "Muskerry-Donegan, a tract lying round Baltimore," but this Muscherie-Dunegan, was "*eastward*," where the three cantreds "fell to Fitzstephen's lot."

so widely distant from each other in the province of Munster."

William Barry, whose war cry, "*Boutez-en-avant,*" gave name to Buttevant, founded the priory of Ballibeg, for St. Austin Canons, the revenues of which were enlarged by his son David, in 1231.

King John also made royal grants to Adam de Rupe, or Roche, to Richard de Cogan, to Robert Fitz-Martin, and to Henry and Maurice Fitz-Philip, who were brothers.

"To Adam de Rupe, (or Roch,) the cantred of Rossclibir, with its appurtenances, save the demenses of the bishop of that see, by the service of five knights." Ros-ailither, the "Wood of the Pilgrims," now Rosscarbery, is described in the life of Saint Fachtna, the patron of the district,* as *in australi Hiberniæ parte, juxta mare,* "in the southern part of Ireland, near the sea."

The O'Learys, the O'Heas, the O'Flynns, and the O'Deasys, were the original proprietors of the district. These names prevail in this part of the country to the present day. The Right Honorable Rickard Deasy, of Clonakilty, our present respected Attorney-general, is a descendent of the Deasys of Rosscarbery and Ibaune. We could also point to numerous instances in which the old Norman and Celtic blood have been united.

Milo de Cogan, who was slain at Lismore, was succeeded by Richard de Cogan, to whom king John made a grant of the cantred of Muscrie O'Mullane,

---

* *The patron of the district.*—We have the death of "Connmhach, abbot of Ros-ailither," recorded in the Annals of Ireland for 824.

lying between the harbour of Cork and the port of Insovenagh; in other words, between the harbours of Cork and Kinsale, in the baronies of Kerricurrihy and Kinnalea. Here the famous Dermot Mac Carthy, king of Cork, had his royal residence. Here, in ancient maps, we find the Danish names of Gowle, Coppinger, and Skiddie. Here, we suspect, lay the Danish cantred, and king John's " demesnes." In granting to De Cogan an additional twenty-five knights' fees,* or thirty thousand acres, there is a " saving to the king and his heirs, the aforesaid harbour and his own demesnes."

The De Cogans built the castle of Carrigaline in this district, the picturesque ruins† of which remain to the present day. Part of the lands in this neighbourhood, as Ballybricken, Fort Prospect, Rinnaskiddy, Corabinny, and Coolmore (which form a peninsula), were called in old manuscripts the *Long-a-Cowgon*, " the ship of Cogan." In the parish of Barnahealy are the ruins of an old castle of the De Cogans, incorporated with a modern structure called Warren's Court. Above a door-way of cut stone we have an effigy of a knight, perhaps Richard or Milo himself; and near by is the grave-yard of Barnahealy, where tradition has buried the elder knight; but this, we think, is a mistake, for Milo de Cogan fell at Lismore. There was a

---

* *Knights' fees* varied in value and extent of land. They sometimes consisted of 800, and sometimes of 680 acres; estimated at £15, sometimes at £20, and in later times at £40 a year.

† *The picturesque ruins.*—Smith, who is generally correct, says (writing more than a hundred years ago)—" the castle is entirely demolished." Another writer, following Smith, informs us there is not a " *vestige*" of the castle in existence. It is still a fine and extensive ruin. It is probable that this castle was built by Richard, and not by Milo de Cogan, who resided, for safety, in the city.

Richard de Cogan, lord of the manor of Barnahealy, in 1536.

The twenty-five knights' fees were to be " set out" to Richard de Cogan, " in some other place," under the advice of John Mareschall, and Meiler Fitz-Henry, Lord Justice of Ireland. We suspect this portion of his inheritance was chosen near the port of Insovenagh, or Kinsale, where we see the name of De Cogan and De Courcy lying together, in ancient maps. Myles de Courcy, the son of the celebrated John de Courcy, married a De Cogan, and built a castle on the Head of Kinsale.

The romantic fortunes and misfortunes of John de Courcy, the ancestor of John Constantine de Courcy, the present lord of Kinsale, are more strange, and apparently extravagant, than any fiction ever penned; but they, notwithstanding, form a veritable part of history. We have an impression, though we are unable at the present moment to give our authority, that Merlin, a Welsh bard or seer, had predicted the conquests of the knight above whose helm three eagles* were displayed.

The De Courcys claim alliance with most of the royal families of Europe, paternally, through the Dukes of Lorraine, and maternally, through the house of Normandy.

John de Courcy was sent to Ireland by Henry II., in 1177, to assist William Fitz-Adelm† in the govern-

---

* *Three eagles.*—The De Courcy, or Kinsale arms are—" Argent, three eagles, displayed, gules, ducally crowned, or. Crest, on a ducal coronet, or, an eagle, displayed, argent."—*Burke's Peerage.*

† *William Fitz-Adelm.*—King Henry the Third made a grant in 1225 to Richard de Burgo, or Mac William, (the son of this William Fitz-Adelm,) of the province of Connaught.

ment of this kingdom. He invaded Ulster at the head of twenty-two knights, fifty esquires, and about three hundred foot soldiers, which he won after some hard fighting, and for which he was created in 1181, Earl of Ulster. He was the first of those Norman knights that received an Irish title from an English sovereign. His honors and success excited the fierce jealousy of Hugh de Lacy, who asserted that De Courcy had publicly accused King John of the murder of his own nephew, Arthur, Duke of Bretagne. When this report reached John's ears, he commanded his faithful friend and servant, Sir Hugh de Lacy, to seize that traitor, John de Courcy, and send him bound to England. But to seize De Courcy was more easily said than done, for he was a man of gigantic stature and strength. Of his opponent, De Lacy's presence, we know nothing. His father is thus described by Holinshed:—"His eyes were dark and deep set, his neck short, his stature small, his body hairy, not fleshy, but sinewy, strong, and compact; a very good soldier, but rather rough and hasty."

De Courcy, hearing of De Lacy's purpose to arrest him, offered him single combat, which he declined, saying, "It was not for him, who represented the king's person, (he was at this time Governor of Ireland) to hazard his life with an inferior," whom he styled a "subject," and a "traitor." His inferior he was not—they were both earls; De Lacy, Earl of Meath, De Courcy, Earl of Ulster. Neither of them were particularly "subject" to the powers that be, any longer than it suited their purposes. His traitorous language was unproved. But De Lacy issued a proclamation, offering a large reward to any one who would deliver up De Courcy, dead or alive. It was Good Friday—*Bad* Friday for De Courcy. On that day, as our Annalists inform us, he bore no arms, and wore no armour, but was wholly given up to divine contemplation. Now pacing, " all solitary," round the church of Downpatrick, and now kneeling before a huge wooden cross, perhaps mentally ejaculating a *Salus in Cruse*, or a *Sub hoc signo vinces*, or his own motto, *Vincet omnia veritas*, when, — " The Philistines are upon thee, Sampson." He tears up the cross, his only weapon, and lays about him with all his herculean might, leaving thirteen of his assailants dead at his feet. But he is at length overpowered by numbers, seized, bound, and shipped to England, where he is condemned to perpetual imprisonment in the Tower of London.

"He lieth low in a dungeon now,
Powerless, in proud despair,
For false King John hath cast him in,
And closely chained him there."

There he lies, and grows gaunt and morose, when a dispute arises between John of England and Philip Augustus of France, on their respective and clashing titles to the Duchy of Normandy. It was resolved to decide the affair by two champions, instead of by a general engagement. The French champion is chosen, and sends his challenge, but there was no knight in England, Ireland, or Normandy, to accept it. Even Hugh de Lacy declines the high honor; when a courtier whispers to king John that De Courcy, who now lies in the tower, is the only man in his wide dominions that is able to meet the French champion. The king sends to the earl, who replies, "Not for *him;* I esteem him unworthy the adventure of my blood. He has rewarded my loyalty to his person, and services to the crown, by imprisoning me, unheard, at the suit of my rival and enemy, Hugh de Lacy."

The king becomes a suppliant, and sends a third time, when the grim features of De Courcy relax, as he replies, " For the crown and dignity of the realm, in which many an honest man liveth against his will, I am contented to hazard my life." The king swallows all this, and a great deal more, with a good grace. De Courcy is released from the tower, made much of, " cherished and fed wonderfully," and attains great bulk by the sudden change " from hard keeping, to so large an allowance of diet."

The day of combat, which is to come off in Normandy, arrives. The trumpets of the heralds sound, and the champions enter the lists, in the presence of the assembled kings and nobles of England, France, and Scotland, surrounded by the chivalry and beauty of the three kingdoms. De Courcy, armed with a tremendous sword, for which he had sent to Ireland, approaches his adversary, eyes him with a "wonderfully stern countenance," not unmingled with contempt, and rides by. That grim look has decided the contest. It froze the Frenchman's blood. When the trumpet sounded for the onset, that Frenchman took to his heels, or more correctly, put spurs to his horse, broke through the lists, and fled into Spain.* The men

* *And fled into Spain.*—Hanmer's description of the combat is very graphic. " The day came, the place and lists were appointed, and the scaffolds were set up. The princes, with their nobility on both sides, waited the issue of the battle.

threw up their caps and clapped their hands, the ladies smiled on the Anglo-Norman, and jeered the poltroon Frenchman. The victory was adjudged to De Courcy, and the Duchy of Normandy to King John.

Philip of France, wishing to see a specimen of De Courcy's great strength and swordsmanship, the King of England ordered a helmet of "excellent proof," and a shirt of mail, to be laid upon a block. The Earl, frowning grimly on their Highnesses of England and of France, raised his sword, and cut helmet and shirt of mail asunder at a blow, striking his weapon so deeply into the timber, that he alone could draw it hence. The kings inquired why he had eyed them with so grim a face? "If I had missed my stroke, I should have cut off both your heads," was his reply, which was taken in good part.

King John restored the champion to his titles and estates, in Ulster, valued at 25,000 marks per annum, and asked him if there was any other favour he could bestow. The favor he asked was, *that he and his successors, for all ages, should remain uncovered in the presence of the king, and his successors.* This request was both willingly and graciously granted by the king, and the privilege is enjoyed to the present

The French champion first sallied forth, gave a turn, and rested himself in his tent. De Courcy was sent for, who was trussing himself up with strong points, and answered the messengers, *that 'if any of their company were to go to such a banquet, he would make no great haste.'* He soon after came forth, gave a turn, and went into his tent. When the trumpets sounded the charge, the champions issued out, and viewed each other. De Courcey eyed his adversary with a wonderfully stern countenance, and passed by. The Frenchman, not liking his grim look, and the strong proportion of his person, stalked still along. When the trumpets sounded to battle a second time, De Courcy drew his sword, upon which the Frenchman clapped spurs to his horse, broke through the barrier, and fled into Spain."—*Hanmer*, p. 184, day, by John Constantine de Courcy, the twenty-ninth lord of Kingsale.*

> "So he gave this graceful honor,
> To the bold De Courcy's race,
> That they ever should dare, their helms to wear,
> Before the king's own face,
> And the sons of that line of heroes,
> To this day their right assume,
> For when every head is unbonnetted,
> *They walk in cap and plume.*"

When William III., Prince of Orange, inquired the cause why Almericus, the twenty-third lord of Kinsale, appeared covered in his presence, this Irish nobleman replied, "May it please your Majesty, my name is De Courcy, and I am lord of Kinsale, in the kingdom of Ireland. The reason of my appearing covered in your Majesty's presence is, to assert the ancient privilege of my family, granted to Sir John de Courcy, earl of Ulster, and his heirs, by John, king of England, for him and his successors for ever."† William graciously acknowleged his right, gave him his hand, and said: "*I now remember to have had such a nobleman.*"

This privilege or practice of wearing the hat, in the presence of royalty, is not altogether unique, or confined to this family, or these countries. A grandee of the first class in Spain is privileged to remain covered before the sovereign. A grandeeship, or any number of grandeeships, may be inherited, "without merger," through males and females. Hence the phrase of a noble's having so many "hats," that is, so many rights and privileges to wear his hat in the presence of royalty.

---

* *Lord of Kingsale*, from *Cean-Saile*, "the Head of the Sea."

† Almericus *had been* in rebellion, and outlawed, for his adhesion to James II. William was pleased *not to remember this*.

Notwithstanding the royal pardon, Sir John de Courcy lost the earldom and estates of Ulster, which were claimed by Hugh de Lacy, who said, as De Courcy had never returned to Ireland, to have his outlawry reversed, that he would maintain and retain the grant in Ulster which the king had made him. De Courcy had fifteen times attempted to cross into Ireland, but was put back by contrary winds ; upon which he altered his course and went to France, where, it would appear, he was slain by Walter, Earl of Meath, and Hugh, Earl of Ulster, the two sons of Hugh de Lacy. The murder of this noble knight seems to have excited the indignation of the king. We find the following passage in the Annals of Kilronan :—

"A.D. 1210.—Johannes, the son of Fitz-Empress, king of England, came to Ireland with a great fleet this year. On his arrival he levied a great army of the men of Ireland, to march them to Ulster, to take Hugh de Lacy, and to take Carrickfergus. Hugh departed from Ireland; and those who were guarding Carrickfergus left it, and came to the king. The king marched from Dublin into Meath, and dispatched a large fleet northwards, to a fortress of the English, called Carlingford, to command the sons of Hugh de Lacy, viz., Walter, Lord of Meath, and Hugh, Earl of Ulster, and then Lord, Deputy of Ireland, to appear before him, *to answer for the death of the valiant knight, John De Courcy, who was treacherously slain by them.*"

De Courcy left issue by his wife, Africa, the daughter of Godfrey, king of the Isle of Man, Myles de Courcy, who was created Baron of Kinsale the 29th of May, 1223. This Myles married a De Cogan, built a castle near the old Head of Kinsale, and another at Ringrone, where he and De Cogan slew Reann Roin, or Ringrone Mac Carthy.

Myles was succeeded by his grandson, Sir John de Courcy, who built the castle of Kilbrittan, of which he was afterwards dispossessed by Mac Carthy Reagh, by whom he was slain, in the island of Inchedonny, in the harbour of Clonakilty, in 1295.

Walter de la Haye, the king's Escheator in Ireland, took possession of the De Courcy property, and made it over, for a composition, £12 12s. per annum, on James Keating, "for the use of the heir of the said John Lord Courcy."

According to this deed, the De Courcy property consisted of "The manor of Kilbrittan, Ringrone, with the mills and fisheries; the lands of Carrotsheran, Holderness, Liffynin, Fathax, Lyside, and Kingsale, in the county Cork; and the country of Glynardall and other lands in the county of Kerry."

The title of Baron, or Viscount Kinsale, was fraudulently assumed by Sir Dominick Sarsfield, in 1627. John, Lord Courcy, and his son Gerald Courcy, petitioned the king against the pretender to the title. The petition was referred to the judges, who made the following report:—

"According to your majesty's pleasure, and upon a full hearing of the council, learned on both sides, we find it apparently proved, by ancient records, entries in parliament, etc. that the Lord Courcy, and his ancestors, have, time out of mind, been styled Barons of Kinsale and Ringroan. Although in some records, he is only called Lord Courcey, and Baron de Courcy, this argument being only grounded on omission, we hold to be of little force, as it is usual where divers baronies are in the same person, for the baron to name himself by the chief barony, and to forbear naming the rest, yet we find the same person, called Lord Kingsale, and baron of Courcey, long before this question was stirred. Then the Lord Viscount endeavoured to carry the barony into another line, and to shew the title was extinct by attainder, but both these allegations were clearly answered, so that we are fully satisfied, the barony of Kinsale anciently belonged to the Lord Courcey. Then it was alleged to have both titles stand, the one to be Viscount and the other to be Baron of Kinsale, which we conceive would be confounding titles of honour, and be of ill consequence; therefore, we cannot advise your majesty to suffer it; but we are of opinion, that Sir Dominick Sarsfield may retain the degree that he now hath, taking his title from some other place in Ireland, or else to be called Viscount Sarsfield. For that your majesty was not informed, that the title of Kinsale was given to any other baron, which the patent may recite; and that, for the future, he shall be stiled by the new title, and not by that of Kinsale; all which we humbly present, and leave to your majesty's good pleasure.

March 19th, 1647." Signed,
MARLBOROUGH,
MANCHESTER,
PEMBROKE,
TOTNESS,
GRANDESONE.

This assumption of Irish titles was by no means a rare occurrence. We find Thomas de Carew, in the reign of Edward III., setting up a title, as heir to Fitzstephen. Carew's right was tried in Cork, before Sir Anthony Lucy, Lord Justice of Ireland. The decision was as follows:—

" That Robert Fitzstephen died seized of the moiety of the estate granted by King Henry II. to him and Cogan; and that the said Fitzstephen was a bastard,* and died without issue of his body; that the claim of Thomas de Carew, asserting that he and his ancestors were heirs to Fitzstephen, could not be true, because the said Fitzstephen was a bastard, and died without heir of his body; and further, that the said Fitzstephen, in his life time, enfeoffed Maurice Fitzthomas, before he was created Earl of Desmond, of the castle and manor of Dunemarke, and the moiety of the estate granted him by King Henry II."

* *Was a bastard.*—A collateral branch cannot be heir to a bastard.

We learn from Odericus Vitalis, a monk of Utica, and a writer of Norman history, that the Carews were descended from Arnolph de Montgomery, by Lafracoth, the daughter of an Irish king. Arnolph built the castle of Pembroke (from which he derived the title of earl), and which he fortified for his brother, the Earl of Shrewsbury, against Henry I. They were both banished the realm in 1112, at which time the castle and estates of Pembroke were forfeited to the crown. Their posterity took the name of Carew, and came to Ireland to improve their fortunes. We do not imagine that they laid claim to the inheritance of Fitzstephen in right of their Irish grandmother, Lafracoth.

Edward II. issued a precept in 1310, authorising Maurice de Carew to distrain the lands of Maurice de Barry and Maurice Fitzgerald, for services and duties to the said Maurice de Carew, as lord of their possessions. Among the Carew papers, in the Lambeth Library (fol. 38), is a note of such lands as Thomas Fitzmaurice held of Maurice de Carew, at the death of said Thomas; which lands were forfeited to the crown, but restored to Carew in 1312. We have also a deed, bearing date 1334, from John de Carew, lord of the manor of Castle-Cork, to Richard Fitz-Peter de Carew, in which he invests him with the custody of all the lands belonging to George Fitzadam.* It appears from another M.S. in the same library, that Castle-Cork, and "lands which amounted to near one-half the county," were delivered into the hands of Richard, the son of Sir Peter Carew, in 1567.

* *George Fitzadam.*—Was this a descendant of William Fitz-Adelm, the ancestor of the De Burgos?

A title to nearly the half of the county was set up by Sir Peter in 1568. Sir Peter sent his agent, John Hooker, to Cork, who had a "solemn meeting" with Mac Carthy Reagh, Sir Cormac Mac Teig, Lord of Muskerry, Barry-Oge, O'Driscol, O'Daly, and others. They proposed, if Sir Peter would live among them, to pay " an annual *reasonable* rent," and to advance 3,000 kine, with sheep, hogs, and corn, to stock his farm. Hooker closed upon this offer, took a house for Sir Peter in Cork, and another in Kinsale. Sir Peter set out to take possession, but fell sick on the way, and died in Ross (in Wexford) the 27th of November, 1575.

CHAPTER III.

THE EARLS OF DESMOND—IRISH LITERATURE AND LAWS.

A.D. 1295—1462.

THE Fitzgeralds became possessed of the largest portion of the estates originally chartered to Fitzstephen, and De Cogan. We learn from the decision of the Chief Justice, Sir Anthony Lucy, given in Cork, (the 31st of August, and 5th of Edward III.) on the claim set up by Thomas de Carew, that " the said Fitzstephen, in his life-time, enfeoffed Maurice Fitzthomas, before he was created Earl of Desmond, of the castle and manor of Dunnemarke, and the moiety of the estate granted to him by Henry II."

There must be a mistake here. Maurice Fitzthomas, who was the first Earl of Desmond, was so created in 1329, that is 144 years after Fitzstephen's death. It was to Maurice Fitzgerald, who came over with Fitzstephen, that "Fitzstephen, in his life-time, enfeoffed" the castle and manor of Dunnemarc.

There were in all eighteen Anglo-Norman earls of Desmond. They traced their descent from the Dukes of Tuscany. They came from Florence to Normandy, and from Normandy to England, with William the Conqueror. Maurice Fitzgerald, from whom the Earls of Desmond were descended, came to Ireland with Robert Fitzstephen, and other Anglo-Norman chiefs, in A.D. 1170, and assisted Strongbow in the reduction of Ireland.

"A man he was, both honest and wise, and for truth and valour, very noble and famous; a man of his word, of constant mind, and of a certain bashfulness; well coloured, and of good countenance; of middle stature, and compact at all points; courteous, gentle and moderate, a pattern of sobriety, and good behaviour; a man of few words; his speeches more full of wit and reason than of words; more wisdom he had than eloquence; in martial affairs bold, stout and valiant, and yet not hasty to run headlong into any adventure, but when an attempt was once taken in hand, he would strictly pursue and follow the same."

Maurice died in 1177, and was succeeded by Gerald, who died in 1205. Gerald left two sons, Maurice, the eldest, and Thomas More. Maurice was the first Baron of Offaly, and Lord Justice of Ireland in 1229. He was the ancestor of the Earls of Kildare, and the Dukes of Leinster. His brother, Thomas More, was the ancestor of the Earls of Desmond. He died in 1260, of extreme old age.

He was succeeded by John of Callan, who was slain in battle in 1261. The Four Masters give us the following description of this battle :—

"A.D. 1261.—A great army was marched by the Clan Gerald into Desmond, to attack Fineen Mac Carthy.* Mac Carthy attacked and defeated them, and in this contest were slain eight barons and five knights, besides others of the English nobles; as also John

* *Fineen Mac Carthy.*—This was Fineen Reann Roin, who was slain this same year by De Courcy and De Cogan, in the castle of Itingrone, near Kinsale.

Fitz-Thomas and Barry More. Countless numbers of the English common soldiers were also killed in the aforesaid battle."

Callan, or Callainn Gleanna O'Ruachtain, where this battle was fought, is in the parish of Kilgarvan, five miles eastward of Kenmare, in the county of Kerry. The Annals of Innisfallen place it under the year 1260; so does Docter Hanmer, from whom we have the following notice :—

"The Carties plaied the divells in Desmond, where they burned, spoiled, preyed, and slue many an innocent. They became so strong, and prevailed so mightily, that for the space (so it is reported) of twelve yeeres, the Desmond durst not put plow in ground in his owne country. At length, through the operation of Satan, a love of discord was thrown betweene the Carties and the O'Driscoles, Odo:.ovaines, Mac Donoch, Mac Mahonna, Mac Swines, and the inhabitants of Muscrie, in so much, that by their cruell dissention they weakened themselves of all sides, that the Desmond in the end overcame and over-topped them all."—*Hanmer's Chronicle, Dublin edition of* 1809, *p.* 400.

John of Callan had five sons—Maurice, who was slain in 1261, with his father, Maurice, the ancestor of the Knights of Kerry ; Gibbon, the ancestor of the White Knights, (hence the surname of the family of Fitzgibbon) ; John More, the ancestor of the Knights of Glyn, and Thomas, the ancestor of John of Kerry.

Maurice, the eldest son, who was slain in 1261, left two sons, Thomas Na n-appadh, who died in 1296, and Sir Richard, the ancestor of the Seneschal of Imokilly.

Thomas *Nappagh* (" of the Apes"), was the father of Maurice, the first Earl of Desmond. He (*i.e.* Thomas Nappagh,) was Baron of Offaly, and Captain of Desmond, and so powerful as to be styled Prince, or

Ruler of Munster. He was surnamed Nappagh, (na n-Appadh,) from a remarkable circumstance which occurred to him in Tralee, when only nine months old. On the news of his father's death, (who was slain at Callan, in 1261), the nurse rushed out of the house, leaving the child alone. A large monkey seized the opportunity of carrying off the child, and of taking it up to the top of the castle. After some time, it brought it back, and deposited it safe in the cradle. From this time, the monkey has held an honorable place in the armorial bearings of the family.

Maurice, son of Thomas of the Apes, was created Earl of Desmond in 1329. He is styled by Doctor Smith "the most active nobleman in the kingdom." Being summoned by the Lord Justice Sir John D'Arcy, to suppress rebellious septs in Leinster, he came into the field at the head of a thousand men, and routed the rebels. For his thousand men he had the promise of the king's pay, but the revenue of the kingdom * being unequal to such an expenditure, he introduced the custom of imposing coin and livery, that is, horse-meat, men's-meat, and money for other expenses. It is asserted, that by such extortions his income rose from one thousand to ten thousand marks a year.

His ambition rose with his income. He rejected the English laws, and claimed the right of governing the counties of Cork, Waterford, Limerick, and Kerry, by what Cox and Smith style "the barbarous customs of the Irish." Upon his refusing to swear fealty to

---

* *The revenue of the kingdom* of Ireland in the 29th of Edward III. was £2,285 less than its expenses. The following year the deficiency amounted to £2,880; the next year it was £1,808; nor did Ireland pay for *its keep* during any one year of the next reign, that of Richard II.

the English crown, he was committed (by the Lord Justice, Roger Outlaw,) to the custody of the marshal of Limerick, from whom he escaped. He was retaken soon after by Sir Anthony Lucy, and released upon a solemn oath of fidelity. His sincerity being suspected, he was retaken, and confined for eighteen months in Dublin castle, till he found security for his future good behaviour.

Edward III. having discovered that the over-large grants of land made to Anglo-Norman lords, had raised them to the position of Irish kings, and produced the same insubordination and anarchy which had existed before the conquest, attempted to curtail, and in some instances to nullify and resume these lordly inheritances, which produced a rebellion among Irish lords that was headed by the Earl of Desmond. The king sent over Ralph Ufford, who summoned a parliament to meet in Dublin, on the 7th of June, 1345. The Earl of Desmond not only refused to attend,* but summoned an opposition parliament to meet at Callan, in the county of Kilkenny, which so provoked Ufford, that he confiscated Desmond's lands, and attempted to seize his person, but not succeeding, took two of his castles, Iniskysty and Island Castle, and hung three of his followers, Sir Eustace Power, Sir William Grant, and Sir John Cotterel.

These severe measures of the Lord Justice, who is described as "over rigorous, greedy of amassing wealth, and an improper person," were discountenanced by

* *Refused to attend.*—To refuse to attend these parliaments was esteemed a very high misdemeanour. A fine of 200 marks was imposed on Lord Roche for refusing to attend a parliament convened the 20th of Edward II. The son of this Lord Roche got the fine reduced to £10 by Edward III.

nearly all the other Irish knights and noblemen, twenty-six of whom bound themselves for Desmond's appearance at an appointed day.

A parliament was called the next year, 1346, which Desmond also refused to attend, uniting with his cousin, the Earl of Kildare, in calling a council in Kilkenny. Here articles were drawn up, which caused the removal of the Lord Justice. He was replaced by Sir Walter Bermingham, who procured the earl liberty to manage his cause. Desmond went to England, was kindly received by the king, and allowed twenty shillings a day to defray his expenses. "Being very active in his own cause, he obtained satisfaction for the wrongs done him by Sir Ralph Ufford, so that in the year 1352 he was restored to all his castles and jurisdictions."

He was, after this, made Lord Justice of Ireland for life. He died in Dublin Castle, the 25th of January, 1355, and was buried in the church of the Black Friars, and thence removed to the Dominican Abbey in Tralee. He married Margaret, daughter of Richard de Burgo, Earl of Ulster.

Maurice Oge, the eldest son of the first earl, succeeded his father, but he enjoyed the property and the title but three years, during which he seems to have waged fierce war with the De Burgos and Poers. Lord Arnold Poer had called his father a *rhymer*. Perhaps the old earl made but indifferent verses; but the son could not brook the taunt, so to war they went. He is supposed to have died at Castlemaine in 1358.*

---

* *Castlemaine in* 1358.—O'Flaherty adds to the year 1357, in II. 2. 11 :—
" Comes Desmonia transfretando submersus."

Edward III., on account of the disturbed state of Munster, granted to John, his brother (who afterwards succeeded to the title), the serjeantcies of the counties of Cork, Kerry, and Waterford, and the custody of all Maurice's castles and lands, "with the exception of the dower of Aveline, widow of said Maurice, and Beatrix, widow of said earl." These privileges had been previously conferred on Maurice, on the payment of one rose per annum. John died in 1367.

John was succeeded by his brother Gerald, or Garrett, the poet, who became Lord Deputy of Ireland in 1368, a dignity which he enjoyed but one year, giving place to Sir William de Windsor. The poet was taken prisoner, with other noble persons, on the 6th of July, 1370, near the monastery of Maio, in the county of Limerick. His captors were O'Brien and Macnamara, of Thomond. He is described as a man of gaiety and affability, an Irish scholar and poet, and the most distinguished of the English in Ireland. "The Lord Garrett, earle of Desmond, a nobleman of wonderful bountie, cheerfulness in conversation, charitable in his deeds, easy of access, a witty and ingenious composer of Irish poetry, and a learned and profound chronicler; in fine, one of the English nobility that had Irish learning, and professors thereof, in greatest reverence."—*Annals of Clonmacnoise.*

These Geraldines were becoming, at this early period, as Irish as the Irish themselves—Irish in the highest and best sense of the term, in their love and appreciation of Irish literature and literary men. Irish chieftains, from a very early period, practised the humility of keeping wise and learned men near their persons, while English princes, to a later period—from excess of wisdom, no doubt—retained the services of court fools.

We learn from our Annals, that Irish society was divided into seven classes, which were distinguished by the number of colors in their garments. The garments of a slave contained but one color, those of a peasant, two; a soldier, three; a brughaidh, or public victualler, four; those of a chieftain, five; of an ollamh, or brehon, six; of a king or queen, seven; which seems to have been the number of perfection.

The Four Masters, under date A.M. 3664, give Tighearnmas the credit of introducing the purple, blue, and green dyes, but add—"Eochaidh Eadghadhach, who reigned eight years later, was so called, because it was by him the variety of color was first put on clothes in Ireland, to distinguish the honor of each by his raiment, from the lowest to the highest." The Four Masters make a seven-fold distinction, thus:— "One color in the clothes of slaves, two in the clothes of soldiers, three in the clothes of goodly heroes, or young lords of territories, six in the clothes of ollamhs, and seven in the clothes of kings and queens." The list is not complete, but it is probable that the robes of kings and queens were distinguished by the seven colors, that for them the royal purple was reserved.

The veneration entertained for the character of both brehon and ollamh (judge and poet), and the position which they held in kings' palaces, contrasts curiously with the otherwise barbarous condition of society, and reflects somewhat to the disadvantage of a later age. The ancients clothed their wise men in purple and scarlet, and adorned their persons with collars and chains of gold; the moderns "build their sepulchres." When a brehon or ollamh died the circumstance was deemed of sufficient importance to be entered in the Annals of the Kingdom. " A.D. 1166, Raynall O'Daly, Ollamh of Desmond, died."

These learned men received substantial rewards while living. We read as late as A.D. 1578, " John, the son of Donal, son of Teige Mac Clancy, chief professor of Brehonism to the Earl of Desmond, died. There was not a brehon or judge in the territory of Ireland at this time who had *a better landed property and mansion than he had.*" O tempora! O mores! But truth compels us to record, that Hugh, son of Boethius Mac Clancy, a distinguished brehon, who died in 1575, was not only a " Professor of Poetry and Brehon law," but also " *a buyer of wine,*" and we conclude, a *seller* of the same article. He would have ranked as a *vintner* in the present day.

The profession of Ard Brehon, or Chief Justice, was deemed of sufficient honor to be adopted by kings' sons:—

" Age of Christ, 14.—Cairbre Caitcheann, after having been five years in the sovreignty of Ireland, died. Son to this Cairbre was *the very intelligent Morann.*"

We learn from the *Leabhar Gabhala*, that after the inauguration of Fearadhach, (who succeeded Morann's father as monarch of Ireland,) Morann was appointed as chief, or *Ard-Breilheamh.*

This Morann had a chain, or sin, called Ith-Morann,* which had an extraordinary effect upon the witness. When put round the neck of a guilty person, it squeezed him to suffocation, and when put about the neck of an innocent person, it expanded so as to reach the earth.

We are disposed to conclude that the links of the chain employed by Morann, were composed of close arguments, or perhaps, cross-examinations (vulgarly styled cross-hackling,) in the use of which our modern brehons, or lawyers, are adepts

It is by no means improbable, that Irish judges, as well as kings and chieftains, wore golden collars, or muntorcs.† We are told by the historian Rollin,— but he does not mention his authority—that thirty judges were selected out of the principal cities of Egypt, to form a body or assembly for judging the whole kingdom. The president of this senate wore a collar of gold, set with precious stones, at which hung a figure represented as blind, this being called the emblem of *Truth*. When the president put on this collar it was understood as a signal to enter upon business. He touched the party with it who gained the cause, or in other words, had Truth on his side; this was the form of passing sentence.

We find from a state paper, (Number 186,) that the brehons and their laws were in full operation in 1557, and recognised, or at least winked at by the

---

* *Ith-Morann*:—" Moranus ille Carbri filius judiciis ferendis a Rege adhibitus, observantissimus æquitatis cultor, anulum habuit ea virtute præditum, ut cujus vis judicii sententiam pronuntiaturi, vel testis testimonium prolaturi collo circumdatus arctè fauces stringeret; si latum unguem ab æquo ille, vel hic a veritate discederet. Unde vulgari diverbio testium colla Morani anulo cingi exoptamus." *Lynch*, p. 128.

† *Muntorcs* were collars for the neck. The bracelets and anklets for the arms and legs were called *failghes*.

government. In the towns, the king's laws were usually found to prevail, but out of them, either the brehon law, and the statutes of Kilcash, were exclusively obeyed; or the lord (of the soil) exercised the option to enforce the one or the other, as he thought most beneficial to himself.

The fees of brehons were regulated by scale, though they sometimes deviated from it. They were paid by both plaintiff and defendant. We discover, from a presentment made at Waterford, that the "Brehon, who was ordained by Lady Katherine Poer, took for his judgment (called *eylegeag*) 16d. of every mark sterling both of the plaintiff and defendant."

This would be 2s. 0d. in the pound in money transactions, and would amount to a large sum in the year. But if this covered *all* the expenses of plaintiff and defendant, *they* had cause to bless their stars.

The brehon fines were—for stealing a sheep, 5 marks; for drawing a weapon, 20s.; for cutting a joint—a *human* joint we conclude—100s. We could cut a joint for less money in the present day. We conclude from these fines, that when an Irishman aimed a blow, which he did not intend to be mortal, it was at the joint he struck, thus maiming his opponent for life. The loss of an arm or leg in those days was deemed worthy of public record. In a battle fought between the Geraldines and Mac Carthys, of Carbery, we read—"Two or three hundred of the valiant forces of the Geraldines were either slain or drowned; and although the Carbians were victorious, they sustained a great loss in that battle, for Torlough Mac Sweeney lost a hand and a foot, and was obliged to use a *wooden leg* to carry him from that time to his death." It appears from the fines enumerated, that the eric or lex talionis was in full operation among the brehons. Neither the rope, which some consider the perfection of our penal code, nor any other kind of capital punishment, was much in vogue. Even in the case of *fiongail*, the murder of a relative, lord, or priest, they were rather disposed to leave the murderer to the judgment of God.*

The eric, or punishment by fine, existed in Ireland from a very early period. It was similar to the *were* or *wergild* of the Saxons. The Normans, who were a people of precise honor, imposed a penalty of five sous (twopence halfpenny) for a tweak of the nose, and ten sous for *un coup au derrière*. The practice of demanding eric for injuries inflicted was adopted by the church. The following is an interesting example of the pertinacity with which an Irish abbot demanded *éric* for his alumnus or pupil, who had been suffocated in a church fired by O'Conor. The abbot was not at home, but, returning next day, was greatly incensed at the death of his ward, and demanded his eric from O'Conor. O'Conor asked what was his own award. "My award," replied the abbot, "is the very best man among you." "That is Mahon," (the lieutenant) replied O'Conor. "No, but the chief captain, O'Conor," replied Mahon. "I will not go without my eric,"

---

* The extent to which the belief of God's retributive judgment (especially in the case of an injury or an injustice done churchmen or their property) prevailed, is illustrated by a story told by Sir Richard Cox. Philip of Worcestor, Lord Justice or Governor of Ireland, came over, accompanied by one Hugh Tirrel, a man of ill report. Tirrel stole a brewing pan from the priests of Armagh. What was the consequence? The house where he lay was burned, along with the horses in the stable, and Philip of Worcestor had *a severe fit of the gripes*, " so he was fain to leave the pan, for want of the carriage," *i. e.* the means of carrying it away.

cried the abbot. The army marched out of the town, and the abbot followed it. In crossing a river, which had overflowed its banks, they had to construct a bridge; they pulled down the chapel-house of Saint John to provide the material. Mahon, who directed the party, was killed by the falling of a rafter; his sudden death, while engaged in this sacrilege, so affected O'Conor, that he gave three times the full of the king's bell, but we are not told of what—perhaps wheat—together with thirty horses, as an offering for his soul; and thus it was that the abbot, the coarb of St. Caillin, obtained eric for his ward.

In a tract on the brehon laws in Trinity College, Dublin (class H. 3, 18, p. 426), we have the fine for a cow's killing a bondsman or bondswoman:—

"If it be a bondsman or bondswoman that has been killed by a cow, the cow is forfeited. Thirty sigals of silver is the fine."

Doctor Petrie is of opinion that the *sigal* here mentioned was a small piece of silver, weighing twenty-four grains, about equal in value to the Roman denarius. "*Thirty pieces of silver*" was the value of a bondsman or bondswoman among the Jews. "So they weighed for my price thirty pieces of silver." It was for this sum that our Saviour was sold by Judas. Joseph was sold for twenty pieces, but the Midianite merchantmen, who trafficked in slaves, got Joseph under the market price.

The brehon law was in full operation throughout Ireland during the reign of Henry VIII. The poet Spenser, who flourished during Elizabeth's reign, was under the impression that the English law was inapplicable to Ireland:—

"The common law is of itself most rightful, and very convenient *for the kingdom for which it was first devised;* for this I think seems reasonable, that out of the manners of your people and the abuses of your country, for which they were invented, they take their first beginning. Now then, if these laws of Ireland be not likewise applied and fitted to that realm, they are very inconvenient."

We are not, therefore, surprised, when such opinions prevailed, to find the English law falling into disuetude, and the halls or courts of justice falling to decay. We find the following complaint, on this score, in a state paper of Henry VIII.

" And in anywise some order to be taken immediately for the building of the castle hall, where the law is kept, for if the same be not builded, the majesty and estimation of the law shall perish, the justices being then enforced to minister the lawes upon hylles [hills] as it were brehons, or wylde Irishemen, in their *eriottes.*"*
—*State papers, vol.* ii., *p.* 501.

Sir John Davies, the Irish Attorney-general to James I., who should know all about the administration of the law, informs us, that during Sir John Perrott's presidency of Munster, the English law was not in operation, and that "the people were left to be ruled by their own barbarous lords and laws."† Had the Attorney-general been better acquainted with the Irish brehon laws, he would not have styled them barbarous. Sir John Davies himself was on one occasion beholden to a brehon for important information. It was at the assizes of Fermanagh, where the judges and Chancellor were sitting. The difficulty was to discover the tenure

* *Eriot,* a meeting or council, at which the brehons administered their laws.

† *Barbarous laws.*—We cannot quarrel with the Attorney-general for speaking thus, as we find Morrough O'Brien, last king of Thomond speaking of the "*naughty laws and customs of Ireland.*"

by which Maguire held his lands. O'Breslin, the brehon, was sent for. He was a feeble old man. The judges demanded his roll, which he refused; but on the Lord Chancellor taking an oath he would return it safe, the brehon drew it from his bosom, and handed it up to the court. We are told in one of Sir John Davies' tracts, that it was well written, and contained a correct account of the tribute paid to Maguire, which consisted of cattle, cows, hogs, meal, and butter. Davies took a copy of the roll, which he afterwards lost in Dublin.

Garrett, the poet Earl of Desmond, whose love of Irish literature has produced this long dissertation, died or disappeared (perhaps to cultivate the muses,) in 1398. Doctor O'Donovan says, "Tradition still vividly remembers this Garrett; and it is said his spirit appears once in seven years, on Lough Gur, where he had a castle." It would be a happy circumstance for Celtic literature if his spirit appeared every year. There was a spirit abroad lately which recommended the abolition of the professorships of Celtic literature in the Queen's Colleges. We should warn this anti-Irish spirit not to wander, after nightfall, on the margin of Lough Gur.

In order that the poet's son, James, should receive a thoroughly Irish training, he sent him to Thomond to be educated. For this he required the king's permission. This permission was graciously granted him, as a reward of his loyalty, though so genuine an Irishman; for the two things are not really incompatible. On a Patent Roll of the 8th of December, 1388, and 12th Richard II., we find a license from the king to Gerald Earl of Desmond, in the following words:—

"The king having been credibly informed of the constant good repute which Gerald Fitzmaurice, Earl of Desmond, held and supported, above all others of his part of Ireland, for fidelity to him and his liege subjects in Munster, and on that account, and for the better preserving the peace and the said liege people for the future, being willing to shew him favour, did, at his request, grant him license to send his son, James,* to Conor O'Brien, of Thomond, an Irishman, to be brought up or educated, and there to remain as long as he should think fit, notwithstanding any statutes made to the contrary."

This royal confidence was fairly merited by the poet.

"A.D. 1377.—Gerald, Earl of Desmond, having come to the city of Cork, at the command of the justices of Ireland, with a great force of men, and having remained there for several days, at his own expense, was paid ten marks, to remunerate him for the same, and as a compensation for his servant having been drowned by accident, when riding over a piece of water, near the city, on a horse belonging to the earl, of the value of two marks."

"A.D. 1381.—O'Brien of Thomond, with an excessive force, endeavoured to make a general conquest in the counties of Limerick, Kerry and Cork; in consequence of which, and the Justice's being unable to remain in Munster without inconvenience to the king, it was agreed that Gerald Fitzmaurice, Earl of Desmond, should go towards Limerick 'to assuage their malice;' and 200 marks were directed to be paid him for one quarter's salary, and commissions of oyer and terminer were granted to him and Walter Coterell."

"A.D. 1386.—The king appointed Gerald, Earl of Desmond, and Robert Thame, Sheriffs of the county, deputies of Philip Courtenay, the Lord Lieutenant, for the defence of Munster."

"A.D. 1391.—Gerald, son of Maurice Earl of Desmond, and Patrick Fox, were appointed overseers of the conservators of the peace, and also conservators themselves, in the counties of Cork,

* *James.*—This James was the poet's youngest son. He succeeded his nephew, Thomas, the sixth earl, who was displaced for marrying Cormac' daughter.

Limerick, and Kerry, with power to compel the sheriff, conservators of the peace, and other the king's assessors, to muster the men at arms, &c., and to marshal them into thousands, hundreds, and twenties, and to lead them wherever there might be occasion, for defence of the marches."

The condition of Cork and the surrounding country at this time may be judged of from the following address of the inhabitants to Lord Rutland:—

"MAY IT PLEASE YOUR WISDOMS, to have pity on us, the king's poor subjects within the county of Cork, or else we are cast away for ever."

The address gives the former revenues of the lords, knights, and gentlemen of the county :—

"First, the Lord Marquis Caro; his yearly revenue was, besides, Dorzeyhaven, and other creeks, £2,200 sterling; the lord Barnewale of Beerhaven; his yearly revenue was, besides Bearehaven and other creeks, £1,600 sterling: the lord Vggan of the great castle; his yearly revenue was, besides havens and creeks, £1,300 sterling; the lord Balram of Emforte; his yearly revenues, besides havens and creeks, £1,300 sterling: the lord Courcy of Kilbrittain; his yearly revenue, besides havens and creeks, £1,500 sterling: the lord Mandeville of Barrenstelly; his yearly revenue, besides havens and creeks, £1,500 sterling: the lord Arundell of the Strand; his yearly revenue, besides havens and creeks, £1,500 sterling: the lord Baron of the Guard; his yearly revenue, besides havens and creeks, £1,100 sterling: the lord Sleynie of Baltimore; his yearly revenue, besides havens and creeks, £800 sterling: the lord Roche of Poole castle; his yearly revenue, besides havens and creeks, £1,000 sterling. The king's majesty hath the lands of the late young Barry, by forfeiture, the yearly revenue whereof, besides two rivers and creeks, and all other casualties, is £1,800 sterling."

The address goes on to say, that the power of these English lords was at one time equal to their property; that they had succeeded in hunting down the Irish, and driving them, like a pack of hungry wolves, into a valley called Glanehought, between two great mountains, where they fed on "*while meat*,"—rabbits, we conclude,—but now the whole country is subject to them.

"Lord Roche, lord Courcy, and the lord Barry only remain with the least part of their ancestors' possessions, and young Barry is there upon the king's portion, paying his grace never a penny rent; wherefore we, the king's poor subjects, of the city of Cork, Kinsale, and Youghal, desire your lordships to send hither two good justices, to see this matter ordered, and some English captains, with twenty Englishmen, that may be captains over us all, and we will rise with them to redress these enormities, all at our own costs; and if you do not, we be all cast away, and then farewell Munster for ever; and if you will not come nor send, we will send over to our liege lord the king, and complain on you all."

Campion says the inhabitants of Cork

"Were forced to watch their gates continually, to keep them shut at service times, at meals, from sunset to sun arising, nor suffer any stranger to enter them with his weapon, but to leave the same at a lodge appointed. They walked out at seasons for recreation with strength of men furnished, they matched in wedlock among themselves, so that well nigh the whole city was allied together."

Sir John, the fifth earl, succeeded his father, the poet, in 1398, and was drowned at the ford of Ardfinnan, on the river Suir, the next year, 1399, while in pursuit of the Butlers.

Of Thomas, the sixth earl, who died in 1520, we have a sadly interesting tale. When hunting on the banks of the Feal, near the town of Listowel, in Kerry, he strayed from his companions, and lost his way, and being benighted, took shelter in the house of Mac Cormac, one of his dependants. Mac Cormac had a fair daughter, *Catherine*,* with whom the young earl

* *Catherine* Ni William Mac Cormac : Cox.

became suddenly enamoured. He wooed and won her heart, and married her; but his alliance with the humble maiden excited the brutal pride of his followers, who regarded the indulgence of his honorable love as an unpardonable offence; they, therefore, deserted his person and pennon, and selected his uncle, James, as chief. He, with a broken heart, fled with his beautiful bride to Rouen, in France, where he died. It is to the honor of the heroic and chivalrous Henry V., of England, who was then in France, that he expressed his admiration of the young earl's character, conduct, and choice, by attending as chief mourner at his grave. Moore has immortalised the memory of the banished earl, whom he represents as thus addressing his followers:—

> You who call it dishonor
> To bow to this flame—
> If you've eyes—look but on her
> And blush, while you blame.
> Hath the pearl less whiteness,
> Because of its birth?
> Hath the violet less brightness,
> For growing near earth?

James, the young man's uncle, and the poet's son, who had been fostered by O'Brien, assumed the title of the seventh earl, and was called the *Usurper*. This is scarcely fair, inasmuch as the Irish not only exercised the power of electing, but also of dethroning their princes or chieftains. We learn from O'Flaherty, the author of *Ogygia*, that " any male relative," be he " uncle, brother, or son, might succeed to the chieftainship."

" It is to be imagined," says Hume, speaking of the Saxon government, " that an independent people, so little restrained by law, and cultivated by science, would not be very strict in maintaining a regular succession of their princes. Though they paid great regard to the royal family, and ascribed to it an undisputed superiority, they either had no rule, or none that was steadily observed, in filling the vacant throne; and present convenience, in that emergency, was more attended to than general principles. We are not, however, to suppose, that the crown was considered as altogether elective; and that a regular plan was traced by the constitution for supplying, by the suffrages of the people, every vacancy made by the demise of the first magistrate. If any king left a son of an age and capacity fit for government, the young prince naturally stepped into the throne: if he was a minor, his uncle, or the next prince of the blood, was promoted to the government."

Mr. Hallam argues, with his usual wisdom, for the necessity of an elective monarchy among a semi-civilised people : " In a state of civilisation so little advanced as that of the Anglo-Saxons, and under circumstances of such incessant peril, the fortunes of a nation were chiefly dependant upon the wisdom and valor of its sovereigns."

This James, the Usurper, was in bad odour with the Irish, which may be explained by the following notice in the Annals of Ireland :—

" A. D. 1414.—The Earl of Desmond came to Ireland, bringing with him many of the Saxons to devastate Munster. The Earl of Ormond came to Ireland from the king of England."

These Norman knights must have gone to England for succour. They found it difficult at this period to keep their own; if we may style it *their own*. "A great defeat was given to the English at Meath, where the Baron of Ikreen, together with a great number of nobles and plebians, were slain ; and where the son of the Baron of Ibane was taken prisoner, for whose ransom fourteen hundred marks were obtained."

Those great defeats induced the king to strengthen the hands of the Anglo-Norman earls, by an importation of Saxons. He also sent over Sir John Stanley as deputy.

"A.D. 1414. John Stanley, the Deputy of the king of England, arrived in Ireland, a man who gave neither mercy nor protection to clergy, laity, or men of science, but subjected as many of them as he came upon to cold, hardship, and famine. It was he who plundered Niall, the son of Hugh O'Higgin. The O'Higgins, with Niall, then satirised John Stanley, who lived after this satire but five weeks, for he died of the virulence of the lampoons."

This was the second poetical miracle performed by this Niall O'Higgin, the first being the discomfiture of the Clan Conway the night they plundered Niall at Cladann.

Irish poets, or rhymers, possessed great power in this way, from time immemorial. Once upon a time the great and distinguished Seanchan, with his troop of subordinate ollamhs, paid a visit to Guaire, king of Connaught. The cross old man being displeased with the fare at court, refused the rations provided for him. After a three days' fast, his wife persuaded him to try an egg. By some neglect of the servants, the mice had sucked it. The rhymer was so exasperated that he vowed to satirise the mice, but, upon reflection, determined to lampoon the cats.

Irish poets were fond of this sort of thing, but they did not confine it to the cats; they more frequently satirised men, and very often great men. We read in the *Book of Ballymote* (fol. 77, p. 2, col. b.) of a poet named Athairne, of Binn-Edair, (now Howth) satirising the men of Leinster for having killed his only son. "He continued for a full year to satirise the Leinstermen, and bring fatalities upon them, so that neither corn, grass, nor foliage grew for them that year."

There was an impression abroad at this time, that poets could satirise people to death. The wife of Caier, king of Connaught, conceived a criminal passion for the poet Neidhe, and offered him a ball of silver; but he, like a second Joseph, rejected her advances, till she offered him the kingdom. "How can that be, seeing the king is living?" said Neidhe.—"It will be easy enough," replied the queen, "for you are a poet, and can *rhyme him to death*, or bring a blemish on his cheek. A man with blemish cannot enjoy the kingdom." The poet went to work, and composed an *aeir*. The king went to the well next morning, to wash his face, and drawing his hand across his cheek *felt three great boils*.

If Irish poets could satirise Irish kings and Irish deputies after this fashion, we are not surprised to find the English government making laws and regulations against them.

"Item, that no yryshe mynstrels, rymours, shannaghes, ne bardes, unchaghes, nor messenges, come to desire any goodes of any man dwellinge within the Inglyshrie, uppon peyne of forfayture of all theyr goodes and theyr bodyes to prison."—*State Papers*, vol. ii, p. 215.

We read in the Four Masters, under date 1576, of Sir Henry Sidney, " suppressing the custom of keeping poets and literary men."

But poets and satirists laugh at penal laws. The famous Florence Mac Carthy, who knew this as well as any man in Ireland, wrote a letter, (which is still preserved in the State Paper office,) in which he pretty broadly recommends the government to employ the poets, for he knew they were a class of men who might be tempted to direct their Greek fire against each other, and their own chieftains.

"The two sorts of people of the greatest abilty and authority to persuade the Irish gentlemen, are the priests and the rimers. The priests may not be trusted to do service to the queen,* while of the rimers, only some may, if employed by those gentlemen whose followers they are by lineal descent."

Mac Carthy then goes on to say, (and we blush for Florence's sake, to quote his words) that "*I mean to employ one of special trust and sufficiency.*" It is supposed that he here refers to the famous Irish poet, Aenghus O'Daly, who wrote the fearful lampoon on the poverty, meanness, and want of hospitality of Irish chieftains, for which he paid the penalty of his life. He was stabbed to the heart in the house of O'Meagher, chief of Ikerrin, in the county of Limerick.

The terrific satire for which he met this fearful death, is entitled the *Tribes of Ireland*. It has been translated from the Irish, and annotated by Doctor O'Donovan. We may have occasion to quote from it,

---

* *Do service to the queen.*—Considering the kind of service required, this must be viewed as a compliment to "the priests."

"There is certainly no family," writes Doctor O'Donovan, "to which the bardic literature of Ireland is more deeply indebted than that of O'Daly." They are descended, according to O'Flaherty, from the race of Maine, son of Niall of the Nine Hostages. We discover from the Irish annals of 1213, that an ancestor of Aenghus O'Daly, who was also a poet,—the profession was hereditary in the family—slew a churl servant of O'Donnell, who insulted him. O'Donnell pursued the poet and caused him to flee to Clanrickard, to Richard De Burgo, for protection. Here he composed a poem, in which he expresses the utmost astonishment that anything so trifling as the murder of a clown, should produce a difference between him and O'Donnell. We give our own *free* translation of one of the verses :—

> A trifling difference,—you see,
> Your shepherd was affronting me;
> I raised my axe, and killed the clown;
> O God! and can this cause a frown.

O'Donnell, who was foolish enough to take the thing seriously—perhaps he viewed it as a personal insult—obliged the poet to flee for his life to Scotland. But there he composed a poem, which smoothed the raven-down of darkness from the chieftain's brow: "O'Donnell kind of hand. He obtained peace for his panegyric. "O'Donnell received him into friendship, and gave him lands and possessions as was pleasing to him."

Nearly two hundred years after this (in 1394), we read of an O'Daly slaying "Teig O'Haughian, a learned poet," in a squabble about "the Ollamhship of O'Neill." A fruitful branch of this poetic and pugilistic family settled in Munster as early as the twelfth century, and became Ard-Ollamhs in poetry to the MacCarthys, kings of Desmond. One "Raynall O'Daly, Ollamh of Desmond in Poetry, died," as we have seen, in 1161. From this man the O'Daly's of Muinter-Bhaire, in the south-west of the county of Cork, are descended.

Sir John Stanley, who was satirised to death, was succeeded by Sir John Talbot,* called Lord Furnival. He was styled the English Achilles, on account of his bravery in the French wars, during the reign of Henry V. He landed at Dalkey, in September, 1414, and remained in Ireland six years, preying and spoiling like any Irish chieftain. "He carried off great preys of cows and horses, and cattle, and plundered Mic nam-Breathnack (the sons of Welshmen), and hanged Garrett, the son of Thomas Ceach, of the Geraldine blood." He also plundered a great number of the poets of Ireland. Talbot left Ireland, we are told, "being runne much in debt for victuall and divers others things, carrying along with him the curses of many." He left his brother Richard, Archbishop of Dublin, as deputy in his stead.

The incidents recorded during the earlship of James the Usurper, who reigned "nearly" half a century, are very few. The following is to his credit:—

"Anno 1418.—The manors of Moyallow, [Mallow] Broghil, and Kilcolman, were assigned to Maurice, the son of Thomas, the sixth Earl of Desmond, by his uncle [granduncle] James, who usurped the earldom."

* Sir John Talbot married the eldest daughter of Sir Thomas Neville, by Joan, the sole daughter and heiress of William, the last Lord Furnival.

This Maurice was the son of the banished earl, who married Cormac's daughter.

There is an entry in the year, 1418, of the deaths of Bishop O'Driscoll, his brother, Maccon O'Driscoll, lord of Corca Largh, and Dermot Mac Carthy, Tanist of Hy-Cairbre, or Carbery.

There were four branches of this distinguished Irish family, namely—the Mac Carthy More, principally of Kerry, the Mac Carthys of Muskerry, the Mac Carthys of Carbery,* and the Mac Carthys of Duhallow. The Dermot Mac Carthy, whose decease is here recorded was the *Tanist* of Carbery. We shall explain the meaning of this term.

We have already stated that the chieftain was elected by the tribe. In the state of society which then existed, the death of a chieftain,—and their lives were always in jeopardy,—would have produced great confusion, if not anticipated by the previous nomination or election of his successor. The person so nominated was called the *Tanist*.†

"On choosing the prince, a successor was at the same time appointed, who, in case of the decease of the former, should assume the sovereignty. This person might be either the son, or brother, or some other of the worthier descendants of the family, and was styled the *Tanist*, a designation adopted from the ring finger, which, as in length and position, it was next to the middle—so the Tanist was next to the prince in position and authority. And from this circumstance, Davis and Ware derive the origin of the law of tanis-

* *Mac Carthys of Carbery.*—This branch of the family was originally seated along the river Maigue, whence they were driven, by the Fitzgeralds, into Carbery, which had been originally in the possession of and ruled over by the O'Donovans. We learn from the Annals of Innisfallen that Auliffe O'Donovan was king of Hy-Cairbre in 1201.

† *Tanist.*—Skinner thinks *tanist* comes from Thane; and Spencer, from Tania, a province, as Aquitania, Lusitania, or Brittania, or from "*Dania*, that is the Danes."

try. Each of the remaining members of the family was styled Righdamna, that is, the *material* of a king, or one who was capable of being selected to exercise the functions of royalty."—*O'Flaherty's Ogygia.*

The following interesting passage is from Spenser's *View of the state of Ireland*, written before the end of the sixteenth century :—

" EUDOXUS—What is this which you call *Tanist* and *Tanistry?*

IRENEUS—It is a custom amongst all the Irish, that presently after the death of any of their chief lords or captains, they do presently assemble themselves to a place generally appointed and known unto them, to choose another in his stead, where they do nominate and elect for the most part, not the eldest son, nor any of the children of the lord deceased, but the next to him of blood, that is, the eldest and worthiest; as commonly the next brother unto him, if he have any, or the next cousin, or so forth, as any is elder in that kindred or sept; and then next to him, do they choose the next of the blood to be Tanist, who shall succeed him in the said captainry, if he live thereunto.

EUDOX.—Do they not use any ceremony in this election, for all barbarous nations are commonly great observers of ceremonies and superstitious rites ?

IREN.—They used to place him, that shall be their captain, upon a stone, always reserved for that purpose, and placed commonly upon a hill, in some of which I have seen formed and engraven a foot, which they say was the measure of their first captain's foot, whereon, he standing, received an oath to preserve all the ancient former customs of the country inviolable, and to deliver up the succession peaceably to his Tanist; and then hath a wand delivered unto him by some whose proper office that is, after which, descending from the stone, he turneth himself round, thrice forward, and thrice backward.

EUDOX.—But how is the Tanist chosen?

IREN.—They say he setteth but *one* foot upon the stone, and receiveth the like oath that the captain did.

EUDOX.—Have you ever heard what was the occasion and first beginning of this custom ?

IREN.—I have heard that the beginning and cause of this ordinance amongst the Irish was specially for the defence and maintenance of their lands in their posterity, and for excluding all innovation or alienation thereof unto strangers, and specially to the English. For when their captain dieth, if the seigniorie should descend to his child, and he perhaps an infant, another, peradventure, would step in between, or thrust him out by strong hand, being then unable to defend his right, or to withstand the force of a foreigner; and therefore they do appoint the eldest of the kin to have the seigniorie, for that he commonly is a man of stronger years, and better experience to maintain the inheritance and defend the country, either against the next bordering lords, which used commonly to encroach one upon another, as one is stronger; or against the English, which they think lie still in wait to wipe them out of their lands and territories. And to this end, the Tanist is always ready known if it should happen the captain suddenly to die, or to be slain in battle, or to be out of the country, to defend and keep it from all such doubts and dangers. For which cause the Tanist hath also a share of the country allotted unto him, and certain cuttings and spendings upon all the inhabitants under the lord."

We read under date 1421, that one Cormac na Coille Mac Carthy (or Cormac of the Wood), of Carbery, was slain, by the sons of Owen Mac Carthy.

Sir John Talbot, or rather his brother, Richard, Archbishop of Dublin, who acted as his deputy, was succeeded in 1425, by Mortimer, Earl of March, who died of the plague the same year. His short sojourn in Ireland, and death, are thus described by an Irish chronicler:—

"A.D. 1425.—Mortimer, that is Earl of March, came to Ireland this year, and many Saxons came along with him. This earl had the guardianship of the King of England, and of the greater part of France, and of all the English of Ireland; for the King of England was left a child, and the Earl of March had his guardianship and protection. Many of the chiefs of Ireland came to the house of that earl, and returned with great satisfaction and honour. When they had completed their treaties with the earl, they set out for their homes, but before they were outside Meath, the earl died of the plague."

It was this same year that "Rory Roe O'Higgins, a learned poet, died." Was this a descendant of the famous rhymer O'Higgins, that satirised Sir John Stanley to death?

"A great war broke out" in 1430, between Mac Carthy Reagh, and James, the Earl of Desmond, called the Usurper. The castle of Cill-Britain* was taken by the earl from Mac Carthy Reagh, and given to his brother Donough, who united with Desmond in storming it. The ruins of this old Irish fortalice are still in existence. Beside them stands the modern residence of Colonel Alcock Stawell.

Two years after this, in 1432, we have the arrival of Sir Thomas Stanley, as new Lord Deputy. He was the son of Sir John Stanley, who died of the lampoon.

In June, 1438, Robert Fitz-Geoffry de Cogan made a grant of all his lands in Ireland to this seventh Earl of Desmond. Some time after this he obtained a royal patent for the government of the counties of Cork, Waterford, Limerick, and Kerry.

Two years later, in 1440, we have James, the old Earl of Desmond, in the field.

"A. D. 1440.—O'Conor Fahy, his sons and brother, went *upon* a predatory excursion into Leix, O'Moore's territory, and after having sent the prey on before them, they were overtaken by the Earl of Desmond, who defeated O'Conor, and killed his son Con, with sixty of his soldiers."

* *Cill-Britain.*—Now Kilbrittan. It is described as "a fair town in the barony of Carbery, and county of Cork."

The year 1442 was particularly fatal to the Mac Carthys :—

"A. D. 1442.—Mac Carthy Reagh, lord of Isaragh, died. The Abbot Mac Carthy died. Donell Glass; Mac Carthy, lord of Hy-Carbery, died."

Five years later, in 1447, Edmond, the son of Mac Maurice, or Fitz-Maurice, of Kerry, was slain by Cormac, the son of Owen Mac Carthy.

A. D. 1449 was a great year for Ireland. "The Duke of York came to Ireland, with great glory and pompe, and the commissioners of Ireland came to his howse. And the Irish came to his howse, and verry many beeves were given him for the mainteynance of the king's kitchen."

There were also this year great wars in Desmond, between Mac Carthy Rivagh and Thady Fitz-Cormac Mac Carthy. And Diarmaid Mac Carthy More's son was slain, and O'Sullivan More's son was taken prisoner, with Daniel Fitz Cormac Mac Carthy, *et alii multi nobiles et ignobiles.*

The last entry of importance in the reign of this old Earl of Desmond records the death of two of his sons:

"A. D. 1452.—Maurice, the Earle of Desmond's son, being slaine on Vaithney, by Conner O'Maelrian, after the castle of Uaithne was broken on Connor by the two earls. Maurice returning, unknowne to his owne men, one of the pursuers wounded his horse, and he fell down and was killed. John Cleragh, son to the said earl, died."

The old earl, James, died about ten years after this, considerably over eighty, and was succeeded by his more distinguished grandson, who was beheaded at Drogheda.

CHAPTER IV.

THOMAS OF DROGHEDA—IRISH POETS AND POOR SCHOLARS.

A. D. 1462—1468.

THOMAS, the grandson of James, the Usurper, was the Eighth Earl of Desmond. Dowling denies that "Thomas, *of Drogheda,*" could be earl at all, his father, Garrett, the son of old James, being alive. He refers to the pedigree :—" Vide pedegrew Desmonia quod non fuit comes, pater tum nevebat et cetera." He says the father predicted he would have " *an ill end.*"

There may be something in what Dowling says, for Garrett, the father of Thomas, was made prisoner by the Butlers, about the time old James the grandfather died, and Thomas, as tanist, may have assumed the earldom, and, as a consequence, have brought down upon his head a malediction which was fearfully verified.

The battle at which his father, Garrett, was made prisoner, was one of the fiercest ever fought between the Ormonds and the Desmonds. It may have laid the foundation of that permanent animosity and jealousy, which made Ireland too narrow for them both. The battle was fought at Baile-na-phoill, or Pilltown, near Carrick-on-Suir, in the county Kilkenny.

" A.D. 1462.—The young Earle of Ormond, came to Ireland in this yeare, with a multitude of Englishmen. Then great warr was raysed betwixt the Earles of Ormond,* and Desmond. Gerott, son to the Earl of Desmond, was taken prisoner by the Butlers. Portlargy, [Waterford] was taken by them, but afterwards, they on both sides ordained to decide their variances by sett battle, and soe they have done; meeting each one, with an odious irefull countenance; nevertheless, it was against the Earl of Ormond's will Mac Richard went to fight that day, for Englishmen were accustomed not to give battle on Munday, nor after noon any day; but Mac Richard respected not that their superstitious observation, but went on, though he had the worst, he being defeated and taken prisoner also, and after the account of them that knew it, there was the number of four hundred and ten of his men buried, besides all that was eaten by the doggs, and by foules of the aire."

The general on the Butlers' side is styled Mac Richard. His name was Edmond Butler. He was the son of Richard, the son of James, the son of *Iarla Balbh*, or the "Stammering Earl." This Mac Richard was in possession of a copy of the Psalter of Cashel, which he was obliged to deliver up to Thomas, the Earl of Desmond, for obtaining his liberty. This was a high price for a book, if we estimate its value by the amount paid in 1414, for the ransom of the son of the Baron of Slane, namely, fourteen hundred marks.† The Danes, who captured Mahon, Lord of Bregia, in 1029, exacted for his ransom, twelve hundred cows, seven score horses, three score ounces of gold, sixty ounces of white silver, along with the sword of Carlus, and other small etcetera.

That the Psalter of Cashel was accepted by Thomas, Earl of Desmond, as the full price of the ransom of

* *This Earl of Ormond* was considered one of the most accomplished gentlemen of his age. Edward IV. said, "If good breeding and liberal qualities were lost in the world, they might be all found in the Earl of Ormond." He died in 1478, on a pilgrimage to Jerusalem.

† *Marks.*—A mark was 13s. 4d, but a shilling then was worth a pound now.

Edmond Mac Richard Butler, appears from a fragment of a copy of the Psalter, preserved in the Bodleian Library at Oxford. In the margin of fol. 110, p. b. is as follows :—

"This was the psalter of Mac Richard Butler, until the defeat of Baille-an-phoill was given to the Earl of Ormond and to Mac Richard by the Earl of Desmond, (Thomas) when this book and the Book of Carrick were obtained in the redemption of Mac Richard, and it was this Mac Richard that had these books transcribed for himself; and they remained in his possession until Thomas, Earl of Desmond, wrested them from him.

In the genealogical work by Mac Firbis "a blessing is pronounced" on the soul of the Archbishop of Cashel, Richard O'Hedigan, *for it was by him the owner of this book was educated, Edmond, son of Richard,* son of James.*" It is then added, "Let all who read this give a blessing on the soul of both."

We conclude that the education of the principal Irish families, both Norman and Celtic, was at this time in the hands of churchmen, but there were regularly endowed teachers, whose emoluments were by no means contemptible. We discover from a tract on brehon laws, in the library of Trinity College, Dublin, H. 2, 16, and also in the *Book of Ballymote*, that the wages of a teacher, or an ollamh in poetry or language, were the same as those of an architect and builder, or as he is styled "AN OLLAVE PROFESSOR OF TRADES," who received as a reward for "the versatility of his ingenuity, and for his perfect knowledge of dissimilar arts," *twenty-one cows*, and "*a months refection to him.*"

---

* *Edmond, son of Richard.*—"Richard, the son of Edmond Mac Richard Butler, was slain in the door-way of the church of St. Canice," the cathedral church of Kilkenny, "by Fineen, one of the Ossorions," in 1478.

"If he be an ollave professor of trades, who is entitled to twenty cows as his pay, *i.e.* if he be an ollave who possesses the mastership of trades, it is ordained that twenty-one cows be his pay. These are twenty-one cows for the ollave of trades. And a month's refection to him, that is, a month is his full allowance of food and attendance; for although of old the ollave tradesman was entitled to more than this, in reward for the versatility of his ingenuity, or for his perfect knowledge of dissimilar arts, still the author of this law refused to allow him more than the ollave in poetry, or the ollave in language, or the teacher."

We may judge of the *style* in which some of these ollamhs lived, by the following notice:—

"A.D. 1496.—O'Duigennan of Kilronan, ollav of Muinter-Mealmain, a learned historian, who kept a house of general hospitality, and the richest of the literati in Ireland in flocks and herds, died in his own house at Kilronan, at a venerable age, after winning the goal from the world and the devil."

The teacher or schoolmaster was abroad at an early period in Ireland. *Abroad* in reality, for those who adopted the profession were of an itinerant, or wandering habit. In the cod. Clarend., tome 49, they are called "*Strollers.*"

"In the same year [1169] Rory O'Conor, King of Ireland, granted ten cowes yearly, from him and every king after him, in honor of Patrick, for learning to the strollers of Ireland and England."

The Annals of Ireland say this endowment was to the Rector of Ard-Macha, or Armagh, where these strolling scholars may have received lectures, for there was nothing low about a wandering life in these days. The following is the extract of a letter from Gerald Byrne to Sir John Perrott, dated 18th April, 1590, in which we find the harper riding his hackney:—

"When I saw the company of horsemen in my way, I made toward them to see what they were, and there I found him and another horseman, well furnished with horse and armour, and a harper riding upon a hackney with them; and asking them from whence they came, and whither they wolde, they said, that they came from my howse, and wolde that night lie at Morgh Mc Edmund's howse, a neighbour of mine, whose daughter was married to Feagh Mc Hugh's son; from thence they wolde go to Feagh Mc Hugh's howse."

This treatment of the ollamh in poetry, so late as the end of the sixteenth century, reminds us of Sir Walter Scott's beautiful lines, in the "Lay of the Last Minstrel":—

> "No more on *prancing palfrey borne*,
> He caroll'd light as lark at morn;
> No longer courted and caressed,
> High placed in hall, a welcome guest,
> He poured to lord and lady gay
> The unpremeditated lay.
> Old times were changed, old manners gone,
> A stranger filled the Stuarts' throne;
> The bigots of the iron time
> Had called his *harmless art a crime;*
> A wandering harper, scorned and poor,
> He begged his bread from door to door,
> And tuned, to please a peasant's ear,
> The harp a king had loved to hear."

Mr. T. W. Atkinson, in his "*Travels in the Upper and Lower Amoor,*" teaches us how the warlike passions of a clan, or tribe, were excited or controlled by the bard, or "shepherd poet." We find it difficult to believe that the following sketch is a true picture of life in the nineteenth century.

"Two Kirghis presently met me, and led me to their chief, whom we found sitting at the door of his yourt, like a patriarch, surrounded by his family, having in front his poet singing the great deeds of his race. He rose to receive me, gave me a seat on his own carpet, and then the bard continued his song. This family group, the glowing sky, and the vast plain, with the thousands of animals scattered over it, formed a charming picture. Homer was never listened to with more attention than was this shepherd poet, while singing the traditions of the ancestors of his tribe. Whatever power the old Greek possessed over the minds of his audience, was equalled by that of the bard before me. When he sung of the mountain scenes around, the pastoral habits of the people, their flocks and herds, the faces of his hearers were calm, and they sat unmoved; but when he began to recite the warlike deeds of their race, their eyes flashed with delight; as he proceeded, they were worked up into a passion, and some grasped their battle-axes, and sprang to their feet in a state of frenzy. Then followed a mournful strain, telling of the death of a chief, when all excitement ceased, and every one listened with deep attention. Such was the sway this unlettered bard held over the minds of his wild comrades."

The following picture of an Irish school for "strollers" is drawn from another point of view, and in a different spirit. "They grovel upon couches of straw, with their books to their noses; themselves lie flat prostrate, and so they chaunt out with a loud voice their lessons piecemeal, being the most part lusty fellows of twenty-five years and upwards."

This is not a very pretty picture, by Stanihurst, but we conclude that these young men lay down in the straw, with their books to their noses, for lack of forms and desks, which are modern inventions. These "lusty fellows" were the "strollers," who, in course of time, became hedge schoolmasters.

The "poor scholar" is not yet extinct. He goes about the country with a few books in a satchel or strap, and will *accept* a few pence *for paper and pens*. I knew one of them, a few years ago, and tried to put him through his moods and tenses, and found him to be a *very poor scholar* indeed.

Thomas, the Eighth Earl of Desmond, was a distinguished patron of literature, as we may imagine from his accepting the Psalter of Cashel as a full ransom for Mac Richard Butler.

The College of Youghal was founded by him, in 1464. The Four Masters style him "the most illustrious of his tribe in Ireland, in his time, for his comeliness and stature, for his hospitality and chivalry, his charity and humanity to the poor, and the indigent of the Lord." They praise him for his "bounteousness in bestowing juels and riches on the laity, and clergy, and poets, and his suppression of theft, and immorality."

He was a great favorite with Edward IV., King of England, and stood in the relation of godfather to George, Duke of Clarence. He went to England in 1464, and returned Lord Chief Justice of Ireland, which high honor must have begotten no small jealousy in the bosoms of the Butlers, and other Irish and English lords; but some repaired to his court in Dublin.

"A.D. 1464.—Mac William Bourke and O'Donnell, and many of the English and Irish, went to Dublin towards Thomas, Earle of Desmond, Lord Deputye of Ireland, and adheared to him. Nine of the Lord Deputye's men were slaine in Fingall, through the instigation of the Bishop of Meath. The Deputy and Bishop aforesaid, and the Preston, went to their king's house, condemning each other."

Some are of opinion that it was his close adhesion to the Burkes, O'Donnells, O'Briens,* Kildares, and other Irish lords, which lost him royal favor, and finally his head; but a more interesting, and perhaps probable explanation is given of this tragic affair.

* *O'Briens.*—The Earl of Desmond relinquished his claim on Clanwilliam, in Tipperary, and any claims he possessed on the county of Limerick, to O'Brien, in 1466.

Leland and Cox say he lost his head for calling Edward's queen (the beautiful Elizabeth Woodville) " a tailor's wife." But his offence was of a more serious character. Before leaving England the king entreated him, in the privacy of friendship, to say " whether he saw aught amiss in his conduct, or in the administration of the offices of his kingdom." The earl assured him he knew of nothing but his unwise marriage with the widow of Woodville, Lady Elizabeth, whom the king had clandestinely espoused ; " Wherefore, I think," said the earl to his Majesty, " you would do well in divorcing the present queen, and forming a new alliance with some powerful princess." This advice, which the king took in good part, afterwards cost this earl Thomas his head ; for during some bitter altercation with his queen, the king said to her : " Had I hearkened to my cousin Desmond's advice, I should have humbled thy proud spirit."

" What advice ? " said she.

" It matters not now," said he, but, pressed hard, he told her all, for he deemed his friend Desmond, who was then the Deputy of Ireland, safe from her hands. But in the course of time, she obtained his removal, and had Tiptoft, my Lord of Worcester—a friend of her own—appointed in his place, who on his arrival, arraigned the Earls of Desmond and Kildare, of "alliance, fosterage, et alterage avecq les Irois enemies du Roy comme en donnant a eux chevaulx et harneis et armors et supportant eux envers les foilax sujects du Roy."

They brought the order for beheading him to the king, who refused to sign to it ; but the queen, who hated Desmond as bitterly as Herodias did John the Baptist—and with far better reason—obtained the signet by stealth, and placed it with her own fair hand on the paper, and sent it to Worcester, who instantly acted on it. He laid claim to some of the earl's estates. When Edward IV. was made acquainted with the treachery, he became so enraged with the queen, that she had to leave the court, and fly to a place of safety. Worcester was beheaded himself shortly after. The doom of Tiptoft is thus described in the Four Masters :—

"A.D. 1470.—The Earl of Warwick, and the Duke of Clarence, cut into quarters the wreck of the maledictions of the men of Ireland, namely, that Saxon Justiciary; and it was in revenge of the death of Thomas, Earl of Desmond, that this ignominious punishment was inflicted on him, and the Earl of Kildare appointed in his stead."

"Much destruction," we are told, in the same annals, " was caused by Garrett, the son of the Earl of Desmond, in Munster and Leinster, in revenge of the death of Thomas the Earl." The Earl of Ormond thus describes the effect of the murder of this earl—for we can call it nothing else—upon his followers:—"They have such a cankered malicious rebellion rooted in them, evye sithens the putting to execution of Thomas, Earle of Desmond, at Drogheda, that they ben as far seperated from the knowledge of any duty of allegiance that a subject oght to owe his prince, as a Turk is to believe Christianity. Thei blaspheme the king, and have their ears and eies open every day, gaping to have assistance in this open rebellion out of Spain."

The following anecdote of this earl is worthy of record. It ocurred at Mogeely Castle, on the banks of the Bride. He had a steward as famous at expedients as he of Ravenswood. The steward, without his master's permission, gave an invitation to a number of the chiefs of Munster, to spend a month at the castle. The invitation was accepted with alacrity; the Fitzgeralds came in crowds, nor could the earl say them nay, though the castle was not overstocked with provisions. The servants informed him one day there was nothing for dinner, that the Irish chieftains had fairly eaten themselves out. Here was a predicament! The honor of his house and his character, for hospitality, were at stake. He invites them to a hunt, commanding the servants to set fire to the castle in his absence. He looked on his return for the flames; could see none, but met the steward, who told him to cheer up, that he had been out and taken a prey of corn and cattle, (probably from the lands of some of his guests) which would sustain both his castle and credit for months.

Donald Roe Mac Carthy, of Desmond, contended with Maguire, prince of Desmond, in the beginning of the fourteenth century, for the palm of hospitality. A bard was engaged to spend a year at each of their houses. He adjudged the prize to Maguire, declaring, that although he possessed less territory, he exceeded Mac Carthy in the number of his servants and retainers, and the quantity of food consumed in his house. The Desmond, or Mac Carthy's country, is thus bitterly described by an Irish poet, who passed through it at a much later period:—

"But of all places, Desmond in truth takes the lead
In fasting. I pray God it may win its just meed.
If a pilgrim gain heaven for sandal and scallop,
Then Desmond, methinks, should come in at a gallop."

CHAPTER V.

STATE OF SOCIETY—LAMBERT SIMNEL AND PERKIN WARBECK—CITY CHARTERS.

A.D. 1468—1497.

THE year after the death of the Anglo-Norman Earl of Desmond the following entry occurs in our Irish Annals :—

"A.D. 1469.—Mac Carthy More, lord of Desmond, died." In 1471—" The son of the Earl Thomas was *styled* the earl, but was soon after taken prisoner by the Mac Carthys." In 1472—" The young earl was set at liberty by the Mac Carthys."

There were at this time four distinct chieftaincies of the Mac Carthys; the Mac Carthys More, or lords of Desmond, and their off-shoots, namely, the Mac Carthys Reagh of Carbery, the Donough Mac Carthys of Duhallow, and the Mac Carthys of Muskerry. The Mac Carthys Reagh, with Donnell Gud, as their chief, branched off in 1185, during the lifetime of Donnell More na-Curra, lord of Desmond; the Duhallow Mac Carthys, soon after, with Donough for their head, in the lifetime of Cormac Fune, lord of Desmond; and in the fourteenth century, the Mac Carthys of Muskerry, with Diarmaid More as their chieftain, during the lifetime of Cormac Mac Donnell Oge, lord of Desmond. The following entry refers to the Mac Carthys of Muskerry :—

"A.D. 1467.—The Monastery of Cill-Credhe,* in the diocese of Cork, was founded for Franciscan friars by the Mac Carthys; and they erected an honorable tomb† in it for the interment of their gentlemen and chieftains."

The Castle of Blarney, as well as Kilcrea Abbey, two of the finest structures of the kind of the period, were both erected by Cormac Mac Carthy, surnamed *Laider*, "the Strong." His strength seems to have been displayed in works of patriotism, taste, and piety, as well as war.

Both Anglo-Norman and Irish chieftains seemed about this time to be emulating each other in deeds of blood and barbarous cruelty. James, Earl of Desmond, is no sooner liberated, than he disables or maims his uncle Garrett,—probably by "cutting a joint." Garrett is slain, and eighteen of the Geraldines "put to death" in 1477.

"A. D. 1477, Cormac, the son of Donough, son of Mac Carthy Reagh, was taken prisoner by Cormac, son of Teige, son of Cormac, son of Dermot Reamheer, of Muskerry, and by the sons of Dermot an-Duna, the sons of his father's brother."

He was afterwards blinded. The Dublin copy of the Annals of Ulster say emasculated. We should not have suspected Mac Carthy Laider, the founder of Kilcrea, of countenancing such barbarous conduct. But the times were barbarous.

---

* *Cill-Credhe.*—Anglicised Kilcrea, the cell or church of St. Credh, a virgin, who had a nunnery here at an early period.

† *An honorable tomb.*—The founder, Cormac Mac Carthy, surnamed Laider, or "the Strong," was buried here in 1495. Charles Mac Dermot Mac Carthy, lord of Muskerry (a Protestant), was interred here in 1616. The Barretts, and other principal persons, were also interred here.

This fearful and inhuman habit of blinding was resorted to in Ireland to disqualify for kingship or chieftainship. We read of Roderick O'Conor, the "Last Monarch of Ireland," blinding his own brother, Brian. But the practice was not confined to Ireland. Shakspeare gives us a horrible example in his King Lear, where Cornwall plucks out Gloster's eyes, and tramples upon them.

> GLO.—" If wolves had at thy gate howl'd that stern time,
> Thou should'st have said ' *Good porter turn the key.*'
> All cruel's else subscrib'd. But I shall see
> The winged vengeance overtake such children.
>
> CORN.—*See it !* Thou shalt never. Fellows, hold the chair.
> Upon these eyes of thine I'll set my foot."

We read, a few years after this, of Donough Oge Mac Carthy, or young Donough Mac Carthy, lord of Ealla, killing "Barry More John, the choicest of the English youths in Ireland," on a Christmas-day.

In 1487, James, the Earl of Desmond, was treacherously slain by his own people, at Rathkeale, at the instigation of John, his brother. The murderers were banished by Maurice, the earl's son.

Next comes the murder of Mac Carthy Laider himself :—

> "A. D. 1495.—Cormac Mac Carthy, the son of Teige, son of Cormac, lord of Muskerry, was slain by his own brother Owen, and his (Owen's) sons. He was the exalter and reverer of the church, the first founder of the Monastery of Cill Chreidhe, and a man who had ordered *that the sabbath should be strictly observed throughout his territory.* Owen, son of Teige, assumed his place."

Con, the son of Donnell, paid a visit to Mac Carthy's country this year, and took a prey at the head of his "*great little army.*" If Con be a fair specimen of a Northern chieftain, the South was the more civilised part of Ireland. Con never assembled more than twelve score axe-men for a standing fight, and sixty horsemen for following up the route. Hearing that Mac Keon of the Glins had the prettiest wife, the best dog, and fastest steed in the country, he resolved to visit him. He did so, but asked for the steed only, for Con had a conscience. The churl, Mac Keon, refused, so Con assembled a troop of horse, and carried off the three, with all the property. The story goes, that Con made full restitution to Mac Keon's wife of all *her* property. Whether he ever made restitution to the husband of his property *in his wife* is not stated. He divided the spoil which he took from the Mac Carthys and Mac Keons among the men of Ulster.

If such raids, burnings, and taking of preys, did not bring a curse in the shape of blighting or mildew, they were well calculated to produce famine.

The Annals of Ireland for 1497, records a fearful famine:—

"A.D. 1497.—A great intolerable famine throughout all Ireland this year, the likeness of which the people of that time had never seen, for there was scarce a corner or angle of all Ireland in which many persons did not die of that famine. Throughout Meath generally, a peck of wheat was purchased for five ounces, and a gallon of ale for sixpence, and among the Gaels, a small *beart* of oats, containing ten meaders, was purchased for an in-calf cow, and a beef was sold for a mark, and a milch cow for two in-calf cows, and a shilling more."

Henry VII., Duke of Richmond, was proclaimed King of England, in 1485. We learn from the Annals of

Ulster,* that the impression abroad throughout Ireland at this time, was, that Henry, Duke of Richmond, was not the true heir to the throne; that the real prince was Lambert Simnel, the son of a tradesman at Oxford. This young man was set up by Margaret, Duchess of Burgandy, sister to Edward IV., as her brother, the Duke of Clarence's son.

"A.D. 1485.—The King of England, Richard, was slain in a battle, in which fifteen hundred were slain, and the son of a Welshman, [Henry VII. Duke of Richmond,] by whom the battle was fought, was made king. But there lived not of the royal blood at the time but one youth, who came the next year in exile to Ireland.

The son of Clarence was likely to be received with open arms in Ireland. It was Clarence that avenged the murder of his godfather, Thomas of Drogheda, Earl of Desmond, and procured Desmond's friend, Garrett, Earl of Kildare, to be appointed Chief Justice, in place of Tiptoft, Earl of Worcester, by whom Desmond was adjudged to death. We are not therefore surprised to find Simnel, (the supposed son of Clarence), received in Dublin, by the Earl of Kildare, who was then Lord Deputy; by the Chancellor, the Treasurer, Lord Lovel, Lord Lincoln, and many other nobles and chief men, lay and clerical. He was crowned in Christ Church, and carried thence in triumph to the castle of Dublin, on the shoulders of a gigantic Irishman, named Darcy. It is said that the diadem used on the occasion, was taken from the statue of the Virgin, kept in a church near Damesgate.

As Henry VII. had the real son of the Duke of

* *The Annals of Ulster* were compiled, to a great extent, by Cathal Mac Manus Maguire, who was Archdeacon of Clogher, in 1486.

Clarence under bolt and bar, in the Tower, he displayed the magnanimity of pardoning Simnel, and making him a turnspit in his kitchen.

"A.D. 1497.—Great famine throughout all Ireland this and the following year, *so that the people ate of food unbecoming to mention, and never before heard of as having been introduced on human dishes.*"

These words have a ghoulish import. We learn from Spenser, that the people fed on human flesh and human carcases raked out of their graves, about a century after this.

We have an account about this time, of a man raked or dug out of his grave, but for another purpose:—

"A.D. 1500.—Barry More was slain by his own kinsman [or brother] David Barry, Archdeacon of Cloyne and Ross. David was slain by Thomas Barry and Muinter O'Callaghan. The Earl of Desmond disinterred the body of David in twenty days, and afterwards burned it.

The Dublin copy of the Annals of Ulster say the Earl of Desmond made "*meal and ashes,*" of the fratricide's bones. The Thomas Barry who united with O'Callaghan in revenging the death of Barry More, by slaying the Archdeacon, seems to have been engaged in the Simnel rebellion, and was obliged to take a new oath of allegiance.

Sir Richard Edgecomb, who had been employed to receive the oaths and allegiance of the Irish lords who had espoused the pretensions of Lambert Simnel, arrived in the harbour of Kinsale on the 27th June, 1488. He had five ships and five hundred men. He, notwithstanding, refused, at first, to land, but compelled Lord Thomas Barry, or Barry Oge, to attend him on board ship, and there renew his oath of allegiance, and do homage for his barony. Sir Richard was prevailed on the next day to land and enter the town, where he was met by the Lord de Courcy and others, who did homage in the church of St. Multosius.

The Earl of Desmond, who had the body of David Barry disinterred, was Maurice, the tenth earl. This Maurice united with the famous Perkin Warbeck, who assumed to be the Duke of York, or second son of Edward IV., who is generally believed to have been murdered with his elder brother, in the Tower of London, at the command of Richard III.

Perkin Warbeck arrived in Cork from Lisbon in 1492, where he was kindly received by the citizens, and "caressed," as Doctor Smith says, by John Walters, an eminent merchant, who was Mayor in 1490 and 1492. Perkin Warbeck wrote to Garrett, Earl of Kildare, at this time Lord Deputy, and to the Earl of Desmond, informing them of his arrival; but before he got their replies, he had received a letter from the French king, inviting him to visit France, for which he set sail, and was "royally entertained," till such time as a treaty of peace was concluded between France and England, when he received intimation that his presence could be dispensed with. He went from France to Flanders, to visit his supposed aunt, the Duchess of Burgundy, where he remained for three years. He set sail from Flanders in 1495, with six hundred men, and made a landing on the coast of Kent, where a hundred and sixty of his followers were made prisoners, and afterwards hanged.

Not liking this sort of treatment, he resolved to try

Cork a second time, where he met much kindness, but little aid; so he determined to try Scotland. Here he married a daughter of the Earl of Huntley, and persuaded the Scots to invade England; but a " treacherous peace" having been concluded between the two countries, he resolved, for the third time, to visit his Irish friends.

He arrived in Cork in July, 1497, and was joined by the Earl of Desmond and the Duke of Lincoln in the siege of Waterford. The account of this siege is thus recorded in Doctor Ryland's *History of Waterford:*—

"In the year 1497, it was again the good fortune of the citizens of Waterford to manifest their loyalty to the king; for which, among other honours, they received the following motto—' *Intacta manet Waterfordia.*' On this occasion they communicated to his majesty the intelligence of the arrival of Perkin Warbeck at Cork, and assured him of their loyalty and affection.

"An opportunity was now afforded them to prove the sincerity of their professions, and the extent of their devotion, for immediately on his landing, the whole strength of the rebel force was directed against Waterford. Perkin Warbeck, and Maurice, Earl of Desmond, with an army of 2,400 men, advanced to the city, and on the 23rd of July prepared to invest it. This force was intended to assault the western division, while a fleet of eleven ships, which arrived at Passage, was ordered to engage from the river; there was also a body of troops landed from the fleet, who were to proceed in the direction of Lumbard's Marsh, and co-operate with the land forces.

" To prevent the junction of these two divisions, the

ponds of Kilbarry were kept full, the besieged having raised a large mound of earth to stop the course of the river, which flows from Kilbarry into the Suir. The necessary preparations being completed, the siege was vigorously commenced and carried on, for eleven days, with great zeal and activity. In the many skirmishes and sorties which took place, the citizens were generally victorious, and routed or captured their opponents. In the field, the citizens covered themselves with glory; but it is to be regretted that after the fight their valiant hearts had no touch of pity. On one occasion, after a successful sortie, in which they committed great slaughter, they returned to the city with a numerous band of prisoners; they carried them to the market place, chopped off their heads, and fastened them on stakes, as trophies of their victory. Their valour and the dread of their cruelty could no longer be resisted, the besieged became the assailants; the enemy were repulsed in every direction, and what served to ensure the victory of the citizens, the cannon planted on Reginald's Tower, after many days' hard firing, beat in the side of one of the ships, when the entire crew perished.

"The enemy, disheartened by all these untoward occurrences, and fearing to await the vengeance of the enraged citizens, raised the siege, and on the night of the 3rd of August, retreated to Ballycasheen, from thence they proceeded to Passage, where Perkin Warbeck embarked, and fled to Cork. The citizens pursued him, with four ships, and, after an eager chase, followed him to Cornwall, where he landed. When this intelligence reached the king, who was then at Exeter, he ordered the pursuit to be continued, and Perkin was at length apprehended.

"The loyalty and courage of the citizens of Waterford were duly appreciated by the monarch, who, in addition to other marks of favor, was pleased to honor them with two letters."

Doctor Ryland does not inform us, that after the siege of Waterford, Perkin visited Cork, where the Earl of Desmond raised a hundred and twenty men, and procured vessels to enable him to make a descent upon Cornwall. Here he was well received, and joined by thousands. He assumed the title of Richard IV., and laid siege to the city of Exeter, which shut its gates against him. He was compelled, on the approach of the king's troops, to raise the siege, and flee from the royal ire to the sanctuary of Beaulieu. After a time he surrendered himself, and was imprisoned in the tower, with the young Earl of Warwick. Perkin escaped from the tower, was retaken, and hanged.

We omit the "*two letters*," as we are not writing the history of Waterford, although they are very complimentary. Henry, like a wise monarch, reserved his more substantial favors for his enemies. The Earl of Desmond, who provided both men and arms for the siege, was not only pardoned, but received "a grant of the customs of Limerick, and other the king's heriditaments in the ports, city, and towns of Cork, Kinsale, Baltimore and Youghal."

David, Archbishop of Cashel, and the Bishops of Cork and Waterford, were also compromised in this foolish rebellion, but were pardoned, "the better to quell the contrivances and designs of Perkins' friends."

John Walters, Mayor of Cork, was treated somewhat differently. He was tried at Westminster, by a jury of twelve men, found guilty of high treason, and hanged at Tyburn, in November, 1499, with his friend and protege, Master Perkin Warbeck. Their heads were afterwards set up on London bridge. Philip Walters, the Mayor's son, who was implicated, received the royal pardon, though Lord Bacon says he was executed with his father.

We learn from Campion, who wrote his *Historie of Irelande*, in 1570, that Perkin Warbeck made the following declaration before his execution :—

"I, being born in Flanders, in the town of Tournay, put myself in service with a Breton called Pregaut Meno, who brought me with him into Ireland, and when we there arrived, in the town of Cork, they of the town, because I was arrayed with some clothes of silk of my said master, threaped upon me that I should be the Duke of Clarence his son, that was before-time at Dublin; and forasmuch as I denied it, there was brought unto me the Holy Evangelists, and the cross, by the mayor of the town, called John Lavallin,* and there I took my oath that I was not the said duke's son, nor none of his blood. After this there came unto me an Englishman, whose name was Stephen Poyton, with one John Walter, and swore to me that they knew well that I was King Richard's bastard son; to whom I answered, with like oaths, that I was not: then they advised me not to be afraid, but that I should take it upon me boldly; and if I would so do, they would assist me with all their power, against the king of England, and not only they, but they were assured that the Earls of Desmond and Kildare should do the same; for they cared not what part they took so they might be avenged on the king of England; so against my will, they made me to learn English, and taught me what I should do and say; after this, they called me Richard, Duke of York, second son

---

* *The Mayor of the town, called John Lavallin.* He was mayor in 1492, 1496, and 1498. There was a Richard Lavallin, mayor in 1455, very likely John's father.

to King Edward IV., because King Richard's bastard son was in the hands of the king of England; upon this they entered upon the false quarrel, and within short time after, the French king sent embassadors into England, viz., Lyot, Lucas, and Stephen Frayne; and so I went into France, thence to Flanders, thence into Ireland, from thence into Scotland, from whence I passed into England, thence back into Ireland, and so into England again."

The city of Cork lost its charter for the part it took in this rebellion, but it got a new and better one, the charter of *Inspeximus*, which gave enlarged privileges to the corporation. Cork got its first charter while John was deputy, in the reign of Henry II. It runs thus:

"I have granted and given, and by this my charter confirm, to the citizens of Cork, all the fields held of my city of Cork, and the ground on which the city is, now for my benefit to increase the strength of the citizens. This is to them and their heirs, to hold of me, and my heirs, and to remain in frank burgage, by such custom and rent as the burgesses of Bristol, in England, pay yearly for their burgages, and to secure my city of Cork, I grant this to the same my citizens of Cork, all the laws, franchises, and customs or freight which are in Bristol, on whatsoever sails. And firmly commanding that the aforesaid, my citizens of Cork, and their heirs, and their successors have the aforesaid city of Cork, of me and my successors, as is aforesaid, and have all the laws and franchises, and frank customs of Bristol, and as those were wont to be used and written in my court, and in my hundred of Cork, and in all business."

We discover from the terms "in my Hundred of Cork," that the court of *D'Oyer Hundred* was in existence at this early period. *D'Oyer* is an old French word, signifying "to hear." This corporation court of a hundred *hearers* has become a court of about half this number of *speakers*.

This charter of Henry II. is lost, but a copy of it

is preserved among the Harleian MSS. in the British Museum.

The earliest existing Cork or corporation charter is that of Henry III. This charter granted to the citizens, or rather *let* to them, for eighty marks annually, an exemption from toll and all other customs throughout his majesty's dominions, with prisage of wine, custom and cocket,* within the jurisdiction of the port.

Edward I. granted two charters, in the nineteenth and thirty-first years of his reign. The last enacted that *murage*† should be collected by the bailiffs of the city, for six years. We conclude from this that the city walls were in a dilapidated state.

In the charter of the 11th of Edward II., the office of *Mayor* is, for the first time named. The next year, there was an enactment passed which abolished the necessity of the elected Mayor's going to Dublin, to be sworn in before the Barons of the Exchequer, his predecessor in office being authorised to receive the necessary oaths.

Charters were granted in the 4th and 5th of Edward III., in the 5th of Richard II., and in the 2nd of Edward IV. This last, after reciting that the Mayor and commonality had eleven parish churches within the city, which extended, with the suburbs, a mile in every direction, and which had been, for fifty years preceding, destroyed by Irish enemies and English rebels, remits all arrears, and grants them the cocket of the city for the construction of the walls, till such

---

* *Cocket* was a seal belonging to the king's customs. To grant cocket meant to forego customs.

† *Murage.*—Money paid to keep the city walls in repair.

time as they should be able to travel peaceably one mile beyond them. This looked like granting cocket, or foregoing customs, in socula seculorum. It was a hundred and forty years after this that Sir Warham St. Leger was killed within a mile of Cork.

We learn from a curious letter written by "John Deythyke, Prest," that Dublin, in 1533, was even worse than Cork at this time :—

"Your mainstership knoweth their accostomed ceremonie is to refrain from flesh on Wednesday; but now they be much more full of devotion, for they not only abstain on Wednesday, but also Sunday, Monday, Tuesday, and Thursday. I trust to Jesus, ye may have many saintes amonge them. But they play the foxe's parte when he could not reach the hens. All the butchers in Dublin have not as much beefe to sell as would make one mess of browse. The cause whereof is, they are *nyghtly robbyd*. There has been *five or six prayes taken out of Saynt Thomas*' [*parish*] *within this ten dayse*. Another cause is the country is so quiett, they dare not ryde one myle out of town to buy any maner of vyttles.—*See State Papers, vol.* ii, *p.* 180.

In the 15th of Edward IV., all former charters were confirmed, and the Mayor and citizens enjoyed their franchises within both city and suburbs, and through the entire port. — *Vide p.* 22.

It then releases, during pleasure, all arrears of the rent of eighty marks, and grants that the corporation, in lieu thereof, shall in future, render at the exchequer, twenty pounds of wax.*

Henry VIII., in the first year of his reign, granted a " *Confirmatory Charter*," and in the twenty-eighth, a charter, which conferred on the Mayor " one decent

* *Wax.*—The breath from our mountains are to the present day as fragrant of wild honey, as the heights of Hymettus. We have purchased the best maiden honey in the county for twopence and threepence a pound.

sword sheathed," and upon the sword-bearer a *remarkable cap.**

" We grant and give license to our well-beloved subject, William Coppinger, now mayor of our said city, and his successors, mayors of Cork, that he, as long as he shall continue mayor within said city, may and can have borne and carried before said mayor, and all other mayors for the time being, within said city and liberties thereof, one decent sword, sheathed, and our will is that the sword bearer be adorned with a remarkable cap, when they think fit, for the cause aforesaid."

It is not perfectly clear, from the wording, whether this " remarkable cap " is to be mounted when the mayors or the sword-bearers " *think fit.*"

By a charter of the 18th of Elizabeth, the Mayor, the Recorder, and the four senior Aldermen who had filled the office of mayor, were constituted justices of the peace, both of land and water.

The charter of 6th of James I. released the corporation from the impost of twenty pounds of wax. By this charter, the city and surrounding district, marked out by commissioners, became a distinct county, called the county of the city of Cork, over which the power of the justices of the peace for the city extended.

* *Remarkable Cap.*—Waterford also had its remarkable cap. "And now at this time, as a remembrance and evident token of our favours, we have sent you by the bearer, a *Cap of Maintenance,* to be borne at all times thought fit for you, and necessary before you, our mayor, being our officer, of that our said citie, and our successors, officers of the same."—*Ryland's Waterford,* p. 40.

CHAPTER VI.

THE NORMANS—THE COMMONERS—THE ARMY—THE CHURCH.

A.D. 1515—1535.

WHEN Henry VIII. ascended the English throne, the Irish Norman knights and their followers had become as rebellious, and every whit as Irish as the Irish themselves. The Norman invasion produced no really social or permanently political revolution in the country. The conquerors became in their turn conquered, absorbed in the mass of the people, and leavened by their laws, religion, manners, and customs. The English knights intermingled their blood with that of Irish families, and became no more nor less than Irish chieftains, with English names; Irish in heart and soul; Irish from their beaver to their brogue:—

> " Those Geraldines, those Geraldines, not long our air they breathed,
> Not long they fed on venison, in Irish water seethed;
> Not often had their children been by Irish mothers nursed,
> When from their full and genial hearts, an Irish feeling burst.
> The English monarch strove in vain, by law, and force, and bribe,
> To win from Irish thoughts and ways, this *more* than Irish tribe;
> For still they clung to fosterage, to brehon, cloak, and bard;
> What king dare say to Geraldine, your Irish wife discard ?"

In a state paper, which the poet Spenser must have seen before he wrote his "*View of the State of Ireland,*" we read:—

"Ther is more then 30 greate captaines of the Englyshe noble folke, that folowyth the same Iryshe ordre, and kepeith the same rule, and every of them makeith warre and pease for hymself, without any lycense of the king, or of any other temperall person, saive to hym that is strongeyst, and of suche that may subdue them by the sword. Ther names folowyth immedyat:—

"The Erlle of Desmounde, lorde of the countye of Kerye; the Knight of the countye of Kerye; Fytzmawryshe, of the countye of Kerye; Syr Thomas of Desmounde, knyght; Syr John of Desmounde, knyght; Syr Gerald of Desmounde, knight; the Lorde Barrye; the Lorde Roache; the younge Lorde Barrye; the Lorde Courcye; the Lorde Cogan; the Lorde Bareth; the Whyt Knyght; the Knyght of the Wall*; Syr Geralde of Desmoundi's sonnes, of the countye Waterford; the Powers, of the countye of Waterford; Syr William Bourke, knight, of the countye Lymryk; Syr Pyers Butler, knight, and all the captaines of the Butlers of the countye of Kylkennye, and of the countye of Fyddert."

Then follow the names of the "countyes that obey not the kinge's lawes, and have neyther justice, neyther shyryffs, under the king."

" The countye of Waterfford; the countye of Corke; the countye of Kylkenny; the countye of Lymbryk; the countye of Kerye; the countye of Conaught; the countye of Wolster; the countye of Charlagh; half the countye of Uryll; half the countye of Meath; half the countye of Dublyn; half the countye of Kyldare; half the countye of Wexford. All the Englyshe folke of the said countrys ben of Iryshe habyt, of Iryshe

---

* *Knight of the Wall*, or valley, pronounced *walley*, for the Normans preserved their *pronunciation* intact. By the Knight of the Walley, or valley, we understand the Knight of Glin.

langage, and of Iryshe condytions, except the cyties and the walled townes."

We find the very Lord Deputies themselves riding forth at the head of wild troops of Irish kerne and galloglasses, making raids, taking preys, and insisting on black mail, or that "damn'd impost of coyne and lyverye."

"Some say the kinge's Deputye is the cause, that all the said common people, be so poor, so feeble, and soo Iryshe; for where sometimes, in our days, the kinge's Deputye used always have about him, whereever he did ride, a strong guard on horseback, of spears and bows, well garnished after the Englyshe manner, that paid truly for ther meate and drynke, wherever they did ride, now the guard of the kinge's Deputy is none other, but a multitude of Iryshe gallowglasses, and a multitude of Iryshe kerne and speres, with an infinite number of horse-lads, and with the said guard, the kinge's Deputye is ever moving and stirring from one place to another, and with extortion of coyne and lyverye, consumeth and devoureth all the substance of the poor folk, and of the common people of all the kinge's subjects."

"The Irish in the middle ages," writes Dr. Smith, "employed two sorts of foot soldiers; one called galloglasses, armed with an iron head-piece, and a coat of defence stuck with iron nails, wearing a long sword by their sides, and bearing in one hand a broad axe, with a very sharp edge, after the manner of those ancient Gauls mentioned by Marcellinus. This kind of foot were thus armed by the Irish in imitation of what they saw used by the English, as appears from the name gallo-glass, from Gallo-glagh, *i.e.* an English servant."

Stanihurst says, the galloglasses were "grim of countenance, tall of stature, big of limb, burly of body, well and strongly timbered; feeding on beef, pork, and butter." The same writer describes the food of the people as consisting of "watercresses, which they term shamrocks, roots, and other herbs; oatmeal and butter they cram together. They drink whey milk and beef broth; flesh they devour without bread, and that half raw, the rest boileth in their stomach with aqua vitæ, which they swill in after such a surfeit by quarts and pottles. They let their cows' blood, which grown to a jelly, they bake and overspread with butter, and so eat in lumps. No meat they fancy so much as pork, and the fatter the better."

"The *kerne*, the light armed foot, signifieth shower of hell, because they are taken for no better than rakehells, or the *devil's blackguards.*" We may conclude from this description, that the kerne was a sort of *Irish Zouave*. Spenser describes them as "very valiant and hardy, great endurers of cold, labor, and hunger, very active and strong of hand, very swift of foot, very vigilant and circumspect in their enterprises, very present in perils, and very great scorners of death."

Dr. Smith's description is more classical. "Kernes were, among the Irish, light arm'd foot, perditis Levis Armaturæ, called by Henry of Marlborough, Turbiculi, and by others Turbarii. But their common names were kernes, from the Irish keathern, which signifies a company of soldiers. They wore head pieces, fought with darts and javelines, to which a thong was fastened. They had also swords, knives or skeynes."

The Irish kernes were often employed as mercenary troops, by English monarchs. They generally fought well, even out of Ireland, when led by their native chieftains or captains, who let themselves and their men out to hire. We find among the State Papers (No. 437) a curious letter from O'Reilly, to King Henry VIII., who brings his majesty in debtor in the sum of about six hundred pounds, for the service of a hundred men in England, but O'Reilly is willing to take "the little farm that Prior Ford had" as a set off against this demand.

"JESUS!

"TO THE RIGHT HONORABLE AND HIS VERY GOOD KING HARRY, KING OF HIGLAND, FRANSE AND HIRLAND.

"Right Honorable Noble King Harry. After my most bounden dutie premised, may it please your noble grace, the cause of my writing at this time, is to beseech your majesty to be so good to your pore servant as to consider the great coste I was at for the 100 men that I shent [sent] to your grace into Hyngland. I certify your grace that my 100 men coste me about £600 for going and coming, and there are 8 vyke* [8 weeks] of their wages unpaid yet, because they were so long at Shester, [Chester] and Hollyhead, the wind being contrary. Now I desire your noble grace for that same costes, and for the service I du your grace and your deputy in Hirland every day, to *shend me a lytell ferym*, within my own land, to have for myself, and my son after me, that every man may know I have your grace's wages in Ireland."

He goes on to mention a farm that the Prior Ford had, for £18 a year. Whether the prior had been

---

* "8 *Vike*":—We suspect O'Reilly got a Welshman to write this letter. We have cut it down, and improved the spelling.

dispossessed or not, we cannot say, but O'Reilly puts in a good word for him in the end.

"Also I desire your grace to be so good that same pore chaplain,* for God's sake, and for the service sake that he has done your grace. I testify your grace, that that pore chaplyn was taken into Scotland, and that he paid 8 nobyll for his ransom, and I know there are many men in Hirland that have 2s. and 3s. a day, that will not do more service to your grace than he has done. For God sake, and for me, let him have some living in Ireland. Finally, God save the King!

Your obedient tryu servant,
Thy Lord O'Reilly."

We read among the minutes of council in this monarch's reign of "William Keating, who hath been capitain of the kern, to have lands of £10 Irish by the year, to him during his life, and after him to such, for the time till that matter of the kern be reformed, shall have the office."—*State Papers, vol.* iii. *p.* 584.

Spenser speaks in the following terms of the Irish horse soldier, or dragoon. "I have heard some great warriors say, that in all the service they have seen abroad in foreign countries, they never saw a more comely man than the Irishman, nor that cometh on more bravely in his charge, neither is his manner of mounting unseemly, though he lack stirrups, for in his getting up, his horse is still going, whereby he gaineth way, and therefore the stirrup was called so in scorn, as if it were a stay to get up, being derived of the old English word, sty, which is to get up, or mount."

The horsemen were accompanied by *horseboys*, who are thus described by Spenser. "After the Irish

---

* *Pore Chaplain.*—We conclude this Prior Ford was chaplain to the troop, and that the pay of such chaplains was 2s. and 3s. a day.

kerne, methinks the Irish horseboys would come well in order, the use of which, though necessity (as times now be) do enforce, yet in the thorough reformation of that realm, they should be cut off. For the cause why they are now to be permitted, is want of convenient inns for lodging of travellers on horseback, and of hostlers to tend their horses by the way. But when things shall be reduced to a better pass, this needeth specially to be reformed. For out of the fry of these rake-hell horseboys, growing up in knavery and villany, are their kern continually supplied and maintained. For having been once brought up an idle horse boy, he will never after fall to labour, but is only fit for the halter. And these also (the which is one foul oversight) are, for the most part, bred up amongst the Englishmen, of whom learning to shoot in a piece, and being made acquainted with all the trades of the English, they are afterwards, when they become kern, made more fit to cut their throats."

After the horseboys come the *daltins*. "The basest sort among them are little young wags called daltins. These are lackeys, and are serviceable to the grooms and the horseboys, who are a degree above the daltins." This word "daltin" has an English look and sound; it should probably be spelt *Dalton*. The descendants of the English, Welsh, and Flemings who came to this country in the pay of the Normans, had long ere this intermarried with the Irish, and had sunk down to their condition. While the Saxon in England had been gradually rising in the scale of society, the Saxon in Ireland had been as certainly sinking; for the Celtic chieftain as well as Norman knight, had no idea of a middle class, called *commoners*. A State Paper, written during the early part of the reign of Henry VIII., thus describes the condition of this class in Ireland :—

What pyttye it to hear, what rueth to reporte, there is no tounge can tell, ne penne that can wryte it; it passyth far the oratours and the musies all to shewe the conduct of the noble folke, and how crewell they enterith [enlisteth] the poore *comyn people*, when danger is to the king."

These poore comyn people who were enlisted or "pressed," in time of danger to the state, were of English descent. The writer of the State Paper just quoted, makes the following most noble comparison between the commons of England and Ireland :—

"What comyn folke in all this worlde maye compare with the comyns of Ingland, in ryches, in fredom, in lyberty, welfare, and in all prosperytie? Who richeith the Kinge's treasor, and repayreith his cofers with golde, sylver, and precyous stones, save the comyns? Worsshipeith [supporteth] the prelates and the clergye of the churche, save the craftye [clever] peoplle, and the carlyshe rurall folke of the realme of Inglande.

"What comyn folke in all this worlde is so power, [poor] so feble, so ivyll besyn in town and fylde, so bestyall, so greatly oppressid and trodde under fote, and farde so evyll, with so great myserye, and with so wrecheid lyff, as the comen folke of Irelande?

"Hit is a comyn tome of olde date, 'as the comen folk fareith, so fareith the kinge;' that is to say, riche comen, a riche kinge; poore comyn, poore kinge; feble comyn, a feble kinge; strong comyns, a strong kinge: ergo it folowyth, a riche kinge and comyns in Ingland, a poore kinge and comyns in Ireland. What comen folke in all this worlde is so mightty, and so strong in the fylde, as the comyns of Ingland? What comyn folke in all this worlde is soo feble, and soo evyll besyn in towne and in fylde, as the comyns of Ireland?"

We suspect it was from these poor Anglo-Irish commoners that our "little young wags," or daltins, or devil's imps, (who were employed by the horseboys in cleaning boots and spurs) were descended. Some of these Daltins or Daltons took to "the road." There was one so famous as to have his heroic deeds recorded in the Irish Annals. The Four Masters, under date 1414, tell us of a *Henry Dalton* who plundered the king's people, and gave part of the prey or spoil to that distinguished Irish poet, O'Higgins, who "satirised" the king's Lord Deputy "to death." Dalton must have had a love for lampoons, to share his prey with the poet. We suspect that some of the "little young wags" were his lineal descendants.

In the State Paper under date 1515, from which we have already quoted, inquiry is made why the "Iryshe folke" is grown so strong, and the "king's subgettes," that is the Normans or English, so feeble, and fallen into so "great rebellyon." One of the reasons runs thus:—

"Some sayeth, that the cause the English men be so feeble, and Irish men be so strong, is, that English men hath refused their own armour and weapon, that is to say, spears and bows, after the English manner, wherewith they did win and conquer the lands, and hath chosen to them harness and armour, spears and bows, after the Irish manner, whereby they hath lost unto little all the land; for Irish men be in number ten against one, be more cunning and better in their own war, than English men."

Another cause of the weakness of the English government in Ireland, mentioned in this State Paper, was the inactivity and worldly-mindedness of churchmen, who were, for the most part, English. If a good bishopric was to be had, they were all on the qui-vive. In a letter " scribled at Dublin, the 27 day of August, 1520, Surrey writing to Wolsey, says:—

"Also plesith it Your Grace to understonde, the Busshop off Cork is ded; and grete sute is made to me to wright for men off this contre; some say it is worth 200 markes by yere, some say more. My poure advyse shuld be that it shuld be bestowed upon sum *Inglish man*. The Busshop Leygblyn, your servaunte, havyng bothe, methynk myght do gode service here. I beseech Your Grace *let none of this contre have it*, nor none other, but such as woll dwell thereupon, and such as dare, and woll speke, and roffle, when nede shalbe. Yours most bownden,

T. SURREY."

On the 6th of September, Lord Surrey concurred with his council in a letter to Wolsey, (which is among the Cardinal's correspondence in the Chapter House, vol. xi. part 2, leaf 22.) recommending " Waltier Wellesley, Priour of a House of Chanons, called Conall, a famous clerc, notid the best in the land, a man of gravitie and vertuous conversation, and a singular mynde having to Englishe ordre," to succeed to the vacant see, which is stated to be under a hundred marks value. Wellesley refused to take the bishopric, unless allowed to keep his priory in commendam. In 1531 he was made Bishop of Kildare, and retained the priory. He held both these benefices till his death, in 1539.

Two years after, we find the Earl of Kildare asking for the avoidance and denomination of the bishopric of Kildare, for "Maister Edward Dillon, who is of vertuous living, and English name and condition."

Robert Cowley, writing to Wolsey respecting the appointment, says, "Anthony Knevit had obtained the bishoprick of Kildare to a simple Irish priest, a vagabonde without learnyng, maners, or good qualitye, not worthy to be a *Hally water clerc.*"*

The earl informs Wolsey that the income of the bishopric does not exceed a hundred marks sterling, "the substance hereof lieth in the Irishry, *and will not be lightly had, but by temporall power.*"

We may judge how this temporal power was exercised by a letter from Archbishop Allen, or John Dublin, to Cromwell. This John Allen was also Chancellor † at "fortie marke" ‡ a-year, but he had received nothing from this office for two years and a-half.

"Sir, afor God I desire no translation nor any manner of benefice or cure, nor yet dignity, but only (if it might please the king's highness to have some compassion on me,) a prebend, *which should cause no murmer of absence, whereby I might keep a dozen yoemen archers, in wages and livery, when I lie in the marches upon the church lands,* to keep me in the king's service from his Irish enemies, and English rebelles, and ever among them to do some little reparation."

We conclude the "little reparation" here mentioned, was to be done on the bodies, and not on the souls of

---

* *Hally-Water clerc.*—The office of Holy-water clerk, or Aquæ-Bajulus, in plain terms, a "Water-porter," was conferred by Boniface on poor clerks or curates.

† *Chancellor.*—He was appointed Lord Chancellor, September 19, 1528, while Archbishop elect. He was displaced from the chancery in July, 1532. There was a John Allen, a relative of the Archbishop, we conclude, who was "Maister of the Rolles" in 1532.

‡ *Fortie marke.*—Doctor Robert Wreston, Chancellor in 1567, prays Queen Elizabeth to pardon him the 100 marks she lent, and the first-fruits of a deanery.—*Calender of State Papers*, 1509-1573, p. 345.

these Irish enemies, and English rebels. The allusion to his lying out in the marches proves that John Dublin dared to "roffle" when need be.

The Archbishop concludes his letter by promising Cromwell, when he is "half ought of dett, one hobby, one hawk, and one Lymeryke mantle, which are things for a gentleman's pleasure in these partes." Sad to say, John of Dublin was murdered at Artane, in 1534, by John Telying and Nicholas Walter, at the instance and procurement of Lord Thomas Fitzgerald, better known as Silken Thomas,* whose father, at this time, lay prisoner in the Tower. Allen, who had been chaplain to Wolsey, was the enemy of the Fitzgeralds. Silken Thomas suspected that his father's imprisonment was owing to him. Allen was brought as a prisoner before the young Geraldine, then in arms and rebellion. *Beir naim an bodach,* "Remove the churl from my presence," said the enraged young noble, pointing to Allen. His men removed him *with a vengeance.* Thomas, with his five uncles, were afterwards executed at Tyburn.

The state paper, No. 81, is "The copie of the *curse given Thomas Fitzgerald and others for kyllyng the Archbusshop of Dublyn,*" which is hot and heavy enough.

If the following be a true description of the clergy at this time, we are not astonished they had to resort

---

* *Silken Thomas.*—He was so styled from his silken banners, and the beautiful and embroidered dresses of his cavaliers. He was the brother of the Fair Geraldine, of whom Surrey writes:—

> "From Tuscane came my lady's worthy race,
> Fair Florence was some time their ancient seat;
> Foster'd she was with milk of Irish breast,
> Her sire an earl, her dame of princes' blood."

to, or employ temporal power in the collection of their incomes :—

"Some sayeth that the prelates of the church, and clergye, is muche cause of all the miss-order of the land; for ther is no archbysshop, ne bysshop, abbot, ne pryor, parson, ne vycor, ne any other person of the churche, highe or lowe, greate or smalle, Englyshe or Iryshe, that useyeth to preache the worde of Godde, saveing the poore fryers beggars; and when the worde of Godde do cesse, ther can be no grace; and without the specyall grace of Godde, this lande maye never be reformyd; and by preacheing and teacheing of prelates of the churche, and by prayer and oryson of the devoute persons of the same, Godde useyth alwaye to graunte his aboundante grace; ergo the churche, not useing the premysseis, is muche cause of all the said mysse-ordre of this lande.

"The parsons of the churche crowd more by the lucre of the ploughe rustycall, then by lucre of the ploughe celestyall, to whiche they hathe streccheyd ther handes, and loke always backwarde. They tende muche more to lucre of that ploughe (whereof groweth sclaunder and rebuke) then to lucre of the soules, that is the ploughe of Cryste."

But we are not without examples of noble disinterestedness on the part of churchmen. The Pope, for some reason or other with which we are unacquainted, suspended the bishop of Kilmore, and conferred the bishopric on a poor priest named John Brady, who, thinking an injustice had been done his diocesan, surrendered the bulls which had been drawn in his favor to be cancelled, and "without interruption per-

mytted the said bishop quyetely to enjoye the same."
St. Leger was so much pleased with his noble conduct,
that he applied to the king, Edward VI., on the death
of the bishop, to have Brady appointed.—See *Calendar
of State Papers*, 1509-1573, p. 109.

Such was the state of things, and the general
misgovernment, or want of government, both civil and
ecclesiastical, in the beginning of the reign of Henry
VIII. In fact, the country had all but passed from
the hands of the English monarch, who had no party
there. An English party or interest in Ireland is of
more modern growth. If it had not been for the
natural antipathy of race which existed between the
Celt and the Norman, the English king and government
would have had no party in Ireland upon which
to depend, and the country must have been reconquered.

The Earl of Ossory, writing to Cowley in 1535,
says—" Then in January also, many of the McCarthies
and the Geraldynes of Mounster, began to murmor and
swell, whereupon I, with my retenue, sowed such stryff
betwene them, as they do continue in the same, full of
warr and debate, the one destroying the other."

CHAPTER VII.

THE EARLS OF DESMOND, ORMOND, AND KILDARE.

A.D. 1520—1524.

MAURICE, the friend of Perkin Warbeck, the Tenth Earl of Desmond, died in 1520. He was, at an early period of his life, nick-named "*The Bacach,*" for he was lame, which caused him to be carried to the field of battle in a chariot, on which account he was styled *Maurice an Charbaid,* " of the chariot." He was succeeded by his son James, who commenced his reign by making fierce war on Cormac Oge Mac Carthy, ravaging and laying waste the territory of Muskerry.

"This year [1520] James, the Earl of Desmond, began to ravage and lay waste the barony of Muskerry, belonging to Cormac Oge Mac Carthy, with fire and sword. The archbishop of Dublin, William Rokesby, with other commissioners, went from Dublin to Waterford to appease him, but in vain, for Desmond persisted to burn and destroy Mac Carthy's lands, who was not backward in his turn, to revenge the injury, and confederating with Sir Thomas of Desmond, the earl's uncle, (but implacable enemy) they came to a pitched battle with the earl in September, which proved a bloody engagement, wherein Desmond's soldiers forsaking him, he was obliged to save himself by flight, having lost above a thousand men, and had two of his uncles, John and Gerald, made prisoners." This battle was fought, according to some writers, between Cork and Mallow, near Mourne Abbey. Mac Carthy Reagh, with the Carbery forces, assisted his kinsman in this battle. The victory, according to the same author, was chiefly owing to Sir Thomas, the earl's uncle, who charged at the head of the horse, and broke the earl's main body of galloglasses.

We have the following account of the battle in a letter from Surrey and the Irish council to Henry VIII.:

" Please it, your most noble grace, to be advertised, that this day came unto me a messenger from the Earl of Ormond, with a letter, expressing of a great discomfiture lately given upon the Earl of Desmond, on Friday last past, by Cormac Oge, Mac Carthy Reagh, and Sir Thomas of Desmond ; as by the contents of the said letter, which I send unto your grace, herein closed, plainer it may appear. And as the messenger reporteth, in the said conflict were slain of the said Earl of Desmond's party, 18 banners of gallowglass, which be commonly in every banner 80 men, and the substance of 24 banners of horsemen, which be 20 men under every banner, at the least ; and under some, 30, 40, and 50. And among others was slain the said earl's kinsman, Sir John Fitzgerald; and Sir John of Desmond taken, and his son slain ; and Sir Gerald of Desmond, another of his uncles, sore wounded and taken ; with many others, where of the certainty appeareth not yet.

"Sir, any ways it is no great hurt that he is punished, for of late he hath lent more to the counsel of Irishmen than of me, your grace's lieutenant, and of others of your grace's counsel here.

"Another way his discomfiture and loss may be right hurtful. The most part of them that overthrew him be Irishmen, and I fear it shall cause them to wax the more prowder, and also shall cause other Irishmen to take pride therein, setting the less by Englishmen. Notwithstanding the said Cormok, who was chief captain, is the man of all the Irishmen of the land, save O'Downyl, that I think would most gladly fall to English order.

"And, undoubtedly, if the said earl had not invaded his country, and burnt and destroyed the same, he would not have attempted any thing against him, and this discomfiture was in the said Cormac Oge's own country."—*State Paper*, vol. ii, p. 46.

Writing to Wolsey shortly after, he says :—"Since writing our letters to the king's grace, we have heard divers ill reports of the Earl of Desmond in his moving war against divers of the king's subjects, and other Irishmen lately sworn to his highness." He requests, in the same letter, to be furnished with "Northumberland speris and Welsh speris, and not bowes on horsbak," and acknowledges the truth of the report that he had discharged "divers tall men, and taken in their stedis many symple personages"; perhaps the "light-armed skipping kernes."*

Surrey, writing to Wolsey, April 27th, 1521, says, "There came thidder to me Cormok Oge and Mac Carthy Reagh, two Irish lordes of great power, and they have put pledges in my hand to keep peace to the Earl of Desmond and his adherents, and to be ordered

---

* *Kernes.*—We find the Irish council directed to send over these Irish troops to assist the king in his Scotch wars.

by me in all causes between them." Writing again to Wolsey he says, "a great capteyne of Irishmen, called Cormocke Oge, dwelling nygh Cork, who is a *sadd wise man*, and very desirous to become the king's subject, as an Englyshman, offering to take his landes of the king; but what yearly rent he would give I am not certain; desiring also to be made a baron, and to come to parliamentes and counsailes. He hath shewed me a great charter, granted to his grandfather by the king's noble progenitors, under the great seal of England." Surrey, after duly examining the charter, recommends that he should be encouraged, and adds, " surely he is substantiall of his promyse."

One Richard Peper, of Calais, who had been robbing on the high seas, was brought into Cork in 1521, with twenty of his companions. Surrey wrote to the king to know what he should do with them, adding, " I have noon authoritie to put them to deth, and the long keeping of them will be chargeable to your grace. I have none of their names, but Rychard Peper, wherefore, if your grace would have them put to deth, there must be lefte a blanke in the comyssion for their names to be put in."

We cannot imagine what brought this Richard Peper from Calais to Cork. The French were ever ready to foment dissension in Ireland, and we suspect that the favour shewn that " sadd wise man," Cormac Oge Mac Carthy, excited the slumbering wrath and rebellion of the Earl of Desmond, who had entered at this time into a treaty with the French king, for the subjugation of Munster, and the confiscation of the Mac Carthy property.

A paper in the British Museum,* Titus, B. xi. leaf 352, said to be collected by Sieur de Tillet, out of the records in France, and written in his book, entitled " Le Recueil des Roys de France," states, that in June, 1523, Francis I. made a treaty with James, Earl of Desmond, (styled a prince in Ireland,) by which the earl engaged to make war, in person, and at his own charge, against Henry VIII., as soon as the French army should land in Ireland; and to bring into the field four hundred horse, and ten thousand foot, and, when need should require, to aid the French with fifteen thousand foot or more, and to furnish horses for the draft artillery; and the king engaged to pay the wages of the troops at certain stipulated rates. The objects of the war were, to conquer Desmond's country,† and to place the Duke of Suffolk (Richard Pole) on the throne of England; and it was provided that the Earl of Desmond should hold his country to his own use and benefit, except one of the three ports of Kinsale, Cork, or Youghal, which Francis was to reserve for ever, for the security of his ships.

Another source of rebellious feeling in the minds of the Earls of Desmond, was the general preference or precedence given to the Earls of Ormond, who lived nearer the pale, and were more frequently consulted on state affairs. When Surrey left Ireland, an Earl of Ormond was appointed Deputy in his stead, and, if we are to believe the State Papers of the period, employed his power to cut down both the great

* *British Museum.*—A copy of the treaty, dated the 23rd of June, 1523, may be seen in the Bibliothèque Impériale, Paris.
† *Desmond's Country.*—The Mac Carthys More were called the Lords of Desmond, the Fitzgeralds, the Earls of Desmond.

branches of the Geraldine tree. They succeeded in destroying one branch only—the Desmond branch. The other branch, that of Kildare,* or Leinster, we rejoice to say, is green and fruitful. And fruitful in more ways than one.

The Earl of Kildare, writing to Henry VIII., says: "Having heard there was a Britton ship laden with Gascon wine, at your town of Craguergerise, [Carrigfergus] I addressed myself unto it." On his return he discovered that the "said Deputie's retynue" had carried off five hundred mares and colts. "Since it was bruted here that your grace minded to amove [remove] him from the deputacion, [deputyship] he hath been nothing in effect ruled by your Council, but hath made bonds with divers of the Irishry." The earl's wife, Elysabeth Kyldare, writes to Wolsey on the same subject:—

"In my most humble manner I commend me to your grace, beseeching you to be a good and gracious lord to my lord and husband, for as yet my lord and husband has not had any great profit by me, yet I find him as good and kind unto me always as eny man may be to hys wyf. Humbly thanking your grace to remember me to my moder,† [mother] *as tucheng my maryag mone.*" [marriage money.] She then goes on to say she is in continual fear of the king's Deputy. "It is commonly noised, that if the said Deputy might have my said lord at any advantage, he would utterly

* *Kildare.*—The present Marquis of Kildare, who has been so happily styled the "*First Irish gentleman,*" is as distinguished for his literary taste as for his urbanity. His history of the Kildare family is a valuable contribution to Irish literature.

† *My moder.*—Elizabeth, Countess of Kildare, was daughter of Thomas, second Marquis of Dorset, by Margaret, his second wife.

destroy him; of which I have known him twice in one morning warned, er he rose owte of hys bed."

We meet immediately after this, an "Indenture" of peace made between the Deputy Ormond and the Earl of Kildare; and the next year, 1524, an indenture between the king and Kildare, who is appointed Deputy in the place of his old enemy the Earl of Ormond. So much for "hys wyf" Elizabeth's letter to Wolsey. Ormond, writing to his son, Lord Butler, who was in London, tells him he must have "good, secret, and diligent espyall" over the king's letters, and adds, "Whereupon you must devise in my name to the king and my lord cardinal, as my trusty servant, Robert Cowly, shall penn and endite;" or, in other words, that the old earl's secretary should carry on the war in penmanship at court, while the father made war in Munster.

Robert Cowley's letters must have told, for the next paper from Henry directs the new deputy, Kildare, to pay our right trusty, and well-beloved cousin, the Earl of Ormond, the sum of eight hundred pounds, "one half of our subsidie there," which we conclude was the balance of his salary.

The Earl of Kildare replies that "the said earl was clierly payed the same subsidie, and all other revenues unto him due, which amounted not to the said somme, as shall appere by the accompt of your under treasurer here."

On the heels of this demand come "*Articles* towching the mysdemeanour of the Earl of Ormond," for taking coyne and livery from the king's subjects; for occupying the king's manors and lands, without the king's letters patent; for joining the king's enemies against the king's deputy, and sending O'Carroll four gunners, with guns and powder, to defend the said O'Carroll's castle; for permitting the late bishop of Leghlyn to be heynously murdered by the abbot of Duske's son [Maurice Kavanagh]; for burning, robbing, and spoiling the deputy's town, called Lyvetiston; murdering and burning seventeen men and women, divers of them being with child, and one of them that fled out of the fire to the churche, slayne on the high auter [altar]; for keeping a warde of evill disposed persounes that only robbe and spoyle and ravish women, maydens, and wydowes; for allowing churches to go to extreme decaye, without making provision for divine service, so that few or none laboureth to the appostill, without the consente of the said earl and his wyf, by whom he is ruled;* for imposing a subsidie of *four pence* on the king's subjects, passing the age of twelve years, within the county of Kilkenny, towards his charges into Englande; and finally, for sending over to one Robert Cowley, to indite complaintes and diverse untrothes against the Earl of Kildare, he the said Robert Cowley, " having with hym a signet of the said Earl of Ormondes, to seale the same."

This state paper concludes thus:—" In case the Earl of Ormond make any new matter of the letter which

* *By whom he is ruled.*—" She was man-like, and tall of stature, and very liberal and bountiful, a sure friend, a bitter enemy. Hardly disliking where she fancied, not easily fancying where she disliked. She was a good help-mete in those days, whereby her husband's country was brought to civilitie. The Earl and Countess planted great civilitie in the countie of Tipperary and Kilkenny, and to give good example to the people, brought out of Flanders and other countries, divers artificers, who were daily at work in the castle of Kilkenny, where they wrought diaper, tapestry, turkey carpetts, cushions, and other like workes, whereof some do remaine as yet with the now Earl of Ormond,"—*Vide British Museum, MSS.* 4792, *by Robert Rothe, in* 1616.

the Earl of Kildare sent to the Earl of Desmond, the trouth thereof was this :—Notwithstanding the wars between the Earl of Kildare and the Earl of Desmond, the said Earl of Kildare wrote to the said Earl of Desmond to meet him at a certain place, where he desired his aid against the king's rebels, as Mac Carthys, Cormok Oge, and other the king's Irish rebels. At the writing of which letter the said Earl of Kildare knew nothing of the said Earl of Desmond's mysdemeanure towards the king's grace ; which letter Lady Ormond caused to be taken from the Earl of Kildare's servant, who lodged at her house ;* the said letter was shewn to the commissioners by the Earl of Ormond, who, no doubt, endeavoured to implicate the Earl of Kildare in the Earl of Desmond's treason with the King of France. But to prove that the Earl of Kildare is a true man, and no traitor, ' when it shall please the king's grace to command him (the Earl of Kildare) to do anything for his (the Earl of Desmond's) reformation or punysshement ; then it shall well appere whether he shall do his devour to accomplisshe the same or not.' "

He went to Munster after writing this letter for the ostensible object of arresting Desmond, but did not succeed ; for the Earl of Desmond kept out of the way, alleging his privilege of not coming before any governor, unless he listed. Ormond accused Kildare of playing a double game. He was ordered to London, where Wolscy said, " Had you lost a cow or horse of your own, two hundred of your retainers would have rescued the prey. Earl !—nay, *King* of Kildare—for when you are disposed, you *reign* more like, than rule the land."

* *Who lodged at her house.*—Margaret, the Countess of Ormond, was sister to the Earl of Kildare.

A letter from Archbishop Juge and the Lord Chief Justice Bermingham, to Wolsey, under date 1528, informs us that the Deputy,* Earl of Kildare, "for som of his mysdemeanours of late, is committed to the Tower," and that James Butler is in persuit of the Earl of Desmond, "whois person it will be harde to take, as we suppose, but by trayn."

It was James Butler who was caught by "trayn," but we shall not style it *trayn precogitate*. It took us greatly by surprise to find the famous penman, Robert Cowley, the Earl of Ormond's and his son James Butler's, private secretary, writing this very year to Wolsey, and complaining that "James Butler is the grettist freende, alye, and succour, that the Earl of Desmond hath," till we remembered that the Earl of Desmond had an only child, a daughter named Joan, who married one James Butler, who afterwards became Earl of Ormond. We are disposed to conclude from the venom with which the secretary abuses the Archbishop of Cashel, that it was he who tied the knot.

"The Archbishop of Casshell, by subtill synestre means, without knowledge of your grace, and in a maner in contempt of your grace's mynde and assent, makith at court immediate and importunate suit for sundry unreasonable grants and privileges, for the maintaining and fortifying and erection of the Earl of Desmond."

Again, "This Archbisshop and Sir James, by the seducious practice of the man that your grace knoweth, have *bounde to giddress*, [bound together] the one with his spirituell power, and the other with his strenght,

---

* *The Deputy.*—Richard Nugent, Lord Delvin, was vice-deputy.

that my said lord or his son should not be hable to doo the king service against the Earl of Desmond."

The said lord spoken of was Sir Thomas Fitzgarret, or Fitzgerald, Earl of Ossory, and brother to the imprisoned Earl of Kildare. He was chosen by the Irish council* to guard the state, in the absence of the Vice-deputy, Lord Delvin.

This Lord Delvin, or Richard Nugent, had been made prisoner by O'Conor, the Earl of Kildare's son-in-law, who expected that his grace [the king] would be thereby moved to release the earl "from his duresse, and send him to rule here againe."

"Divers times," says the council," we have advertised the Vice-deputie to beware of the said O'Conor, and to have *paid him the waiges* that he and his predecessors have long had, rather than to rynn to further daunger or warr." The *waiges*, we conclude, was a sort of black mail.

This O'Conor and his friends made the country almost too hot for the council. "Almightie God grant that our sovereigne lorde may provide breve remedye, or else this poor Englishrie is like to have such ruin, that it will not be repaired in any man's days living; for the Hirishmen being never so strong as now, have spied their time, and our debilitie never more than this houre. The Holy Trinitie defend us, for here is none other hope of socoure."

---

* *Chosen by the Irish Council.*—It is erroneously supposed he was elected as Deputy. The Irish Council had no power to elect a Deputy. "The strenght, if any be, is by the Garrontynes [Fitzgeralds] be reason whereof we are compelled to make Sir Thomas Fitzgarret a *Generall Captaine.*"

CHAPTER VIII.

THE OLD COUNTESS OF DESMOND—THE COURT PAGE.

A.D. 1524—1534.

SIR WILLIAM SKEFFYNGTON was made Lord Deputy[*] in 1524. It was at this time the Earl of Kildare was enlarged from the Tower on promise of future good behaviour. The Deputy was instructed to do his utmost to promote "good unite, love and concorde" among the Irish lords, and chiefly between the king's right well-beloved cousins, the Earls of Kildare, Desmond, and Ossary.

James, Earl of Desmond, died 1529, and was succeeded by his uncle, Sir Thomas Maol, third son of Thomas of Drogheda. This was the Thomas who united with Cormac Oge and Mac Carthy Reagh, against his nephew, James, the eleventh Earl of Desmond, at the battle of Mourne Abbey, near Mallow. "In nine battles he wore the palm," and was celebrated by bards as the *Victorious*. He was even more distinguished as the husband of the old Countess of Desmond, who lived to the age of a hundred and sixty-two, or three. I knew the old countess," says Sir Walter Raleigh, in his *History of the World*, "who lived in the year, 1589, and many years since, and who was married in Edward the Fourth's time, and held her jointure

---

[*] *Lord Deputy.*—He was not Deputy to the king, but to the Duke of Richmond, the king's natural son, who was appointed Lord Lieutenant of Ireland on the 22nd of June, 1529, and held office till his death.

from all the Earls of Desmond since then; and that this is true, all the noblemen and gentlemen in Munster can witness." If she was married even at the early age of fifteen, in the last year of Edward IV., and if she died in 1614, the year Sir Walter Raleigh published his History of the World, she must have been no less than one hundred and forty-seven—two years older than old Parr.

There is a story current that she danced with Richard III., and that she affirmed "he was the handsomest man in the room, except the king, his brother Edward, and he [Richard] was very well made." Some venerable Sir Walter St. John, and old Lady Dacre are reported to have conversed with the Countess of Desmond, and to have handed down to posterity, this corrected judicium in refutation of the spretæ injuria formæ of the caluminated Richard, Duke of Gloucester. Rous says, "He was small of stature, with a short face, and unequalled shoulders, the right being higher than the left." Miss Strickland says—and ladies understand each other best—"the testimony of the old Countess of Desmond ought not to invalidate the statement of Rous, for many a lady would think any prince handsome who had danced with her."

The Right Honorable Colonel Herbert, of Muckross Abbey, near Killarney, has in his possession a portrait of the old countess, stated to have been executed during her final visit to London. The following appears to have been painted on the back of the picture, the time the likeness was taken:—

"Catherine, Countess of Desmond, as she appeared at ye court of our Sovereign Lord, King James, in this present year, A.D. 1614, and in ye 140th yeare of her age. Thither she came from Bristol, to seek relief, ye house of Desmond having been ruined by attainder. She was married in ye reigne of King Edward IV., and in ye course of her long pilgrimage, *renewed her teeth twice*. Her principal residence is at Inchiquin, in Munster, whither she undauntedlie proposeth (her purpose accomplished) incontinentlie to return. Laus Deo."

The death of this famous old lady is ascribed to an accident. "She might have lived much longer, had she not mett with a kind of violent death, for shee must needs climb a nutt-tree, to gather nutts; soe falling down, she hurt her thigh, which brought on fever, and that brought death."

But tradition and merry poets assert that it was not from a nut, but from "a *cherry* tree," planted by Sir Walter Raleigh, that she fell, having been tempted by the beautiful fruit.

> "And as old
> As the Countess of Desmond, of whom I've been told
> That she lived so much more than a hundred and ten,
> And was killed by a fall from a cherry tree then!
> What a friskey old girl!"

The parish of Affane, where Sir Walter Raleigh first planted the cherries * which he imported from the Canary islands, is within two or three miles of Dromana, the residence of the old countess's family. The Lord of Decies presented Sir Walter with Affane "for a breakfast."

Sir Thomas, the husband of this old lady, was Earl of Desmond from 1529 to 1534. He had been frequently "out" before he attained the earldom. On one of these occasions he slew his wife's father with his

---

* *Cherries.*—Edmund Spenser mentions cherries in his *Epithalamion:*
"Her forehead ivory white,
Her cheeks like cherries, charming men to bite."

own hand, but we learn from the same authority, that it was not his *reigning wife's* father; for on attaining the title in 1529, he made a grant in perpetuity of the country of the Decies, to his "reigning wife's father, Sir John Fitzgerald, of Dromond," or Dromana. The Countess Catherine Fitzgerald was his second wife. This venerable pair, for the earl lived to a very great age, lie buried at Youghal, where their monuments or effigies in stone, with the heraldic monkey at their feet, may be seen to the present day.

The earl had a son Maurice, by his first wife Ellen, the daughter of Mac Carthy of Muskerry, but he died before his father, leaving one son named James, known as the *Court Page*, but how he came to attain this title requires explanation.

Various plans had been proposed for the conversion of the English or Norman lords from their Irish habits and feelings, which had become ingrained. Many elaborate State Papers had been written on the subject, the general tenor of which was to foment bad feeling between the English and the Irish, who could be destroyed by neither the sword nor famine. The sword was a weapon at which the Irishry had become adepts, and as for starving them out, as Sir Warham St. Leger had to confess, the thing was impossible, their powers of endurance put starvation at defiance: there they remained, corrupting the minds of the Englishry, and encouraging the Norman knights in their rebellion. A remedy must be provided. It was hit upon by, we suspect, the astute Crumwell, "my singular good master of the king's most honorable council," whose word, at this time, was law with

Henry VIII. We quote only a portion of the State Paper No. 64, bearing date 1533 :—

"The thing most necessary to be devised is to increase the English order, habit, and manner, and to expel and put away the Irish rule, habit, and manner; which must be, principally, with good and genteel entertaining by the king's highness, of such as may be brought to that purpose. But before the king's grace should enterprise any general reformation, it must be first devised that his grace's English subjects, which are bounden to due obedience to his grace, wherein now they are savage, be brought to reconciliation.

"And surely such of the Englishrie as are in Munster are furthest from good order or obedience, so that no difference is betwixt them and the mere Irishmen, but only the very surname. Therefore it should do well, that the Lord Barry's son and heir, the Lord Roche's son and heir, the son and heir of James, son to Sir John of Desmond, knight, the Lord Fitzmaurice's son and heir, Theobald Burke's son and heir, Gerald Fitz-John of Desmond's son and heir, together with the Earl of Desmond's heir, being with such a Deputy, and brought up in his house, should be a means to keep and continue their fathers and kinsmen in good peace, and be a good and honourable breaking in, or training for them. Cormac Oge, who hath obtained his liberty, and his denizen, his son is of too great age to be brought to that purpose; but his sonne's son, whoe is but yonge, may be had thereto, for that lordship goeth always by lenial descent* of inheritance,

* *Goeth always by lineal descent.*—Not always, but we conclude the law of tanistry was not in operation at this time among the Mac Carthys of Muskerry.

otherwise than any other lordship among the wild Irishrie."

The plan for catching and breaking-in these wild young Irish sons and heirs took Henry's fancy. He resolved to adopt it, and wrote to the old Earl of Desmond to send his grandson to court. The Patriarch Jacob did not feel a deeper pang, when asked to send Benjamin down to Egypt. He replied thus :—

"I submit myself to your grace as I did to your noble, *direst* [dearest] fadere, of famous memory,—whose soul Jesu pardon,—trusting for to shew myself the same man, according to my bounden dutie of allegiance during my life, by fulfilling all my promises to my power, *saving one*, of which I desire your grace me to pardon, as I have promised to send myne herre [my heir] to your grace. I being well stricken in age, having none other but only he, my lordship [inheritance] under your grace, beinge far assundere, having sondry mortall ennymies, considringe myn anciente and his tendere aige, your grace may consider, that we bothe has moche adowe for to kipe our oune; and if he were absent, bothe in daunger of the see, and other mischaunces, I should had much adowe."

But he had much more adowe to appease the wrath of the king and his enemies at court, who accused him of "untrewly transgressing his most solemne othe," so he was obliged to send the lad. The king took a fancy to him, and made him one of his pages, instead of casting him into the Tower, as his daughter, Elizabeth, did the "*Parliamentary Earl.*" The old earl outlived his favorite grandson's departure but a few months. He died in 1534.

CHAPTER IX.

SIR JOHN OF DESMOND—THE COURT-PAGE—JAMES FITZ-JOHN, THE PRETENDED EARL.

A.D. 1534—1540.

THE grandson's inheritance was seized upon, and the title assumed by an old savage* grand-uncle, Sir John of Desmond, the late earl's brother, and a son of Thomas, who was beheaded at Drogheda.

The charge brought by the old man against his grand-nephew, when sent over to take possession of his estates, was, that *"he spekes very good Ynglyshe, and keepeth his hair and cap after the Ynglyshe fashion."* We conclude this charge was made to his Irish tenants, but they knew better, for his grandmother was a Mac-Carthy, of Muskerry, and he had enough of her Irish wit, notwithstanding the cut of his hair, and the fashion of his cap, to marry the daughter of that "sadd wise man," Mac Carthy Oge.

A law was passed at this time, (1536) 28th Henry VIII., for enforcing the "English order, habit, and language" in Ireland, which provided that no one should be shorn or shaven above the ears, or use the wearing of hair upon their heads like unto long locks,

---

* *An old savage*.—This old man was engaged in the murder of his own brother, James, the ninth Earl of Desmond, at Rathkeale.

called glibbes,* or have or use any hair growing upon their upper lips, called a crommeal, or to use or wear any shirt, smock, kercher, bendel, neckercher, mocket, or linen cap, coloured or died with saffron, or use or wear in their shirts, or smocks, above seven yards of cloth. The women were also prohibited from wearing any kirtle or coat tucked up, or embroidered, or garnished with silk, or couched or laid with usker, after the Irish fashion. And all were prohibited from wearing any mantle, coat, or hood, made after the Irish fashion. There was a previous act against having a beard on the upper lip.

Sir John Perrott, writing to Burghley, at a later period, says, " Amonges the rest of my doings heare, I have caused all the Irishry in this province to forgoe theyr glybbes; and have waded *into a farder daynger*, as in vanishinge all the GREAT ROWLES from the wearinge of ladies, gentlewomen, townswomen, and others in all places, by which meanes *I am assured to have no wyfe in thease partes.*"

If we may believe ancient chroniclers and poets, our Irish kings and queens wore mantles of the richest silk, fringed with lace, and fastened at the neck with golden buttons. The chieftains' shirts, of *thirty* ells of linen, saffron dye; leather girdles round the waists, and red cloaks, with a hood and border of shagged hair, drawn together at the breast, with a silver fibula

---

' * *Long locks called Glibbes.*—These long locks were deemed sufficiently graceful to inspire our national poet, Moore, who has put the following words into the mouth of an Irish maiden :—

"And I'll gaze on thy gold hair, as graceful it wreathes,
And hang o'er thy soft harp, as wildly it breathes ;
Nor dread that the cold-hearted Saxon will tear
One chord from that harp, or *one lock from that hair.*"

or buckle, short boots of untanned skin, and long beards running to a point. When mounted on their wild horses, with their brazen swords and golden-bitted bridles glistening in the sun, they must have presented a bright array.

The Court-page, or James, the Earl of Desmond, acting, it would seem, under the advice of his father-in-law, Cormac Oge, sent a Catholic priest with letters to the king, informing his Highness of the base treatment he had received at the hands of his grand-uncle, Sir John. The Lord Chancellor Audeley wrote as follows :—

"Pleaseth your majesty, the *Irishman* who sued to your highness at Mr. Secretaries, hath informed me there is a priest coming with letters to your grace from James of Desmond, and from one Cormoke Ogge, a knight, whose daughter the saide James hath maried. The opinion of this Irishman is that whatsoever suits shall be made to your majestie by the said James and Cormock Ogge, or the said Sir John Desmond, that your highness should, in this time of contention in your said land of Ireland, abstain to grant your favour to any of them to be Earl of Desmond, but to give the priest that shall come to your highness in this behalf, fair dulce words, till your grace may know more of their demeanour and service towards you in your said land.

" He also delivered me a letter sent unto your highness from the mayor and counsil of your town of Youghal, in your said land; the effects of which consisteth, that they declare themselves to be your true subjects, and the great pains they have taken in defence of your said town against your enemies, making humble requests that your grace would send to them some ordinance and power ; for they think themselves sufficiently furnished with men to keep the walls of your said town."

William Cowley, writing to R. Cowley shortly after, says, " Last week, Sir John of Desmond came to

Yowghill,* but was kept owt; but he manages, with much people, to annoye them"—the townsmen. He then adds, "Without doubt this Sir John is one of the worst that ever grew of that blood. He praiteth, and is so proud of the little sodain overflowen power that is shed to him. Sir, it will be right necessary and expedient (standing with the king's pleasure), that this young gentleman, James of Desmond, be retourned home with letters of justice in his favours."

This hint was acted on. Captain Ap. Parry, who was in the service of Lord Leonard Gray, thus describes the visit of the "young gentleman" to Cork :—

" Upon a hill, half a mile or more, Cormac Oge was with his host, so down came Cormac Oge into the valley with a certain, and my Lord James with a certain, and so they met together, and fell to parleying. And after they had parleyed, my lord went into the town with all his host, and the mayor of the town, with his brethren, received him in ther skarlet gowns and ther typetts of velvett, after the English fashion, and was very glad of us, Englishmen, *and made us the beste chere that ever we had in ower lyves.*

"And on the morrow came Cormac Oge to the town end, and brought with him the ywng gentylman wych chalengys to be the Earl of Desmond. This ywng man speaks very good Ynglysche, and keepith his hair and cap, after the Ynglysche faschyon, *upon hys hede.*" He is content, with all his heart, if Sir John of Desmond, his uncle, will submit himself to the king

---

* *Youghal.*—A certain captain Ap. Parry, who visited Youghal this year [1535] says, "The first night, from Dungarrvan we went to a towne called Yowhhol, where we had very good cher, and were honestly received, and there they dyd sell a galond of Gasgoyn wyne for 4d. sterlyng.—*State Paper*, v. ii, p. 283.

and his council. He is willing to abide by their decision.—*See State Papers*, vol. ii, p 283.

Upon hearing this, the Lord Deputy demanded that old Sir John should go to London, and lay his claims to the earldom before the King. " What should I do in England, to meet a boy there ?" was his reply. " But give me the Irish horson (horse) Morac Oge, and I will go." We may conclude he got the Irish horse, and set out on his journey, for a State Paper, dated from Waterford, in 1535, reports, "This day came Sir John Desmond. He is an old man, and can speak very good Ynglysche." We cannot say whether he went to London. He died in 1536.

James, his eldest son, set up his title to the earldom. This James was called the Traitor. He is called in public documents the " Pretensid Earl of Desmond." Wise, writing to Crumwell, says, " We are like to have some sporte, *procol ab urbana luxuria*, with the Desmonds and the Breenys." The Deputy, Leonard Gray, marches into his country, and endeavours to "entangle" him, but without success; so he takes his castle at Loughyl, makes a forage on his corn, and carries away " doris and wyndowes, firing the roffe themsilffes."

Notwithstanding, this " Pretended Earl of Desmond," with something of the patience of Job, "shewed himself, in gesture and communication, very reasonable and condescending;" but the Deputy has his suspicions, and does not like to trust him, or encourage his hopes to the earldom, the right heir being in London, preferring his more legitimate claims before the king. The Pretended Earl has a conference with the Mayor of Limerick, the Chief Justice, and the Master of the

Rolls, and offers to deliver his two sons as hostages, and to procure Viscount Barry, Lord Roche, Thomas Butler, and others, as security in the sum of twelve hundred marks, that he will obey the king's laws, and cause them to be obeyed, and leave his claims, with those of the Court-Page, to the decision of the Deputy and his council, who are half won over to his interest; but the Deputy still hesitates. At this crisis the Pretended Earl comes out with a public document, which has the effect of allaying every suspicion, and of securing the Deputy in his interest. Here is the paper :—

"Be it known unto you and every of you, the king's high officers of his grace's cities and towns of Munster, as Limerick, Cork, Youghal, Kinsale, and Kilmallock, that I, James, under God and the king, Earl of Desmond, am willing and content to make restitution and satisfaction unto you, or to any of you, that can prove before the right noble Lord Leonard Gray, the king's Deputy of Ireland, and the king's noble council of the same, of any goods or cattles by me taken wrongfully from you, or any of you, since the time that it pleased God that I have been Earl of Desmond aforesaid. In witness of the premisses, I, the said Lord James, Earl of Desmond, hath put hereunto my signet, the 7th day of December, the 28th year of the reign of our soverreign lord, King Henry the Eight."

This, together with other documents, in which he promises to act fairly by James Fitzmaurice, who "challenges the earldom of Desmond," produced a most eloquent reply from the Lord Deputy, who descants on the excellence and beauty of truth. The earl's " good cher, and gentle enterteignement " of the messenger, Henry Hoke, had its effect. We can give only a part of the Deputy's reply :—

"Right Trusty and Well-beloved—we greet you well. And have received your letters by our servant, Henry Hoke, for whose gentle entertainment and good cheer we heartily thank you; noting therein great kindness on your behalf; desiring you to persuade yourself, and judge in us, that in your lawful, just, and reasonable pursuits and causes, we be, and will be, as favourable unto you, and no less desirous of your weal, than any man, that's living. And before we shall enter to the particularities of your letters, and the paper of your articles, sent unto us, by our said servant, we advise you to remember that truth and honesty excelleth all riches, and other worldly things; and on the other side, if you will be accounted for a noble man, before all things, decree and determine with yourself that truth passeth all things, and is the foundation of nobility. And again look you, never write, nor promise, that thing with your mouth, but that you will perform it in deed effectually; therefore, before you make promise, be well advised, but when you have promised, for nothing break it.

"And concerning the obtaining of your pardon, you shall be well assured, that we will be petitioner and mediator for the same to the king's majesty, to the uttermost of our power, so as, if we obtain not the same unto you, betwixt this and the first day of May next coming, your pledges shall remain no longer, but be delivered to you again, without your own agreement otherwise. Also, except James Fitzmaurice find sureties, according to your demand, we assent that your pledges shall not be returned for any of his demands. Thus committing you to God, who send you grace to do as well as we would wish to ourselves. Written from the king's manor at Manooth, the 28th day of December."

These arrangements, or contracts, appear to have gone no further. It is probable they were not sanctioned by the king, but the Pretended Earl managed to hold his ground. Robert Cowley writes (evidently from England,) to Crumwell, "This James of Desmond in Ireland, who pretendeth to be earl, is of the greatest power, and the best beloved there of any that hath been these many years, nevertheless, for that *this gentleman*,* is here, and seeketh for succour at the king's hands, it shall be for the king's honor he have the *better remedie*. Wherefore, if *he in Ireland*† will come and make any reasonable submission, it would be expedient, (the king's honor saved) to have both their services, which would enfeeble much the Irishry, especially the Brenes, the Mac Carthies, and others."

It would seem from this that the king felt himself bound in honor to support the just claims of the Court-Page, who is so often styled "the gentleman," or the "young gentleman who wears his cap in the English fashion."

Anthony St. Leger arrived in Ireland at this time, (1537) as Lord Deputy, instead of Pour Leonard Gray. In the "instructions given by the king's majesty to his trusty and well-beloved servants, Anthony Sentleger of Ulcome,‡ George Poulet, Thomas Moyle, and William Berners, esquires," some very crooked and partial dealing is recommended the Irish council in deciding between the claims of the two earls. The Court-Page is evidently a great favourite with the King.

"And whereas, the title to the earldom of Desmond dependeth in variance between the son of Fitzmaurice, being here, and the son of Sir John Desmond, called James of Desmond, now by force usurping the said earldom, the king's pleasure is, that the said commissioners shall debate the matter with the Deputy and council, and shall by their advice send for the said James, to appear before

* *This gentleman.*—James Fitzmaurice, the Court-Page.
† *He in Ireland.*—James Fitz-John, the Traitor, or Pretended Earl.
‡ *Anthony Sentleger of Ulcombe.*—William the Conqueror stepped ashore at Bulverhythe, near Hastings, leaning on the shoulder of a St. Leger, afterwards *St Leger of Ulcombe*. Sir Thomas St Leger married Anne, widow of the Duke of Exeter, and sister of Edward IV. "Whether dating from Norman or Plantaganet, the blood of the St. Leger answers to the legend on their shield of arms, ". Haut et bon."—*Athenæum.*

them, for the scanning of the title between him and this young man; and if he shall refuse to come without safe conduct, the Deputy and they shall award him a safe conduct under the great seal there; and if they shall or can thereby induce him to appear before them, they shall first shew unto him that the king's majesty doth much marvel that he useth himself in such a violent sort, and so take upon him to be his own judge, and therewith shew himself to be his highness's rebel; and that his grace hath commanded them expressly to intimate unto him, that unless he will humbly submit himself and desire his pardon for his former offences, and stand to their order upon the examination of his title for the possession of that earldom, his majesty will not fail to take such order for his punishment, as all others of that land shall have cause to beware by his example. And if they shall by this means and by such other good persuasions as they shall think mete, induce him to a conformity therein, they shall then duly and substantially examine the title between him and this young man, *whos parte* they shall avaunce, because he is here with the king's highness, as much as they may without the offence of justice, callyng all men, that can anything say for his parte."

The Pretended Earl must have got some inkling of these one-sided instructions; some member of council, or confidential servant, perhaps Henry Hoke, grateful for his late " good cher and gentel entertainment," let out the state secret. He writes informing the king that he had served him more faithfully than any of his predecessors, since his " grantfather who was heded [beheaded] at Drodagh," save only his father, who was " the leader and forman of the king's hoste in Ireland, especiall in Munster." He greatly marvels that his noble grace should not consider in his heart the extortions, treasons, and rebellions of the " bastarde called Jamys Fitz-Moryce," whom his grace favored, although his father and grandfather were always rebels against the crown, robbing cities and borough towns, and killing merchants and other subjects. Henry VIII. was most anxious, at this time, to promote trade and commerce. As for him (James Fitz-John), with the help of God and three-hundred well-armed men, he would promise to bring the whole of Munster into subjection within two years.

The last sentence had a magical effect on the king. Crumwell writes to St. Leger,— "This shall be to advertise you, that the king's majesty hath received such another letter from James of Desmond. *His hyness desireth you to handell the sayd James in a gentyll sorte*, declaring that his majesty taketh his letters in good parte; and enter with him upon the points of the same, that you may the better *fele* hym and his purpose, what service he shall be able to do, and what recompence he will make to *this young man*." This "young man" appears to be ever and always at Henry's elbow.

St. Leger replies,—"This day we proceed to the survey of the king's lands,* towards the part where James Desmond is, with whom we trust to have communication." Again,—"We further advertise your good lordship, that we have parled with James of Desmond in the fields without the town of Clommell, [Clonmel] and not perceiving any towardness in him, departed without making any conclusion."

Two days after, the earl sent his secretary to St. Leger, with his master's signet, saying that the captain of his galloglasses being present on the former occasion, he durst not proceed to business. The secretary

---

* *Survey of the king's lands.*—Survey here means to see the state of the country and its inhabitants. It was found that all the freeholders, lay and spiritual, charged their tenants with coin and livery.

brought a deed or article, (a copy is in the State Paper office) which may be summed up thus:—

James promises, in the first place, to be a most obedient subject, to assist in maintaining the authority of the king's judges and other law officers; to levy all taxes and benevolences granted to the king's highness; not to ally himself with or support the king's enemies; to defend and maintain the king's cities of Cork, Limerick, Youghal, Kinsale, and Kilmallock, and to protect all merchantmen. If he should get a lease of Croom and Adare, and lands in the county of Limerick, belonging to the Earl of Kildare, he will pay the rents. Finally, although he repudiates the claims of that bastard, James Fitzmaurice, who is a traditor of high treason against the king's majesty, he is content to leave the decision of his right of title to the king.

Crumwell acknowledges receipt of the earl's articles, and directs St. Leger to proceed with him; and "as he alegyth bothe bastardy and trayson against Jamys Fitz-Morys, it is the king's pleasure that he shall article the points of said treason, and write the evidence of the basdardy, declaring himself frankly."

The proofs were not produced. "As concerning James of Desmond, (writes William Brabazon to Crumwell,) he both writeth and speaketh fair, but I can see neither good nor evil that he doeth, but worketh for his own purpose. Howbeit the opinion of many men is that he will do right well, but I am of the contrarie opinion."

St. Leger writes to Crumwell the same year,—"As touching James of Desmond, and his submission under his hand and seal,"—the seal here refers to the signet he sent by his secretary—"as yet we see no part thereof performed. We have despatched another messenger to him with letters, to encourage him fairly to perform his promises, advertising him how the king taketh his submission in good part."

St. Leger's letter to the earl ran thus:—"Right Honorable, after our most hearty commendations, we cannot but marvel, considering your letters to our Lord the king, and your submission, under seal, made to us at Dungarvan, by your loving frynde and felowe, Mr. William Welshe, and your secretorye," you have not performed your promises. On receipt of your letter, dated at your manor of Lorgar, the 8th of November, we wrote to our said sovereign lord as much in your favor as we could, who hath commanded us to treat with you for proof of the bastardye of Jamys Fitz-Morryce, and the traytorous words by him spoken against his grace, and how you will use the three hundred men in case the king's hyness will send them." The letter concludes by entreating him for the love of God to take advantage of the king's favor, who sends his royal pardon by Mr. Wise of Waterford, who is to receive his son as a hostage or security for the performance of his promises and contracts. The "Articles" sent by St. Leger along with this letter to the earl (as I suppose we may call him) for signature, are far more definite, and demand much more than the earl promised. We discover from the first that the king had repudiated the power of the Pope, and required the earl to do the same:—

"First, that the said Lord James do clearly, as the king's true, faithful, and obedient subject, relinquish the false and usurped power and authority of the Bishop of Rome.

"Secondly, that he certify his clear title to the earldom of Desmond, and the basdardy of James Fitzmorice, now in England.

"That if permitted him under the greate seale of Ireland to absent himself from Parliament, he shall bind himself, by writing, duly to keep and perform all laws enacted there." Some Irish lords thought they were bound by no law to the making of which they were not parties.

"That he shall certify, by writing and seale, what entertaynment [allowance] he will give to the finding [support] of James Fitzmaurice, now in England, and what surety the king's majestie will have for the yearly payment of the same.

"That he shall state what he will allow yearly for the forty gunners which he requires for the reduction of Munster.

"Also, what yearly rent he will pay for the lands in Limerick, lately in the possession of the Earl of Kildare.

"And lastly, is he willing to use his persuasion, and, if necessary, power, to bring back Gerald Fitzgerald, the second son of the late Earl of Kildare, who had withdrawn himself from the king, that cherished him, as well as his elder brother and mother, in wealth and honor, in his roialme [realm] of England?"

It is probable that this young Gerald Fitzgerald had the dependant condition of the Court-Page before his eyes (whose acquaintance he had no doubt made at Hampton court), and whose princely inheritance the king was about to make over on his cousin, for some shabby yearly maintenance; and that suspecting a good Irish sword might serve him better than an English cap, he gave his gracious majesty the slip. What had he to expect from a monarch who was at this very time farming out his father's estates to the highest bidder?

James, the Pretended Earl, did not relish the last articles, the first of which required him to repudiate the Bishop of Rome, and the last to kidnap young Gerald of Kildare.* " We as yet fynde no faythe in Jamys of Desmondys, neither in worde or writyng. We have sent to him five or six times, and always received fayre promyse and nothing performed. We have now a messenger with him, *who has been there more than a monyth.*" St. Leger, loosing all patience, concludes "if we have not then, [at the messenger's return,] such assurance as he hath promised, we think it folly to give any further faith either to his worde or wryting."

A better report follows on the heels of this : " Whereas we advised your lordship that small trust and confidence was to be had in James of Desmond, yet nevertheless, he hath not only delivered his son †

---

* *Young Gerald of Kildare.*—He was brother to Silken Thomas and to the Fair Geraldine. The young earl, who was at this time about 13 years of age, took shelter at Kilbrittan Castle, in this county, at the house of Lady Elinor Fitzgerald, his aunt, who was widow to Mac Carthy Reagh. She afterwards married Manus O'Donnel, and made it one of the marriage articles that he should protect her nephew Gerald. She afterwards quitted her husband for endeavour to betray the boy.

† *Delivered his son.*—This was *Thomas*, the eldest son, by Joan Roche, the daughter of Lord Roche, or Viscount Fermoy, whom he divorced in order to marry Maud O'Carrol. Maister William Wise, who was sheriffe of Waterford, in a letter to Crumwell, writes, "James of Desmond has sent over to England his son *Thomas*, whose mother is the Lord Roche's doghter, whom he put away, and now occupyeth O'Karroll's doghter, by whom he hath issue."—*Lamb. Lib.* v. 602, *leaf* 105.—So Henry did not get the right son after all.

into the hands of Maister William Wyse, of Waterford, (for whose coming we look every hour,) but hath affirmed by his secretary, and writing, all that he before promised." Whether this included the repudiation of the Pope's authority, (a point on which Henry was very jealous) we cannot say.

This was one of the last public documents signed by St. Leger before leaving Ireland, the affairs of which he administered with temper and discretion. He was succeeded by a very different man, Lord Leonard Gray, who got into trouble with every one.

Ormond, writing to St. Leger, after he left for England, says, "James of Desmond *hath* put his sonne into the king's hands." But the giving this pledge does not seem to have had the effect of making James a good subject. "James of Desmond laid seige to a castle of the king's grace. Whether he did it for displeasure of one of the Brenes [O'Brien's] havyng ward there, or for what purpose he did it, I cannot certifie to your lordship."

Gray, writing to Henry, in June, 1538, says, "I shall endeavour to allure James of Desmond to repair to your excellent majestie, and have practyst with your grace's servant, William Wyse, for the accomplyshment thereof. Again, "James of Desmond hath written me, grevouslye complaining that the Treasurer, Rychard Butler, and all their retynue, and the retynue of their lord, their father, have invaded and preyed on the country of a servant of the said James." He hopes the variance will be appeased, and asks for more artillery.

Shortly after this comes a State Paper, accusing the

Lord Gray himself of like practices. It is entitled, "Articles of the enormities and abuses of the Lord Leonard Gray, the king's Deputy in Ireland." One of the charges was that he and his retinue made hosting among the poor people, entering the public markets and taking food without payment, and carrying away horses and carriages, "which, if contynued, woll cause many ploughes to be decaided and gevin over."

He is likewise charged with *a want of hospitality!* "Former Deputies have used to kepe honourable [open] houses, having a household of a hundred men [servants.] The said Deputy kepith noo suche house, whereby he should discharge the country of a hundred of the army." The charge, put in plain terms, is— the Deputy is not a "good fellow," but a churl, whom nobody cares to obey.

We find this year, 1538, by a letter from Ormond to the Council, something like the cementing of a union between the Kildares, the Desmonds, and the O'Briens. "Kildare's son-in-law have lately married O'Brene's doghter, and combined with James of Desmond in suche wise, that he have married his sister to the said James, and by such means to enfeeble them that taketh earnest part with the king's majestie." All these alliances were closely scanned and duly reported in state documents.

This daughter of O'Brien was James' third wife. Whether his first wife, Joan, the daughter of Lord Roche, was alive, or he still continued to "occupye O'Carroll's doghter," is not stated. But there was nothing strange in this. We are informed that Ulicke de Burgo, first Earl of Clanricard, had three married wives at the time of his death, and it is added, in the Council Book, "*No doubt he hath maried this last whoman solemply.*" They were, no doubt, walking in the footsteps of their royal master.

The following incident, which occurred this year, is valuable, as illustrating the state of society among men in high places. O'Molrian owed the Deputy, Lord Gray, forty marks, and to secure the payment, put a pledge of forty cows into the hands of James, Earl of Desmond. O'Molrian having paid Lord Gray the forty marks, demanded of Desmond his pledge of cattle, which the earl refused to return. The Deputy went to him, and told him he must deliver the pledge. "You are paid your money," argued Desmond, "the affair is no longer yours." "Whereupon my Lord Deputy and James of Desmond *began to square together*, after such a sort, that all their men, on either side, were harnessed, and put in full redenys to fyghte." Friends interfered, and entreated Desmond "for the love of God," to deliver up the pledge. This little rencontre does not seem to have produced any bad blood beween the pugilists. Gray, writing to the king a few days after, says, "I set forward on my journey with eight days' victuals to meet James of Desmond, who had a good band of men, who diligently served your majestie under me."

In proportion as James of Desmond grew in favor with the Deputy, Lord Leonard Gray, he lost the favor and good will of the Council, who thus describe him in a letter to Crumwell, dated November 28, 1538:—

"Among other things, James, the Pretended Earl of Desmond (by dissimulation, as it were), pretending to the commissioners that he would be ordered in all things to the king's pleasure, and also since my Lord Deputy's last journey into Munster, hath obtained such a strength in Munster, as no Earl of Desmond had there, in no man's remembrance; having constrained and allured to his band the Lord of Kerry, Lord Barry, the Knight of the Valley, the White Knight, and all others of the English blood in those parts, which heretofore, for the most part, were at the king's peace. We do not otherwise perceive, by his new attempts and gestures, but that he intendeth rather to be the king's open rebel and adversary, than the contrary, and having most of the O'Briens, and many other Irishmen, his friends, if he should make an insurrection (as we fear he will,) he may destroy the Earl of Ormond, which thing all we of these parties been not able to let.

And therefore our advice is, that the king's majesty send over *the other James*, which is there, giving him (which as far as we hitherto can perceive, is the very right heir,) aid against the other, whereby the combination and power of the other may be abated and diminished. For much more good wisdom and policy it is to put them two together, the one against the other, whereby this pretended earl may have his hands full, to look to his own defence, than to permit him to aggregate to himself all the strength of the best part of Ireland, wherewith he may, at his sensuall pleasure, return upon the king's subjects, for we see no likelihood, ne esperance, of conformity in him for the king's purpose."

William Wise, the sheriff of Waterford, was evidently no friend to Desmond. There still exists (among the " Depositions in Treasonable Matters") in the Chapter House, a letter from him, in which he endeavours to implicate the Pretended Earl in treasonable practices. The letter is dated Waterford, December 8th, and apparently addressed to the Lord Chancellor Alen :—

" I have spoken to a neighbour of mine, a merchant of this citie, [Waterford] who came from Youghal, where he lately arrived from partes beyond the seas. He shewed me, in a secret manner, that on his coming on land at Youghal, he went to William Walsh's house, and there, in the said William's chamber, James, the pretended Earl of Desmond, the same William, and his wife were together at supper, none other present but themselves.

"And, when he came into the chamber where they were, the said William Walsh did bid him welcome, in Irish, demanding of him from whence he came. He said from parts beyond the sea. Whereupon, James of Desmond said to him. 'How doth the Emperor?' The other answered 'He doth like a noble man, but I have little speech on him, but of my own natural prince, the King of England.' Then said William Walsh, 'But how doth our new pope in England?' He said, 'I know no new pope there, neither no pope, but the king,' Then said William, answering, 'But I will be loath to be of his council, who putteth to death the chief of his kin and council.' The other answered, that he did therein like a prince of justice, and would to God, the like were done in Ireland, then should it be a merry land. Whereunto the said James of Desmond answered, you say like a wise young man, you may depart."

The Pretended Earl sees the storm gathering in the distance, and prepares to meet it; and in order to gratify the royal avarice for church lands, and to clear his own character of the suspicion of treating with the Pope or the Emperor, writes to Sexton thus :—

"If it please his grace to have all the abbeys and fryers in Munster suppressed, I shall bring his comysshners for the suppressing and surveying of the same, and I shall take the same to ferme [to farm,] with my friends and servants, so that it shall be a great revenue to his grace. And for the more trouth of the premysses, and the aforesaid James Fitz-John of Desmond, hirto have sett my seale and signe manuell, the third day of Marche, in the 30th year of the reigne of our Sovereigne lord Kinge Henry 8th."

(Signed,)   J. of D.   (L. S.)

What hope could the Court-Page, James Fitzmaurice, have after this? But this did not satisfy the Pretended Earl. He wrote to Henry himself, utterly repudiating the claims of his cousin, accusing him of abominable and detestable treasons, and traitorous words against the king's noble person; insisting on it that he is a bastard, as there was "no lawful marriage solempnysed between the said Maurice, his supposed father, and his mother, the doughter of the late White Knight."

Four months after the date of the letters to Sexton and the king, it was discovered that Desmond, O'Neil, and O'Donnell, had formed a confederacy with the king of Scotland in favor of young Fitzgerald. The Earl of Ormond, writing to Crumwell, says, "James, the son of John of Desmond, that pretendeth himself an earl, having the permission and manifest bearing of the Lord Deputy, hath won all the strength of Munster." We are not to take all that the Earls of Ormond say for gospel, for there can be no doubt that they hated the Pretended Earl, and all the real earls, and all the branches of the great Geraldine family, with a most sincere hatred. Robert Cowley, writing to Crumwell (Sept., 1539), says, "I trust the new Earl of Ormond will do some good on his part, notwithstanding the great power of the Pretended Earl."

James, Lord Butler, became Earl of Ormond and Ossory the 21st of August, 1539, by the death of his father. The old Earl of Ormond is thus described by Robert Rothe:—"The said Sir Pierse Butler, Earle of Ormond and Ossorie, in all the course of his life was very religious and godly, and as I have heard, by an ancient man that lived in his tyme, he used every yeare, in the last fortnight of lent, to retire himself from all wordly business, and to lie during that time in a chamber nere St. Kenny's church of Kilkenny, called Paradise, and there he use his daily prayers, and gave alms to the poore, and prepared himself to receive the Blessed Sacrament, and upon Easter Eve, in the evening, he returned to his dwelling howse. He was married to the Lady Margaret, daughter to the Earl of Kildare, with whome he lived many years in great honor and prosperitie."

CHAPTER X.

THE PRETENDED EARL—THE COURT-PAGE—LORD LEONARD GRAY—SIR ANTHONY ST. LEGER.

A.D. 1540—1546.

It having been at length resolved by the king, my Lord Privy Seale, *i. e.* Crumwell, and the Irish Council, to displace James of Desmond, James, Earl of Ormond, the hereditary enemy of his house, is employed to hunt him down. But Desmond has, by some means or other, made a fast friend of Lord Leonard Gray ; the latter therefore must be first assailed, and, if possible, removed from office. Ormond, writing to Wriothesley, says—" The eminent danger now might have been prevented if my Lord Deputy had been ruled by the Council, whom the king's grace and my Lord Privy Seale appointed to him, whose advice for the most part he despiseth, adhering to the council of those that are and ever have been *Geraldines.* And of very truth his lordship hateth mortally all those of the king's Council preferred by the means of my Lord Privy Seale, and worketh against them all that ever he can of malice, to withdraw the king's favor from them, to wrap them in his highness's indignation, thinking thereby to have his bridle of willfulness at liberty. His practices are such, and so well known, that he hath brought himself, in a manner, out of credit with all men here, especially with Irishmen, who do not spare to shew the same openly, saying, they marvel why the king putteth such a man in so high trust."

Strong language like this requires some sort of an apology:—" I have written thus largely to my Lord Prive Seale; and I forsake Christe if I do write this against him of any malice that I beare to his person, although I love not dyvers his willful and hedy conditions; yet I take him to be a hardy gentilman, and a paynful; but in my judment, an unmete governor."

Having laid down the pen, which he wielded so powerfully against the Deputy, he takes up the sword against his friend, the Pretended Earl. But James of Desmond is no contemptible opponent. He must be approached cautiously. The Archbishop of Cashel is employed to feel the way. "I sent the Archbishop of Cashel, and others of good indifferency and discression, to treat with the said James. It was appointed that the said James and I, with a few of either party, should meet." Ormond approaches with a slynder company, sparing no jeopardie, and meets the archbishop, ryding at great pace, who tells him to " torne backe," that it " boted him not to tary;" which friendly advice he adopted, writing to Crumwell to send more aid to Cork and Youghal. But in the meantime, not wishing the army to lie idle, he consults with the Lord Deputy, whom he has so lately abused, with Mr. John Travers*—a " well-worthy" man, who has been just appointed one of the Council—and with the Maister of the Rolles, respecting the next move. They passed

* *John Travers.*—This John Travers was Master of the Ordnance, as well as one of the Council.

from the Shannon to Roscrea, from Roscrea to O'Carroll's country, from thence to Cashel, from Cashel to Clonmel, from Clonmel to Youghal, from Youghal to Cork, and from Cork to Kinsale. They were joined at Youghal by three of the sons of Garrett of Desmond. They passed from Youghal to Imokilly, and from Imokilly to Cork, where a large number of castles were delivered into their hands, to be held for James Fitzmaurice, the Court-Page, whose star is again in the ascendant. Lord Barry visited the Deputy in Cork, and bound himself, in three hundred pounds, to send two of his best men as hostages. Hither came also, two of the sons of Cormac Oge, the father-in-law of the Court-Page. In passing through Kercurriry, on their way to Kinsale, they took possession of lands belonging to James Fitzmaurice, in right of his grandfather, Thomas.

At Kinsale, the Deputy and Ormond parted for a while. "My Lord Deputy resting at Kinsale but one night, returned to Cork, leaving me for the coming of Mac Carthy Reagh, in whose country I found much cattle, which I restored to him; by reason whereof, and other fair means, I so allured and persuaded him, that he came with me to the Lord Deputie, and put in his brother and his hostages." Leaving Cork, the Deputy and Ormond repaired to O'Callaghan's country, intending to cross the river Awnmore, or Blackwater, when lo! and behold, upon the other side, stands, in all the panoply of war, the wily and enraged James Fitz-John of Desmond, driven like a lion to its last cover. He had "no manor of towardnes, or any good conformytie." His deportment was threatening, so much so, that "My Lord Deputy, being so moved at his words, returned to Cork again."

Men driven to desperation will resort to any quarter for aid. James of Desmond, young Gerald of Kildare, O'Neill, and O'Donnell, send letters and messengers to the Emperor, the King of France, and other princes, for aid. What is to be done with those rebels? "To exterprize the hole extirpation and destruction of all the Irishmen of the land, would be a marvelous sumptious charge, and great difficultie, considering both the lack of inhabitors, and the great hardness and misery these Irishmen can endure, bothe of hongre, cold, thurst, and evill lodginge, more than the inhabitants of any other land; and we have not heard or redde in any cronycle [chronicle] that at such conquests the whole inhabitants of the lande have been utterly extirpated and banished." Besides, "the land is very large, *by estimation and description as large as England*, so that to inhabit the whole with new inhabitors," would require more subjects than any "prince cristened" could "comodiously spare." For these wise and cogent reasons, it was humanely proposed by the Council, to exterminate *but a portion* of the inhabitants. This they thought could be managed by an additional force of six thousand men, consisting of so many dragoons, gunners, archers, and billmen. This humane proposal was signed, it would appear, by the whole Council, fourteen in number.

The star of James Fitz-John is again in the ascendant, that of James Fitz-Maurice, the Court-Page, sets in blood. "It was reported,"—and the report was true,—that "His Grace's servant, James Fitz-

Maurice, who claymed to be the Earl of Desmond, was cruelly slayne, the Friday before Palm-Sunday, by Maurice Fitz-John, brother to James Fitz-John, then Usurper of the Erledome of Desmond."

This Maurice, as we shall see, was murdered afterwards himself. James of Desmond now feels that the inheritance is his. He posts to Youghal, where he was " wele received and interteyned." After this the whole country lay open before him. " He entered into all the pills and garrisons in the county of Cork," which the Deputy and Ormond had wrested from his grasp. Around his standard gathered my Lords Roche, Barry, the White Knight, Mac Carthy Reagh, and a host of Irish chieftains and captains, who had lately given pledges of obedience to the Deputy. The Deputy is thunderstruck, the Council are trembling in their brogues. The new earl will be up upon them. They must parley and meet him with " dulcie wordes." Ormond resolves to beard the lion in his den. " May it please your good lordship, I have practised to win James of Desmond to serve the king's highness at this point of extremytie. Perceiving he would not trust me, nor yet be allured to any good purpose, I resolved to jeopardy myself in his hands, to win him with familiaritie and persuasion." He therefore passed two nights with him in the heart of his own country.

We suspect that Ormond had some private motive for this visit—that it was on this occasion the marriage between the families was broached. We have a short, friendly, and very badly written letter from Desmond to Ormond, who is starting for London:—" I desyre you, accordinge to my full truste, to bring me in the kinge's fawor [favor] as best ye cane."

St. Leger, who has returned to Ireland a second time, as Lord Deputy, sets out for Cashel, accompanied by the Earl of Ormond, who made him and his fellowes "grete chere" by the way. They meet Desmond in Cashel, who is on his guard, and demands Ormond, who has made him good cheer, as a hostage. Such a thing is not to be thought of—St. Leger refuses, but sends his own brother and the Archbishop of Dublin instead, throwing in John Travers, Master of the Ordnance, to make up the difference. They meet in the house of Sir Thomas Butler, and there, "in the presence of Mc William O'Conor, and divers other Irish gentlemen, to the number of two hundred at the least, he kenelyd down before me, and most humbly delivered his said submission, affirming that it was more glad to him to be reconciled to your favours, than to have any worldly treasure." After this he is appointed one of the Council, in which capacity, St. Leger says, he is "a very wise and discrete gentleman."

But there must be some atonement for all the bloodshed and misgovernment of the last ten or twelve years. Who is to be the scape-goat? The Council have already decided that Lord Leonard Gray, who has been so long running with the hare and holding with the hounds, and playing fast and loose with the Pretended Earl, should bear their sins as well as his own; they accordingly draw out the articles of indictment. They contain *ninety* distinct charges,—for uniting with Irish rebels, for taking them into his confidence and council, and for mal-administration generally. The following are a few extracts, somewhat curtailed :—

"His lordship elected by himself a private councill of the Geraldyne and papisticall secte, by whom he has been ordred and governed ever sithens. My lord sent his newphew to scole to Levorus,* an arrant traitor and a rank papist. His lordship remained for a greate space with an abbot, in the borders of Westmythe, who wrote divers letters to my lord, and my lord to hym, verie lovinglie. My lord had a servant called Robert Walshe, brother to the Prior Walshe, and stand-bearer to the traytor, Thomas Fitz-Gerald, and when the said Thomas Fitz-Gerald was sent to the Tower, my lord employed this Robert Walshe to convey private letters between them, conceiled from the king. My lord fell into a gret familiaritie with O'Brien's wif, who was an intier frend to the traytor, Thomas Fitz-Gerald. My lord passed through the strength of all Thomond upon O'Brien's nude [bare] promyse, having for his salve [safe] conducte a simple galloglagh of O'Brien's, bearing an axe before hym. My lord made a jorney northward, and when he came there, he took preys My lord was accounted a grete frend to O'Neill, and my lord made gossope to O'Neill,†

---

* *Levorus.*—The Lord Deputy Crofts, writing to the Duke of Northumberland in 1551, recommends that Levorus, who was a schoolmaster to young Lord Gerald Fitzgerald of Kildare, should be appointed Archbishop of Cashel. He speaks of him "for learning, discretion, and good living, as the best man in this realm, and best able to preach both in the English and Irish tongue." *Calendar of State Papers*, 1509-1573. The paper is dated Kilmainham, November 11, 1551.

† *Gossope to O'Neill.*—When two persons stand as godfathers or godmothers to the same child, they become *gossips* to each other. Fosterage was esteemed even more sacred than gossipry. When a child was borne to Mac Carthy Mor, he sent a cradle to the person he wished to stand in the relation of fosterer to his offspring. On one of those interesting occasions he sent the cradle to O'Connell,

which in Ireland is the grettist frendship accepted amonges men. My lord sent his servaunts to spoill the O'Reillys, then being at peas, whereby Cahir Modder was mortally wounded. My lord made his his last jorney into Mac Mahon's countrie, and stracke a gentleman named Thomas Nugent, (being the best of the name next to the baron) whereof he toke suche shame and greve, as he never rose after he retorned, till he was dede. Fynally, the pillage and extorcions of my lord and his servants upon the king's poore subjectes, be so many in every quarter, that thei wold not be comprehended in a longe boke."

It was agreed in council in England, that "the Lord Leonard Gray, *led by the affection he bore to the marriage between his sister and the late Earl of Kildare*, had done and committed heinous offences against the king's majesty. We believe the decision was so worded in order to touch the heart of the king, but the heart of the royal monster, was, by this time, callous. Leonard Gray, who was Henry's second cousin, wrote him before he left Ireland, "I do assure your grace, of my pore honeste and truyth, that the tender sucking childe dyd never sorer long for its mother's pap, than my pore heart longeth to see your most gracious presence." His desire was gratified a few months after. He went to England, where he was attainted of treason, and executed on Tower hill, on the 28th of June, 1541.

Although St. Leger had arrived in Ireland, on the 8th of September, of the preceding year, he does not

of Ballycarbery, who returned it by a gillie, with the bloody head of Mac Carthy's messenger. Mac Carthy hung the gillie on his gallows of Park na Crob, on the Lakes of Killarney.

appear to have mixed himself up, in any way, with the proceedings against this wrongheaded and unfortunate nobleman. His object was to produce peace and good will among all parties. To his wise and " genteel handling" we attribute the great improvement in James of Desmond. " Desmond promised to have repaired at this Michelmas to your highness, but suche warres as Mac Cartie hath erected againste hym, and lacke of money, he cannot repaire thider this year, but will send his sonne to your magistie." Desmond probably had the fate of Lord Leonard Gray before his eyes.

St. Leger was accused at this time by Cowley, "late Master of the Rolles," who was evidently a friend of the Butlers, of erecting a new Geraldine band. The wise and dignified defence of the Lord Deputy is worthy of record :—

" It may please your majestie, that where it hathe bene to me reported, that the saide William Cowley, late Master of your Rolles here, shoulde article ageinste me, that I wente aboute to erecte a newe Geraldine band, menyng the same by the Erle of Desmond; the tioute is, I laboured mooste effectuallie to bring him to your perfoicte obedience, to my grete parill and charge; and this, gracious lorde, was the onlie cause I sawe that, nowe the Erle of Kildare was gone, ther was no subjecte of your majestie's here mete nor hable to way with the Erle of Ormonde; who hathe, of your majestie's gifte, and of his owne inherytance and rule, gevin him by your majestie, not onlie fifty or sixty miles in length, but also meny of the cheife holdes of the frontiers of Irishemen ; so that if he, or any of his heiers, shoulde swarve from ther dewtie of allegiance (whiche I thinke verilie that he will never do), it wolde be more harde to daute him, or theim, then it was the saide Erle of Kildare, who had alwayes the saide Erle of Ormonde in his toppe, when he wolde or was like to attempte any suche thing. Therefore I thought it good to have a Rowlaude for an Olyver; for having the saide Erle of Desmond your highnes' assured subjecte, it will kepe theim bothe in staye. And I truste in God, the said erle is nowe so trayned, that your highnes may be assured of him; and I truste in God, he will se your majestie, or it be long. This, as my bounded dewtie, whiche is to allure al men to your majestie's obedynce, was the cawse why I labored the saide erle to the same, and no geele that I have either to Geraldyne or Butler, otherwise then may serve to the sarvice of your majestie, in the whiche I love them bothe; for assuredlie I thinke your majestie hathe them bothe your trew and faithfull subjectes, and I never yet harde that the Butlers offended your majestie, or your noble progenytors, in no poynte of rebellyon, whiche is miche to their prayse."

Desmond goes to England in the summer of 1542, is graciously received at Hampton Court, and has his title of Earl of Desmond acknowledged. St. Leger, writing to the king before him, hopes that he may have a "short retourne," and that his "entertaynment" may do credit to the royal "bountie." St. Leger had already given him a gown, jacket, doublet, hose, and other articles of dress.*

We suspect it was during the earl's absence † in England that St. Leger visited "Desmond's country," and the towns of Cork, Kinsale, and Youghal, the prosperity of which had been retarded, or "long hyndered by the evil behavor of two greate captaynes in these quarters," namely, the Mac Carthys of Carbery and Muskerry.

A formal treaty was made this year with both the English and Irish lords of Munster. The document not only gives Henry his new title of *Fidei Defensoris*,

* *Articles of dress.*—O'Rourke, before attending the parliament of 1541, petitioned for a suit of clothes. He states that he is "a man somewhat gross."

† *During the earl's absence.*—St. Leger visited these towns in the autumn of 1542.

but styles him, under Christ, the supreme head of the church on earth:— "Et in terris, immediate sub Christo, Ecclesie Anglicane et Hibernicane Supremi Capitis." It contains the names of my Lord Barry, and my Lord De Rupe, (alias Roche) my Lord of Muskerry, Mac Carthy Reagh, and Barry Oge, (alias young Barry) and O'Sullivan Beare, an Irish captain, (sue Nacionis capitaneum) and Barry Roe, (alias the Lord Red Barry) and Mac Donogh of Dhuallow, (another Irish captain) and Donald Ochallogan, (O'Callaghan) who is styled "*Nacionis Primum*," and Gerald, the son of John, *militem*. These noblemen understood Latin somewhat better than English. Of their ignorance of English we have a remarkable example. A parliament* was convened in Dublin in the June of the preceding year, at which these "Lordes of Monster," and divers other lords, were present, for whom it was found necessary to translate the Chancellor's opening speech from English into Irish. The speech was "briefly and prudentlie declared in the Irysshe tongue to the said lordes, greatly to their contentation."

Contracts with Irish chieftains were generally drawn in Latin; Conatius O'Neile, in 1541, employs the Latin tongue in renouncing the "Usurpatam auctoutatem Romani Pontifices," and styles the English monarch "Supremum Caput Ecclesie Anglicane *et Hibernicane*, immediate sub Christo."

The document signed by the Munster lords had not the effect of producing that obedience to the king, and

* *A parliament.*—A modern writer erroneously states that this parliament was convened in 1637 instead of 1541.

good fellowship between themselves which was contemplated. St. Leger writing to Henry, the next year, 1543, says:—

"I met the Earl of Desmond, to whom I had before written for the redress of many evil behavours, committed by the Lord Roche and the White Knight, which be two that long have been out of good order, and yet Englishmen, the one having destroyed the other's country; the same earl [of Desmond], according to his bounden duty to your majesty, repaired to their said countries, and took them both, and brought them to me, to your highness's castle of Caterlagh, where he delivered them to me to be punished, as shall appertain; and so I have laid them both in your castle of Dublin, where now they agree very well together, *and lye bothe in one bedde*, that before could not agree in a country of forty miles in length between them, and under their rule. I purpose they shall there remain till their amity be better confirmed, and then, God willing, and your high pleasure so known, I intend to send them home free, and apparel them like Englishmen; for now they be in ther saffren shurtes and heinoghes cotes. I must of force so do, or else drive them to great extremity, for I think they both, with all their riches, would not buy themselves one apparel, and pay for their board in your said castle for one quarter of a year; and yet I am sure their lands, well ordered, would make them both great lordes. I trust in God this shall be to them sufficient warning from hence forth.

"And for that the same Earl of Desmond hath not only been diligent in this, but in all other his proceedings, to do your majesty's service according to his bounden duty, I can no less than humbly beseech your highness to regard him according to your princely goodness, the *man being poor*, and not able to serve your grace as his harte wolde."—*State Papers, vol.* iii., *pp.* 466, 467.

The *poor* man was after this raised to the dignity of Lord High Treasurer of Ireland.

St. Leger's wise and impartial administration, and humane treatment of Irish lords and chieftains, excited the anger and fierce jealousy of James, Earl of Ormond, who made a party in the Irish council against him, and employed Walter Cowley* to "write a boke." He also sent private letters to England, some of which were intercepted. John Alen, Chancellor, and Gerald Aylmer, Justice, volunteer their opinion in a private letter to the king, " they twayne being his grace's olde servauntes, having trayvaited thereto in the affairs of the realme." They request his highness to inquire to what extent his revenues had been increased during the last five years, how much further his "writt rinneth," how the reconciled and ennobled Irishmen demeaned themselves, and what jurisdiction the king had in their territories; what was the strength of the pale, and what barriers were erected in Leinster, "the key and stay of all the rest, for the protection of his majesty's faithful subjects."

Archbishop Brown, who takes the opposite side,† writes *his* private letter, and refers to the "insaciable ambicion" of Ormond, who "rayneth continual quoyn and lyvrie, called extorcion." When sent for, to appear before the Irish council, "he brought with hyme suche a company of galloglas!" "The said earl is more like a prince than a subject, more like a governor than an obedient servant." As this was behaviour which Henry did not like, he sent for Ormond, and his friend Cowley, to meet St. Leger, face to face, in London, and there substantiate their charges. They go, and Cowley is thrown into the Tower, where St. Leger writes to

---

* *Walter Cowley* was the son of Robert Cowley, the "trusty servaunt" of the old Earl of Ormond. We find the father's name, signed "Master of the Rolles" in State Papers, from January 16, 1540. "As for Cowley's *boke*." says Alen, "I take God to record, I would be ashamed to be named to the pennynge of so lewde a boke."

† *Opposite side.*—Archbishop Brown writes five years after this, commending the Lord Chancellor Alen, and accusing St. Leger of "papistical practices."—*State Papers*, July 31, 1551.

him, saying, "If Cowley can shew that *he is not the inventor* of those matters that he had set forth foolishly, he shall have the more favor at the king's hands." Cowley, in reply, expresses his readiness to "declare in open assembly, his foolish attempstate" against St. Leger, "upon false information." He was not privy to the letters found in Ross, and other places. It was Catherine Coke,* one of St. Leger's gentlewomen, who said that the Deputy hated Ormond above all men living. Cowley's wife and household can testify how much he was grieved after his interview with Cantwell.† He explains, "with as sorrowful a hart as ever any pore man had," how one Cantwell, meeting and gossiping with John Conway, the Earl of Ormond's servant, led to all this sorrow.

The curtain drops on this curious and interesting correspondence, (which would furnish material for a romance,) with the death of Ormond, who, along with "James White, steward of his household, and many others of his followers, *were poisoned at a supper at Ely House, in Holborn, on the* 17*th of October*, 1546.

Cowley, writing to the Privy Council, trusts that their "noble hearts will incline to shew mercy to him, whose sorrowful letters cumith to your honorable hands *amidst your noble joyful feuste*." The gentleman who edits the Calendar of Irish State Papers from 1509-1573, asks, "Is it possible that this is the *feast*

---

* *Catherine Coke.*—Was this Catherine Coke the aunt of the Lord Chief Justice, who was born in 1552.?

† *Cantwell.*—This Cantwell must have been in the pay of government, for the king charges the Vice-Treasurer, "to forbear payment of the wages due to William Cantwell, and his man." *State Paper*, April 7th, 1547. Again, "Cantwell to get one of his ears cut off, for counterfeiting the hands of certain of the Privy Council," August 17, 1551.

[the poisoning] referred to above?" We should say not. Feasts were not less common then than now. We are bound in charity to conclude that the *cook*, and not the Privy Council, was responsible for the "*accident*" at Ely House, Holborn.

In the meantime, the Irish lords " take up the cudgels" for St. Leger, and in a fine Latin oration, addressed to the king, nobly vindicate the character of that "INTEGERIUM VIRUM." And Cusake, one of the Irish council, when forwarding the document, says to Paget, " I assure you good mastership, that *ther never lefte Irelande one that hath the prayers of pore people more than he hath.* Pittie it were that the occasioners of our inquyetnes here shoulde not be knowen, that such punyshment might ensue as others shoulde thereby feere to attempte the lyke; for till then men will be more busy than needeth."

But St. Leger is well able to defend himself, and he does so nobly against ten distinct charges tabled by the Lord Chancellor Alen. The charges can be gathered from the replies, which we give in the most condensed form :—

1st.—Farmers, *paying* for their farms, cannot allow to the king the horses and harness which the *owners in fee* did formerly.

2nd.—For the obeying of the king's wrytt, " I think it very little further obeyed than it was four years ago, for it is hard to make wild men, who know neither law nor letter, obey the king's process in so short a time. When I came to this land no man could ride between Limerick and Cashel without a *safe conduct*, and pay a crown for every packe carried a horssebacke."

3rd.—As it regards the augmentation of the king's revenue, St. Leger did his best.

4th.—As it regards Leinster, the power of the O'Byrnes, the Kavanaghs, the O'Mores, and the O'Carrolls had been greatly curtailed. "Old O'More wold ride everie day in the weik with more horsemen than all the O'More's countrie" can now produce.

5th.—As it regards the Irish who have been reconciled, " having been allowed to murder the king's English subjects," he knew of nothing of the sort.

6th.—As for Irishmen not keeping their " pactes," [compacts] " perchance if Englishmen were well examined they all kepe not their promises."

7th.—If Irishmen use their own laws, so does the Chancellor's friend, "the Earl of Ormond, and all the lord marchers in Ireland, and I would fain know when Irishmen so well obeyed the king's commandment."

8th.—To the charge of attempting to "control the king," which looks like an implication of disloyalty, he does not vouchsafe a reply.

9th.—To the charge that " the king is beguiled," he replies, " I know not what he meaneth thereby."

10th.—To the last charge, where the archbishop says he marvels how the whole revenue of Ireland, along with £5,000 a-year, is consumed to maintain the Deputy's estate, St. Leger replies, "*I marvel as much, he is not ashamed to lye*, for he well knoweth there is no such sowme spent there. For my parte, I have not as much as I spend by five hundred marks a yere."

We are not surprised to meet soon after this the following minute of Council: "The king's pleasure to be known for the naming of a new Chancellor."* He was to be an "Englishman of some good behaviour."

It was thus that this wise, noble, and loyal ancestor of the Doneraile family, who are now residents of this county, discharged the onerous duties of Governor of Ireland, and defended himself from his malicious foes. Ireland never had, and never will have, a wiser or a better Lord Deputy.

* *Chancellor.*—Two hundred pounds was added this year, 1546, to the Chancellor's income, making "his office worth £400 as we esteem it." It was also proposed to augment the Justices' fees. "Two hundred markes in this matter would do much to the consideration of them all." This included the Clerk of of Council (who had but £10 a-year) and the Remembrancer of the Exchequer.

CHAPTER XI.

EDWARD VI.—MARY AND PHILIP—THE EARL OF DESMOND.

A.D. 1547—1558.

We have a new king and a new Lord Deputy. St. Leger has been superseded by Sir Edward Bellingham. The principal magistrates of the principal towns, send letters and addresses. The mayor, bailiffs, and council of Cork write to say, they have sent John Coppinger to the king to procure the confirmation of their grants and liberties; the mayor, bailiffs, and council of Youghal, that they have captured a pirate, named Smith, who had plundered their fishing boats, and wish to know what they are to do with him; the Sovereign and council of Kinsale, that all their men have died of pestilence—there was a great plague in the city of Cork this year—that they have a wide and empty town, few men, and naughty neighbours, that their haven is stopped by "eagle's pirates," and that one Richard Colle, or Colley, a pirate with a pinnace, has married Barry Oge's aunt, and lives in his castle, and will not suffer any one to come to the town. They request the Deputy to send letters to Mac Carthy Reagh, Barry Roe,* Barry Oge, and Lord de Courcy commanding them to take the king's coin.

* *The Lord Barry.*—The Editor of the Calendar of Irish State Papers for 1509-1573 erroneously styles this Irish nobleman *Lord Barrymore.* David Lord Barry, Viscount of Buttevant, was created Earl of Barrymore, February 28, 1627. The title Baron Barry was conferred in 1420, and Viscount Buttevant in 1555.

The coin of Ireland, at this time, was not of equal weight, or of as pure a metal, as that in circulation in England. The Irish coinage had to be closely watched by the Lord Treasurer, or there would have been the most flagrant adulteration. Sir Anthony St. Leger, writing to Sir James Croft, from Cork, May 20, 1551, says, " the Master of the Mint is so destitute of bullion, that he hath not wherewith all to furnish his ordinary charges. Although there be here presently [present] an *honest substance* of ore drawen in the mines, which we think would make a good masse of bullyon, yet, for as much as we are not authorized, we forbear to put it in use." Bellingham was greatly annoyed that he should not be privy to the king's treasure in the mint. He neither bought "houses, lands, fee or office, dised or carded, or riotously or laciviously spent the king's treasures."

We meet, a few years after this, with a " common supplication from the Lords Deputy and Council, with the rest of the nobility, gentlemen, and merchants, and divers others of the king's subjects, to the Privy Council," which attribute the universal dearth of all things in Ireland to the money, as the "*furste and pryncipall cawse,* withoute remedye whereof it is thought ympossible to set a staye." They pray that the monies in Ireland may be of the like valuation, weight, and fineness, as in England. No English or foreign merchant could be expected to bring his wares to a port or market notorious for light or bad money.

The mayor and bailiffs of Cork write to complain that Edmond Tyrie, while seeking the rightful possession of lands in Barrie's country, was treacherously "murdrede by twenty-three foynes of an Irish knyffe, given him in the very hart." William Davis, an English gentleman of rank, was cruelly murdered in the city this year, of which the mayor does *not* inform the Deputy, but goes on to say, that O'Sullivan Beare * had accepted a "large ransom" for the liberation of John Tomson and other pirates. They promise that no soldiers or other persons shall leave the realm without special license and passport, and that they will make a strong fortress for the defence of the town. They complain that their harbour, and their whole line of coast, is haunted and harassed by English adventurers. They mention the arrival of a "big ship" at Kinsale, from St. Malo, en route to Galway, with wine and hides, and desire to know the king's pleasure concerning pirates—whether they should apprehend or kill them? They inform the Deputy, that "a great ship of Venice, of seven hundred tons burthen," together with other vessels, laden with Malmsey and Spanish wool, have been driven into Cork harbour by stress of weather. The Malmsey has been seized and sent as a present to the king, which was likely to settle the question of their right of seizure. The letter goes on to state, that certain wild Irish, coming one night to make a prey near Cork, were met by the Lord Barry, *who was going to do the like on certain other wild Irish*, and that the Lord Barry killed eighty of them.

It would appear from a letter, written from Carrigaline, the 2nd of December, 1548, that Maurice of Desmond, the earl's brother, had not the same scruples

---

* *Dermot O'Sullivan Beare* was blown up in his own castle, by accident, with gunpowder, this year, and his brother Amlavus, who succeeded him, was killed soon after.

about "*buying an office*" as the Deputy, and that he understood, even at this semi-civilised period, that ladies managed these things better than their lords. He writes to the Countess of Ormond, who was a Geraldine, that "he is nothing as yet promoted by his lord brother;" if the countess had any place that would suit him, "he will pay such fine as any other man living would give."

It was a falsehood to say he was nothing promoted by his brother, for the earl settled the whole barony of Kerricurrihy upon him, with the castle of Carrigaline, in which he penned this lie. But it is probable he did not esteem this worthy of his services in murdering the Court-Page, and thus opening his brother's way to the earldom. He speaks of being *promoted*. He richly deserved it—at the hands of the hangman. He was slain some time after this, when caught preying on the estates of his son-in-law* of Muskerry.

Patrick Myagh, Mayor of Cork, wrote to the Lord Deputy, stating that one "Tamsin," or Thomson, and Richard Stephenson, lately in the pay of Robert St. Leger, had arrived in Cork, on Christmas-day, in a ship laden with wines, figs, and sugar, offering to trade. Very proper commodities for Christmas, though a day or so too late. The mayor wishes to know whether he is to trade, or seize the ship and apprehend the owners.

"There be land thieves and water thieves," quoth honest Antonio. There were port pirates, and piratical mayors and council men in "*the city*" in those days.

---

* *His son-in-law.*—His eldest daughter married Mac Carthy Reagh, of Carbery; the second married Lord Roche, and the third Dermot Mac Teige, of Muskerry. This Maurice was the father of James, who brought the Italians to Smerwick.

The corporation of Cork laid claim to all such confiscated property; and the St. Legers were not in favor. The Deputy replied that, "Tomson and Stephenson may have probably procured their pardons; that as it does not appear their goods are stolen, the mayor and council may *trade*. The mayor makes inquiry, and finds that Messrs. Tomson and Stephenson are honest merchants, that the people in the adjacent country have long traded in their wares; that other parties have been compelled to return pirated goods to the proper owners. Honest trading must have been a hazardous affair in the harbour of Cork in those days. The traders in Malmsey and Spanish wool would scarcely style it a *Statio bene fida carinis*—a station very faithful to keels or mariners.

Walter Cowley and Sir John Alen, as he is now styled, are again in office, and members of Council. The Council and the Lord Deputy are at loggerheads. William Brereton sets Bellingham against Alen. Alen, with a sneer, says, that Bellingham had been favored by Mars, and wishes that Jupiter and Venus had been as propitious. Bellingham tells the Council it would be "a good turn for the king, if they were all hanged." Such civility could not last very long. Bellingham resigned his Deputyship on the 19th of December, 1549, and Sir Anthony St. Leger was nominated for the third time.

But his old enemy, the Lord Chancellor, is in the field again, preferring charges. He replies to the reports made against his enlightened and impartial administration, that his majesty has now five thousand hearts more in Ireland than at his coming; that "such handling of the wild Irish" as was recommended by certain of the Irish Council hath done much harm in Ireland; that his chaplain, James Bicton, *is no papist,*" as is reported. In writing to Mr. Secretary Cecil, "he is sorry the Privy Council will not appoint his chaplain, James Bicton, to the vacant see of Ossory. He marvels that his *owlde freende,* Mr. Alen, hath wrytten that he is not allowed to counsell here, but that he standeth at the dore emong servants."

His "owlde freende," or enemy, the Chancellor, is doing his best at this time to prevent a marriage which promises to produce lasting peace and harmony between the rival houses of Ormond and Desmond. The widowed Countess of Ormond, whose husband died of the poisoned supper at Ely House, has serious thoughts of giving her hand to Garrett, the second son and *heir* of the Earl of Desmond; but the Lord Chancellor remonstrates, reminds her of her first noble husband, and in the end so persuades her against her will, that she promises "upon hir honour, *she wold live sole* [single] *for oon* [one] *yeare*" more.

The old Earl of Desmond and the Chancellor had become friends at this time. In writing to his brother, Thomas Alen, he requests that thanks and gifts of apparel may be sent Desmond from the king, to animate him in well doing. We find the following "postil," or note of remembrance, among the Irish State Papers for July, 1550:—"Letters to be sent to the Earl of Desmond, the Earl of Thomond, the Earl of Clanrycard, to Mc William, to O'Donnell, or his son, or both of them, to O'Reilly, to O'Kane, and Mac Quillan; and some remembrance, either of scarlet cloth or some piece of plate, whereby they shall the more diligently be inclined to serve the king. *Postilled:* cups to be provided to the value of £100." These presents of apparel and red cloth, to incline them to serve the king, look very childish or savage-civilising. The plate and silver cups are quite up to the mark of the present day.

The Lord Deputy was instructed, in the early part of 1551, to visit Cork, Kinsale, Baltimore, and Beare, and to report what points of the south-western coast required to be fortified; he was also advised that ships had been sent to Waterford with arms and munition. He remonstrated, and expressed his inability of fortifying either Cork or Kinsale without money from the mint. He informs the Privy Council that he has the sons of the Earls of Desmond and Thomond ready to send into England. He acknowledges the arrival of a thousand soldiers and a hundred and twenty pioneers, but has no money to pay them.

St. Leger retired from the Deputyship in the May of 1551, and Sir James Croft was appointed in his stead. Mr. St. Leger, the son, gets the office of Andrew Brereton, who has, as he states, "honestly served." The Earls of Desmond, Thomond, Clanricard and the Earl of Tyrone, with the Countess, his wife, repair to Dublin to welcome the new Lord Deputy. These Irish rebel lords are being converted into courtiers. Andrew Brereton, who has lost office, calls Tyrone a traitor, and says he wrote to the King of France, promising to join him against King Edward. Mac Carthy More submits; an oath of fealty is preparing for his people.

The new Lord Deputy, Sir Thomas Croft, writes to Duddeley, Earl of Warwick, respecting the fortification of Cork, Kinsale, and Baltimore, and recommends the punctual payment of the thousand soldiers and hundred and forty laborers, who are "without money to find them,"—support themselves.

The Earl of Desmond is made Treasurer, "with such pre-eminences and dignities as may stand with the surety of the state." There was a necessity for this saving clause, for at this very time the Lord Deputy had to call Gerald, the earl's son, and Maurice, the earl's brother, before him, "for preys they had taken from the O'Mahons;" and the old earl himself had a dispute with Lord Fitzmaurice, respecting the "liberties" of Kerry. He offers to entertain at his own cost,* the Chief Justice Luttrell, P. Barnewall, Master of the Rolls, or any other judges who can speak the language, that the case may be fully and fairly tried. The earl also lays claim to the manor of Dungarvan, which was wrested from him by the Earl of Ormond; he supplicates the Privy Council, and gets Sir Thomas Cusake, the new Lord Chancellor, to "recommend his suit." This was nothing uncommon in these days.

Sir John Alen, the late Lord Chancellor, had retired on a pension of two hundred marks, and was engaged in making out depositions against St. Leger, on the score of religion. He was unable to go to England, as the surgeon, in attempting to bleed him in the

---

* *To entertain at his own cost.*—About sixty years after this, a Cork Jury says, "We present that all the lords of this country, to color and maintain their own extortions, have wrought such a policy *to entertain all the lawyers of the province*, whereby no freeholder nor poor man can have a lawyer to speak in his cause, be it never so just."

leg,* had hit the wrong vein, or "severed a sinew."
St. Leger was also *hors de combat*. In sending a packet
of letters to the Duke of Northumberland, he says,—
" For thys ij days I have bene so paynyd with the
syatyca, as I ame nether hable well to goo nor ryde."
In the mean time, Alen's case against St. Leger seems
to have broken down, for the king, writing in 1553 to
Con, Earl of Tyrone, who, "through gentill enter-
teignment," was arrested in Dublin, refers him to
" Sir Anthony St. Leger, whom he purposes to send
presently into Ireland as Lord Deputy."

We meet at this time with a " Device for the better
Government of Ireland," in which it is proposed that
no man be Deputy above one year; that every three
years a mere Englishman be Deputy; that after one
year the Earl of Kildare be Deputy. These are among
the last Irish State Papers of the reign of Edward VI.,
and are dated Westminster, June 9th, 1553.

St. Leger was in office for the fourth time in 1553,
when Queen Mary ascended the English throne. The
second Irish State Paper, written in the October of
1553, contains instructions to the Deputy to "restore
the Old Religion." The next is a letter from Conaghor
M'Carthy, clerk, to the queen, praying for permission
to go to Rome, to obtain from the Pope " certain porr
benefices."

St. Leger is assailed in 1555, on the score of expenditure. He says that the queen owes him £3,000,
and that he has borrowed so much he can borrow no
more. He retires from office in the April of 1556,

* *To bleed him in the leg.*—Before the discovery of the circulation of the blood, it was the habit, to abate inflammation by bleeding the part affected. This habit prevails in some parts to the present day.

and is succeeded by "Sir Thomas Radclyff, Lord Fitzwauter."

The Earl of Desmond writes to the queen, 1577, to complain that John Walsh, "by sinister means" has got the manor of Dungarvan. He sends his chaplain, Dorbye ne Royne—Darby Ronan—to insist on his just claims, and his right to the prize wines of Youghal and Kinsale, belonging to the late Earl of Ormond. In all these suits, he says, writing to his chaplain, " My Lorde of Pembrooke, my Lord of Ely"—it was at Ely House, Ormond was poisoned—"and Master Petre, I trust, wyll further youe." He writes under date, March 1st, to the Mayor of Cork, to let him have certain of her majesty's powder and shot, and, if need be, the loan of certain great guns, "to plague disordered people within his rule," or rather, we suspect, to put a bold face on his demands for Dungarvan.

Lord Fitzwauter succeeds to the title of Earl of Sussex. Philip and Mary send a circular to the nobility of Ireland, charging them to further all good order pertaining to piety. The Earl of Desmond replies, (the letter is dated, Youghal, October 13th,) If her majesty would direct letters to John Browne, and Edmond Gowle, [Gould] merchants of Cork, to restore the dissolved house of Friars' Preachers, adjoining to the city walls, (where many gentlemen and lords have their monuments) it would "do moche good emonges her grace's pore savage people in thies partes, that knoweth not decently where to be buryed."

The house of Friars' Preachers, of which the earl speaks, was called the Monastery of the Minorites, or the Friars of Seandun, or Shandon. It was founded by MacCarthy More in 1231, whose tomb stood in the middle of the choir. This convent, on account of its strict discipline, was styled "*The Mirror of Ireland.*" It stood without the city walls, on the north side of the river. Its site is now occupied by the houses of the North Mall, the vicinity of which is still known as the "North Abbey."

It was recovered to the church in Mary's reign, from the hands of John Brown and Edmond Gowle, or Gould, and passed in 1562, during the reign of her sister Elizabeth, into those of Andrew Skiddy,* gent.

"The scite and precinct of the late house of Ffranciscans, neare unto Corke, with the appurtenances, containing one hawle, one kitchen, one cloyster, six chambers, six cellars, one church-yard, one little orchard, and three gardens, the moytie of one water mille, called the Ffrier's milne, and the third part of one watermille there, one fishing place for salmonde, and one salmonde weare, called Gowle's weare, tenn acr of land arr, and x^{ii} accr. of pasc. and xxtie ac. of underwood, wth thapp^t in the town and fields of Templenam-raher, in the aforesaid County of Cork; one half acre and one stagne of land arr. in the aforesaid County, and seven gardens, late belonging to the said house, to the said Andrew Skyddye and heyres males of his body, lawfully begotten in *Capite* per service xx^{mo} parte unius feod mil, rent per annum, ad Recept scij per pmiss l.viij^s viij^d str. at the feastes of Easter and St. Michaell by even porcons."

Andrew Skiddy died in 1596, and by an inquisition taken in the April of this year, his son was found seized in Dominico suo ut de feodo de et in cit circuit ambit et precinct nuper monii sine Domus Frini Franciscanse juxta Corke. Skiddy's interest was purchased by Richard Boyle, first Earl of Cork.

* *Andrew Skiddy.*—We discover from the State Papers that Joan, Countess of Desmond, and Dowager Countess of Ormond, wrote to the Queen in favor of Andrew Skiddy. The letter is dated from Youghal, April 24th, 1562. She also asks for 800 weights of wheat and malt for her own house.

Whilst digging in 1804 for the foundation of the present line of houses on the North Mall, a number of stone coffins were discovered, which no doubt contained the remains of the " many gentlemen and lords" of which the Earl of Desmond speaks. A sceptre is inscribed on one of the coffins, on another, "*Sa Alme hait merci.*"

A small chapel stood on the site of the monastery, in 1690. In this little chapel the ill-fated James II. heard mass. There is a chalice* belonging to this chapel still in existence, engraved "Dna Margareta Sarsfield me fieri fecit pro Fribus Minoribus de Shandon. Anno Domini 1627. Orate pro ea et pro marito ejus Waltro Coppinger."

There was an abbey and fraternity of the same order at Timoleague, in which many eminent persons were buried, among whom we may mention Allen Patrick O'Fihelly, in 1505, "famed for his learning," and Edmond Courcy, bishop of Ross, in 1518, who added a library, infirmary, dormitory, and belfry to the original structure, which was founded by William Barry, in the reign of Edward II., though some give the Mac Carthys the credit of the foundation.

A petition was presented to the queen in 1557, by Robert Gogan, one of the friar preachers of the convent of Youghal, praying for the restitution of the monastery of St. Mary's of the Island, adjoining the walls of Cork, and partly thrown down. This order of friar preachers, or black friars, settled in Ireland, in 1224. The house on the island in Cork,' called

* *Chalice.*—Mr. Windele, writing in 1844, says, the chalice "is in the possession of the Rev. T. R. England, the biographer of the Abbe Edgeworth and Father Arthur O'Leary."—*Guide to the South of Ireland*, p. 72.

"*St. Mary de Insula,*" was founded by Philip de Barry, whose equestrian bronze statue was preserved till the destruction of the convent. David Mac Kelly, dean of Cashel, and bishop of Cloyne, took the Dominican habit in this house, as did also Alan O'Sullivan, bishop of Lismore, and David, archbishop of Cashel, who built for his brethren a beautiful church and abbey near his own cathedral, on the Rock of Cashel.

The Earl of Desmond's chaplain writes, May, 1558, from London to the old earl and countess, saying he has presented their letters to the Secretary Petre, but has not been introduced to the queen, or able to deliver the letters brought to him by Thomas Fanning, the tailor, of Youghal. He then adds, that he is going to Flanders or Brabant, to see Cardinal Caraffa, the Pope's legate, respecting a dispensation for the marriage of their daughter, Onoria, with Mac Carthy More—Cardinal Pole, the queen's cousin, not having as yet received his powers.

We discover by the queen's letters to the Lord Deputy, that she has been made acquainted with "the Earl of Desmond's large requests," respecting the manor of Dungarvan, and declines to give him a patent until he states more minutely the particulars of his demands. The queen, at the same time, recommends that "the earl be treated with circumspection."

About six months after this, the Lord Deputy writes to the queen—"*The Earl of Desmond is now certainly dead.*" This was written on the 31st October, but the earl died on the 14th, at Askeaton, in the county of Limerick. His son Garrett, who succeeded him, is styled "the Great Earl of Desmond," but this

James, without doubt, was the *greatest* of all the earls. His son was great in losing what he was great in winning. He commenced as "James the Usurper," and the "Pretended Earl," and died, at an advanced age, as the Lord High Treasurer of Ireland, with his titles fully recognised, and his princely inheritance widely extended. He was the Solomon, and his son Garrett the Rehoboam of his house.

Queen Mary died on the 17th of the next month. There was a manuscript book " brought out of Ireland," just before her death, entitled—"*Fides Piscorum de veritate carnis et sanguinis Christi in Sacramento Altaris, quam ab ipsâ assensione Dominica semper tenuit Universalis Christi Ecclesia, a vetustissimus auctoribus in suis scriptis nobis relicta.*" It was in the faith thus expressed that Mary breathed her last.

Ireland was not destitute of men of letters, either in the catholic or protestant church at this time. Queen Elizabeth writes to Warham St. Leger in December, 1559, to send over "the books and writings of John Bale, late Bishop of Ossory, a man that hath byn studious in the search for the history and antiquities of this our realme, (which he left behind in the time of our late sister, Quene Mary, when he was occasioned to departe out of Ireland,) for the illustration and setting forth of the storye of this our realme, by him the said Bale."

CHAPTER XII.

GARRETT, STYLED THE GREAT EARL OF DESMOND.

A.D. 1558.—1571.

The Earl of Sussex was Lord Deputy of Ireland when Queen Elizabeth ascended the English throne. About eighteen months after this, (May, 1560,) we meet a memorandum for giving him the title of Lord Lieutenant. But no titles could reconcile him to the office. He requests the queen to allow the Lord Justice, Sir Henry Sydney, who is now in Ireland, as his locum tenens, or deputy, to hold the office. Sir Henry is popular with the Irish, he is joined in gossopryke with Shane O'Neill; he will manage the affairs of Ireland, with its present reduced establishment, better than Sussex, who has his wyef and family, and horses in England, he has three offices already, ys ynough occupare totum hominen—quite enough for one man. But no, go he must, nolens, volens. There was an idea at this time of placing Ireland, as the Cæsars did Palestine, under a tetrarchy. Munster, under the government of the Earl of Warwick, Connaught under Lord Grey, Ulster under the Earl of Sussex, and Leinster under Sir Henry Sydney. Munster was some time after this placed under the government of a Lord President and Council. During St. Leger's deputyship, in 1541, the bishop of Cork and Ross, the bishop of Waterford, and the mayors of Cork and Youghal, were appointed judges and arbitrators of Munster, in all civil and civic affairs.

The corrupt state of the coinage received a great deal of attention at the commencement of Elizabeth's reign. We meet with numerous letters on the subject. There is a memorandum in February 1559, respecting "*Harp money*, made for Ireland in the mint in the Tower of London." The harp money has ever been esteemed in Ireland, rather, we conceive, on account of the purity of the metal, than the poetry of the device. Measures were taken in December, 1560, "to prevent the transportation of base English coins into Ireland. There was then an order for making out an estimate of the base money in Ireland, and directions for "decrying" it, and a proclamation for searching all vessels freighted out of the realm, and if such money be found, to arrest the offending parties. After this comes a memorandum of the things required in the mint in Ireland, for *fining* the metal, and a note of the charge of fining 60,000 lbs. weight into fine money. The next entry may appear somewhat strange to the reader. "A *gain* to the queen's majesty of £2,000 sterling, in refining 60,000 lbs. weight" of Irish harps.* For "refining" we should read *adulterating*. We must conclude that these Irish harps, minted or cast in the Tower, were *recast and somewhat adulterated* in the Irish mint.

A mint was established in Cork in the reign of Edward I. It appears by acts passed, (the 11th and

* "*Irish harps*" were silver coin that passed for *twelve* pence in Ireland, and *nine* pence in England. They bore the queen's head on one side and three harps on the other.

12th of Edward IV.) that a great deal of light and adulterated metal had been coined in Cork. Three coiners, John Fannin, John Crone, and Patrick Martel were indicted, and the Mayor of Cork received instructions, "In case the said coiners do not appear before the Deputy, in parliament, to execute the law on their persons, as traitors attainted." By another act, (16th Edward IV.) the silver money struck in Cork was "*utterly damned.*"

Gerald, the second son of James, has taken the oath of allegiance, and has been admitted to the Earldom of Desmond.* He gets a confirmation of the Regalities of Kerry, to procure which his father offered to entertain the judges; but this does not satisfy him; he seeks the manor of Dungarvan, and the prize wines of Youghal, and disputes with his step-son,† the young Earl of Ormond, the right to some property in the county Waterford. The Lord Lieutenant informs the Privy Council of "a contention between the Earls of Desmond and Ormond," and adds, that some speedy order should be taken for their reformation. This contention did not cease till this step-son, known afterwards as the Black Earl of Ormond, sent the gory head of the Earl of Desmond, "pickled in a pipkin," to the queen. But the two men are well matched; Munster was not wide enough to contain them both. Desmond appears to have been the first assailant.

---

* *Admitted to the earldom.*—The document is dated 5th and 6th of Philip and Mary, for the news of Elizabeth's accession had not reached Ireland. It was to Mary, and not to Elizabeth, that this great Catholic and rebel lord swore allegiance.

† *Step-son.*—Gerald, now Earl of Desmond, married the dowager Countess of Ormond, whose husband had been poisoned at Ely House. She gave her word and honor to the Lord Chancellor Alen to remain "sole one yere," but no more.

The Lord Lieutenant writes (in 1561) to Desmond, to disperse his power, and remain in peace within his own territories. He replies, that the Earl of Ormond lay in wait to surprise him, on his return from the queen's service. Ormond sends pledges to keep the peace. Desmond refuses to do so, till he knows the Lord Lieutenant's pleasure; so they prepare to fight it out, when "the Almighty God sends the Angel of Peace" among them—whose visits to Ireland, at this time, were "few and far between." The affair is thus described by the Four Masters:—

"When these noblemen could not be reconciled, they agreed on a certain time to meet in a pitched battle, and the place of battle which they appointed was *Bothar-mor*," or "Broad-way," where they might have elbow-room. "Each party collected their forces respectively, of both English and Irish, from Bealach Conglais of the son of Duindesa the Fenian, in the west of the two noble provinces of Munster, to the white-blossomed Barrow, and from the lake of Garman Glas, the son of Bomalica, [Wexford] to the foaming broad harbour of Limerick, in the extremity of Hy-Figinta, and of the Lesser Decies, [in Waterford] to Caoil-an-Chosnamba. After those great armies having met face to face, and front to front, the Almighty God sent the Angel of Peace to them, to establish concord among those forces, and having sensibly reflected concerning that battle, they separated without fighting on that occasion."

Ormond, the more politic of these two noblemen, endeavours to keep the ear of the Lord Lieutenant, and writes from Kilkenny:—"The Earl of Desmond has burned a good town and much corn since you departed." The next complaint is for capturing Ormond's servant, near Limerick, and robbing him of five hundred pounds. Nor is he satisfied with making war on Ormond, he attacks the members of his own family: "Maurice Fitz-Desmond and his nephew, the earl, are at hot wars." The Maurice here mentioned is Black Maurice, the freebooter and incendiary, who murdered the Court-Page. His son Thomas, witing to Fitzwilliam, who is now Lord Chief Justice, complains of the "earl's misuse" of his father, the earl's uncle.

This Thomas, son of Maurice Duv, or Black Maurice, would not be his father's son, or first cousin to the earl, if he were not fond of fighting. "Thomas and James, the sons of Maurice Duv, marched with a force into Carbery. The son of Mac Carthy Riavach and Turlough Mac Sweeny, with a party of galloglasses, attacked the plunderers." They pursued them as far as Innishannon, on the Bandon river. The Carbrians were victors. Two or three hundred of the Geraldines were either slain or drowned. It was on this occasion that Turlough Mac Sweeny lost a hand and foot, and was obliged to use *a wooden leg* to carry him to his death.* Thomas, the leader of the Geraldines, died about two years after this. The father's death is thus described by the Four Masters:—

"A.D. 1564.—Maurice Duv, the son of John, went to take a prey in Muskerry. Dermot and Cormac, the sons of Teige Mac Carthy, overtook and beheaded Maurice." Other writers say, those who were left to

---

* *To his death.*—Turlough Mac Sweeny, "*of the wooden leg*," fell by the hand of Brian Mac Sweeny, at the gate of Cork, in 1579.

guard him fell on him and slew him. Thus died Maurice Duv, or Maurice *Tothaire*, "the Freebooter." He resided at Carrigaline castle, in this county. The Four Masters style him "The high-tempered steel of the Geraldines, the plunderer of his enemies, the slayer of his opponents." They place his death in their annals two years later than it is recorded in the State Papers.

The queen, who held the Earl of Desmond responsible not only for his own conduct but that of his house, demanded his presence in England. Fitzwilliam writes him about Ormond's five hundred pounds, and hints that his delay in answering the queen's *lettre de cachet*, must seem strange. He asks if he shall meet him at Waterford. The earl screws up his courage, and promises to go; so the Chief Justice prepares a proclamation for the safety of Desmond during his absence, and the mayor, bailiffs, and council of Youghal write, commending him to the queen, telling of the protection he has given them, and how he drove out a den of thieves from a castle four miles up the river*—when who should cross his path, and decide his doom, but a messenger from the famous Shane O'Neill, who is in rebellion, and desires the aid of an Irish chieftain to put the South in the same commotion as he has put the North. The earl hesitates. A new idea has struck him, so he begins to build a castle in Lord Roche's country. Fitzwilliam writes to Cecil of

---

* *A castle four miles up the river.*—The castle, we suspect, of *Rhincrew*, or the "Firm Promontory," about four miles above Youghal, on the Blackwater. It is supposed to have been possessed by the order of Knights Templars. Raymond Le Gros, who is believed to have been the founder of Rhincrew, died here, and was buried in the neighbouring Abbey of Molana. The ruins are still extensive, containing chapel, cloisters, refectory, kitchen and dormitories.

"Desmond's facteous intention of building a castle," and to Desmond, to hasten his journey. The earl sends Patrick Meagh, late sovereign of Kinsale, to England, to spy out, or pave the way. Meagh carries an address from the council of Kinsale to the queen, which states that the Earl of Desmond is their only help and security against the disorders of the country, and entreats her majesty to "*animate*" him by her favor, on his present repair to her presence. To do him justice, he was never wanting in animation.

He goes, and as he might have suspected, is "sequestered from his liberty," in the house of the Lord Treasurer of England. But the queen is kind to him, and writes to his wife, Joan; and gets him to swear—to which he never objected in his life—that he will confine himself to his own kin and his own affairs, in the counties of Cork, Limerick, Kerry, and Waterford, and no longer molest the "Lord Great Barry, the Lord Roche, Little Barry, Barry Roe, the Lord Courcy, the Lord Fitzmaurice, Sir Maurice Fitzgerald, Mac Carthy More, Mac Carthy Reagh, Teig Cormac Mac Carthy, O'Sullivan Beare, O'Sullivan More, O'Donoghue, O'Callaghan, and others, which oath he faithfully promises to observe. He also promises—the hypocrite—to assist the protestant bishop in the furtherance of religion. But her most gracious majesty, knowing his weak point, and many temptations, furnished him with a bill, in the way of reminder, entitled, "Book of the debt of the old Earl of Desmond, and of Gerald, the new Earl of Desmond, for rents and possessions held of the crown, £1,386 10s. 8d." Perhaps it was to meet this that he sued Ormond for

£4,000, " as the forfeiture of a bond that he would marry his sister."

He procured the queen's pardon on the 21st of July, 1562, at Greenwich, for all his murders, manslaughters, and felonies, and is ready, on his return, to recommence his raids with a clear conscience. But he is still detained in London. Cecil wishes some explanation from him respecting the prize wines of Youghal and Kinsale, and he has none to give, save and except that he views them as his rightful inheritance. He asks permission to return to Ireland, or Bristol; says he has no money to support his retinue, and seeks passports for "Sir Dorby—probably Darby—the styward; Andrew Skiddy, and thirty-seven others, the Earl of Desmond's servants."

He is detained so long in England, that John his brother, and Joan his wife, take the field against the queen, in 1563, and render Munster too hot for her deputy. This was the invariable policy when any of these great Irish lords were either detained, or entertained, too long in England, be their place of residence the Tower, the house of the Lord Treasurer, or Hampton Court. The Lord Lieutenant and Council, writing to the queen, inform her that Nicholas Heron and Edward Fitzsymon have delivered "*a perfect book*" of the hurts committed by the *Countess of Desmond*, and John, the earl's brother. The Lord Roche, Lord Barry, Sir Maurice of Desmond, Teig Cormac, and others, have received "great hurts." The city of Cork is also disturbed. The mayor, bailiffs, and commons of Cork speak of their exposed position, and ask to be protected from pirates, rovers, and malefactors generally.

Immediately after this we find a letter from the earl, thanking Cecil for his enlargement. He should rather have thanked his good wife, Joan, and his brave brother, John. But this enlargement did not allow of his leaving England, for he writes Cecil, (July 4th, 1563,) that "the continued craving of his creditors" prevents his repair to court, and asks for a loan of six hundred pounds. He requests Sir T. Cusake "to further his speedy return," and the month after informs Cecil that he is very sick and low—low in health and pocket—and has not four pounds in the world, and fears he will be arrested by his creditors, on his journey home, which he requests the secretary's services to prevent. To be a prisoner in the hands of the queen is bad enough. He is released in time to spend his Christmas in Ireland, which he gains in despite of his creditors and his hereditary foe, the Earl of Ormond, for we find him on the 20th of December, writing to the Irish Council, informing them that the Irish chiefs will not yield to the "proposed civility," and asking for ordnance and skilful gunners to batter down their forts and castles. He desires license to apprehend malefactors within the liberties of Cork, and other chartered towns, and asks for the manor of Dungarvan, Onought, a castle called Ynyshanon, and the reversion of divers abbey lands.

We meet a document in the calender of the State Papers, (No 74, December 20, 1563,) entitled "orders to be taken by the Earl of Desmond, for such things as he hath voluntarily accorded, and are by him to be observed in Munster," amongst which we find the abolition of brehon laws, the suppression of rhymers, bards, and dice-players, and the payment of *fourpence a cow, annually to the queen.* The queen seems ambitious to walk in the footsteps of Brian Boru. Brian, son of Kennedy, gained the title of Brian Boru, or Boroimhe,* or "Brian of the Tribute," by the imposition of his cow tribute upon Leinster.

The Earl of Desmond, writing to the Marquis of Winchester, the High Treasurer of England, says, he has met the queen's commissioners in Cork, and that the country is willing to perform the articles agreed to by him in England. He informs Cecil, by the same messenger, July 26th, that his proceedings with the queen's commissioners have been most satisfactory.

The accounts from other quarters of the earl's proceedings were not quite so satisfactory. Sir T. Wrothe informs Cecil of his having burned two houses, in an attempt to take the castle of Kilfeacle,† in the county Tipperary. Ormond writes to Cecil to say, that her majesty's subjects under Desmond's rule, are daily invaded by the Earl, his brother John, and their retinue, that he (the Earl of Ormond,) was on the very point of removing the "dam'd impost of coyne and livery," ‡ when the earl's invasions compelled him to continue one evil, in order to meet another. He writes again, (December 4th, 1564,) complaining that his "tenants are spoiled by the earl of Desmond," asking letters to the Lord Justice "to stay the said earl."

---

* *Brian Boru or Boroimhe.*—We find in the presentment of a Cork jury, a complaint that Owen Mac Carthy and Dounell Mac Carthy, "take of the same freeholders and inhabitants a sum of money called *cowe.*"

† *Kilfeacle*—There are the remains of the castles of Grantstown and Castlefield, in this parish, to the present day.

‡ *Coyne and Livery.*—This impost had been frequently condemned by the English government, and Irish lords forbidden to levy it.

As this was more than any Lord Justice in Ireland could do, the Earl of Ormond united with Sir Maurice Fitzgerald, knight, of Dromona,* in the county Waterford, who lived "between the Earls of Ormond and Desmond," to lay a trap to catch him. The trap was set at Affane, where Sir Walter Raleigh first planted cherries. The affair is thus described by the Four Masters :—

"A.D. 1565.—It happened on a certain expedition, the Earl of Desmond, *i.e.* Gerald, the son of James, son of John, had made into the Decies of Munster, that the lord of Decies, namely, Maurice, the son of Gerald, son of John, sent treacherously for the Earl of Ormond, namely Thomas, the son of James, son of Pierce Roe, in order that he might lie in ambush for the Earl of Desmond. The earl (of Desmond) having come to the country, he never perceived until he was surrounded on all sides at a place called Ath Meadhain; the large body of the ambushed troops attacked, wounded, and took him prisoner, and a great number of his people were either slain or taken prisoners along with him. The Butlers were full of joy and gladness, on account of the great booty and the number of prisoners they had taken on that day, and the result of that capture was, that the two earls went to England, by command of the queen, and having remained for some time in London, they returned back in peace and friendship.

The Earl of Desmond was wounded in the thigh by a pistol shot from Sir Edward Butler, and was lame the rest of his life. When the Butlers were bearing him on their shoulders from the field, one of them tauntingly asked,—"Where is the great Earl of Desmond now?"—"On the necks of the Butlers, where he ought to be," was his ready and witty reply.

* *Dromona*, the residence of Sir John Fitzgerald, the father of the old Countess of Desmond. It is in the Decies country, on the northern bank of the Blackwater. The present residence of Lord Stuart de Decies is on the site, and incorporated with the old castle. Nothing can be more beautiful than the demesne and the land up and down the river.

The Four Masters say that Desmond and Ormond went to England by command of the queen, and returned "in peace and friendship." They went to London to criminate each other, but did not return in friendship. Desmond was accompanied by Mac Carthy More and O'Sullivan Beare, who wrote to Cecil from Liverpool for travelling expenses. Ormond was accompanied by Sir Maurice Fitzgerald, of Dromana, whose evidence went to shew that no trap had been laid by Black Ormond for the Earl of Desmond; that Ormond went to Affane in order to protect Fitzgerald's cattle. Fitzgerald, on his own account, petitions the queen against the impositions and exactions of Desmond on the Decies' country, which he holds in fee from the queen only.*

The Earl of Essex also makes some very serious charges against the Earl of Desmond—that he had refused to deliver up offenders; that he had aided rebels against the Earl of Thomond; that he had done violence to Lords Roche, Barry, Mac Carthy More, Teige Mac Cormac, and many others; that, in fact, he had never served the queen faithfully, and that Ormond had ever done so. Similar testimony is borne by others. There are charges and counter charges, fines, and articles for future good conduct, with many queenly injunctions not to fall out for the future.

It was at this time (1565) that Mac Carthy More and O'Sullivan Beare, who accompanied the Earl of Desmond to London, were created, the former an earl, and the latter a knight. Mac Carthy More's new title

* *The queen only.*—"The whole land as far as Waterford, together with the city of Lismore," and everything betweeen Waterford and Lismore, is reserved to the crown, in the charter of Henry II., already quoted.

was under consideration six or seven years before it was conferred. We have it among "*Instructions*" from the queen, dated Greenwich, July 16th, 1559, "Mac Carthy More to be advanced to some degree of honor." The queen, writing to the Earl of Sussex (May, 1561), says, "That Mac Carthy More is *not* to be created an earl; but O'Reilly is to be made Earl O'Reilly; and in July, Sussex acknowledges the receipt of " robes, collars, and coronets," for O'Reilly and O'Donnell. When Shane O'Neill heard that Mac Carthy had submitted to the queen, and received the title of earl, he said, " I keep a lacquey as noble as he. Let him enjoy his honor, it is not worthy of O'Neill." We shall see by and bye that Mac Carthy More repudiated his new title.

Mac Carthy More took the prescribed oath, and did homage to the queen, as Baron of Valentia, and Earl of Clancare. He shortly after addressed the Earl of Leicester to use his influence with the queen to obtain for him the loan of £600, and an annual fee out of the exchequer, or land within the pale, " as is customary for newly-created earls."

Sir Owen O'Sullivan Beare also sends in his little petition, for the loan of £200, and hopes there will be no mistake in the wording of his new patent; that the lands of Beare and Bantry, with its towns and castles, including an area of forty-two miles in length, and twenty-four in breadth, will be properly described. The Earl of Clancare hearing this, petitions the queen, that the services due by O'Sullivan Beare to him as lord paramount, should not be passed over in general words, but fully expressed. He encloses "a schedule of the services, rents, duties, and demands, Sir Owen

O'Sullivan Beare, and his heirs, ought to pay the Earl of Clancare." Every time Mac Carthy More thought proper to go to Berehaven, O'Sullivan had to provide entertainment for him and his followers, for two days and nights. He must also send provender to Pallace,* for Mac Carthy More's riding horses, and pay 3s. 4d. to his groom, and 1s. 8d. to his huntsman, yearly, out of every arable ploughland.† He was also expected to feed his hounds, greyhounds, and spaniels, when they came in his way. This habit was called coshering. In a State Paper for 1534, (No. 69,) we read :—

"Item—The said Erles of Desmond, Kildar, and Ossory, their wiffis, childryne, and servauntes, do use, afftyr the custumbe and usage off wyld Irysh men, to cum with a gret multitude of peple to monasteries and gentylmenys howsis, and ther to contynu 2 dais and 2 nightes, taking met and drink at ther plesurs, and ther horssis and kepers to be sheifftyd and dyoydyt un the pore fermors, next to that place adjoynyng, paieng nothing therefor, so as they be found, in thys maner, in other men is howsis moo then halff the yere, by this wyld Irysh custume off extorcion, and spare ther own howsis."

Stanihurst describes the practice thus:— "Their noblemen and noblemen's tenants now and then make

---

* *Pallace.*—" The word *pailis* is generally applied to old forts, in the sense of palace of the fairies"—*Dr. O'Donovan.* The Castle of Pallace, otherwise Caislean na Cartha, the residence of Mac Carthy More, stood on an eminence to the north of the lower Lake of Killarney, near the entrance to the gap of Dunloe. The field in front is still called *Park-an-eroh*, the " gallows field," that being the place where the Mac Carthy executed *justice !* The castle was destroyed in 1837 by a road-jobber.—*See Windcle's Guide, p. 387.*

† *Ploughland.*—The "summer oats" for each ploughland was restricted to a bushel, or a bushel and a half, but it was often demanded in greater quantity.

[take] a feast, which they call coshering, whereto flock all their retainers, their rhymers, their bards, their harpers, that feed them with music. In their coshering they sit upon straw, they are served on straw, and lie upon mattrasses and pallets of straw. They observe divers degrees, according to which each man is regarded. The basest [lowest] sort among them are the *little young wags.*"

On the 7th of December, 1566, "the Earls of Ormond and Desmond are reconciled, and licensed to depart towards Ireland, and to confer with the Deputy," Sir Henry Sydney. Sir Henry was appointed on the 22nd of June, 1565. The Earl of Desmond is not to depart from Dublin when he gets there—he has not got there yet—till he pays what he owes the queen and her subjects. The murderers of the earl's uncle, Sir Maurice of Desmond, are to be tried and punished; the earl to be provided with a safe guard to come and go, and the outrages committed by John of Desmond, the earl's brother, on Sir Maurice Fitzgerald's tenants, to be redressed. Means are to be adopted to make peace between the two earls, and between the Earl of Desmond and Sir Maurice of Dromana. They are all to pay up their arrears of rent and borrowed money—the severest punishment, with the exception of confiscation or imprisonment, that could have been inflicted. But the Earl of Desmond manages it somehow, for on the 11th of January, 1566, *he hath taken good order with all his creditors*, and goes to take leave of the queen and the nobility; but the queen is not prepared to take leave of him. More than three months have rolled by, and we read, April 25th, "the Earl of Desmond is detained in London."

There was reason for this no doubt. Shane O'Neill had assumed a more threatening aspect. He was in correspondence with Charles IX. King of France, and his Prime Minister, the Cardinal of Lorraine. In this correspondence, he makes mention of the earl's detention in London, the warlike character of his brother John, the claims of Mary Queen of Scots to the English crown, and the necessity of all true catholics uniting in a treaty against Elizabeth. All this had been discovered by the council, which Shane had designated "*stupid.*" Cecil was more than a match for Shane. Just at this time, Mary Queen of Scots has been delivered of a child, but whether it be a *knave child*,* or a lass, is not yet known. Under all these circumstances, it was deemed more prudent to detain the Earl of Desmond a little longer in London. Besides all this, there was a very suspicious character, called Tom Stucly, or Stukely, and by Miss Porter, in her "Don Sebastian" Sir Thomas Stukely, going up and down the country, of whom we may have occasion to speak more at large by and bye.

The case was very different with the Earl of Ormond; he was in the confidence of Cecil, and in high odour with the queen, "in memory of his education with that holly yong Sallomon, King Edward VI.," so much so, that Sydney is suspected of partiality to the Earl of Desmond, for indicting Sir Edmond Butler, who had unlawfully imposed coin and livery. Her majesty

* *A knave child.*—In a translation of the New Testament, made about this time, the Apostle Paul (Rom. i. 1) styles himself, "*Paul, the knave of Jesus Christ.*"

is displeased, and gives her Deputy a check for indicting a Butler, which causes a report that coin and livery are to be reimposed. There is also a report that Sydney is in disgrace, which he confirms by desiring to be recalled.

Shane O'Neill writes in the meantime to John, the earl's brother, that it is the object of the English government to *root* out both Celt and Anglo-Norman; but they have no luck in war; now or never is the time to unite against them. The Earl of Desmond, who has just returned to Ireland, (1566) replies to this invitation by uniting with the Deputy in a general hosting against O'Reilly, who appears to have joined the great rebel of the north, notwithstanding his new English title of Earl O'Reilly.

The year 1567 is memorable for the Lord Deputy, Sir Henry Sydney's tour through Munster, which occupied eleven weeks and two days. He was met on this occasion by the Earl of Clancare and Sir Owen O'Sullivan Beare,—" although prohibited by the Earl of Desmond "—by Sir Donough M'Carthy or M'Carthy Reagh, captain of Carbery, and Sir Dermot M'Carthy, captain of Cork, " verie greate possessioners in that county," who complained of the flagrant injuries and injustice of the Earl of Desmond; that, in fact, they who should be free subjects had become his " thralls and slaves." Sydney, though ever so well disposed to befriend Desmond, could not shut his eyes " on viewe of the bones and skulles of your ded subjectes, who partelie by murder, partelie by famyn, have died in the feldes, as in troth hardelie any christian with drie eies coulde beholde. There were certeyne porr women soughte to have been rescewed, but to late, yet so sone after the horrible facte committed, as their children were felte and seene to sturre in the bodies of their ded mothers; and yet did the Earl of Desmond lodge and banckett, after the facte committed, in the howse of the murderer, a principall servaunte of his."

Sydney had to put down those raids, burnings, and murders with a high hand. "I write not the names of each particular varlet that hath died since I arrived, as well by the ordinary course of the law, as flat fighting with them, *when they would take food without the good will of the giver*, for I think it no stuff worthy the loading of my letters with; but I do assure you the number of them is great, and some of the *best*, and the rest tremble; for most part they fight for their dinner, and many of them lose their heads before they be served with supper. Down they go in every corner, and down they shall go, God willing "—*MSS. Cot. Titus B.* x.

We are not surprised to hear that the earl, who had wrought so much evil, had been arrested* by one who had previously acted as his friend, who had suffered in the queen's estimation for defending him; for those who have read the State Papers with attention can come to but one conclusion concerning this earl, and that is, that he was *a violent and bad man.* The Lord Power, the Lord of Dunboyne, Viscount Baltinglass, and Sir Maurice Fitz-Thomas were arrested at the same time, and carried to Dublin. The queen writes to have Desmond indicted, and if need be,

* *Arrested.*—" The Earl of Desmond was taken prisoner at Cill Mocheallog [Kilmallock] by the Lord Justice, who conveyed him to Limerick, from thence to Galway, to Athlone, and finally to Dublin."—*Four Masters, A.D.* 1567.

arraigned and condemned, but "at all events indicted." The earl writes to the queen, asserting his immaculate innocence, and bewailing his want of education to defend himself. He also writes to the privy council, saying, he had hoped the Deputy would have taken him to England. The queen writes the Deputy to have the earl and his brother, Sir John of Desmond, sent over. But Sir John is at large, so a trap is laid to ensnare him. He gets permission to visit the earl, and is seized, and the two brothers are transported to England. John becomes sick at Lichfield, so the earl writes to Cecil, desiring to be satisfied as to her majesty's pleasure respecting their future residence, which, in the end, proved to be the Tower.

The charges brought against the earl in 1568, were principally for disloyalty in entertaining proclaimed traitors. Cahir O'Conor swore that he, a proclaimed traitor, had been entertained while passing through the earl's country. The earl's servant, Donough, had acted as guide to some of these traitors. Andrew Skiddy, recorder of Cork, who seems to have been in favor with Cecil, denied all knowledge of traitors having been entertained by the earl. Skiddy wrote to Cecil at this time to obtain letters from the queen in his favor, to the mayor of Cork, to grant him his office of recorder for life, with an increase of £10 a-year to his salary. Cecil replies, that Skiddy has been malapert, and has used counterfeit diligence for the Earl of Desmond, which Skiddy indignantly denies.

The earl's brother, Sir John of Desmond, was charged with carrying on some secret and treasonable intercourse with Shane O'Neill against the queen's government. Andrew Skiddy and Richard Creagh, the titular Archbishop of Armagh, who had lately come from Rome, and was at this time a prisoner in the Tower, were examined on this charge, without eliciting anything of importance. Jacques Wingfield was also examined "concerning the confession of a little friar," who had been a messenger between Shane O'Neill, the Earl of Desmond, and his brother John. The earl denied the charges made in the first twenty-two articles, but confessed to the siege of Kilfeacle, and having taken goods in Kilshelan for a distress. Desmond asserts his authority, as Lord Palatine, to rule all Geraldines in Munster. In all causes between two Geraldines he held that he should be judge; but these prerogatives or powers he was now required to resign. He had no choice, while a prisoner in the Tower, but to do so. He is even content that her majesty should take from him a portion of his lands and liberties for the more quiet government of the realm.

Commissioners were appointed to govern Munster during the earl's imprisonment. They arrive in Cork, where they write, January 14th, 1568, to the Lords Justices. "Wood kerne, under Gerot Bracke, one of the Earl of Desmond's near kinsmen, intercepted our letters, certain kerne lay in ambush for us, but Lord Barrymore and John Fitz-Edmund, Dean of Cloyne, met us, and led us to Barry's Court." They had a dangerous and wet journey, and when they got to Cork, none of the Munster chieftains came to meet them. The Countess of Desmond wrote them, January 11th, from Kilmallock: "the country is in such disorder that few can trust a father, a son, or a brother." She herself, could hardly abide two days in one place, trudging by day, and partly by night, endeavouring to appease their lewd attempts. The inhabitants have been so bruised that she cannot take up the duties of her husband's present need.

Her husband, the earl, seems to have been in need of everything. He writes to Cecil, February 8th, 1568, asking for a "table," and furniture for a chamber in the Tower, the charges whereof he will pay to her majesty at a convenient time. He writes on the 26th of August, to both Cecil and the Duke of Norfolk, for "more liberty" in the Tower—his brother is sick with a new ague—and the loan of £100. To his astonishment he gets the £100, and will never be unmindful of Cecil's courtesy—Timeo Danaos et dona ferentes. The very next month the queen instructs her deputy in Ireland, to take order that the revenues of the Earl of Desmond, and Sir John, now prisoners in the Tower, be sequestered for their charges, and order taken for their sustenance during their imprisonment. We meet next with a certificate of the earl's yearly rents, and then with a sum of £50 for the earl's apparel,—was this a tailor's bill?—and then with a letter from the earl, on the 1st of November, in which he complains of the "*cold of the Tower*," and asks for some "honest house," where he may have convenient lodging and sure keeping. In December, he begs, as he has almost recovered his health, that he may go to some place in the Tower, where his friends may visit him.

We meet with no less than twenty letters dated the 18th of November, 1568, but as three of these are addressed to one person, his wife, we conclude they were not all written the same day. He tells the countess to be advised by the Lord Deputy, Sir Warham St. Leger, and Andrew Skiddy, recorder of Cork. He writes Lord Roche on behalf of his man, David Leche, long kept in duress. He now felt what it was to be a prisoner. He requests Skiddy not to slack in his counsel and advice to the countess, and requires Donough M'Crahe to deliver up the manor and castle of Mocollop to his father, John M'Crahe. The same things are repeated over and over again, and in many of the letters he asks for money, and complains to his wife that the "chancellor of Limerick" has kept back his money, and tells Andrew Skidmour, gent., in the city of Cork, not to fail to declare how Sir Donoghowe Casseihe, the chancellor of Limerick, has acted.

The earl and his brother John were allowed to make their submission this year, 1568, and became bound in the sum of £20,000 each for the due performance of the articles of submission. But they still remained prisoners.

Munster was at this period in a very disturbed state. Mr. Jacques Wingfield, writing to Cecil, says, the queen's lands in Cork and Limerick are utterly waste, without a person to inhabit there. He speaks of the extortions of Thomas Roe,* of Desmond, the bastard brother of the earl, and his cousin, James Fitzmaurice, who made a raid into Kerry, which caused the Earl of Clancare to retaliate, by entering Cork and spoiling

* Thomas Roe, of Desmond, was no bastard, but the eldest son of James the Usurper, by Joan, the daughter of Lord Roche.

Lord Roche, who writes, September 14th, from Castletown, "The Earl of Clancarty, accompanied by M'Donoky, O'Kyve, M'Auly, O'Donocowe More, O'Sullivan More's son, Edmond M'Swyny, and others, with six or seven banners displayed, has taken 1,500 kine, burned 7,000 sheep, all his corn, and a great number of men, women, and children." He therefore desires "a commission to *hurt* the said earl."

The Lords Justices write to the Earl of Clancare of the horrible excesses complained of by Lord Roche, trust they are not altogether true, and command him to make restitution to the extent of the injury done. They speak of Lord Roche's loyalty; say that his services merit the protection of the government, and call upon Lord Barry More, Sir Dermot Mac Teig, the mayor of Cork, the sheriff of the county of Cork, the sovereigns of Kilmallock and Kinsale, to aid the Lord Roche against Clancare. Such a call to arms was eminently calculated to foment the dissensions and civil war which the government professed to discountenance, but England possessed no other means of punishing violence or rebellion.

Mac Carthy More—for he at this time, 1569, repudiated his new title * of Earl of Clancare—was meditating rebellion, and carrying on an intercourse with Spain. One John Corbine, who had received a safe pass to travel through his kingdom of Kerry, made some important revelations to Cecil. The south-west coast was much frequented by Spaniards. Every year two hundred sail "fysheth there, and caryeth away

---

* *Repudiated his new title.*—"Mac Carthy More, who refuseth the new title of Earl, and is offended with any one that calleth him Earl of Clancare.—*Mayor of Cork to Sydney.*

2000 beyffs, hydes, and tallow. No due to the queen's majestie knowen." Two Spanish ships, with arms, were expected at Easter. The Mac Sweeneys had galleys which might prove useful to an invading foe.

Mac Carthy Reagh, James Fitz-Edmund, and others, were on the *qui-vive*, waiting the word to start into actual rebellion. It was reported that the Earl of Desmond had sent word to his people to unite with the other Irish chieftains in throwing off the English yoke. Andrew Skiddy, writing to the Lord Deputy, says,—"Yesterday, Mac Carthy More, whom I dare not name an earl, and James Fitzmaurice, spoiled all the inhabitants of Kerrycurrihy, and the farm Sir Warham Sentleger has of the Earl of Desmond, and laid siege to the abbey of Tracton." The mayors and councils of Cork, Youghal, and Kinsale also write. The Lady Ursula St. Leger, who is besieged by the rebels in the castle of Carrigaline, writes the Deputy to this effect:—"On Wednesday, Sir Warham St. Leger, the sheriff of Cork, left for England. The next morning James Fitzmaurice, with 4000 men, spoiled Kerrycurrihy; on Friday they took Tracton, and slew John Enchedon and all his men; on Saturday they laid siege to the castle of Carrigaline." Jaspar Horsey, writing, says, "St. Warham St. Leger's *tall ship** is threatened." Sydney did not lose an hour in marching to the lady's relief. Most opportune, he found four hundred newly arrived troops in Cork. He followed the rebels from Cork to Buttevant, and from Buttevant to Kilmallock, which was burnt before his arrival. The

---

* *St. Warham St. Leger's tall ship.*—The district farmed by St. Leger under the Earl of Desmond, was called De Cogan's ship. It is to a great extent surrounded by water.

mayor and corporation of Cork inform Sydney, that the rebels brag they will take Cork and Kinsale, that help cometh from Spain, and that the Butlers, who boast of their loyalty, are of the rebel confederacy. All the corporate towns are in terror, writing hard for soldiers, fire-arms, and barrels of gunpowder; and not without cause, for that great rebel leader, of whom we shall hear more by-and-bye, writes to the mayor and corporation of Cork, "to aboolissh oute of that cittie that old heresy newely raised and invented, and namely, Barnaby Daaly, and all therein that be Hug-nettes, boothe men and woomen, and Greynvile's wife and his children." Grenville was united with St. Leger in the government of the city and province, and was, we conclude, absent at this time. St. Leger, who is too sick to leave his house at Southwark, London, sends Cecil letters, dated 1569, from his wife from Carrigaline, and adds,—"It is better the queen should spend £40,000, than that Cork should be lost." He proposed to the privy council to raise £10,000 on his lands in England, in order to equip a force of 1,500 men, at his own charge, "for evicting lands from rebels and traitors, to the value of £1,000 a-year."

This rising was not confined to Cork and Kerry. The mayor and corporation of Waterford write, that good subjects in the country were forced by the rebels to join. They who refused were not only spoiled of kine and garrans, but driven naked to the city gates, "not sparing, a most shameful thing to be reported, to use the honest huswives of the countrey in like manner." They were tormented with more cruel pains than "eyther Phalaris, or any of the old tyrants, cowld invent." We find a Pierce Butler among the rebels, preying on Callan, and robbing Fulk Quemerford. The urbs Intacta, or city of Waterford itself, did not behave in the handsomest manner to Sydney, when lying before Clonmel, for it refused him, with rudeness, the aid of a few soldiers in his emergency. It is true that it endeavoured to efface the impression by subsequent civility, but the Deputy did not fail to remind them of their previous bad conduct. There were a few Irish noblemen who preserved their loyalty unsuspected during this rebellion, foremost among whom we may mention, Lord Roche and the Lord Barry. The Viscount of Decies told the rebels to do their worst, that he would be a true servant to the queen.

There was at this time a report that forty Spanish ships had arrived at " Dinglishe," or Dingle, but these reports were so frequent, that like that of the boy who cried "wolf!" they failed to excite alarm. Most of the Anglo-Norman, and some of the Irish lords and chieftains, offered their aid to the secretary, who succeeded in the course of a few months, in bringing the earl of Clancare to his knees, and of causing James Fitzmaurice to change his quarters. H. Gylberte, writing from Limerick, informs the Deputy, that on the 4th of December, the Earl of Clancare and M'Donough, "came in, fell on their knees, and acknowledged their treasons." Gylberte refused parley or peace to any rebel. He would not have them think that the queen had more need of their service than they had of her mercy. Clancare sends Sydney a petition, which he styles "the most humble submission of the most unworthy, and the most unnatural Earl of Clancare,* otherwise called Mac Carthy More."

The Earl of Desmond and his brother John remain, during this rebellion, out of harm's way, in the Tower of London; but very much against their grain. Desmond writes to the queen to write to the Lord Deputy, to write to John Oge, of the Island of Kierrie, to send him as much money as will discharge him, namely, £902 15s., which is owing to her majesty (partly money borrowed, we conclude), and for a quarterly supply for their expenses. But how or where can John Oge, or Young John, be he as active and clever as the friend of bold Robin Hood, raise £902 15s.? Nowhere in Ireland. So Ellinor, the faithful friend and wife of the rebellious chieftain, writes to the earl that she has resolved to repair to her majesty as an humble suitor for her lord's enlargement. The mouse may gnaw the net, which the lion cannot break. The destruction of the country is so great, she can raise no money. How she travelled, or how she speeded on her noble mission, we cannot speak with certainty; but that she succeeded in having the earl removed from the Tower, to the friendly roof of Sir Warham St. Leger, we have positive proof. Desmond writes to Cecil from the Tower, July 5th, 1570, that his wife was not able to follow up her suit, for his deliverance, beseeching Cecil to aid her. Three months after this, on the 17th of October, St. Leger writes, from Leeds castle, for money " for the diets of the Earl and Countess of Desmond, Sir John, and their families,

* *The unnatural Earl of Clancare* was also treacherous. When the Earl of Thomond thought it was *his turn* to go into rebellion, he wrote to Clancare, who sent the letter to Gylberte.

in number thirteen or fourteen persons." He adds that they have not so much of their own as will buy them a pair of shoes, and are in despair of having anything out of their own country. Four months after this, we meet Sir John Desmond at St. Leger's house, at Southwark, writing to Leicester of his poverty, and asking an interview; and in June, 1571, to Burghley, of his "sickness and great misery," entreating to be liberated. St. Leger tells Burghley that an Irish horseboy had brought a message from Turlough Lynagh to the earl, so the messenger was "stayed." Three days after, he writes to say Sir John is better, and that the countess is sick, that they cannot get their health, "being pent up in so little a room."

We conclude that St. Leger was their jailor, and that he did not like his office, for he asks permission to go to Ireland to recover his losses. Writing to the privy council two months after this, he complains that the Earl of Desmond refuses to go down to Leeds castle, in Kent, with him, and that, in his absence, he has rashly ranged abroad in sundry parts of London. The poor fellow was happy to shake a loose leg, without the presence of a keeper, though it was a lame one. St. Leger requests either to be relieved of the charge, or to have command to keep him prisoner, without liberty. This sounds harsh from St. Leger. "Maurice Roche, mayor, and his brethren of Cork," petition the queen, for the Earl of Desmond and his brother to be enlarged. "Michael Roche, soveraigne, and his brethren of Kinsale," memorial the privy council to send over the Earl of Desmond, and Sir John, to assist the president in repressing the rebels, who seek to destroy their town, as they did Kilmallock. The president of Munster, Sir John Perrott, proposes to bring back Sir John of Desmond, and stay the earl, as he is "rash and void of government."—" God kepe both Sir John of Desmond and base money out of Ireland," exclaims the Lord Justice Fitzwilliam. "Yet ar they both at the sea syde, to cum over, if brutes [reports] be trw." Here we shall leave them for the present.

CHAPTER XIII.

IRISH RULERS—LORD PRESIDENT OF MUNSTER—LORD DEPUTY—
MANNERS AND CUSTOMS—DRESS.

REIGNS OF HENRY VIII. AND ELIZABETH.

SIR JOHN PERROTT, the reputed son of Henry VIII., and brother to the queen, arrived in Waterford the 27th of February, 1571, as Lord President of Munster. His appointment dated from the latter end of the previous year. The queen writes from Hampton Court, December, 1570, to the President and Council of Wales, to permit Sir John Perrott, appointed president of Munster, to take thirty-four of his own servants and tenants to attend him into Ireland. We meet with a patent, signed the 1st of January, 1571, authorising him to transport 1,000 quarters of grain, 30 barrels of butter, and 500 stone of cheese yearly. Drury got a similar patent in June, 1576.

It is a received, but erroneous opinion, among Irish writers, that Sir Warham St. Leger was the first Lord President of Munster, in 1567. We do not think that the presidency court of Munster was instituted as early as 1567. We meet among the State Papers, with "Commissioners for Munster," about this time, or in February, 1568, but no presidency court. There is *talk* of establishing a presidency court in Munster, as early as March, 1566, and of making Sir Warham St. Leger president, but to the latter part of the proposition, the queen, in a letter to the Lord Deputy Sydney, dated from Westminster, January 16th, 1567, objects, on the ground that St. Leger is not likely to be "so indifferent," or impartial to the cases of the two Earls of Desmond and Ormond, as is meet. Sir Warham St. Leger was the son of good old Sir Anthony, the friend of the Desmonds. The Ormonds were especial favorites with the queen.

While the whole of Ireland was under the government of a Lord Justice, or deputy—who is now styled "Lord Lieutenant, and General Governor"—the affairs of Munster were administered by a Lord President, who was sort of deputy to the Deputy. The office of president was one of great responsibility and power, for the state of the country was such, as to throw every man invested with authority, upon his own resources. Sudden and unexpected emergencies can only be met by men possessed of actual power.

The powers or prerogative of the President of Munster are contained in Sir George Carew's "*Instructions*," dated the 7th of March, 1599, to which, on account of their great length—twenty-five pages—we must refer the reader.*

Dr. Smith has furnished us with the following synopsis:—

" The power of the Lord Presidents was very great; they had authority to hear and determine all complaints

---

* "Instructions given by us, the Lord Deputie and Councell, to our right trustie and well beloved Sir George Carew, knight, Lord President of her Majesties Councell, established in the province of Mounster." *Pacata Hibernia*, vol. 1. pp. 10 to 34.

throughout the province, as well guildable, as belonging to the franchises of corporations, and might send for and punish any such officer against whom such complaint was made. They had commission of oyer and terminer, as well as of gaol delivery of the whole province, and might hold their courts when and where they thought proper, with power to execute martial law upon all persons who had not £5 of freehold, or goods to the value of £10, and could prosecute any rebel with fire and sword, and for this purpose might array any number of the queen's loyal subjects. They could hear and determine complaints against all magistrates and officers, civil and military, throughout the province of Munster, and the crosses and liberties of Tipperary and Kerry, and might punish the offenders at discretion. They had authority to put persons, accused of high treason, to the torture, and might reprieve condemned persons. They had power to issue out proclamations, tending to the better ordering and regulation of the queen's subjects.

"The president had a serjeant-at-arms to attend him, who carried a mace before him, in the same manner as the lord president of Wales had his borne, such sergeant-at-arms to apprehend all disobedient persons. Thus, the presidency court was a civil jurisdiction, equal, within the district, to the lord lieutenants of Ireland; he being a kind of viceroy, in every circumstance, but in name. He had the power of life and death, could make knights, and was royally attended with guards; and had power, by patent, to command all the forces raised, or to be raised in the province. The Earl of Orrery, in answer to articles exhibited against him before the House of Commons of England, says, "that the presidency court of Munster had an absolute jurisdiction to hear and determine any cause, whereof it had cognizance, without being subject to any other court; and constantly proceeded to the determination of causes, notwithstanding certioraris sent from other courts to remove causes commenced there; and adds, that his predecessors have imprisoned persons who brought such certioraris."

The Lord President's salary was £133 6s. 8d., with a retinue of thirty horse and twenty foot. He had 2s. per diem allowed him for an under captain, and for a guidon and trumpeter 2s. each.

According to an ancient document at Lismore, in the hand-writing of the first Earl of Cork, besides the above salary, the president and council were allowed £20 a-week for diet, and £1 10s. 7d. a-day for retinue of horse and foot.

Morison gives us the establishment of Munster for the year 1598, as follows:—"The Lord President, £130 6s. 8d. per annum; for his diet, with the council at his table, £320 per annum; for his retinue of twenty foot and thirty horse, with the officers, £803. The Chief Justice, £100; the second Justice, £66 13s. 4d.; the Queen's Attorney, £13 6s. 8d.; the Clerk of the Council, £20; the Clerk of the Crown, £20; Serjeant-at-arms, £20; Provost-marshal, £255 10s.; total, £1951 16s. 8d. sterling money."

Sir William Fitzwilliam was appointed Lord Chief Justice of Ireland about the same time that Sir John Perrott was appointed President of Munster. He arrived in Dublin the 29th of January, 1571, where he discharged the duties of Deputy under the title of Chief-Justice. Fitzwilliam, who knew Ireland well, and considered it a sort of penal circuit for those who had lost favor at court, was as much disinclined to assume the office of Chief-Justice as Sir Henry Sydney was loath to relinquish that of Deputy. Sydney had been some eighteen years in harness, and had got to like the duties of his office, and Irish life; besides he was in debt, and did not find it convenient to settle his accounts with the queen, or his Irish creditors. Sir William had served in various offices for thirteeen years, and was glad to return to England. Ireland was never in a more disturbed state, or more difficult to govern. James Fitzmaurice was spoiling Munster. Sorley Boy had returned from Scotland, to spoil Ulster; there were bruits of Spanish invasions, and of the "damnable treasons" of that ubiquitous bugbear, Mr. Thomas Stukely; so Fitzwilliam writes to Lord Burghley, six short weeks after his arrival, entreating, for his health's sake, that he may be recalled. It is reported he is to be superseded by Lord Grey. He is in delight. Grey's coming is "stayed," he is distracted, and entreats to be "revoked," lest he come before he is looked for. He writes to the queen—and gets his son to deliver the letter into her own hands— of his utter unfitness for the government of Ireland, of his impoverishment after thirteen years' service, and the evils which generally grow during the administration of a Lord Justice.

We find Sir John Perrott, who was Deputy many years after, earnestly petitioning the queen to relieve him of a burden which the "perverseness of her subjects in Ireland, *of the English race*, had rendered intolerable." "I can please your majesty's Irish subjects better than the English, who, I fear, will shortly learn the Irish customs, sooner than the Jews did those of the Heathens."

Though a bold resolute man, like his royal parent, he was sometimes checkmated, bearded, and bullied, by members of his own council. We have an account of a scene which occurred at the council board, between him and Marshal Sir Nicholas Bagnal, that is scarcely surpassed in the southern states of America.

"The 15th of May [1587], very angry words passed between the Lord Deputy and Sir Nicholas Bagnal, Marshal, in the presence of the Chief Justice, the Master of the Rolls, and the Secretary of State, upon occasion that one Patrick Cullan (who used to go into England, in the name of O'Neal, with complaints to her majesty against the Lord Deputy) was ordered to be examined before the council. The Marshal required that the Lord Deputy should not be present at the examination; upon which the Lord Deputy, taking it ill to be directed by him, told him, 'That though he would not be present at it, yet he would do what he thought fit.' The Marshal reply'd, 'He mistrusted false measures would be used.' The Deputy said, 'He defy'd him, or any man, who should think any false measure should come by him.' The Marshal told him, 'He defy'd him also.' Hereupon, the Deputy, with the flat of his hand, touched his cheek once or twice, and laying his other hand on his right shoulder, said, 'Well, well, Marshal, if you defy'd a man in my place, in another country, he would have hanged you.' The Marshal hereat held up his staff, as if he would have struck the Deputy; but Mr. Fenton, the Secretary, and Sir Nicholas White, Master of the Rolls, interposing themselves, the Marshal fell back, and rising up said: 'It will be proved you have done ill in this matter.' The Lord Deputy: 'You lye, if you say I have done ill in this matter.' Marshal: 'You lye;' and correcting himself: 'If you were not Lord Deputy I would say, you lye; but I care not for John Perrott.' The Deputy said: 'If I were but Sir John Perrott,* I would teach you to use me thus; and if you did not dote, I would commit you to prison.' 'If you do,' answered the Marshal, 'I wou'd come out, whether you wou'd or no.' The Lord Deputy said: 'Get you hence, for 'tis no reason to talk with you, for a man would think you were drunk.' 'You are drunk,' reply'd the Marshal. What was the end of this discourse is not known, nor the cause of it, only 'tis believed that the Marshal was a great friend to Cullan."

The difficulty of governing the country at this time, is well expressed by Spenser, in his "View of the State of Ireland:"—

"The governors are usually envious one of another's greater glory; which, if they would seek to excel by better governing, it should be a most laudable emulation; but they do quite otherwise. For this, as

---

* Sir John Perrott was too honest by half for his time and his office; he was allowed to die in the Tower, though half brother to the queen. He attributed his disgrace to his old enemy, Sir Christopher Hatton, whom he despised as a carpet knight. When he heard he had been condemned to death: "God's-death!" exclaimed he, "will my sister sacrifice her brother to his frisking adversaries?" When Elizabeth heard these Tudor-like words, she refused to sign his death-warrant, saying, "They are all knaves that condemned him." But she, notwithstanding, allowed him to pine out his life in prison.

you may mark, is the common order of them, that who cometh next in place will not follow that course of government, however good, which his predecessors held, either for distain of himself, or doubt to have his doings drowned in another man's praise; but will straight take a way quite contrary to the former: as, if the former thought, by keeping under the Irish, to reform them; the next, by discountenancing the English, will curry favour with the Irish, and so make his government seem plausible, as having all the Irish at his command; but he that comes after will, perhaps, follow neither the one nor the other, but will dandle the one and the other in such sort, as he will suck sweet out of them both, and leave bitterness to the poor country; which, if he that comes after shall seek to redress, he shall perhaps find such crosses as he shall hardly be able to bear, or do any good that might work the disgrace of his predecessors. Examples you may see hereof in the governors of late times sufficiently, and in others of former times more manifestly, when the government of that realm was committed sometimes to the Geraldines, as when the house of York had the crown of England; sometimes to the Butlers, as when the house of Lancaster got the same, and other whiles, when an English governor was appointed, he, perhaps, found enemies of both."

There now prevailed as many and as contradictory opinions regarding the true mode of governing Ireland, in the reign of Elizabeth, as existed fifty or sixty years ago. Some, like Lord Grey of Wilton, and his secretary, the poet Spenser, were for the iron hand;

others for kindness, and more, like Sir George Carew, for the "divide et impera," policy. Sir John Perrott was for kindness, which policy the poet condemned. He would have given the deputies more power than they usually possessed, and would not have allowed them to be crossed and check-mated as they were, by the ministers who stood between them and the queen:—

"The chief evil in that government is, that no governor is suffered to go on with any one course, but upon the least information here, of this or that, he is either stopped, and crossed, or other courses appointed him from hence which he shall run, which, how inconvenient it is, is at this hour too well felt. And therefore this should be one principle in the appointing of the Lord Deputy's authority, that it should be more ample and absolute than it is, and that he should have uncontrolled power to do anything that he, with the advisement of the council, should think meet to be done; for it is not possible for the council here, to direct a government there, who shall be forced oftentimes to follow the necessity of present actions, and to take the sudden advantage of time, which being once lost, will not be recovered; whilst through expecting direction from hence, the delays whereof are oftentimes through other greater affairs most irksome, the opportunities there in the meantime pass away, and great danger often groweth, which, by such timely prevention, might easily be stopped.

"And this (as I remember) is worthily observed by Machiavel, in his discourses upon Livy, where he commendeth the manner of the Romans' government, in giving absolute power to all their counsellors and governors, which, if they abused, they should afterwards dearly answer. And the contrary thereof, he reprehendeth in the States of Venice, of Florence, and many other principalities of Italy, who use to limit their chief officers so strictly as that thereby they have oftentimes lost such happy occasions, as they could never come unto again; the like whereof, whoso hath been conversant in the government of Ireland, hath too often seen, to their great hinderance and hurt."

The deputy's commission was to make war and peace, to punish or pardon—treason against the queen's person, or counterfeiting money, only excepted—to impose fines, dispose of the estates of rebels, to assemble parliament—with her majesty's privity—to confer all offices, except Chancellor, Treasurer, three Chief Judges, and Master of the Rolls; and to collate and confer all spiritual promotions, except archbishops, bishops, and deans. In a word, to do all things that the queen would do if present. Although it was decided by Henry VIII., in 1541, that deputies should not appoint to "bishopricks or deaneries," they employed their influence in recommending to these offices. The Lord Deputy Sydney wrote to Cecil, December 26, 1569, to get his chaplain, Richard Dixon, appointed bishop of Cork and Cloyne, "the yearly value of which did not exceed £40." He was appointed, but the appointment was unfortunate, for in April 16, 1571, we find the Lord Chancellor Weston, Adam Loftus, Archbishop of Dublin, and the Lord Justice Fitzwilliam, writing to Lord Burghley, that "Richard Dixon, Bishop of Cork, less than twelve months, who has a married wife, has under color of matrimony retained a woman of suspected life as his wife; that they have compelled him to do penance in the cathedral of Dublin, but fearing to exceed their commission, desire instructions as to depriving him." Weston, writing to Burghley, November 26, 1571, recommends Matthew Seyne to the bishoprick of Cork, "vacant by the deprivation of Richard Dixon."

Doctor Smith and others, we know not on what authority, say that Dixon was "deprived for popery." No such charge could have been brought against his successor, Matthew Seyne or Sheyne, for this was the bishop who "publicly burnt the image of Saint Dominick at the High Cross of Cork, to the great grief," as Smith says, "of the superstitious Irish of that place." Sheyne was succeeded by the famous William Lyon.*

There was persecution at all sides, and great irregularity in church affairs at this time. Edward Staple, Bishop of Meath, complained, December 16, 1558, " The Lorde Cardinall [Pole] Layed Agaynst me for A grevous Article that I presumed in my sermond to pray for our olde master's sole." The "olde master" was Henry VIII., who had been excommunicated. Essex received instructions from Elizabeth (State Paper, dated May 22, 1561) to repair the jails, and commit such as do not go to church.

---

* *The famous William Lyon.* — There is a story told that Lyon had been an English admiral, who had done distinguished service against the Spanish Armada; that the queen asked what she could do for him, and that he replied, "Make a bishop of me;" that he was accordingly made Bishop of Cork and Cloyne. There is no foundation in truth for this story. Lyon had been previously Bishop of Ross. The see of Ross was united to Cork and Cloyne in his time, the 17th of March, 1583. He held the three sees until his death, which happened in 1617.

Laymen were sometimes appointed to church offices. Robert Weston,[*] who got Dixon deprived of Cork, was appointed to the deanery of St Patrick, of which Archbishop Loftus, who had been previously Dean, complains, and hopes, when the appointment is again vacant, it will not be given to a layman.

Men were appointed to livings and bishopricks who were totally ignorant of the language of the people. Alexander Craik, Bishop of Kildare and Dean of St. Patrick, writing to Duddeley in 1561, desires to be "discharged," as he cannot speak to the people, or the people understand him. The queen endeavoured to mitigate this evil by advancing money for an Irish Testament. "Idem, whereas her majestie hath paid £66 13s. 4d. to the bushoppes there for the making of carecters for the Testament in Irishe, that oneless they doe presently put the same in print, her majestie may be repaid." The Lord Deputy Croft (in November 11, 1551) recommended a schoolmaster to be made Archbishop of Cashel, because he was able to preach in the English and Irish tongues. Mr. Brown was recommended to the bishoprick of Down in 1573, as being "discreet and learned in the Irish language."—*See State Papers, vol. 39, Feb. 19, 1573.*

The low value of these high appointments was perhaps the cause of schoolmasters and humble men getting them. The bishop of Cork and Ross could not be styled even in 1571, "passing rich on forty pounds a year." We discover from certain rolls forming part

[*] *Weston.*—This Robert Weston seems to have been a favorite with the queen. He writes at one time to Cecil, complaining of the smallness of his fee, as Lord Chancellor, and the impoverishment of his deanery of St Patrick, and prays the queen "to pardon him the 100 marks she lent, and to forego the firstfruits of the deanery, and the yearly 20th part," which she grants.

of Pope Nicholas' taxation in 1291, that at this early period the income of the Bishop of Cloyne was rated at a hundred and eighty-five marks, £123 7s. 0d. per annum, and that of the Bishop of Cork at £90 6s. 8d. per annum. The State and the early reformers laid a greedy hand on church property. The Irish deputy and council, writing to Henry VIII. from Dublin, April 20, 1537, say,—"Your revennues be worth seven thowsande marckes by the yere, besides your furste-frutes, tenthe, and souch other things as ye be entitled unto, which will amounte to asmych more." This would give a revenue, the mark being 13s. 4d., of less than £10,000 per annum. The annual value of the land at this time, subject to the impost of first-fruits, was under £50,000 per annum. The king complains of the small revenue and heavy outlay. The estimates of Irish expenditure for the half year ending the 4th of July, 1567, was £83,876 12s. 5d. We are not, therefore, surprised to find the small salaries of government employees in arrear for years. The salaries of the "Lord Deputy, chief officers, and others," were in arrear from May 24th, 1560, to September 1st, 1567. The arrear[*] amounted, according to a book kept by Thomas Jemyson, to £31,606 2s. 4d., which was under £5,000 a-year, for the Irish vice-regal expenditure. We meet in the State Paper office with "a warrant," dated August 11th, 1545, " to increase the salary allowed John Goldsmyth, clerk of the council, (the Irish under-secretary in modern days,) who

---

[*] *The arrear.*—Fitzwilliam writes to Burghley, April 15, 1572, that he must "sell Milton;" and in July of the same year, that his "wife must sell the stock of Milton." He writes in August, praying Lord Burghley to preserve him from beggary, and help him out of his office of deputy.

has only £10 per annum." The whole sum drawn from the queen's coffers in England, for the affairs of Ireland, from Michaelmas, 1565, to December, 1571, was £201,891 12s. 9¼d. This sum was intended to cover not only the civil, but military expenses of the country. £5,000 is voted in 1571, for the soldiers in garrison. The army at this time was almost *nil*—a mere handful of men, not sufficient to guard even the pale, let alone to keep the Fitzgeralds, the Butlers, the O'Neills, the Mac Carthys, and other Irish chieftains, in check.

We have no better description of Munster in the latter half of the sixteenth century, than that contained in the letters of Sir Henry Sydney, who was an eyewitness of what he describes. He arrived in Youghal the 20th of April, 1565, which he calls "a very proper town," but of late decayed by reason of pirates, and no less annoyed by the landlords of the country, under the rule of the Earl of Desmond.

He travelled from Youghal to Cork, from Cork to Kinsale, and from Kinsale to Limerick, and says, "As I never was in a more pleasant country in all my life, so never saw I a more waste and desolate land."

He gives a sad, but we believe an exaggerated description of the manners and morals of the people:— "Surely there was never a people that lived in more misery, nor, as it should seem, of worse minds, for matrimony is not regarded; perjury, robbery, and murder, are counted allowable. I cannot find that they make any conscience of sin." He doubts whether they christen their children, as he could find "no place where it should be done." Stanihurst says, "In one corner of the land"—he does not condescend to say in *what corner*—"they used a damnable superstition, leaving the right arms of their infants unchristened, to the intent that they might give a more ungracious and deadly blow."

Hooker gives quite an Arcadian or Millennial description of Munster the year after this. We shall put one over against the other. It was intended as a compliment on Sir John Perrott's administration:—

"Now every man, with a white stick only in his hands, and with great treasures, might and did travel without fear and danger where he would; and the white sheep did keep the black,* and all the beasts lay continually in the fields without any stealing or preying." Perrott, writing from Cork, July 2, 1573, says, that he knows "not one evil man at present in rebellion, or any two picking thieves within his province."

Every country under heaven has had its golden age. We are told that Rollo, the ancestor of the Conqueror, suspended a valuable bracelet from an oak in a forest near the Seine, and that it remained there for three years. Bede says, that a woman with a new-born child might travel through Northumberland, in the reign of Edwin, without fear or insult. The conversation of the Irish in A.M. 3960, "was as sweet a harmony to one another as any music." We suspect that Hooker's description of the man travelling with the *white stick*, gave Moore the idea of the lady with the " snow white wand : "—

* *The white sheep did keep the black.*—This must be figurative. It needed but the lion to lie down with the lamb to complete a picture of peace, which might rival that of Landseer.

> " Rich and rare were the gems she wore,
> And a bright gold ring on her wand she bore ;
> But oh ! her beauty was far beyond
> Her-sparkling gems, or snow white wand.
>
> Lady ! dost thou not fear to stray,
> So lone and lovely, through this bleak way ?
> Are Erin's sons so good or so cold,
> As not to be tempted by woman or gold ?
>
> Sir Knight ! I feel not the least alarm,
> No son of Erin will offer me harm ;
> For though they love women and golden store,
> Sir Knight, they love honor and virtue more !
>
> On she went, and her maiden smile,
> In safety lighted her round the green isle ;
> And blest for ever is she who relied,
> Upon Erin's honor and Erin's pride !"

Sir Henry Sydney paid a second visit to Munster, in 1575. He arrived in the city of Cork the 23rd of December, and " was received with all joyfulness, tokens, and shews, the best the citizens could express of their dutiful thanksgiving to her majesty." They lodged and entertained his English footmen and galloglasses for six weeks, "without grudging or complaint, either of townsmen or of soldiers, the townsmen receiving in ready money the one-half of the soldiers' wages for his board, fire and lodging, wherewith he held himself very well satisfied, and the soldiers in like manner well contented to give it."

Sir Henry writes the privy council :—" The good estate and flourishing of that city well approveth the good effects of resident authority amongst them ; for it is so amended as in a few years I have seldom seen any town. I was, for the time of my continuance there, very honourably attended and accompanied by the Earls of Desmond, Thomond, and Clancarre, the

Bishops of Cashel and Cork, and the Elect of Rosscarberry,* the Viscounts of Barry and Roche, the Barons of Courcy, Lisnard, Dunboyne, Power, Barrie-Oge, and Lowthe."

He was visited in Cork on this occasion by "divers of the Irishry not yet nobilitated; the lord of Carbery, called Sir Donald Mac Cartie, and the lord of Muskerry, called Sir Cormac Mac Tiege Mac Cartie, neither of these, but in respect of their territories, was able to be a viscount; and truly I wish them both to be made barons, for they were both good subjects, and in especial the latter, who, for his obedience to her majesty and her laws, and disposition to civility, is the rarest man that ever was born in the Irishry, but of him I intend to write specially, ere it be long, for truly he is a special man.

"There came to me also Sir Owen O'Sullivan, and the son and heir of O'Sullivan More, the father not being able to come by reason of his great years and impotency. Sir William O'Carroll of Ely, O'Carroll and Mac Donogho, never one of them, but for his lands, might pass in the rank of a baron either in Ireland or England.

"There were in like manner with me of the Irishry O'Kyne and Mac Fynnen, the sons or heirs (as they would have them) of Macaulay and O'Callaghan, the old men not being able to come by reason of their age and infirmity. O'Mahon and O'Driscolls (each of them) have land enough, with good order, to live like a baron either here or there."

Lord Burleigh, in a private document, written but a

* *The Elect of Rosscarberry, i. e.* the *Tanist* of Carbery.

few years after this, gives a very different account of these Irish lords and captains:—" Sir Cormac Mac Tiege, whoe was of late honorablie used of the quene's highnes in England, hath quite forgotten the same; Sir Owen M'Cartie, beinge a simple man, is so addicted to one sept of the Mac Swyns as he is to be directed by them as they list; Omahound, his follower, match of his imperfections, a man of small force, although a proper countrie; Barioge, a poor beggarlie captaine of a countrie betweene Cowrk and Kinsale, called Kynoley, whose simplicitie is such as hee maketh of a propper sort of a countrie nothinge to bee accompted on; Mac Donough, his countrie so nere the rebells as I feare he is infected with their treasons; O'Kieff, if there were want of theves in this province, he might be aptly termed a theef."

If there be any truth in the following lines, translated or paraphrased from the Irish of Aenghus O'Daly, there is some palliation for O'Keeffe's thieving propensities:—

> " The ragged O'Keeffe, he shivers and shakes;
> The sad ragamuffin, he hasn't got stuff in
> His carcase to battle with agues and aches.
> But I spare him, the luckless;
> Poor devil—the cloakless are always the pluckless.
> Poor little red robin, the snow hides the ground,
> And a worm or a grub is scarce to be found;
> Still don't visit O'Keeffe, rather brave the hard weather,
> He'd soon bring your breast and your backbone together."

Sir Henry Sydney goes on to speak of the English or Anglo-Norman race. "Sir Norris Fitzgerald, brother of the Viscount Decies; Sir Theobald Butler, whose uncle and cousin were barons of the Cayre, whose lands he lawfully and justly enjoyed, and better deserveth that title of honor than any of them ever did, for whom I intend more specially to write, for truly he is worthy any commendation."

"There came to me also many of the ruined relics of the ancient English inhabitants of this province, as the Arundels, Rochfords, Barretts, Flemings, Lombards, Terries, and many others whose ancestors (as it may appear by monuments, as well in writing as of building) were able, and did live like gentlemen, and knights some of them; and now all in misery, either banished from their own, or oppressed upon their own."

"Lastly, there came to me five brethren, and the sons of two other brethren of one lineage, all captains of galloglass, called Mac Swynes,* who, although I place them last of the rest, yet are they of as much consequence as any of the rest, for of such credit and force were they grown into (although they were no lords of lands themselves), as they would make of the greatest lords of the province, both in fear of them, and glad of their friendship.

"And the better to furnish the beauty and filling of the city, all these principal lords had with them their wives, during all the Christmas, who truly kept very honorable, at least very plentiful houses. And to be brief, many widow ladies were there also, who each had been wives to earls and others of good note and account."

Two young people met at this grand vice-regal assembly, or coshering, whose romantic wooing affected

---

* *Mac Swynes.*—Spenser says the Mac Swynes were anciently of the Veres [De Veres] of England. "Proud hearts do oftentimes, like wanton colts, kick at their mothers. So they say did these Mac Swynes and Mac Mahons, or rather Veres and Fitz-Ursulas, for private despight turn themselves against England."

not only their fortunes, but the affairs of Munster for many years; one of these was Lady Ellen, the daughter of Mac Carthy More, the Earl of Clancare, by his countess, the Earl of Desmond's sister; and the other was the famous Florence Mac Carthy, the son of Sir Donogh Mac Carthy Reagh, of Carbery. As we are writing history, and not romance, we shall not anticipate the regular sequence of events. We shall take up their story at some future time, and allow Sir Henry Sydney to conclude his interesting letter.

"It may please your lordships to understand what this company did, and what I, with the assistance of such others as I named in my former letters, together with Mr. Dowdall and Mr. Walsh, whom I found commissioners in this province, what we did; and for them they seemed in all appearance generally to loathe their vile and barbarous manner of life. Such as already do not yield rent or service desire to yield both, and agreed to deliver in the names of their idle men, and then to answer for them, and if any were found unbooked, to be used as a felon or vagabond.

"I caused daily sessions to be held in that city, from the morrow after Twelve-day till the last of January, in which appeared very honest and good juries, sound and good trial made by them, a number of civil causes determined and ended, and above twenty-four notable malefactors condemned and executed. Condon or Canton Armou attainted and adjudged to die, yet stayed from execution; but his lands, which were great, were escheated. A younger son of the Viscount Roche was endicted, arraigned, and condemned to die, but stayed for execution; for as the world goeth here, his fault was very small." Perhaps sporting an Irish *glibb*, which Spenser describes as "a thick curled bush of hair hanging down over their eyes, and monstrously disguising them," as one of the most "vile and barbarous" habits referred to by Sydney in this passage. I think it was the President of Connaught who wrote to the Lord Deputy in 1572,— "Such as doo come in to us, we cause to cutt ther glybbez, which we doo thynke the ffyrst token of obedyence." *

Campion, at this time, describes the dress of Irish chieftains. "Linen shirts the rich do wear for wantonness and bravery, with wide hanging sleeves plaited; thirty yards are little enough for one of them." He says, in another place, "they have now left off their saffron, and learne *to wash their shirts four or five times in the year.*"†

The cloak was in vogue among the Irish at this time, and, if we are to believe Spenser, was applied to far more useful purposes than Diogenes' dish, which was a cup, a cap, a measure, a water-pot—and, as an auctioneer's advertisement would say—a number of other articles too numerous to mention:

"First, the outlaw, being for his many crimes and villainies banished from the towns and houses of honest men, and wandering in waste places, far from danger of law, maketh his mantle his house, and under it covereth himself from the wrath of heaven, from the

---

* *Ffyrst token of obedyence.*—The rebel of 1798 was called a *croppy*, on account of his *short* hair. Many a man was hanged or shot for want of glibbes or long locks in these latter days.

† *Wash their shirts four or five times in the year.*—Fynes Moryson says, "You could not get a bed in any inn, even in the town of Cork, without being swarmed with lice."

offence of the earth, and from the sight of men. When it raineth, it is his pent house, when it bloweth it is his tent, when it freezeth it is his tabernacle. In summer, he can wear it loose; in winter, he can wrap it close; at all times he can use it, never heavy, never cumbersome.

"Likewise for a rebel, it is as serviceable; for in this war that he maketh (if at least it deserve the name of war), when he still flieth from his foe, and lurketh in the thick woods and strait passages, waiting for advantages, it is his bed, yea, and almost his household stuff; for the wood is his house against all weathers, and his mantle is his couch to sleep in; therein he wrappeth himself round, and coucheth himself strongly against the gnats, which in that country do more annoy the naked rebels, whilst they keep the woods, and do more sharply wound them than all their enemies' swords and spears, which can seldom come nigh them; yea, and oftentimes their mantle serveth them when they are near driven, being wrapped about their left arm, instead of a target, for it is hard to cut through with a sword; besides, it is light to bear, light to throw away.

"Lastly, for a thief, it is so handsome, as it being, as they commonly are naked, it is to them all may seem it was first invented for him, for under it he may cleanly convey any fit pillage that cometh handsomely in his way, and when he goeth abroad in the night in freebooting, it is his best and surest friend, for lying, as they often do, two or three nights together abroad, to watch for their booty, with that they can prettily shroud themselves under a bush or a bankside, till they can conveniently do their errand."

The poet, in the end, hands it over to the women, and concludes: "How handsome it is to lie and sleep in, or to louse themselves in the sunshine, they that have been but a while in Ireland can well witness."

English sovereigns laid great stress on the influence of dress in civilising the wild Irish, and bringing them into a state of subjection. Queen Elizabeth, with all a woman's tact, endeavoured to suppress two rebellions, that of Turlough O'Neill, in Ulster, and of Garrett, Earl of Desmond, in Munster, by making their wives presents of handsome gowns. The queen imagined it would add to the favor to send dresses she had worn herself. When the gowns (which were to be presented by the chancellor) came to hand, they were found to be "slobbered in the front breadth." These were replaced by new materials, and the dresses presented in due form. We learn that *after* this, "the Countess of Desmond greatly disapproved of her husband's disloyal conduct." *Her* gown was "cloth of gold."

CHAPTER XIV.

THE LANDING AT SMERWICK—LORD GREY—SPENSER—RALEIGH—LORD ROCHE—THE DEATH OF THE EARL OF DESMOND.

A.D 1573—1583.

We find, from the account of Sir Henry Sydney's visit to Cork, that the Earl of Desmond was at large, and in high favor in 1575. He was brought from London to Dublin in 1573, where he was kept prisoner. It would seem as if his wife, the countess, had also been a prisoner, for we find them both, October 12, 1573, sueing for enlargement, and complaining shortly after, that they got neither favor nor liberty; they therefore resolved to liberate themselves.

"It happened," we are told by the Four Masters, "through the miracles of God, and the intercession of James"—not James, the Apostle, but James Fitzmaurice, the great Irish rebel—that "the Earl of Desmond and his brother John, who had been prisoners in London for six years, were liberated. The earl was put under arrest in the town [Dublin], and John was permitted to visit the fair plains of Munster."

The earl, who appears to have been on a sort of parole, under the custody or care of the mayor of Dublin—but this sort of thing was not well understood in those days—took advantage of a hunting excursion to turn his horse's head to the South. He, and a few followers, travelled for three nights, and arrived unexpectedly in the midst of the Geraldines, November, 1573, who received him with wild cheering.

In the course of one month he expelled the government forces from the chief towns of Munster, taking the castles Baile na Martra [Castle Martyr], in Cork, and Castlemaine, in Kerry. He did not leave a resident chief in any town in the country, from the meeting of the Three Waters [at Waterford] to Bealach Conglais, that he did not bring under subjection in one month.

Sir John Perrott left for England in the autumn this year. We are told by the Four Masters that his "departure was lamented by the poor, the widow, the infirm, and the unwarlike."

The office of president of Munster appears to have been vacant for about three years, and was then filled, in 1576, by Sir William Drury, who "took a circuit," like Sir Henry Sydney, of all the great towns of Munster, "to confirm laws and regulations." He destroyed malefactors and robbers, and put to death Barrett, of Cork, and two noble and distinguished young constables of the tribe of Maolmurry, or Mac Sweeney." He proceeded thence to Limerick, where he hung "a number of chiefs and of the common people."

We conclude it was during this tour that the Earl of Desmond invited Sir William to his castle at Tralee. He came, accompanied by a hundred and twenty men. The earl assembled eight hundred to *meet*, some say to *surprise*, the Lord President. He made a rush or charge at the wild kerne and galloglasses, and drove them to cover. He then rode up to the castle, and demanded an explanation. He was met by the countess, who solemnly assured him that the men he took for enemies were a hunting party, who had approached to give him a "bene venu," or welcome, into that part of Munster; and "she so wiselie and modestlie did behave herself," that Drury believed, or seemed to believe her. We think it was shortly after this, in 1577, that the president made a prisoner of John, the earl's brother, and sent him to Dublin.

Drury was raised to the dignity of Lord Chief Justice, with the authority of a Deputy, in 1578. There was an impression abroad at this time that the office of lord president of Munster was to be abolished. Captain Malby, who is styled president of Connaught, acted as a sort of vice-president of Munster during Sir William Drury's tenure of office, which, as we shall see, was of short duration.

Desmond was known to be deeply compromised in two landings of Spanish and Italian forces, on the south-western coast of Ireland. The first expedition was undertaken by the earl's cousin, James Fitzmaurice. This James, the son of Maurice Duv, was a very remarkable man. We find him in 1575, after various successful forays, and as many failures, retiring with his wife and children to France, his cousins, the earl and the earl's brother, John, having made peace with a government which had often deceived them, in which James had no confidence, and against which he had vowed eternal warfare. The second imprisonment of John brought the earl to the same way of thinking, and remembering the effective aid which James had afforded both him and his brother on a former occasion, he employed his secretary to pen the following letter :—

"WILLIAM OF DANUBI, *servant of the Earl of Desmond, to* JAMES FITZMAURICE. *July* 18, 1579.

"Life and health from William of Danubi to James, son of Maurice, and be it known to James that my master sent him his blessing, and that unless James relieves us soon we are undone; for John is in prison awaiting my master, and so watched and warded that he may never get away again. And therefore, I beseech you, in the name of God, and in the name of my master, to bring relief soon, or you will not be able to overtake the relief of him, and to co-operate with the good helps, [which now offer] such as the sons of the Earl of Connaught, and many others of the men of Erin. And moreover, be it known to you, that *whatever Edmond Brown has said, nothing shall be wanting of it, whatever may be added to it;* and be assured of it, that we cannot tell how much we are in want of you; and though we would like that a host of men should come along with you, that we would be exceedingly glad that yourself [alone] should come to our aid; and be not dismayed by what hardship you have seen, for we think that the greater part of the men of Erin are ready to rise with ourselves, and we would be much the better of you. And do not wait for the harvest, for there is danger that the whole affair may be set aside by that time. And we would incite you more than this, if we thought that you would respond to us the sooner.

"And be assured that I do not write this of my own accord, but at the request of my master, and that it is dangerous to write from Erin to you; for the letter which the Seneschal wrote at Ballynaskellig, to be sent to you by the merchant of San Malves, [miscarried;] that merchant, and Mac Carthy, who was that merchant's gossip, betrayed the Seneschal, and Mac Carthy brought the letter to Portlairge, where the Justice and the President were. And the form that was in it was:—' Life and health from John, son of William, to James; *and be it known to James, that the wheat of the friars has grown well, and that the wheat of the country has failed.*' And God saved the Seneschal on that occasion.

"I have no news, except concerning the death of Mac Carthy Reagh; and that Rory Oge O'More has not left a stake or a scollop in Naas-of-Leinster, or in twenty miles on every side of it; and not only this, but that the flame of war has grown up in many of the men of Erin against the Saxons, if they could [but] get help.

"That is enough; but give a blessing in the name of my master to the King of France."

The King of France, to whom the master of Danubi sends a blessing, received James Fitzmaurice rather coolly, he therefore applied to the King of Spain, but Philip had lately concluded a peace with England; he however gave him letters to Pope Gregory XIII., by whom he was favorably received.

There is no reply from James to this letter extant, but we have a letter from him bearing the same date, addressed to Mac Donnell, a leader of the Munster galloglasses, which announces that James had "come safe to Erin:"—

"JAMES FITZMAURICE *to* AUSTIN KITTAGH MAC DONNELL. *July* 18, 1579.

"Life and health with thee, O writing, to Austin Kittagh Mac Donnell, from his own friend and companion, i. e., from James, son of Maurice, son of the earl. And be it known to him, that I have come safe to Erin with power, after all I have travelled and traversed of foreign countries; and for this reason I implore of him to come to me with as many bonaghtmen as he can bring with him; and moreover, be it certain unto him, that he never came to any war coming into which he should have greater courage, than this war, for many reasons: first, inasmuch as we are fighting for our faith, and for the church of God; and next, that we are defending our country, and extirpating heretics and barbarians, and unjust and lawless men; and besides, [let him understand] that he was never employed by any lord who will pay himself and his people their wages and their bounty better than I shall, inasmuch as I never was at any time more competent to pay it than now, thanks be to the great God of mercy for it, and to the people who have given me that power, under God, and who will not suffer me to want from henceforth. And this is enough; but let him not neglect coming, that he may get some compensation for all the toil and labour that he suffered in my cause before now; let him request his brethren, and the gentry of his territory, to respond to the time, and to rise with one accord for the sake of the faith of Christ, and to defend their country; and moreover, that all their bonaghtmen will get their pay readily;* and that we shall all get a place in the kingdom of heaven, if we fight for His sake."

There is a second letter, a sort of duplicate of the above, written at the same time, and sent, perhaps, by a different messenger. We conclude that both were intercepted by English detectives.

The next letter or billet in which we have the same curious personification is addressed to Randal Mac Donnell, no doubt another leader of galloglasses:—

"JAMES FITZMAURICE *to* RANDAL MAC DONNELL, *July* 31, 1579.

" The custom of the letter [i. e.] salutation, O billet, from James, son of Maurice, son of the earl, to his friend and companion Randal, son of Colla Maeldubh, and tell him that I told him to collect as many bonaghtmen as he can, and to come to me, and that he will get his pay according to his own will, for I was never more thankful to God for having great power and influence than now. Advise every one of your friends (who likes fighting for his religion and his country better than for gold and silver, or who wishes to obtain them all [i. e., to fight for his religion and country, and also for gold and silver] as his wages) to come to me, and that he will find each of these things."

James had met the famous Tom Stukely on the continent, who had promised to join with him in his Irish expedition. If we meet with Stukely's name in one, we meet it in one hundred state papers, and always as the bugbear of some French, Spanish,

* *Their bonaghtmen will get their pay regularly.*—These bonaghtmen were a sort of hired or mercenary soldiers.

or Italian invasion. We are greatly surprised he was never apprehended by the English government. He was held by some as a natural son of Henry VIII.; by the mother's side, a descendant of Diarmaid Mac Murrough, king of Leinster. He is styled Thomas Stucley, late of Enniscorthy, gent., seneschal of the county of Wexford. Under date May 2, 1571, "Stucley's man's examination, declaring his departure for Spain." May 15th, "Examination of a mariner returned from Stucley." Same date, "Stucley has a collectorship of the Pope in Spain." March 5th, 1672, a notice of "Stucley's expected arrrival in Ireland; Viscount Barrymore, O'Neill, and Mac Mahon, to rise on his landing." March 30, 1572, the examination of a French merchant at Kinsale, who reports that Don John of Austria has overthrown the Turks in a great naval engagement; that Stukeley was in the fight, the bravest of the brave, that he has been created Duke of Ireland, with 1000 ducats a-week.

When James Fitzmaurice was prepared to sail, Stukely deserted him, and embarked his forces with those of the Portuguese monarch, for the coast of Africa, where he fell at the battle of Alcazar, along with the heroic Don Sebastian, king of Portugal, Mahomet, son of Abdallah, king of Fey, and Abimeleck, king of Morocco.

James Fitzmaurice, with three ships and a hundred men, made a landing in Smerwick, on the west coast of Kerry, in July, 1579. He was accompanied by three famous English churchmen, Doctor Saunders, as Papal Nuncio, a Jesuit named Allen, and O'Mulrian, the Catholic Bishop of Killaloe.

Mageoghegan says that Saunders was "Anglios de nation, et Legat Apostolique en Irelande." He describes him "un homme d'une vie exemplaire, et très zélé pour la cause catholique."* But adds, "Il est peint sous d'autres couleurs par les auteurs Protestants, qui le qualifient de traitre, et d'archi-rebelle." Cox, to whom Mageoghegan probably refers, styles him "a malicious, cunning, and indefatigable traytor."

Saunders, O'Mulrian, and Allen, marched in canonicals at the head of the invaders, preceded by two friars, bearing the Pope's standard (with a picture of the crucifixion), which had been especially consecrated for the expedition. Watchfires blazed on the mountains, and swift heralds passed through the country announcing the place of gathering. The new slogan, or war-cry, was PAPA ABOO !

> "Then Roderick, with impatient look,
> From Brian's hands the symbol took ;
> Speed, Malise, speed ! he said, and gave
> The crosslet to the henchman brave ;
> The muster place is Lanark mead—
> Instant the time—speed, Malise speed."

The first operation of the invaders was to raise a fort on the peninsula, where they landed; which was duly consecrated. Sir William Drury, who was at this time in "Great Cork of Munster," and who should have gone in person to oppose the foreigners, sent Henry Davells, the constable of Dungarvan, and Arthur Carter, the provost-marshal of Munster, with commands to the Earl of Desmond to besiege and

---

* *Très zélé pour la cause catholique.*—" Ce saint homme epuisé par la fatigue et par la chagrin de voir triompher l'impiété, mourut d'une flux de sang, dans un bois, où il manquoit de tout secours, exeepté le spirituel, qui lui fut administré par Corneille, Eveque de Killalow, qui ne le quitta, qu'à la mort."— *Mageoghegan Hist. Irelande,* tom. iii., p. 448.

raze the fort. Desmond and his brother John, at the head of some Irish kerne and galloglasses, "made a show" of attacking it. The Earl of Clanricarde did the same, but was persuaded by Desmond to go home.

Davells and Carter, who were imprudently inquisitive, and had learned more of the earl's disloyalty than it was desirable they should carry back to Cork, were followed by John and James, the earl's brothers, to Tralee, and murdered in a house or inn near the earl's residence. Another writer says, they were "beheaded while asleep in their beds," in the house or castle of the earl. Doctor Smith calls Henry Danvers, or Davells, "an English gentleman, who was gossip to Sir John of Desmond," and "high sheriff of the county of Cork." He also mentions a Justice Mead as one of the murdered party. Their servants or attendants were also murdered. The professed or pretended provocation was their going to Tralee, to hold a gaol delivery in the Desmond palatinate. It is more than probable that they were looked upon as little better than spies, and dealt with accordingly. O'Sullivan styles this murder "facinus dignum." Camden says that Saunders called it "Suave Deo sacrificium." But every right-minded man will say with the dying patriarch, "*Cursed be their anger, for it was fierce, and their wrath, for it was cruel.*"

These men being despatched, Fitzmaurice prepared to march into the county Limerick. From thence he intended to visit Connaught, taking Holy-Cross, in Tipperary, in his way, in order to accomplish a vow he had taken in Spain. His men began to plunder the country, and offer violence to females; Fitzmaurice commanded that one of the ringleaders should be hung, but John of Desmond would not hear of it. In passing through the baronies of Connello and Clanwilliam, the people assembled to oppose them, headed by Theobald and Ulick, the sons of William Burke. They overtook the invaders, who had halted in a wood. Fitzmaurice, at an early period of the engagement, received a ball in the chest; the wound was mortal, but it fired him to a last effort; so clearing a passage through the enemy's forces, he rushed up to Theobald Burke, and with one blow of his sword, clave his head in twain.* This decided the battle in his favor. But he had not passed far from the scene of his conquest, when the langour of death came over him. He made a will in a few words, and ordered his friends to cut off his head after his death, lest his enemies should know him, and mangle his remains. O'Daly informs us that his kinsman, Maurice had ordered his head to be cut off, and his body to be concealed under an aged tree,† where, not long after, it was found by a hunter, brought to Kilmallock, hung on a gallows, and fired at by a heretic.

Queen Elizabeth, to express her sympathy with the sorrow of Sir William Burke, and her sense of his sons' services to the state, created the father a peer of the realm, under the title of Lord Baron of Castle-Connell. Camden remarks, that the old man died

* *Clave his head in twain.*—O'Daly, who compares Fitzmaurice to Achilles, says he slew William as well as Theobald Burke:—" He made a lane for himself to where Theobald Burke stood, and with a single blow cleft his skull in twain, and with another stroke killed his brother William."—*O'Daly*, c. 22. The Four Masters mention only Theobald. Camden speaks of two brothers falling:— " Theobaldus et alter fratribus cum nonnullis suorum occubuerunt."

† *Aged tree.*—Smith says the *head* was left " wrapped in a blanket, under an old oak."

soon after, overcome by joy—*gaudio perfusus*—of his new title.

Sir William Drury, accompanied by the Earl of Kildare and Sir Nicholas Malby, left Cork, and pitched his camp in the neighbourhood of Kilmallock. "Hither the Earl of Desmond came to meet them, and endeavoured to impress on their minds that he had no part in bringing over James Fitzmaurice, or in any of the crimes committed by his relatives, and he delivered up to the Lord Justice his only son and heir as a hostage, to ensure his loyalty and fidelity to the crown of England. A promise was thereupon given to the earl that his territory should not be plundered in future, but although the promise was given, it was not kept, for his people and cattle were destroyed, and his corn and edifices burned."

Sir William Drury left the camp of Kilmallock at the head of four hundred men, to search the wood of Kilmore [Coill Mhor] in the county Cork. They fell in with John and James Oge at Gort na Tiobrad, the "field of the spring," or Springfield. A fierce engagement ensued, in which the Lord Justice was defeated, three hundred of his men and three of his captains (namely Herbert, Eustace, and Price) having been slain. The remnant of his army fled back to the camp near Kilmallock. Sir William left Kilmallock for Athneasy,* a ford on the Morning-star river, about four miles to the east of Kilmallock. Here he took his death sickness. Leaving Captain Malby to prosecute the war against the Geraldines, he was conveyed in a chariot to Waterford, where he died.

* *Athneasy*, anciently Bel-atha-na-n Deise, *i.e.*, the mouth of the ford of Deis.

He was succeeded by Sir William Pelham, who was elected by the Irish council * on the 11th of October, 1579, in Christ Church, Dublin. Pelham is described by the Four Masters as "a gentleman of the queen's people, who had come from England that very week." The Earl of Ormond returned to Ireland the same week, after a sojourn in England of three years. Ware informs us that Ormond was, at this time, elected governor of Munster, and Sir Warham St. Leger provost-marshal. Ormond was unleashed when Desmond broke cover, and he held on his track, and was in at the death.

Captain Malby, who was left in command by Drury, followed the Geraldines to Askeaton, and overtook them at Monaster-Neva,† about five miles to the northwest of Bruff. We learn from the Four Masters that the Irish forces were routed, with the loss of Thomas, son of John Oge, and that "great spoils, consisting of weapons and military attire," were left on the field. Leland, who had the English and Irish accounts of the battle before him, gives us the following, which appears the most circumstantial:—

"The [English] army consisted of nine hundred foot and fifty horse. Of these three hundred infantry and fifty horse were left in garrison at Kilmallock; and on intelligence received that Sir John Desmond lay a few miles distant from Limerick, with a considerable body, Malby marched to attack him with the residue of his

---

* *Elected by the Irish council.*—This election could have conferred no more than a temporary authority, till confirmed by the privy council and Queen of England.

† *Monaster-Neva.*—It was anciently called Aenach-beag, in the barony of Pobble-Brien, in the county Limerick. Here are the ruins of a magnificent abbey.

forces. In a plain adjoining to an old abbey, called Monaster-Nena (recté, Monaster Neva) he found the rebels in array, to the number of about two thousand, and prepared to give him battle. The papal standard was displayed, and Allen, the Irish jesuit, went busily through the ranks distributing his benedictions, and assuring them of victory. Their dispositions were made, by direction of the Spanish officers, with an address and regularity unusual to the Irish, and their attack was so vigorous, and so obstinately maintained, that the fortune of the day seemed doubtful. The valour of the English at length prevailed; the rebels were routed, and pursued with considerable slaughter, and among the slain was found the body of Allen, who, not content with exhortation, had drawn the sword in the cause of Rome."

When the Lord Justice, Sir William Pelham, came to the South, the Earl of Desmond refused to join him. He, with James, his brother, were, with sound of trumpet, proclaimed traitors, on the 1st of November, 1579. He was now a desperate man. He raised the standard of rebellion on the Ballyhowra mountains, in this county, from which he descended like a torrent, sweeping flocks and herds before him, not always discriminating between friends and foes. He took his first preys from the lands of the Lords Roche and Barry. He then visited the town of Youghal (the mayors of which had ever acted as his friends), and sacked it in the most ruthless and savage way.

"They encamped before Youghal, and finally took that town, which at that time was full of riches and goods. The Geraldines seized upon all the riches they found in this town, excepting such gold and silver as the merchants and burgesses had sent away in ships before the town was taken. Many a poor indigent became rich and affluent by the spoils of this town. The Geraldines levelled the wall of the town, and broke down its courts and castles, and its buildings of stone and wood, so as that it was not habitable for some time afterwards."*—*Four Masters*, A.D. 1519.

Holinshed's description is more circumstantial:—
"The proclaimed traitor of Desmond and his brothers, not able anie longer to shrowd his treacheries, went with all his forces to the towne of Youghall, where against his comming the gates of the towne were shut, but yet it was thought but colourable, for verie shortly after, without deniall or resistance, the earl and all his troupe of rebels entered the town and took it, and there remained about five daies, rifleing and carrieing awaie the goods and household stuff to the castell of Strangecallie and Lefinnen, the which then were kept by the Spaniards."

The Earl of Ormond dispatched a barque, with Captain White, from Waterford, "a very valiant man of a stout stomach," to retake the town. He entered by the water-gate, and took some pieces of ordnance. He was attacked by the seneschal of Imokilly, at the head of a superior force, whom he charged more "rashlie than consideratlie," and was very soon surrounded and slain; and with much ado did a few of his company gain their ship.

* *Not habitable for some time afterwards*.—" The Lord Governor, when he came to the town, found it all desolate, rifled, and spoiled, and no man, woman, or child therein, saving one friar, whom he spared, because he had fetched the body of Henrie Davels, from Traleigh, and had it carried to Waterford, where it was buried in the chancel of the cathedral church."—*Holinshed.*

Shortly after this, Mr. P. Coppinger, the mayor of Youghal for this year, 1579, fell into the hands of the Earl of Ormond, was tried by court-martial, and hung before his own door. He had, previous to the sacking of the town, refused to admit an English garrison, promising to defend the place to the last extremity; but on Desmond's approach, yielded it up, with a mere semblance of opposition.

Holinshed says the Earl of Desmond carried the "goods and household stuffe to the castle of Strangecallie and Lefinnen, *which were then kept by the Spaniards.*" The ruins of Strancally castle are on the Blackwater, between Youghal and Lismore, Doctor Ryland, in his "History of Waterford," makes this castle and cave quite a Giant Despair's residence. We must take the following description *cum grano salis:*—

"The castle of Strancally is situated on a high rock on the bank of the Blackwater, which is here of considerable breadth. The castle enjoyed a bold and commanding situation, was fortified, and in every respect a place of strength. From the foundation on which it stood, an extensive subterranean cave, with a passage communicating with the river, was cut through the solid rock, and thus provided, the worthy lords of Desmond were no contemptible imitators of the ancient giants. It was the custom of these gentle lords to invite their wealthy and distinguished neighbours to partake of the festivities of Strancally, and having thus gotten them into their power, the victims were carried through the rocky passage into the dungeon, where they were suffered to perish, and from thence, through an opening which is still visible, their corpses were cast into the river; thus disposed of, their fortunes became an easy prey. These practices continued for a long time, until at length, one more fortunate than his fellow-prisoners, escaped the final doom, and gave information of the facts to government. The castle and cave were immediately ordered to be demolished by gunpowder."

To find Spaniards in the keeping of two strong castles, like Strancally and Kilfinan, must have stamped the Earl of Desmond as a traitor in the eyes of a sovereign and people who had so lately escaped a great Spanish invasion. Strancally was taken from the Spaniards soon after the sacking of Youghal:—

"The Spaniards, who kept alwais good watch, and had also verie good espials abrode, they were forthwith advertised that a companie of souldiers were drawing and marching towards the said castell, and when they themselves saw it to be true, and had discovered them, they began to distrust themselves, and to doubt of their abilitie how to withstand them. Wherefore, abandoning and forsaking the castell, they passed over the water, thinking to recover the woods, and so to escape the present danger. But Sir William Stanleie, Capteine Zouch, Capteine Piers, Capteine Roberts, and all their companies, did so egerlie follow and pursue them, that in the end they overtook them, and slue all or the most part of them, and so tooke the castell, wherein the Lord Governour placed a ward."

We have an account next year, 1580, of the capture and death of James Oge, one of the Earl of Desmond's brothers, who made a raid into Muskerry. He was captured and bound by a blacksmith, and hid in a bush till the skirmish was over, and then delivered into the hands of Sir Cormac Teige Mac Carthy, Lord of Muskerry. Smith says, that for this service he was knighted by the Chief Justice, and made High Sheriff of the county. We think this is a mistake. Sir Cormac Teige was knighted by Sir Henry Sydney in 1575,* on the occasion of his visit to Cork. In describing this visit, Sir Henry Sydney calls him *Sir* Cormac Teige, and wishes him to be made a *baron;* and says, that for "loyalty and civil disposition" he was the "rarerst man that ever was born of the Irishry."

"A.D. 1580.—James Oge set out in rebellion to seek a prey in Muskerry, but Cormac, the son of Teige Mac Carthy, lord of the country, had all his forces assembled to oppose him. Cormac being informed that James had passed by him, proceeded to a certain place through which he knew James would pass, and he soon perceived James coming towards him with a prey, and he attacked him, and slew and destroyed the greater number of his people. James himself was taken, and sent to Cork to be imprisoned. He was [confined] nearly a month in this town, daily preparing himself for death, doing penance for his sins, and asking forgiveness for his misdeeds. At the end of that time a writ arrived from Dublin, from the Lord Justice and the council, ordering the mayor * to put

* *The mayor.*—This should be the marshal, Warham St. Leger, to whom a commission of martial law had been given, February 11, 1579. Cox says, that Sir James was brought to Sir Warham St. Leger and Captain Sir Walter Raleigh, who caused him to be hung, drawn, and quartered. We doubt that Sir Walter Raleigh, who came to Ireland in the Autumn of 1580, with Lord Grey, could have had anything to do with this execution.

that noble youth to death, and cut him in quarters and little pieces. This was accordingly done."

James Fitzgerald, the son of John Oge, and James, the son of Maurice, were slain the same year. The former fell in a skirmish in Limerick, with Brian Duv, the lord of Pobble-Brien, and the latter was shot in the gateway of Youghal.

Sir William Pelham now opens a fearful campaign against the Earl of Desmond, and all his kith and kin. He writes to England, requesting that an admiral, with a fleet containing ordnance and provisions, should sail round to the coast of Kerry. Vice-Admiral Winter is despatched to cruise about a coast upon which a Spanish or Italian landing was daily and hourly apprehended. Sir William commences his muster, and enrols beneath his standard "all who were subject to the laws, from the Boyne to the meeting of the Three Waters." The Earl of Ormond joined this muster with an immense host. The camp was pitched in Hy-Connello. It was "cold spring." Marauding parties were let loose in Kilmore and the wilds of Delliga, and in Kilbolane, who shewed mercy to none. "It was not wonderful they should kill men fit for action, but they killed blind* and feeble men, women, boys and girls, sick persons, idiots and old people, carrying off their cattle and provisions." In some instances, the people retaliated, and a great number of the English were slain.

The Lord Justice and the Earl of Ormond marched

---

* *Blind.*—"He put to death Faltach of Dun-Maolin, a man who had been blind from his birth. He also killed John Supple, of Cill-Mochna, whom it was not becoming to have killed, for he was upwards of one hundred years of age."— *Four Masters*, A.D. 1580.

from Cork to Tralee. The Earl of Ormond lost a number of his men on the march, from fatigue and scarcity of food. They were seized in Buttevant with a strange sickness called the "*gentle correction.*" Cox says the whole army was affected by it, but none died.

The Four Masters' description of the Lord Justice's artillery, at the siege of Carrig an Phuill, or "the Rock of the Hole," is amusing:—"When the warders of Askeaton and other castles heard the tremendous terror-waking roars of those unknown guns, the like of which had never been heard before, they began to demolish their castles with their own hands, leaving the gates of these which they could not demolish wide open to the conqueror. There was not a solitude, a wilderness, a declivity, or woody vale, from the Cearn of Breas to Cnox-Meadha-Sieril, in which the roar of these wonderful cannon was not heard, and all who heard trembled. James Eustace, son of Roland, son of Thomas, broke down his castles."

The new Lord Deputy, Arthur Lord Grey, came to Ireland the 12th of August, 1580, to supersede the Lord Chief Justice, Sir William Pelham. Pelham went to Dublin the 6th of September, and surrendered the sword of office (which he had sharpened and used with tremendous effect) into the hands of his successor. Lord Grey, as the Four Masters observe, was "of higher title and honors" than Sir William, but there never came to Ireland an Englishman more energetic or triumphant than the latter. Grey was accompanied by Captain Sir Walter Raleigh, and the poet, Spenser, as his secretary.

A hosting was made this year, 1580, by the Lord Deputy and Captain Malby, against the Kavanaghs, Kinsellaghs, O'Byrnes, and O'Toole's, who had flocked round the standard of James Eustace. Eustace had just renounced the "reformed faith," and his allegiance to the queen. It was on this occasion that Peter Carew, the elder brother of Sir George Carew (of whom we have much to say) was slain, with Master John Moor, Master Francis Cosby, and many other gentlemen who had come from England with Lord Grey.

A fleet, composed of Italian and Spanish troops, landed at *Dun-an-Oir*,* or the "Fort of Gold," in the harbour of Smerwick, in Kerry, this year. The fort stood on a small islet, whose perpendicular sides rise fifty feet above the sea.

The Lord Deputy writes to Burleigh for aid, and tells him to stand stoutly to the helm, as a great storm is at hand. He could not borrow more than two hundred pounds in Dublin on the security of the state. He adds, "I will visit the guests with the adventure of my life."

The Earl of Ormond, of whose generalship or courage we have no great opinion, mustered his forces and advanced into Kerry, and marched up the hill which commanded the fort, marked its deep trenches and impregnable ramparts, and then marched down again, and away. A fine army of the Geraldines were there to meet him, but they did not come to blows.

The Lord Deputy resolves to visit Kerry against

---

* *Dun-an-Oir*.—It is thus described by O'Sullivan Beare: "Est in eo portu Arnacantum, qui Anglis Smeruic vocatur juxta Danguinam oppidum scopulus Aureum Munimentum vocant accolæ naturâ satis munitus, partim mariuis fluctibus allutus, partim rupibus altis præcissus, cum continenti sublicio ponte conjuctus."

the advice of Ormond. He approaches the fort, and sends chosen parties to reconnoitre each day. The place seems impregnable. It cannot be stormed. They play on it for "four days," says Camden, for "forty days," says O'Daly. Hard shot has no effect on these Italians or Spaniards. They must try soft words. Communications are opened between the governor of the fort and the Lord Deputy. Sebastian, or Stephen de San Josepho, whom Camden calls "*homo imbellis*"— it is difficult to imagine what brought a homo imbellis there—accompanied by Hercules Pisano and the Duke of Biscay, waited on Lord Grey, and were graciously received, and honorable terms promised on surrender. San Josepho surrendered, was made, with his friends, prisoners of war, and *every soldier in the fort, to the number of seven hundred, butchered in cold blood.*

Edmund Spenser, Lord Grey's private secretary, emphatically denies that their lives were promised. Grey was Spenser's beau ideal of a warrior; he figures in the "Fairie Queen" as his "Talus with the Iron Flail." The poet's friend, Sir Walter Raleigh, was also mixed up with this bloody affair. But let us hear Spenser, for he was in Grey's camp, and present at the conference between the deputy and the officers from the fort. The account occurs in the imaginary dialogue between Ireneus and Eudoxus :—

"EUDOX. — But in that sharp execution of the Spaniards at the fort of Smerwick, I heard it specially noted, and if it were true, as some reported, surely it was a great touch to him in honor, for some say that he promised them life, others, at least *he did put them in hope thereof.*

"Iren.—Both the one and the other is most untrue; for this I can assure you, myself being as near them as any, that he was so far either from promising, or putting them in hope, that when first their secretary (called, as I remember, Signior Jeffrey), an Italian, being sent to treat with the Lord Deputy for grace, was flatly refused; and afterwards their colonel, named Don Sebastian, came forth to entreat that they might part with their arms like soldiers, at least with their lives, according to the custom of war and law of nations, it was strongly denied him, and told him by the Lord Deputy himself, that they could not justly plead either custom of war or law of nations, for that they were not any lawful enemies, and if they were, he willed them to show by what commission they came thither into another prince's dominions to war, whether from the Pope, or the King of Spain, or any other.

"When they said they were only adventurers, come to seek fortune abroad, and to serve in wars amongst the Irish, it was told them that the Irish themselves, as the Earl and John of Desmond, with the rest, were no lawful enemies, but rebels and traitors, and therefore they that came to succour them, no better than rogues and runagates, so as it would be dishonorable for him, in the name of his queen, to make any terms with such rascals; but left them to their choice to yield or submit themselves, or no. Whereupon, the said colonel did absolutely yield himself and the fort, with all therein, *and craved only mercy;* which, it being not thought good to show them, for danger of them, if, being saved, they should afterwards join the Irish."

But we have higher authority than Edmund Spenser,

the Lord Deputy's secretary, and that is *the Deputy himself*. He told the Spanish commander, San Joseph, that "no condition or composition were they to expect, other than they shuld *simplie render me the forte, and yield themselves to my will for lyf or deth.*" He then goes on to say,—"Morning came; I presented my forces in bataille before the forte; the coronel, with ten or twelve of his chief gentlemen, came trayling their ensigns, rolled up, and presented them to me with their lives, and the forte. I sent straighte certeyne gentlemen to see their weapons and armoires laid down, and to guard the munition and victual then left from spoyle. *Then put I in certeyne bandes, who streighte fell to execution.* There were six hundred slayn."

Cox, who had no love for either Spaniard or Italian, says, that the garrison "yielded at mercy, which was too sparingly extended towards them." Leland says, "The garrison was butchered in cold blood;" nor is it without pain that he finds "a service so horrible and detestable committed to Sir Walter Raleigh." We are informed by the same writer that the queen expressed the utmost concern and displeasure at this barbarous execution. The faith of Lord Grey, or "*Fides Greia,*" was long after this for a proverb and a bye-word in Munster. This nobleman lived long enough to lose all favor at court, and what is more remarkable, was found to be deeply implicated in the "Treason of the Bye," or the "*Priests' Treason.*" He expected to be made Marshal of the Horse under the new régime. It was well named, with such an agent, the "Surprising Treason."

We find Captain Raleigh in Cork this year. He seems to have had a constable's commission for arresting persons suspected of disloyalty, and, to do him justice, manifested as much zeal as foolish daring in the discharge of his office. He sets out from Cork to Dublin to make a complaint to his patron, Lord Grey, of the Barrys and Condons, for assisting the rebels, and receives instructions to besiege the castle of Barrys-Court, which he sets about with a will. But he had to deal with resolute and cunning men. Lord Barry fired his castle of Barrys-Court, and his friend, Fitzgerald, the seneschal of Imokilly, set an ambush for the English captain on his return. They lay on the banks of the stream, near the old abbey from which Midleton derived its ancient name of *Chore Abbey*.* The place where Raleigh crossed (near Mr. Murphy's distillery) is pointed out to the present day. Holinshed's account of the affair is amusing enough:—

"Captain Raleigh, not mistrusting any thing, had with him only two horsemen, four shot on horseback, and a guide, who was servant to John Fitz-Edmonds, of Cloyne, then a good subject to the queen, and who knew every corner of the country. Being arrived at the ford, the seneschal observing him alone, having outrode his men, clapt spurs to his horse, and crossed him in the water; however, Raleigh regained the other side, at which time his guide thought proper to forsake him, and fled towards an adjacent ruined castle for shelter.

---

* *Chore Abbey.*—The neighbouring village of Ballinacurra derived its name from a ford on the same stream. It was anciently called *Bally na-chore*, or the " Town of the Ford."

"Henry Moile, one of Raleigh's servants, riding about a bow-shot before the rest of his company, was, by this time, got into the middle of the water, when his horse foundered, and threw him; and being afraid of the seneschal's men, he cried out to the captain to save his life, who returned, and recovered both him and his horse; and then Moile, being over eager to leap up, sprung over the horse, and fell into an adjacent mire; and the horse ran away full speed. Raleigh, with his staff in one hand, and his pistol cocked in the other, continued to wait in the ford, till the arrival of his four men, and his servant Jenkin, who had about two hundred pounds in money about him; and though the seneschal had with him twelve horse, and several shot, yet neither he nor any of them, though twenty to one, durst attack him; but continued to abuse him, with scurrilous speeches, until the arrival of his men."

Raleigh met the seneschal soon after, and charged him with cowardice, in the presence of the Earl of Ormond, to which Fitzgerald made no reply. He afterwards sent him a challenge by the White Knight, offering to meet him, man for man, and cross the river at the same place, which Fitzgerald—deeming prudence the better part of valour—declined. That the seneschal was no coward, but a man of personal daring, is evinced by his assault on the town of Youghal, two years after this, in 1582.

Sir Walter Raleigh's next daring and unwise expedition was against Lord Roche, whom Doctor Smith styles a "nobleman well-beloved in the country." We have a State Paper by Lord Burleigh, containing his opinion of the "suspected lordes and captains" of Munster. "The Earl of Clancare never was good, and never will be. The Lord Barrymore, the subtlest foxe that ever Munster bredd. The Lord Roche, amongst manie bad, *I thinke the best.*"

Raleigh left Cork at ten o'clock at night, with ninety men, for Castletown, the residence of Lord Roche. He approached the gate as a benighted traveller, and asked admittance. When the gates were opened, he and his party pressed in. He saw Lord Roche, and was invited to supper. He supped, and *after supper* informed his hospitable host, that he had orders to convey him and his lady to Cork. The seneschal of Imokilly and David Barry, prepared a force to intercept them. It was a tempestuous and rainy night, on which no lady should have been asked to travel. Raleigh gained the city by day-break. There is but one apology for Raleigh's unknightly conduct, but it is a good one:—"Zouch *ordered* him to take Lord Roche and his lady prisoners, and bring them to Cork." The same excuse holds good as it regards the massacre at Smerwick—*Raleigh acted under orders.* The little we know of Raleigh in Ireland is not to his credit, *if we except the introduction of the potato.* But this should cover a multitude of sins.

The Captain Zouch, under whom Raleigh acted, was made Governor-General of the province under the Deputy Lord Grey. Hearing that Sir John of Desmond, the Earl's brother, and James Fitz-John, his warder of Strancally castle, were in the neighbourhood of Castle-Lyons, he resolved, if possible, to seize them. John is described by the Four Masters at this time as a sort of Irish Robin Hood, "a roving and wandering plunderer."

"The manner in which John lived on his mountain was worthy of a true plunderer, for he slept upon couches of stone or earth, and drank of the pure cold streams, from the palms of his hands or his shoes; and his only cooking utensils were the long twigs of the forest for dressing the flesh meat carried away from his enemies." The following is the Four Masters' account of his death:—

"John set out, accompanied by four horsemen, for the woods of Eatharlach, to hold a conference with Barry More, with whom he had entered into a plundering confederacy. He proceeded southwards across the river Avonmore, in the middle of a dark and misty day, and happened to be met, front to front and face to face, by Captain Siuitsi [Zouch] with his forces, though neither of them was in search of the other. John was mortally wounded on the spot, and had not advanced the space of a mile beyond that place when he died. He was carried crosswise on his own steed, with his face downwards, from thence to Cork, and when brought to that town, he was cut in quarters, and his head was sent to Dublin* as a token of victory."

The Four Masters are in error in saying that neither was in search of the other. A spy, named Richard Mac James, induced one of Desmond's followers to accompany him to Captain Zouch, who bribed Mac James to report that he, Zouch, was on the point of

* *His head sent to Dublin.*—His body hung in chains at one of the gates of Cork for three years, and one stormy night was blown into the river, and carrie d to the sea.—*Vide O'Daly, c.* 23. *O'Sullivan Beare Hist. Cathol. Iber. fol.* 99.

starting for Limerick. This report put John of Desmond off his guard. O'Daly says, that Thomas Fleming, formerly a servant of Sir John of Desmond, plunged a spear into his master's throat; that Zouch wished to take him alive. James Fitz-John, the warder of Strancally castle, was slain at the same time.

The condition of the old outlawed Earl of Desmond was almost desperate. His pursuers, headed by this Captain Zouch, were every day narrowing the circle around him. But he generally managed to break through, and either to distance his pursuers or keep them at bay. He was surrounded by a band of desperate men, called the "Old Children of the Wood," who betook themselves to the wilds near the Lakes of Killarney. It was before dawn on Sunday morning, the 4th of January, 1581. The encampment was near Aghadoe. The remains of a round tower now mark the spot. The earl and countess, who had sat by the watch fires all night, were buried in deep sleep when they were startled by the cry of alarm, and the hoofs of Captain Zouch's cavalry. They barely escaped—he in his shirt—to the bank of the neighboring river, where they remained for two or three hours "up to their chins in water." Desmond took the earliest opportunity of revenging this surprise.

A.D. 1581.—" A hosting was made by the Earl of Desmond, at the end of the month of September, into the plains lying far and wide around Cashel, in Munster, and into Cashel itself. His forces seized upon great quantities of all sorts of property, such as copper, iron, clothing, apparel, and great and small cattle." They were pursued by a large force, on which the earl turned, slaying four hundred men, and increasing his plunder " with many steeds and other spoils."

In the summer of the next year he made a successful hosting into the country of his old foes, the Butlers, and left the hill on which he fought "speckled with the bodies of the slain." In the autumn he made an incursion upon the O'Keeffes of Kerry, who rose *en masse* against him:—" When the earl heard the bustling of the kerns, and the report of their ordnance, he rose up suddenly, rushed upon O'Keeffe, and routed him back the same passage by which he had come, and almost all the pursuers were slain. O'Keeffe himself, *i.e.* Art, the son of Donnell, son of Art, and his son, Art Oge, were taken prisoners, and Hugh, another of his sons, was slain. The son of the Vicar O'Scoly was also taken prisoner on this occasion, and was afterwards hanged."

Desmond had become nothing more nor less than a lawless bandit, preying upon all, and, as a natural consequence, hunted down by all. "The earl, without rest anywhere, fleeth from place to place, and maketh mediation for peace by the countess, " whose abundance of tears bewrayeth sufficientlie the miserable state both of herself, her husband, and their followers." "Again the earl is unhowsed of all his goods, and must now tread the woods and bogs, which he will do as unwieldly as any man in the world of his age. He shrowded himself in glyns and swamps, and in the winter, 1582, kept a cold Christmas in Kilqueg woods." But let us hasten to the close.

" A.D. 1583. The Earl of Ormond was governor of

the two provinces of Munster this year, and the Earl of Desmond became confirmed in his treason and insurrection, and proceeded to ravage the country during the winter and the spring of the following year. His people, however, were so much in dread and awe of the law and the sovereign of England, that they began to separate from him, even his own married wife,* children and friends, so that he had but four persons to acompany him from one cavern of a rock, or hollow of a tree, to another.

The Earl of Ormond writes the queen :—

"ORMOND *to the* QUEEN,

"There have been six score traitors put to the sword and executed since my coming. Desmond being long since fled over the mountaine into Kerrye, is now gone to seek relief by such spoils as he can take from the Earl of Clancartie, (his brother-in-law), Captain Barkley having followed him thither, to aid the Earl of Clancartie. I have sent Sir Cormok Mac Tiege and Sir William Stanley towards Castlemaine to lie for him thereabout (if, in the meantime, they met him not), myself with my horsemen intend to lie out this side of the mountaine for him. I find your majesty's opinion proveth true, for since I kept him from the counties of Waterford and Tipperary, his men have been forced many times to eat horses and carrion, and being now kept from cows in the mountains of Desmond, famine will destroy them as daily it doth. *God send them all the plague I wish them*, and bless your majesty with a most happy reign.

"THOS. ORMOND & OSS.

"Cork, 24 April, 1583."

His death is thus described :—

"When the beginning of winter and the long nights set in, the insurgents and robbers of Munster began to

* *His own married wife.*—We look upon this as a foul slander of the Four Masters. This lady was the daughter of Lord Dunboyne. She was the mother of James, the Parliamentary Earl, and five daughters. She married a second time, O'Conor Sligo, and lived till 1636.

collect about him, and prepared to rekindle the torch of war. But God thought it time to suppress, close, and finish this war of the Geraldines, which was done in the following way:—A party of the O'Moriartys, of the Mang's side, of the race of Aedh-Beannan, took an advantage of the Earl of Desmond, whom they found in an unprotected position; he was concealed in a hut, in the cavern of a rock, in Gleann-an-Ghinntigh. This party remained on the watch around this habitation of the earl, from the beginning of the night to the dawning of day; and then, in the morning twilight, they rushed into the cold hut. This was on Tuesday, which was St. Martin's festival. They wounded the earl, and took him prisoner, for he had not along with him any people able to make fight or battle, excepting one woman and two men servants. They had not proceeded far from the wood, when they suddenly beheaded the earl."

The Four Masters say, that the Moriartys "took advantage of the Earl of Desmond." It has been long doubted whether the Moriartys knew it was the Earl of Desmond till after he was slain. But this doubt is removed by a letter from Ormond to the privy council, in the State Paper office:—

"ORMOND *to the* PRIVY COUNCIL.—Nov. 15th, 1583.

"In my way now from Dublin I received news of the killing of the traitors Gorehe, McSwiny, (captain of galloglass,) the only man that relieved the Earl of Desmond in his extreme misery; and the next day after my coming hither to Kilkenny, I received certain word that Donall Moriarty, (of whom at my last being in Kerry, I took assurance to serve against Desmond,) being accompanied with 25 kerne of his own sept, and six of the ward of Castlemaine, the

11th of this month at night, assaulted the Earl in his cabin, in a place called Glanageenty, near the river of the Mang, and slew him, whose head I have sent for, and appointed his body to be hung up in chains at Cork.

"Thos. Ormond et Oss."

O'Daly, who calls Owen Mac Daniel Moriarty an inhuman villian, has to admit that the earl's people acted barbarously, and gave the traitor great provocation:—"It unfortunately happened, that those who were sent by the earl to seize the prey, barbarously robbed a noble matron, whom they left naked in the field." This noble matron, or as she is styled by Cox, "a poor woman of the Moriartas," was Owen Moriarty's sister. We learn from the same writer, that it was a soldier named Kelly* who actually slew the earl. With the first stroke he almost cut off his arm, when the old man cried—"I am the Earl of Desmond, spare my life!" Cox says, "Kelly would have spared him, were it not that he bled so fast that he could not live, therefore he *immediately cut off his head.*" It would appear from this, that the earl was decapitated before Moriarty had entered the hut.

The head was carried to the Earl of Ormond, the Earl of Desmond's step-son, who had it pickled and placed in a pipkin, and forwarded as a present to the queen. It was a dish fit for Herodias. It was accompanied by the following letter:—

"Ormond *to* Walsingham,

"I do send Her Highness, (for proof of the good success of the service, and the happy end thereof), by this bearer, the principal

* *A soldier named Kelly.*—The queen, in a letter dated December 14th, 1585, ordered that "Her well-beloved subject and soldier, Daniel Kelly, who slew the late traytor, Desmond, for his very good service therein, should have, at least, for thirty years, without fine, so much of her lands, spiritual or temporal, as should amount to £30 sterling per annum."

traitor, Desmond's head, as the best token of the same, and proof of my faithful service and travail; whereby her charges may be diminished, and as to her princely pleasure shall be thought meet.

"THOS. ORMOND ET OSS.

"Nov. 28th, 1583."

The head was impaled on London bridge. The people of the district still point to the spot where the earl was killed, called Bothar-an-Iarla, in the townland of Gleann-an-Ghinntigh, now Glanageenty, about five miles to the east of Tralee; and to an old tree, beneath which his body lay concealed, till it was carried away for interment to the small chapel of Kilnamanagh, near Castle-Island.

Thus miserably perished Garrett, the sixteenth Earl of Desmond. His fate makes a mournful page of Irish history, although "he was given to plunder and insurrection." The great house or family of Desmond fell with him. He left a son, James, called the *Parliamentary* Earl of Desmond, and a nephew, James Fitz-Thomas, called the *Sugan* Earl, but Garrett may be styled the last.

> "Of their names in heavenly records now
> Is no memorial; blotted out and rased,
> For their rebellion, from the Book of Life."
>
> *Milton's Paradise Lost.*

The Four Masters record this year the deaths of David Lord Roche, his wife Lady Ellen, and Eveleen Roche, the Countess of Thomond, and sister of David Roche.

"A.D. 1583. Roche, *i.e.* David, son of Maurice, (son of David son of Maurice) and his wife Ellen, the daughter of James, son of

Edmond Mac Pierce, died in the one month, in the spring of this year. There did not exist of all the old English in Ireland, a couple possessing only a barony, of more renown than they."

We learn from this that Lady Roche was a Fitzgerald. The Four Masters, speaking of James, the Bishop of Kerry, who died this year, 1583, say, "This bishop was a vessel full of wisdom. He was of the stock of Clan-Pierce, of the race of Raymond, the son of William Fitzgerald, the brother of Maurice, who came from the king of England at the time of the first invasion of Ireland."

"A.D. 1583. The Countess Roche [recté Countess of Thomond]* namely, Eveleen, the daughter of Maurice, son of David Roche, and wife of the Earl of Thomond (Donough, the son of Conor O'Brien) died in the summer of this year at Clonroad, and was buried in the monastery of Ennis."

The death of Sir Cormac Mac Teige, of whom Sir Henry Sydney said "for his loyalty and civil disposition, he was the rarest man that ever was born of the Irishry," is thus recorded: "Cormac, son of Teige, son of Cormac Oge Mac Carthy, lord of Muskerry, a comely-shaped, bright-countenanced man, who possessed most *white-washed edifices*, fine built castles and hereditary seats of any of the descendants of Eoghan More."

We conclude that *white-washing* houses was introduced into Ireland about this time, by the English. An Irish poet, speaking of the death of Hugh Maguire, Lord of Fermanagh, who slew Sir Warham St. Leger near Cork, says,—" *The memory of the lime-white mansions his right hand hath laid in ruins, warms the hero's*

---

* *Reeté Countess of Thomond.*—The habit of calling women by their maiden names after marriage prevails to some extent in Ireland even to the present day.

heart." James, the younger brother of the Earl of Desmond, found the "white-washed edifices" of Sir Cormac Mac Teige, of Blarney, no more than "whited sepulchres." Sir Cormac was sheriff of the county when that "noble youth" was put to death, and cut in quarters and little pieces. Desmond was caught taking a prey on Sir Cormac's lands.

His principal residence was Blarney castle. We have no hesitation in saying, that the word *blarney* has derived its peculiar significance from this loyal, rare, civil, comely-shaped, bright-countenanced man.

Aenghus O'Daly, when describing the reception he received from Sir Cormac Teige's successor, says, "Flattery I got for food in Great Musgraidhe of Mac Diarmoda." Doctor O'Donovan, who has edited this interesting poem of the "*Tribes of Ireland,*" says, "This is the earliest notice of the *bladhmann* or blarney of Munster we have yet read." Clarence Mangan's versified paraphrase of the Irish, with a few variations, runs thus:—

> "Mac Dermod of Muskerry, you have a way,
> Which at least I must term odd. You gave me, Mac Dermod,
> With a great deal of blarney, a wine-glass of whey.
> Before I could reach *Ballincollick*,
> I thought I'd have died with your frolic."

CHAPTER XV.

A PARLIAMENT—THE UNDERTAKERS—FLORENCE MAC CARTHY—
O'NEILL AND O'DONNELL.

A D. 1584—1598.

SIR JOHN PERROTT returned to Ireland the 21st of June, 1584, in the capacity of Lord Deputy, and was sworn in the 26th of June. He was accompanied by Sir John Norris as the President of Munster. "A general peace was proclaimed throughout all Ireland, and the two provinces of Munster* in particular, after the decapitation of the Earl of Desmond." The very embers of rebellion seemed to have been trodden out by the Earl of Ormond's and Captain Zouch's cavalry, and quenched in the blood of the outlawed and decapitated earl. There was not a single Geraldine able to bear arms in Ireland, who did not become obedient to the law, except Maurice Fitzgerald,† and he fled, with a company of five persons, across the "green-streamed Shannon," to Sorley Boy, son of MacDonnell, from Sorley Boy to Scotland, and from Scotland to Spain, where he died.

* *The two provinces of Munster.*—The part of Munster south of the Blackwater, and middle Munster, between the Blackwater and Limerick.

† *Maurice Fitzgerald.*—The Four Masters style him Maurice, the son of John Oge, son of John, son of Thomas, the earl—that is Thomas Moyle, the 12th earl of Desmond.

The time had, therefore, arrived for summoning a parliament, and for confiscating Garrett's vast estates. A large number of Anglo-Norman lords, English adventurers, and Irish chieftains, were in attendance. "Where the carcase is, there will the eagles be gathered together."

"A.D. 1585. A proclamation of parliament was issued to the men of Ireland, commanding their chiefs to assemble in Dublin precisely on May-day, * for the greater part of the people of Ireland, were, at this time, obedient to their sovereign; and according they all, at that summons, did meet in Dublin, face to face."

The parliament assembled in Dublin, the 26th of April. The Four Masters mention the names of a number of Irish chieftains, who repaired to this parliament, although they did not take their seats † as members.

"To this parliament repaired some of the chiefs of the descendants of Eoghan More, ‡ with their descendants, namely, Mac Carthy More* (Donnell, the son of Donnell, son of Cormac Ladhrach;) Mac Carthy Cairbreach, (Owen, son of Donnell, son of Fineen, son of Donnell, son of Dermot-an Duna,) and the sons of his two brothers, namely, Donnell, son of Cormac-na-h-Aine, and Fineen, the son of Donough.

Thither also went the two chiefs who were at strife with each

* *Precisely on May-day.*—According to a document in the Roll's Office, Dublin, this parliament assembled on the 26th of April, 1585. It was prorogued the 29th of May, of the same year, and dissolved the 14th of May, 1586.

† *Take their seats as members.*—See list of Lords spirituall and temporall that were "summoned unto the parliament holden before the Right Honorable Sir John Perrott, Knyght, Lord Deputie Generall of the realme of Ireland, XXVI° die Aprilis, anno regni regine nostre Elizabeth vicesimo septimo;" printed in the third appendix to Wardiman's edition of the Statue of Kilkenny, p. 139.

‡ *Eoghan More*, the ancestor of all the principal Irish chieftains of the "kingdom of Cork," was king of Munster in the third century.

other concerning the lordship of Duhallow, namely, Dermot, the son of Owen, son of Donough-an-Bhothair, son of Owen, son of Donough, and Donough, the son of Cormac Oge, son of Cormac, son of Donough.

Thither likewise went O'Sullivan Beare, (Owen, son of Dermot, son of Donnell, son of Donough, son of Dermot Balbh;) O'Sullivan More, (Owen, the son of Donnell, son of Donnell, son of Donnell-na-Sgreadaighe;) O'Mahony the Western, namely, Conor, the son of Conor Fin Oge, son of Conor Fin, son of Conor O'Mahony; and O'Driscoll More, (Fineen, the son of Conor, son of Fineen, son of Conor.)

None of the Munster lords who are here stated to have repaired to this parliament took their seats, as members, with the exception of Mac Carthy More, Earl of Clancare. The county Cork was represented by Sir John Norris, (lord president of Munster), Wm. Cogan, or De Cogan, and John Fitz-Edmond Fitzgerald.

An act was passed that "all conveyances made, or pretended to be made, by any person attainted of treason, within thirteen years before the act, shall be on record in the exchequer within a year, or be void."

This enactment, the object of which was to allow of the confiscation of the late Earl of Desmond's vast estates, was opposed by John Fitz-Edmond Fitzgerald, one of the three members for the county of Cork. His opposition might have proved successful, and, as Cox says, have "baffled the expectations of the undertakers, if Sir Henry Wallop had not gotten a document which proved that the earl had entered into a confederacy of rebellion with the very persons to whom he conveyed the estates, (of whom John Fitz-Edmond was one), two months before the conveyance; but that upon the producing of the document, and the discovering of the fraud and subtlety, the honest part of the house were ashamed to abet so ill a cause, and that accordingly the act was made to prevent the like contrivances."—*Hibernia Anglicana, vol.* i., *p.* 384 ; *and Moryson's History of Ireland, edition of* 1753, *vol.* i., *pp.* 8-9.

The "patrimonian lands" of the late earl extended, according to the Four Masters, from Dun-caoin, in Kerry, to the meeting of the Three Waters, at Waterford, and from the Great Island of Ard-Nemidh (on which Queenstown stands) in Hy-Liathain, to Limerick, consisting of over a million acres, of which 574,628 were forfeited to the crown by a special act of attainder passed against him in 1583.

"This is the quantity of land which the Earl of Desmond had before he opposed the sovereign, *i.e.* $3555\tfrac{3}{3}$ seisreachs [ploughlands]. According to the English, he had 106,606 seisreachs. This was his royal rent, at half a rialo per acre, six thousand pounds a-year. And this was the earl's rent at thirty pound per seisreach, *i.e.* 106,570. There were 343 castles on the lands of the Earl of Desmond."—*Duald Mac Firbis.*

This hundred and six thousand five hundred and seventy pounds per annum, would be worth more than *a million* per annum of our money.

This vast property was apportioned out among English undertakers.*

The following list was made out by Sir Edward Phyton. It gives the names of the undertakers, the number of acres, the rent, and the number of English to be located upon the lands.

* *English undertakers* were so styled from a clause in the deed in which they undertook the performance of certain duties. It is strange this term should now mean a person who superintends funerals, inasmuch as the original undertakers left the bodies of the Irish, whose lands they possessed, uninterred, to the vultures and wild dogs.

THE ENGLISH UNDERTAKERS.

"This was the relation and state of English in Munster given to her majesty's Attorney-General (Sir John Popham,) and Sir Edward Phyton the last summer, and sithence—

TABLE OF UNDERTAKERS IN FEBR^{Y.} 1589.

In Kerry and Desmond at Eight Pence an Acre.

	Acres.	People.	Rent.
Sir Valentine Browne,	6000	20	£100
Sir Edwd Denny,	6000	,,	100
Sir William Herbert and Sir Charles Herbert,	18000	,,	300

Conelogh [Connilloe] at Four Pence an Acre.

Mr. Trencher,	12000	37	150
Sir Willm Courtney,	12000	,,	150
Mr. Oughtread,	12000	22	150
Mr. Billingsby,	12000	137	150
Sir Edwd Barkley,	12000	,,	150

Cork at One Penny an Acre.

* Hugh Cuffe,	12000	74	66 13 4
Arthur Hyde,	6000	24	23 6 8
Phaane Beacher,	12000	12	66 13 4
Hugh Worthe,	12000	,,	66 13 4
Sir Warham St. Leger and Sir Richd Grynfield,	12000	,,	33 6 8
Arthur Robyns,	4000	"	22 4 5
George Robynson,	4000	12	22 4 5
Mr. Read,	3000	,,	16 14 0

Limerick at 2^{d.} ob. (2¼.)

Tipperary and Waterford at 1^{d.} q^{r.} (1^d¼.)

Sir Edward Phyton, and Richd Bould, and Thos Preston,	11000	60	80
Richd Phyton and Alex^{r.} Phyton,	2000	20	
The Earl of Uremont (Ormond,) (he entered but lately,)	3000	,,	16 13 4
Thomas Fleetwood,	3000	22	16 13 4

* *Hugh Cuffe*, of Cuffe's Wood. This family was elevated to the peerage in 1733, under the title of Baron Desart; and was raised to the dignity of Earl of Desart in 1793.

	Acres.	People.	Rent.
Marmaduke Redman, but now dispossessed by Patrick Condon. His petition is with Mr Secretary,	3000	22	16 13 4
Sir Walter Raleigh and his associates,	36000		
My Lord Chancellor,	6000	200	33 6 8

"Mr Attorney (Popham), Mr Edward Rogers (Popham's son-in-law), and Mr Warre have had above sixty Englishmen there these two years, and now for want of land are driven to call them home again; besides there were divers women and servants. Also Sir Warham St. Leger, Sir Walter Raleigh, Sir Edw$^{d.}$ Denny, Sir William Herbert, Sir Thomas Norreys, Sir George Bourchier, Sir Edw$^{d.}$ Barclay, Denzill Hollis, Arthur Robyns, and Mr Read have no English people numbered by us, because we have not been informed of them.

"Also, that the rent of Sir Walter Raleigh, Sir Edw$^{d.}$ Denny, Denzill Hollis, and Rich$^{d.}$ and Alex$^{r.}$ Phyton are not rated, because we know them not.

"Note also, the chargeable lands are not valued, nor many other parcels lying dispersed.

"E. PHYTON.
"J. POPHAM.

"People, 661.
"£1674 14 10."

These grants were ready for signature when James Fitz-Thomas, the nephew of Garrett, the late earl, and the son of Garrett's elder brother, [Thomas,] presented himself before the queen, as the true and legitimate heir of the property. James Fitz-Thomas, better known as the Sugan Earl, is described by Cox as "the handsomest man of his time." His father, Thomas, was the eldest son of James, the fifteenth earl, by Joan, the daughter of Lord Roche, whom he divorced on the plea of consanguinity, marrying a daughter of

O'Carroll. Elizabeth perfectly understood this, but she remembered that Catherine of Arrogan, the first wife of Henry VIII., was alive when her father married Anne Boleyn, so Fitz-Thomas returned as he went, a *Sugan* Earl, or man of straw. He lived long enough to prove that straw is highly inflammable. His father, Thomas, did not concern himself in his brother's or his son's rebellion, but lived peaceably in his castle of Connough.*

An inquisition was held in Shandon castle, in the city of Cork, the 9th of September, 1588, on the conduct of all those who were in any way concerned in, or connected with the Earl of Desmond and his risings, or rebellions. A large number were found guilty and attainted by act of parliament. The inquisitors also, furnished a list of all persons suspected of being ill-disposed to the government. These lists contain as many Anglo-Norman as Celtic names. We do not find among them the name of any of the four great branches of the Mac Carthys, namely, the Carthy More, the Mac Carthy Reagh, Donogh Mac Carthy of Duhallow, or the Lord of Muskerry, although their properties were very extensive.

We may judge of the power of those Irish chieftains from the following list of horse and foot they were able to bring into the field. The list is given by Sir George Carew : —

* *Connough*.—Here he died, anno 1593, and was interred among his ancestors, in the Franciscan abbey at Youghal. It appears by a paper in the Bodleian Library, that his father, the fifteenth earl, made him a grant of the barony of Kinsatalloon, and the manor of Castlemore, near Cork. He left three sons, James, John, and Gerald, and one daughter, who married Donald Mac Carthy Reagh.

LIST OF THE IRISH FORCES IN DESMOND.

	Horse.	Galloglass.	Kerne.
Mac Carthy More, Prince of that portion,	40	160	2000
Mac Carthy Reagh, Lord of Carbry,	60	80	2000
Donogh Mac Carthy of Dowallie,	24	80	200
Teig Mac Cormac of Muskry,	40	80	200
O'Keefe,	12	0	100
Mc Awliffe,	80	0	60
O'Donovan,	6	0	60
O'Driscols of Collimore and Baltimore,	6	0	200
O'Mahon of Ivaghe,	26	0	120
O'Sullivan Beare and Bantry,	10	0	200
O'Donogh More of Lough Lene,	12	0	200
O'Mahoni of Brin,	46	0	100
O'Dwyre of Kil-na managhe,	12	0	100
McTeig McPhilip of Kilnaloghengarty,	6	0	40

The last two were not followers of Mac Carthy.

It appears from a letter bearing date July 25th, 1583, and a bill of expenses* furnished by Mac Carthy Reagh to the queen, that his followers had been employed by her majesty during the Desmond rebellion:—

1583. *July 25th.* SIR OWEN MAC CARTHY REAGH *to* HER MAJESTY.

" My most humble and bounden duetie to yor Excellent Majestie premissed. I thought it good to signifie unto yor Highness whate I and my countrey have employed for the better furtherance of yor Majesties service during the rebellion in Mounster, the particulers wherof appeareth in a schedule herein inclosed; and as Capteine Barkley may certifie the same unto yor Matie, who behaued himselfe verie well in the said contrey, not doubting but yor Highnes (according your accustomed bountie) will haue consideracion of the same, moste humby beseeching youre royall Majestie to grant unto me suche resonable requests as mine agents will pticulerly declare to yor Highnes on my behalf; and thus (with all due reverence) I

---

* *Bill of expenses.*—A little bill of this kind was, as we have seen, furnished to his " very good king Harry," by the Lord O'Reilly; but his kerne were employed in England.

moste humbly take my leave. At your Maties citie of Cork the 25th of July, 1583.

"Yo^r Highnes' Faithful Subject,

"OWEN CARTY."

A *briefe selection* of suche payments as Sir Owen McCarthy Knight and his countrey of Caribrie in the Countie of Cork haue paid for the furtherance of Her Maties Service sence the first of the Rebelion of James Fitz Mores.

In primes. In the tyme of the Government of Sir John Perott Lord president of Mounster, for the better mainteynance of her Maties Garisons being then here, paid in byfs, and cesse taken upp of the said countrey, the som of a thousand Pounds st^s.

Item, after to the Earle of Ormonde, being then L. Genl of Mounster, in money and byfs taken upp of the said contrey, the som of £700 st^s.

Item, to Sir William Drury L. president of Mounster for cesse of 16 horsmen, being towe yeares in the said contrey, viz. to every horsman 5^s st. per diem, amountith to the som of £1147 st^s.

Item, more to the said Sr William in money towards Hir Maties charges, and to be released of the cesse of the said Horsemen £1000 st^s.

Item, the said Sir Owen McCartie paid to Patrick Shearlock of Waterford for the nomber of thrie score kerne cessed upon his said contrey £50.

Item, besides the pmisses the said Sir Owen (of his own goode will) for the better furtherance of Hir Maties Service, have kept in his contrey aforesaid sence the begynning of the rebellion of the Earle of Desmond 100 Englishe soldiers footmen, and paid there Capteyns yearly £1200 vizt.

Item to Capteyn William Aplsey,	£1200
Item to Capteyn Fenton,	1200
Item to Capteyn Barkley,	1200
The totall Som amounteth to,	£7497

It was the original policy of England to cut down and root up the great Irish chieftains by Norman and

Saxon swords. This policy was persevered in to the reign of Henry VIII., till the Norman lords attained an ascendancy which rendered them more difficult to govern than the Irish chieftains whom they were employed to destroy. The policy was then reversed. The forces of the Mac Carthys were in government pay for the suppression of the Geraldines, but the Geraldines being subdued, the question again arose, how are these great Irish lords to be disposed of; for the English sovereigns never contemplated more than the Cyclopean gratitude of eating them last.

The late outlawed Earl of Desmond had one son, whom the queen had caged up in the Tower, with her lions, tigers, and other dangerous animals. Mac Carthy More, Earl of Clancare, also had one son, but what became of him is a perfect mystery. That the English ministry had their meshes spread around his path is evident from the following correspondence:—

1584.* *July 9th. From* TREASURER WALLOP *to* Sir F. WALSINGHAM.

"My Lo. Deputie hath sent the Earls of Desmond and Clancarty their sonnes to the Court by two of my men, whom I beseeche you to discharge of them as sone as they come to the Court w'h them."

1584. *Nov. 28th.* WATERHOUSE *to* WALSINGHAM.

"The other two letters are from the Earl of Clanrickarde; the one, as I learn (both from himselfe and Sir Richard,) is to exhort his son, the Baron of Dunkellin, to beware of such advice as hath been given to the young Baron of Valentia for his undutiful *departure into France.*"

* 1584.—The Earl of Desmond delivered up his son to Sir William Drury at Kilmallock in 1579. He must have remained five years in Dublin—till after his father's death—before he was sent to England.

1586. *January* 19*th.*

"I have no other newes besydes those I sent you lately, save that one Barry, who was the enticer and conveyor away of the Lord of Valentia from here, is of late taken by the Earl of Glencarre. who had intelligence of his coming over into the country, disguised like a beggar, to see how he could procure some relief for the young Lord. I have given order to have him safely sent hither unto me: when I have him I will learn of him what I may.

"From the Castle of Dublin."

1586. *Feb.* 12. NICHOLAS SKIDDY *to* WALSINGHAM.

"Rt. hon.: My humble and most bonden duty premised. Finding this bearer, my cousin, James Meagher, repairing towards the Court, I thought good to write your Honor these few lines, declairing that William Barry the man that brought the Earl of Clancarre's son into France, is apprehended in Desmond, and now brought to Cork. I offered to bring him to your Honor, wherein I could not prevail, by reason that my Lo. Deputie did write for him; and it is meant that the said Barry shall be sent to Dublin."

It appears from these letters that Barry, having conveyed the boy from London to France, returned to Ireland, disguised as a beggar, "to procure some relief for the young lord." What became of the lad after this, we know not; perhaps he died.

Mac Carthy More also had a daughter, Ellen. She was heiress to a princely inheritance. Irrespective of his own personal estates, the Mac Carthy More derived, as lord paramount, the following items of income from subordinate lords and chieftains in the counties of Cork and Kerry. The following is extracted* from papers sent to Burleigh:—

* *Extracted.*—We are indebted for this and other valuable information to the labors of Daniel Mac Carthy (Glas) Esq., who is engaged on a life of Florence Mac Carthy.—See journal of the Kilkenny Archæological Society, vol. ii., new series.

Extracted from the first of three Tracts sent to BURLEIGH.

"The Earle of Glyncarr, before Her Ma'tie created him Earle, was by Inheritance Mc Cartie Moore; by wch amonge the Irishe he was accounted the cheefest in this Province, as descended from them that before they were subdued to the Crowne of England, weare the Kinges of the greater parte thereof; and at the tyme of his creation and surrender of his former titles, he had, and ever synce claymeth under his jurisdiction and dominon *fourteene severall countries*, beside som of lesse quantitie; most of them possessed by such as have descended out of his house, from every of wh^{ch} he demandeth sondrie duties and services, whereof many are abolyshed by statute.

"The First is the countrey of Mc Donochoe (called Duallo,) wch hath w'hin it thre other countreis. O'Chalachan's countrey, M'Aunlief's countrey, and O'Keif's countrey. He claymeth in these countreis the gevinge of the Rodd to the chieffe Lords at their first entrie, who by receiving a whit wande at his handes, for wch they are to paie him a certen dutie, are thereby declared from thenceforthe to be Lords of those countreis. He claymeth allso that they are to *rise out* with him when he makes warre; to maintaine for him seaven and twentie Galleglasses, besides to finde him for a certen tyme, when he cometh to their countreis.

"The Seconde—The country of Muskerie, a very large countrey, wherein *five other* countreis are conteyned; he claymeth of them risinge out, the keapinge of *thirtie galleglass*, and findinge of him for a certen tyme. The Lordes of this countrey, by taking L^{rs} Patents of the Kings of England, have exempted themsealves from him, as they affyrme.

"The Third countrey is O'Sullivan Moore's. It conteyneth two hundred ploughlandes. He claymeth there the geavinge of the Rodd, the findinge of Fiftie Gallyglasses, Risinge out, and in yearely spendinge the value of £20.

"The Fourthe is O'Sullivan Beare's countrey, which conteyneth allso 160 ploughlands; he claymethe there Risinge out, the findinge of 50 Galleyglas, the geavinge of the Rodd, and to the value of £40 a yeare in spendings and refeccons.

"The Fyft is O'Donochoe Moore's countrey. It conteyneth 45 ploughlands, and it is nowe all in the Earle's handes, by Her Ma^{ts} gyft.

"The Sixt is the Lord of Cosmaignes countrey. It conteyneth 84 ploughlands. It is now all in the Earle's hands by Her Ma⁺⁺ gyft, or y° most part thereof.

"The Seaventhe is the Lord of Kerelawny's countrey, otherwise called Slight Cormak. It contayneth 35 ploughlands, whereof some are in the Ile of Valentia. He claymeth there the geaving of the Rodd, risinge out, the findinge of 40 Galleyglass, and to the value of £40 a yeare in spendinge.

"The Eight is the countrey of [Mac] Gelccuddè. It contayneth 46 ploughlands. He claymeth there risinge out, the gevinge of the Rodde, the findinge of 30 Galleyglas, and to the value of £20 a yeare in spendinge.

"The Ninthe is Mac Fynin's countrey [in Glenaraught, Co. Kerry]. It conteyneth 28 ploughlands. He claymeth the givinge of the Rodd, the finding of 15 Galleyglas, risinge out, and to the value of £24 yearly in spendinge.

"The Tenthe is the countrey of Clondonoroe. It contayneth 24 ploughlands. He claymeth theare risinge out, and it is in the Erle's hands by Her M¹ˢ Gyfte.

"The Eleaventh is the countrey of O'Donocho-Glan.* He hath there no other dutie but only six and fortie shillings fourpence of yearelie rent. The countrey contayneth 20 ploughlands.

"The Twelueth is the countrey of Clan-Dermonde. It conteyneth 28 ploughlands. He claymeth risinge out, the keepinge of 16 Galleyglas, and in yearlie spendinge to the value of £40.

"The Thirteenth is Clanlawra's [in O'Sullivan Beare's countrey]. This countrie conteyneth 32 ploughlands. It is all in the Earle's hands by Her Ma¹ˢ gift.

"The Fourteenthe in the countrey of Loughlegh, in Kerry, or of Teignitowin. It conteyneth 32 ploughlands. The Earle claymeth it to be excheated unto him for want of Heires right and legitimate.

"Moreover, the Earle hath in Chief Rents yssuing out of Barrett's countrey, by the cyttie of Corke, £11 a yeare; out of the Abbey of Killaha, £4 a year or thereabouts; out of Ballenskellig yearly as much; out of certen churchland in Beare the like some; besides he hath in demayne land, in the hundreds of Maygonie and Euraught, about his castle of the Pallace [in Kerry], his castle of

* O'Donoghue of Glenflesk, in Kerry.

Ballicarbery, castle Lough, and the Abbey of Vriett [Muckrus] three score ploughlands or thereabouts; in O'Sullivan Beare's countrey, Muskery, and Duallo, or in Donochoe's countrey, certen ploughlands; also in each of them demayne lands.

"All his Lands and Territories lieth in the counties of Desmond and Cork, and some parte in the county of Kerrie. The most parte of his land is waste and uninhabited, wch hath growne partly by the calamities of the last warres, partly by the exactions that he hath used uppon his tenants.

"It is of great consequence and importance unto our inhabitation there, that the Earle's estate be not enlarged, to the ende that after his decease, Englishe Gentlemen may be there planted, and all his dependences brought to hould onely of Her Ma'tie; unless it so weare that by Her Highnes fav^r and good likinge, *his daughter weare maried to som worthy English Gentleman*, and his lands assured after his deceasse to the heires male of their two bodies. In wch case allso I wishe the keapinge of Galleyglas, risinge out, and ceassinge of souldiers to be wholly extinguished, the spendings and refeccons to be reduced to som money rent; the gevinge *of the Rodd to be abolished*,* and all those meane Lords to hould their lands of Her Highness."

The queen, who had a strong penchant for match-making, adopted the hint here thrown out, of marrying the earl's daughter to "some worthy English gentleman." She resolved to wed the fair young girl to the younger son of Sir Valentine Brown; to which the young heiress, and her mother, the countess, were greatly opposed. The father, who appears to have played a cautious game throughout, assented, we are told, " for money."

We gather from Sir Warham St. Leger that the great objection made by the countess and the Kerry

---

* *The gevinge of the rodd to be abolished.*—The Irish chieftains received a white rod at their installation. To receive this was an emblem of their power over their clan, and of their submission to the lord paramount, by whom it was bestowed.

cousins to the match, was a want of "nobilitie of bloud" in young Nicholas Brown.* His father, Sir Valentine Brown, was at this time engaged with Sir Henry Wallop, in surveying the forfeited estates.

"The countess and the young lady came to me, and divers of the gentlemen of the country, to acquaint me of their disappointment; and some other of the best in those parts discovered gneffes by their letters. They desired that she mought be matched to some one of a noble howse." St. Leger himself says, "There is nothinge the Irishe more esteme than the nobilitie of bloud, preferringe it farre before eyther vertue or wealth; so abhorre they nothinge more than disparagement, more odious unto them than death, which well appeared in the late communicacion of mariadge between the Earle of Clyncarr's daughter and Sir Valentine Brown's younger sonne."

Sir Warham, who seems to have sympathy with this objection, on the score of "nobilitie of bloud," wrote to his old friend, Sir Thomas Norris—through whose veins flowed the best blood in England†—"Yf he like of such a matche." He declined, being otherwise disposed to bestow himself, so the young lady, or rather her friends, must be satisfied to take young Brown. Matters were in this state when Florence Mac Carthy stepped in, and, like young Lochinvar, carried off the prize, and married her in an "old

---

* *Young Master Nicholas*, afterwards Sir Nicholas Brown, of Rosse, in Kerry, married a daugh'er of O'Sullivan Beare, to whom Florence had been affianced. Sir Valentine Brown, a descendant of Sir Nicholas, was created Baron of Castlerosse, and Viscount Kenmare, the 29th of May, 1689.

† *The best blood of England.*—Sir Bernard Burke says that the Jephsons, through their descent from the Norreys, partake of the "most illustrious blood in England—of Plantagenet, De Clare, Marshall, Strongbow," &c.

broken church" in Kerry. "I verilye thinke yf it were duly examyned, he was marryed with a mass." He suspects the Earl of Clancare, as well as the countess, as privy to it. "I do thinke in my conscyence yt is a secrete practyce betwene the earl and his wyfe." The dangers to be apprehended from this union between two great Irish families are summed up thus:—

"The perills that may accrue by the match are these, viz:—
1st, The saied Florence, alias Fynian, is dyscended of the doughter of Morrys of Desmonde, uncle of the late wicked Earle of Desmonde, cousyn germain to James Fytz-Morrys, sonne now in Spaine, and likewise to Morrys of Desmonde, Traytor, also in Spaine.

" 2nd. He is alsoe cosyn germain to him that is nowe Lo: of Muskerye, whoe is sonne to the said Fynian's mother's sister.

" 3rd. He is alsoe cousyn germain to the L. Rotche that now is, whoe haith marryed the syster of the saied Fynian's mother; by which kyndred he is stronglie allyed.

"4th. He is also lyke, after the decease of Sir Owen Makertie, who is a man in yeares, and growne latelie sicklie, and thereby not likelie to lyve manye yeares, to have by Tanyshipp the goverment of the countrie of Carburye; unless he be prevented thereof by Her Ma'tie's assystinge Donnell Mack Kertie, who in right ought by Tanyshipp to have the goverment of Carburie before him, in as much as he cometh of the elder brother of the Macke Kerties of Carburye, and besides that his tytle of Tanyshipp he ought to have the countrie before Finian."

Finian, Fineen, or Florence, who stood a head and shoulders above his brethren, and whose mental endowments and education qualified him for a far higher station than that of chieftain to an Irish sept, was the eldest son of Sir Donough Mac Carthy, Lord of Carbery, whose principal residence was Kilbrittan castle, on the west coast of the county Cork. Sir Donough was succeeded, according to the laws of tanistry, not by his son, but by his brother, Sir Owen Mac Carthy; and Sir Owen Mac Carthy, whom St. Leger describes as a man of years, was succeeded, not by his son, but by Donnell na-Pipy,* the son of his eldest brother, who had died; and Donnell na-Pipy, not by his son, but by Florence, the son of the second eldest brother.

But there were more serious objections to Florence than these. Sir Thomas Norris, writing to Walsingham under date July 1st, 1558, says:—"By his own private disposition he hath always shewed himself dearly well affected and inclined to the Spaniards." Again,— "He hath by all means laboured to be interested in the *Old Head of Kinsale.*" This was the year of the Spanish Armada. For all these reasons, it was deemed prudent to arrest him.

"Him now I have according to Her High. pleasure committed, as also according to y^r later direccion in yor lp's l^{rre} of the 4th of the last moneth, have caused the countesse, Mac Finin, Teig Merrigagh, and such others as I could learne to have bene privy to the practise to be apprehended, as I could come by them; and doe not doubt but very shortly to come by the rest likewise, of the wch I understand that O'Sullivan More was the greatest forwarder and nearest of councell, though indeed all the chief of that countrey were wrought by Florence to consent thereunto, who (as I am left to understand) before the marriage, gott all their hands to firme that agreement, by a generall confirmacion of them; and soone after accomplished the said marriage in an old broken church thereby, not in such solemnity and good sort as behoved, and as order of Law and Her Mat' injunction doe require."

These allusions of Sir Thomas Norris to Spain and

* *Donnell na-Pipy* was so called, because in his time some pipes of wine were cast on shore at Burrin, and consequently were his right, being a wreck, and accordingly he had them, which, in those superstitious times, was reckoned very fortunate, the wreck being esteemed, as the Cornishman's phrase is—*God's goods.* —*Smith's History of Cork,* vol. i., p. 27.

the Old Head of Kinsale, (the most likely port for a foreign landing,) were fearfully damaging to poor Florence. Norris, no doubt, felt greatly nettled at the way in which the astute young chieftain, whom Sir George styles a Michavellian ambo-dexter, had taken him in, or thrown him off the scent:—

> "Upon the first arrivall of the sayd Florence here, coming unto me he gave no signe of any such purpose, as sithens fell out, but to give color (as semes) to his entent, and to draw me ye further from suspicion thereof, through his seeming conceived unkyndness against ye Earle, he then discovered unto me some ill dealing of the sayd Earle towards him, namely, how, that being bownd to him in great bands for assurance of certein lands, and for performance of some other condicions, amongst wch one was, that he should give him his daughter in mariage, he neverthelesse had broken with him, and therefore offered me (Yf I should so lyke) the benefitt of the forfeitures of the sayd lands: wch speaches (as sithens as I conceived) sceme to have proceded of some further matter in ye secret of his harte, those his words being so contrary to that wch he eftesoones did attempt."

For the queen to seize and imprison an Irish chieftain for marrying his own cousin, may sound rather strange to our ears, but it was not unusual in those days. Sir Walter Raleigh was imprisoned in the Tower for marrying Elizabeth, the daughter of Sir Nicholas Throckmorton. Florence remained in custody for eleven years, till the rebellion of the Earl of Tyrone spread to the south, when, for state reasons, it was deemed expedient to send him to Munster, and pit him against James Fitz-Thomas, the Sugan Earl of Desmond, and Donnell Mac Carthy, the Earl of Clancare's "base-born" son. To understand this portion of the history of Cork, we must turn to the north, where the storm arose.

The illegal kidnapping and unjust imprisonment of Hugh Roe O'Donnell, by Sir John Perrott, * led to much evil. This noble young Irish chieftain never forgot nor forgave what he endured on that occasion. It was the recollection of all he suffered while a mere youth that hastened his march, at the head of an army, to aid the Spaniards at Kinsale. Treachery in rulers is short-sighted policy. The English government feared, if the lad arrived at maturity, he would join with his brother-in-law, O'Neill, whose loyalty was strongly suspected; it was therefore resolved to remove him from the north. A ship arrives at Lough Swilly, some of the crew come ashore in a small boat, as merchantmen; they have wine to sell. The inhabitants of the neighbourhood buy, and drink to intoxication. The young chieftain comes up and is invited, with a select party, aboard. The invitation is accepted. In the midst of their conviviality, the hatches are closed, and the vessel sails out of the harbour.

The Dublin council are "rejoiced at the arrival of Hugh," and order him to be confined in a "strong stone castle,"—the Bermingham Tower. After three years' imprisonment, he attempts to escape,† but is retaken and loaded with irons, to the "grief, indignation, and despair" of his people. He tries again, and succeeds. It is night. Hugh, with Henry, and Art,

* *Sir John Perrott* was succeeded by Sir William Fitz-William, who was sworn in the 30th of June, 1588. "He had formerly been a very good governer of Ireland, but being answered at Whitehall, when he sought some reward for his services, that the government of Ireland *was a preferment, and not a service*, he ever after endeavoured to make his profit of that office."—*Cox's Hibernia Anglicana*, vol. i., p. 397.

† *Attempts to escape.*—It is the opinion of Fynes Moryson, Cox, and Leland, that the Lord Deputy Fitzwilliam was privy to this attempt. "It was evidently concerted between Fitzwilliam and Hugh, Earl of Tyrone, who buried the secret *in altitudine profunda animi.*"

the sons of O'Neill, catch their keeper napping. They manage to knock off their irons, to scale the walls, and cross the ditch, and away to the wilds of Wicklow. It is a winter's night; the snow falls heavy on their thin garments, as they cross the Red Mountain. Hugh, though the youngest, bears up manfully, but Art is exhausted, and can proceed no further. They cannot desert him, so they all lie down beneath the shelter of a rock, and send a faithful messenger to the house of Fiagh O'Byrne, of Glenmalur, * for aid. The aid is willingly afforded, but it comes too late for Art. His body lies in its white shroud of snow. They buried him where he died, and bore Hugh, more dead than alive, to the house, with his feet fearfully frost-bitten. When able to ride, he pushed on through Meath, to the banks of the Boyne, where he was met by his brother-in-law, Hugh O'Neill, who had a ferry-boat in waiting to convey him to the other side of the river; and from thence, through a dense grove, " to a fine mansion-house belonging to a distinguished English youth, † who was a particular friend of O'Neill."

It was by such base and treacherous conduct that the Irish or English governments of those days put an edge on the weapons of Irish chieftains. Sir John Norris, and his brother, Sir Thomas, the President of Munster, are now about to measure swords with these

---

* *Fiagh O'Byrne of Glenmalur.*—" Fiagh, son of Hugh, son of John, [O'Byrne] from Glenmalure, was slain in the first month of this year, having been treacherously betrayed by his relative, at the bidding of the Chief Justiciary of Ireland, Sir William Russell.—*Four Masters, A.D.*, 1597.

† *Distinguished English youth.*—The Four Masters do not give the name. The biographer of Hugh Roe O'Neill says, the mansion was at, or near, the Abbey of Mellifont, where Dervorgill, the Helen of Irish history, died.

two outlawed and desperate men. Let us see how they fare.

Sir John Norris, and a new Lord Justice, Sir William Russell, arrived in Ireland in 1595. O'Neill, who had heard of Sir John Norris' fame as a general, sent to O'Donnell to assemble his forces at an appointed rendezvous. *"When the Lord Justice* heard they were both in readiness to meet him, he remained in Dublin for that time."*

"A.D. 1595.—For some time after this the English did not dare to bring any army into Ulster, except one hosting which was made by Sir John Norris and his brother, Sir Thomas Norris, the President of the two provinces of Munster, with the forces of Munster and Meath, to proceed into Ulster. They marched to Newry, and passed from thence towards Armagh. When they had proceeded near half way, they were met by the Irish, who proceeded to annoy, shoot, pierce, and spear them, so that they did not suffer them either to sleep or rest quietly for the space of twenty-four hours. They were not permitted to advance forward one foot further, and their chiefs were glad to escape with their lives to Newry, leaving behind them many men, horses, arms, and valuable things. The general, Sir John Norris, and his brother, Sir Thomas, were wounded on this occasion. It was no ordinary *gap of danger* for them to go into the province after this."

Soon after this, Sir Thomas Norris returned to Cork to his duties of Lord President, where he hung Conor

---

* *Lord Justice*, Sir William Russell, arrived in Dublin the 31st of January, 1594. He was the youngest son of Francis, Earl of Bedford.

O'Brien, (in 1596) who was taken preying in Coill Mhor, or the Great Wood, near Charleville.

The next year a new Lord Deputy was sent to Ireland, in the person of Lord Borough. He is described as a man "almost wholly ignorant of the military art." He, notwithstanding, deprived Sir John Norris—whom Camden styles "Vir sane magnus, et inter maximus nostræ gentis hoc ævo duces celebrandus,"—of the office of Commander-in-chief in Ireland, which affront, he adds, together with the disappointment of the chief government, which he knew he merited, and earnestly expected, and the many baffles Tyrone had put upon him, broke his heart. Sir John's great success, previous to his meeting O'Neill, had been such, that it was currently reported he had sold himself to the devil, who appears to have forsaken him in the *gap of danger*. O'Sullivan Beare concludes that O'Neill had not only defeated General Norris,* "*sed ipsum etiam diabolum.*" The Four Masters make the following entry of his death:—

"A.D. 1597.—Sir John Norris, who had been general of the queen's army in France † and Ireland, was deprived of his office by the new Lord Justice who had last arrived in Ireland, and went to Munster, where he remained with his brother, Sir Thomas Norris, who had been previously President (under him) of Munster for the period of twelve years. John was seized with a

---

* "General Norris pertissimum Anglorum imperatorum omni pugnandi apparatu superiorem *sed ipsum etiam diabolum*, qui illi expacto fuisse opitulatus creditur viceret."—*Hist. Cathol. Iber. Compd.*, tom. iii., l. 3, c. x.

† *General of the queen's army in France.*—More correctly in Holland. It was he who placed the crown of Portugal on the brow of John of Braganza, by whose descendants it is still worn.

disease, and died suddenly* in the autumn of this year, and Sir Thomas was the heir to his property. Sir Thomas continued in the same office after the death of his brother."

The Annals of Ireland record, under the same year, 1597, the deaths of the Earl of Kildare, the Lord Justice, and his wife's brother. The Lord Justice fell in with a troop of O'Neill's horse, on the banks of the Abhainn-Mor, or Blackwater, where he was wounded. He was carried in a litter to Newry, where he died. The sword of state was therefore entrusted to the Lord Chancellor, the Chief Justice of the Queen's Bench, and Sir Robert Gardiner, till a new Chief Justice or Deputy was appointed. Thomas, Earl of Ormond was appointed Generalissimo, who concluded an armistice with O'Neill. When the armistice concluded, Marshal Bagnell, whose sister had eloped with and married O'Neill, met this redoubtable chieftain between Lough Erne and Dundalk, and fell, mortally wounded, at the famous battle of the Yellow Ford.† It was fought on the 10th of August, 1598. The account of this battle, in which the English were defeated, spread like wildfire through the South, and kindled a warlike flame in the bosom of James Fitz-Thomas, the Sugan Earl of Desmond, who considered himself the legitimate heir to the title and vast estates of his outlawed uncle, Garrett. He and his brother John opened the campaign in Connello. Sir Thomas Norris, President of Munster, was lying at Kilmallock. The Earl of

---

* *Died suddenly.*—O'Sullivan Beare tells a story of Sir John and the devil, which Doctor O'Donovan says would do credit to the author of Doctor Faustus.

† *Yellow Ford.*—Beal an-atha-buidhe, *i.e.,* mouth of the Yellow Ford.

Ormond, hearing of the sudden rising, hastened, with his troops, to join the president. The Irish leader, nothing daunted, marched upon Kilmallock. "Upon seeing them, the lords, (*i.e*, the earl and the president), agreed to avoid meeting them, and turned off towards Magh Ealla,"* now Mallow. The Geraldines "persued them to the gate of Magh Ealla" and dared them to battle, saying, they never had a better opportunity. Notwithstanding, "the two great men" determined, that the one, Sir Thomas Norris, should repair to Cork, and the other to the territory of the Butler.

We conclude that this piece of poltroonery was arranged by Ormond, the Generalissimo of the queen's forces in Ireland. He left Marshal Bagnell to fight the battle of the Yellow Ford, while he went preying and spoiling in Leix, and in Leix he left the post of danger to his brother, James, who was slain by Brian O'More. The earl was informed there were only a few to guard the territory. He ordered his brother, James, to enter the pass before him. It was Sunday morning. James was loath to go; but set out at the earl's command. He fell mortally wounded. Brian O'More died soon after of his wounds. Brian was succeeded by Owny, the son of Rory O'Moore, who had his revenge on Ormond. The story is told in the *Pacata Hibernia*. Sir George Carew, the new lord president of Munster, is passing through Kilkenny, on his way to Cork. Here he meets Ormond, who tells him he has arranged a parley with Owny Mac Rory O'Moore. The place of parley is Corronneduff, eight

---

* *Magh Ealla*, the "Plain of the Ealla." The country higher up the Blackwater is called Dhuhallow, or the Black Allo. The river above Kanturk, to its source, is still called the Allo. We have the "Allo Bridge" at Freemount.

miles from Kilkenny. The earl asks the president to accompany him; Carew consents. They meet O'Moore on a heath in the midst of a bog, surrounded with shrubs. Behind the shrubs lie a number of bonnoughts and skipping kerne. Ormond asks to see "that infamous Jesuit, Archer." We suspect that Ormond went to the parley with the design of arresting Archer. The churchman comes forward, and is called a "traitor," and accused of making rebels, under the guise of religion. The Irish are indignant, and rally round their priest. The earl's party are surrounded. "We were environed, and stood as if we had been in a fair." Sir George Carew and the Earl of Thomond, who was of the party, turned their horses' heads for flight. Ormond does the same, but is seized, and unhorsed. "His lordship was in a moment drawn from his horse. We had more hanging on than is creditably to be believed; but our horses were strong, and by that means did break through them, tumbling down those that were before and behind; and thanks be to God, we escaped the push of their pikes, which they freely bestowed, and the flinging of their skeins, without any hurt, saving that I, the Earl of Thomond, received with a pike, a wound in the back." The Earl of Ormond remained for sometime a prisoner in the hands of O'Moore. *

This Owny Mac Rory O'Moore was employed by O'Neill to fan the rebellion which had broken out

---

* *A prisoner in the hands of O'Moore.*—It is thought he was converted to the Catholic faith, (during his incarceration,) by Archer, the Jesuit. Ormond lived to the age of 82, and at the close of his life became blind. He was succeeded by his nephew, Sir Walter Butler, the 11th Earl, styled "Walter of the Rosaries," who was also a Catholic. Walter was succeeded by his grandson, James, styled "the Great Duke of Ormond."

in the South. Fynes Moryson mentions him and Captain Tyrrell, as deputies employed "to trouble the province of Munster."

"After the defeat at the Blackwater, Tyrone sent Ony Mac Rory O'More, and one Captain Tyrél, (of *English* race, but a bold and unnatural enemy to his country and the English,) to trouble the province of Munster, against whom Sir *Thomas Norris*, Lord President, opposed himself; but as soon as he, upon necessary occasions, had withdrawn his forces to *Cork*, many of the *Munster* men now, first about *October*, 1598, broke into rebellion, and joined themselves with *Tyrone's* said forces, spoiled the country, * burnt the villages, and pulled down the houses and castles of the *English*, against whom (especially the female sex,) they committed all abominable outrages.

"And now they raised James Fitz-Thomas, to be Earl of *Desmond*, (which title had, since the wars of Desmond, been suppressed,) with condition that (forsooth,) he should be vassal to O'Neal. The Munster rebellion broke out like a lightening, for in one month's space, almost all the Irish were in rebellious arms — the *English* were murdered, or stript and banished. Thus having inflamed *Munster* with the fire of rebellion, and leaving this sedition to be cherished and increased by this new Earl of *Desmond*, and other rebels of that province, the Ulster forces returned back to Tyrone. The infection which *Munster* men have drawn from the corrupted party in rebellion

---

* *Spoiled the country.*—"At this time they offered and sold at their camp, a stripper, or cow-in-calf for six-pence; a brood-mare for three pence, and the best hog for a penny; and these bargains were offered and proclaimed in every camp in which they were.—*Four Masters*, 1598.

did more and more spread itself, so as the old practices, long held by the arch-traitor *Tyrone* to induce them to a revolt, now fully attained their wished effect, to the working whereof, in the hearts of the seditious, there wanted not many strong motives, as the hatred which those *Geraldines* bear to those undertakers, (of whom I formerly spoke in *Desmond's* war,) which possessed their ancestors' lands."

CHAPTER—XVI.

THE POET SPENSER.

ONE of the undertakers so burnt out, was Edmund Spenser, the poet. He came to Ireland, as we have already stated, in 1580, as secretary to Lord Grey. He received a grant of three thousand acres of the forfeited lands of the Earl of Desmond, with the castle of Kilcolman, near Doneraile, in the county Cork. Here he wrote his "View of the State of Ireland," the "Faerie Queene," and "Colin Clouts come Home againe." Here he was visited by his friend Sir Walter Raleigh. The poet represents himself as a shepherd seated at the "foote of Mole," (the Ballyhoura mountain,) when Raleigh comes up, with whom he does not appear acquainted—but this is a feint, for Spenser and Raleigh came to Ireland together—

> "One day, quoth he, I sat (as was my trade)
> Under the foote of Mole, that mountain hore,
> Keeping my sheepe amongst the cooly shade
> Of the greene alders by the Mullaes shore;
> There a strange shepheard chaunst to find me out;
> Whether allured with my pipes delight,
> Whose pleasing sound yshrilled far about,
> Or thither led by chaunce, I know not right:
> Whom when I asked from what place he came,
> And how he hight, himself he did ycleepe,
> The Sheppard of the Ocean by name,
> And said he came far from the main-sea deepe."

Raleigh, the shepherd of the ocean, sits down in the shade beside the shepherd of the hills, and plains, and running streams, and provokes him to "plaie a pleasant fit," and in the end is so charmed and excited, that he takes the pipe to play himself :—

> "And when he heard the musicke which I made,
> He found himselfe full greatly pleased at it:
> Yet, æmuling my pipe, he tooke in hand
> My pipe, before that æmuled of many;
> And plaid thereon; (for well that skill he cond;)
> Himselfe as skilfull in that art as any.
> He pip'd, I sung; and, when he sung, I piped;
> By change of turnes, each making other mery;
> Neither envying other, nor envied,
> So piped we, until we both were weary."

During this pleasant interchange, or rivalry, a bonie swaine, named Cuddy, comes up, and asks Colin for some hymne or morall laie, or carol made to praise his loved lasse. The poet thus replies,

> "Nor of my love, nor of my lasse (quoth he,)
> I then did sing, as then occasion fell:
> For love had me forlorne, forlorne of me,
> That made me in that desert choose to dwell.
> But of my river Bregog's love I soong,
> Which to the shiny Mulla he did beare,
> And yet doth beare, and ever will, so long
> As water doth within his bancks appeare.

The description of the loves and union of these two mountain streams, the Bregog and the Mulla, and the wrath of father Mole, "that mountain hore," when he learns it, is inimitable. The old man or mountain had resolved to wed his daughter, Mulla, who is "fresh as flowre of May," to the Allo, or Blackwater—"Broadwater called farre"—a richer and more important river :—

> "Full faine she loved, and was belov'd full faine
> Of her own brother river, Bregog hight,
> So hight because of this deceitfull traine,
> Which he with Mulla wrought to win delight.
> But her old sire, more carefull of her good,
> And meaning her much better to preferre,
> Did think to match her with the neighbour flood,
> Which Allo hight, Broad-water called farre:
> And wrought so well with his continual paine,
> That he that river for his daughter wonne:
> The dowre agreed, the day assigned plaine,
> The place appointed where it should be doone.
> Nath'lesse the nymph her former liking held;
> For love will not be drawne but must be ledde;
> And Bregog did so well her fancie weld
> That her good will he got her first to wedde.
> But for her father sitting still on hie,
> Did warily still watch which way she went,
> And eke from far observ'd with jealous eie,
> Which way his course the wanton Bregog bent;
> Him to deceive, for all his watchfull ward,
> The wily lover did devise this slight:
> First into many parts his streame he shar'd,
> That, whilst the one was watcht, the other might
> Passe unespide to meete her by the way;
> And then, besides, those little streames so broken
> He under ground so closely did convey,
> That of their passage doth appear no token,
> Till they into the Mullaes water slide."

But father Mole has his revenge on the sly Bregog:—*

> "Yet not so secret, but it was descride,
> And told her father by a shepheard's boy,
> Who, wondrous wroth, for that so foule despight,
> In great revenge did roll down from his hill
> Huge mightie stones, the which encomber might
> His passage, and his water courses spill.
> So of a river, which he was of old,
> He none was made, but scattered all to nought;
> And, lost emong those rocks into him rold,
> Did lose his name: so deare his love he bought."

* *Sly Bregog.*—Spenser says it was called Bregog "because of this deceitful traine," or course. *Breag*, in Irish, means "a lie," and *breagan*, "deceptive."

We have the parish of Bregog, or Bregogue, in the barony of Orrery and Kilmore, and Bregogue castle, but the river which has given name to both, has disappeared. Whether this has resulted from the wrath of father Mole, or the drying or drainage of the soil, we must leave for the present undecided.

Spenser sent a copy of this poem to Raleigh, with the following letter. As the letter was written at his house at Kilcolman, it merits a place in the history of the county. —

> To the Right Worthy and Noble Sir Walter Raleigh, Captain of Her Majesties Guard, Lord Warden of the Stanneries, and Lieutenant of the County of Cornwall.
>
> SIR,
>
> That you may see that I am not alwaies ydle, though not greatly well occupied, nor altogether undutiful, though not precisely officious, I make you present of this simple Pastorall, unworthie of your higher conceipt for the meannesse of the stile, but agreeing with the truth in circumstance and matter. The which I humbly beseech you to accept in part paiment of the infinite debt in which I acknowledge myselfe bounden unto you for your singular favours, and sundrie good turnes shewed me at my late being in England; and with your good countenance protect against the malice of evill mouthes, which are alwaies wide open to carpe at and misconstrue my simple meaning. I pray continually for your happiness. From my house of Kilcolman, the 27. of December, 1591.
>
> Yours ever humbly,
>
> ED. SP.

Spenser could never write as he has done of our rivers and mountains, if he did not love the country—we do not say the people—of his adoption. He calls it "as beautiful and sweet a country as any under heaven." When describing the "Sposalls betwixt the

Medway and the Thames," he would fain introduce our Irish rivers, and he does it with a hearty appreciation which is positively refreshing in an Englishman:—

> "Ne thence the Irishe rivers absent were,
> Sith no lesse famous than the reste they bee,
> And joyne in neighbourhood of kingdome nere,
> Why should they not likewise in love agree,
> And joy likewise this solemne day to see?
> They saw it all, and present were in place:
> Though I then all, according their degree,
> Cannot recount, nor tell their hidden race,
> Nor read the salvage countries through which they pace.
> There was the Liffy rolling downe the lea;
> The sandy Slane; the stony Aubrion;
> The spacious Shenan, spreading like a sea;
> The pleasant Boyne; the fishy fruitful Ban;
> Swift Awniduff, which of the English man,
> Is cal'de Black-water;* and the Liffar deep;
> Sad Trowis, that once his people over-ran;
> Strong Allo tombling from Slewlagher steep;
> And Mulla mine, whose waves I whilom taught to weep.
> There also was the wide embayed Mayre;
> The pleasant Bandon cround with many a wood;
> The spreading Lee, that like an island fayre,
> Encloseth Corke with his divided flood."

If by jolly Hobbinal, and all the shepherd's nation, he intended to represent the Irish nation, the poet must have been under the erroneous impression that he was as much beloved as he was hated.† Colin has just returned from England:

> "Colin my life, how great a losse
> Had all the shepeard's nation by thy lacke,
> Whilest thou wast hence all dead in dole did lie.

---

* *Blackwater.*—This river is called the "Great River" *Abhainn Mhor*, by the Four Masters. It flows for several miles between the counties of Tyrone and Armagh.

† *As he was hated.*—Cromwell writing to the council in favor of William Spenser, the poet's grandson, says, "his grandfather was that Spenser, who by his writings, touching the reduction of the Irish to civility, brought on him the *odium* of that nation.

> The woods were heard to waile full many a sythe,
> And all the birds with silence to complaine;
> The fields with faded flowers did seem to mourne,
> And all their flocks from feeding to refrain.
> But now both woods and fields and floods revive,
> Since thou art come, their course of merriment,
> That us late dead hast made again alive."

If Spenser had only written poetry, or had *never* written his "View of the State of Ireland," his memory and genius would be revered in this country. Even Ware, who edited the work, says, "It was to be wished that some passages in his View of the state of Ireland had been tempered with more moderation." It was Spenser's impression that this country could never be reformed or civilised till the wretched inhabitants had been driven by English soldiers into the woods and morasses, and left there to starve. This idea had been broached in State Papers fifty years before Spenser wrote his work.* We are happy to reflect that this work has not the merit of being original. We doubt that the poet's mind was capable of originating anything so fiendlike or ghoulish; it was bad enough in him to adopt it. His own experience of what the people suffered during the Desmond rebellion should have softened his heart. It is with unmingled regret that we quote the following passage. Would we could blot it out of the page of Irish history.

"The end will, I assure me, be very short, and much sooner than can be in so great a trouble as it seemeth hoped for, although there should none of them fall by the sword, or be slain by the soldier, yet thus being kept from manurance, and their cattle from running abroad, by this hard restraint, they would quickly consume themselves, and devour one another. The proof whereof I saw suffi-

---

* *Wrote this work.*—Spenser wrote his View of the state of Ireland, in 1596. It lay for many years in MS., in Archbishop Usher's library, till published by Sir James Ware, in 1633. It was dedicated to Lord Wentworth, Lord Deputy.

ciently exampled in these late wars of Munster; for, notwithstanding that the same was a most rich and plentiful country, full of corn and cattle, that you would have thought they should have been able to stand long, yet ere one year and a half they were brought to such wretchedness, as that any stony heart would have rued the same. Out of every corner of the woods and glens they came creeping forth upon their hands, for their legs could not bear them; they looked like anatomies of death, they spoke like ghosts crying out of their graves; and if they found a plot of water-cresses or shamrocks, there they flocked as to a feast for the time, yet not able long to continue there withal; that in short space, there were none almost left, and a most populous and plentiful country suddenly left void of man and beast; yet sure in all that war there perished not many by the sword, but all by the extremity of famine, which they themselves had wrought." — *View of the state of Ireland.*

How any man could describe a state of things which he says would have melted a "stony heart," *in order to show how the thing could be done again*, is almost incredible. His heart must have been iron and not stone.

Two years after writing this book, the poet was burned out of Kilcolman Castle, one of his children perishing in the flames. A year after this, in 1599, he died of starvation, in London, for "lake of bred," as Ben Johnson says.

It is evident that Spenser made enemies in England by his works. In his letter to Raleigh from Kilcolman, he speaks of the "malice of evil mouths, which are always wide open to carpe at and misconstrue his simple meaning." He refers to the "Faerie Queene," which he had lately published in London. He seems to have apprehended something of this kind, for in dedicating the poem to Sir Walter Raleigh, he says, "knowing how doubtfully all allegories may be construed, and this book of mine, which I have entitled the " Faerie Queene," being a continued allegory, or dark conceit, I have thought it good, as well for avoiding of jealous opinions and misconstructions, as also for your better light in reading thereof, to discover unto you the general intention and meaning." He then informs us that the book "is to fashion a gentleman or noble person in virtuous and gentle discipline."

One of his modes of doing this is by instituting a comparison between the two churches. This comparison runs through the whole book. It is Dryden's milk-white fawn and impure panther reversed. The " Faerie Queene " is generally as intangible and shadowy a personage as Prince Arthur himself, but she now and then comes out with all the distinct lineaments of the Queen of England. He is thought, on the other hand, to have represented Mary, Queen of Scots, under the character of the false but fair Duessa. It is difficult to say whether the following lines are intended as a description of the rival queens or rival churches. We doubt if these destinctions were well defined in the poet's mind.

> "So doubly lov'd of ladies unlike faire,
> The one seeming such, the other such indeede,
> One day in doubt I cast for to compare
> Whether in beauties glorie did exceede;
> A rosy girlonde was the victor's meede.
> Both seemde to win, and both seemde won to be;
> So hard the discorde was to be agreede.
> Fralissa was as faire, as faire mote bee,
> And ever false Duessa seemed as faire as shee.
> The wicked witch now seeing all this while,
> The doubtful baullance equally to sway,
> What not by right, she cast to win by guile;

> And, by her hellish science raised streight way.
> A foggy mist that overcast the day,
> And a dull blast that breathing on her face,
> Dimmed her former beauties shining ray,
> And with foule ugly forme did her disgrace:
> Then was she fayre alone, when none was faire in place."

If James VI. of Scotland, now on the point of ascending the throne of England, believed the following lines as intended to describe his mother, Mary, Queen of Scots, (and State Papers lead to this conclusion,) neither he nor his friends could countenance the poet :—

> "Thensforth I tooke Duessa for my dame,
> And in the witch unweeting joyd a long time;
> Ne ever wist, but that she was the same:
> Till on a day (that day is everie prime,
> When witches wont do penance for their crime,)
> I chaunst to see her in her proper hew,
> Bathing her selfe in origane and thyme:
> A filthy foule old woman I did vew,
> That ever to have toucht her I did deadly rew.

Shakespeare, in his "Midsummer Night's Dream," speaks of the rival queens more like a gentle knight and poet. The following description is intended for the Scottish queen :—

> OBERON.—"My gentle Puck come hither, thou remember'st
> Since once I sat upon a promontory,
> And heard a mermaid on a dolphin's back,
> Uttering such dulcet and harmonious breath,
> That the rude sea grew civil at her song;
> And certain stars shot madly from their spheres,
> To hear the sea-maid's music."

Nothing can be more beautiful than the following description of our maiden queen, although it contains none of the fulsome and extravagant flattery of Spenser :—

> "Flying between the cold moon and the earth,
> Cupid all arm'd. A certain aim he took
> At a fair vestal throned by the west;
> And loos'd his love-shaft smartly from his bow,
> As it should pierce a hundred thousand hearts;
> But I might see young Cupid's fiery shaft,
> Quench'd in the chaste beams of the wat'ry moon,
> And the imperial *vot'ress* passed on,
> In maiden meditation, fancy-free.
> Yet mark'd I where the bolt of Cupid fell:
> It fell upon *a little western flower—
> Before, milk-white; now purple with love's wound.*

The "milk-white flower, now purple with love's wound," we take to be Mary, purpled with the blood of Darnley, and with the blood of Norfolk, and with her own blood. Love, unhappy love, had wrought all this ruin. But how superior this description to Spenser's picture of that most fair, amiable, and erring princess.

The rising sun has more worshippers than the setting sun. Elizabeth's ministers were at this time carrying on a private correspondence with James VI. of Scotland, and would not be likely to cherish the man who had villified his mother. But the poet may have injured himself just as much by his foolish laudations of Lord Grey—his Talus with the iron flail—who, notwithstanding his zeal in the massacre of the Spaniards and Italians at Smerwick, was in the end attainted of treason. His praises of this nobleman must have nettled Elizabeth. He fell between two thrones.

Of Spenser's genius as a poet there can be but one opinion. It was of the very highest order. Kings and queens and politicians may have been frowning when he died, but, as Camden says, the Muses were smiling at his birth:— "Musis adeo arridentibus natus, ut omnes Anglicos superioris ævi Poetas, ne Chaucero quidem concive excepto, superaret." Spenser sent a portion of the "Faerie Queene" to Sir Philip Sydney, in manuscript. After reading a few stanzas, he ordered his steward to give the bearer fifty pounds. After reading a few more, he directed him to double it. He read on, and told him to make it two hundred, but added,—" Prithee, be expeditious, or I shall give him my whole estate." When Essex heard—too late —of the poet's distress in London, he sent him twenty pieces, which Spenser refused, saying he had no time to spend them.

Did he intend this as a reproof for previous neglect? Spenser was as proud as he was poor. To beg he was ashamed, as we may conclude from the following lines in " Mother Hubberd's Tale : "—

> " Most miserable man, whom wicked fate
> Hath brought to court to sue for that which
> Few have found, and many a one has missed.
> Full little knowest thou, that hast not tried,
> What hell it is, in suing long to bide:
> To lose good days, that might be better spent;
> To waste long nights in pensive discontent;
> To speed to-day, to be put back to-morrow;
> To feed on hope, to pine with fear and sorrow;
> To have thy princess' grace, *yet want her peers;*
> To have thy asking, yet wait for many years;
> To fret thy soul with crosses and with cares;
> To eat thy heart thro' comfortless despairs;
> To fawn, to crouch, to wait, to ride, to run;
> To spend, to give, to want, *to be undone.*"

The queen had ordered that Spenser should get £100 for one of his poems. "What!" exclaimed the Lord Treasurer Burleigh, "all this for a single song?"

"Then give him what is reason," replied Elizabeth. The poet waited for some time, and got nothing, when he wrote her majesty the following lines, which procured the poet his money and the peer a rebuke.

> "I was promised on a time
> To have '*reason*' for my rhyme;
> From that time unto this season,
> I received nor rhyme nor reason."

The poet left a widow and four children—three sons and a daughter. We learn from the "Amoretti" that his wife's name was Elizabeth. The following lines do him high honor as a son, a subject, and a husband:

> "Most happy letters! fram'd by skilfull trade
> With which that happy name was first desynd,
> The which three times thrise happy hath me made,
> With guifts of body, fortune, and of mind.
> The first my being to me gave by kind,
> From mother's womb deriv'd by dew descent;
> The second is my sovereigne queene most kind,
> That honour and large richesse to me lent:
> The third, my love, my lifo's last ornament
> By whom my spirit out of dust was raysed:
> To speak her prayse and glory excellent,
> Of all alive most worthy to be praysed.
> Ye three Elizabeths! for ever live
> That three such graces did unto me give."

If we can receive a lover's description of his bride, she was very beautiful, though but a "countrey lasse," and as good as she was fair. We have the following description in the "Faerie Queene:"

> "Yet was she certes but a countrey lasse,
> Yet she all other countrey lasses farre did passe:
> So farre as did the daughter of the day
> All other lights in light excell;
> So farre doth she in beautiful array
> Above all other lasses bear the bell,
> No lesse in virtue that beseemes her well

Doth she exceede the rest of all her race;
For which the graces, that here wont to dwell,
Have for more honour brought her to this place,
And graced her so much to be another grace."

We are disposed to conclude she was a Cork woman, for the poet, on his wedding morning, invokes the "scaly trouts" of *Mulla* to be present,

"To help to decke her and to help to sing,
That all the woods may answer and their eccho ring."

It is not improbable that the marriage was celebrated in the city of Cork, of which the poet was sheriff in 1597.

"Tell me, ye merchant daughters, did ye see
So fayre a creature in your town before?
Her goodly eyes, lyke saphyres shining bright,
Her forehead ivory white,
Her lips lyke cherries charming men to byte."

Spenser's widow, who seems to have regained the Kilcolman estate, was married a second time in 1603, to Roger Seckerstone. We cannot say whether it was her interest in the Kilcolman property, or her beauty which charmed Seckerstone "to byte."

Sylvanus, the poet's eldest son, who felt that his rights had been compromised by this marriage, petitioned the Lord Chancellor—the original petition is in the Rolls Office, Dublin—who issued an order for an inquisition. The inquisition was taken in Mallow, in the county of Cork, the 7th of August, 1611.

"The said Jurors doe finde and present that the p. te or p. econ (part or portion) of a seignory granted by these patents from the late Queene Elizabeth unto Edmond Spencer, late of Kilcolmayn, in the Countie of Corke, Esquire, deceased, after his death descended unto Sylvanus Spencer, his sone and heire, whoe doth nowe possesse and enjoy the same, in manner and forme as followeth, viz. :—The

THE KILCOLMAN PROPERTY. 309

said Sylvanus Spencer is seized in his demeasne as of fee of the Castell of Kilcolmane, with ccc. acres of land p. cell of the said seignory, being the demeasne lands of the same."

The "Search," or "Inquisition," goes on to say that other portions of the property were "set and leased to Edward Henton, who had 400 acres; David Lowes, who had a house and 100 acres; Geffrey Hoorde, who had 100 acres; John Liech, who had a house and 100 acres; John Ridgwaie, who had 400 acres; John Roche, who had a house and 100 acres."

The Inquisition goes on to say, that " The said Jurors doe finde that the two ploughlandes, called Ballyellish Ardgilbert and Ardadame, containing VI. c. [600] acres of land, or thereabouts, part of the seignory of Kilcolemane, were evicted by Nicholas Shyname from the said Edmond Spencer, before Sr Thomas Norreis, Knight; Sr Robert Gardener, Knight, and other Commissioners for the Province of Munster. And that upon the said order an abatement of the rente hath been given to Sylvanus Spencer, viz.:—£VI VIs. VIIId. The said Jurors doe also finde that John Power, of Doneraile, doth withholde the ploughlande and half of Carrigyus and Keylme Enyth, containing ccc. acres of lande, or thereabouts, from the said Sylvanus Spencer, by what title we know not; and we also finde that the said Sylvanus Spencer hath noe abatement of rent for the said ccc. acres of lande."

Sylvanus Spenser married the eldest daughter of David Nagle,* of Monanimy, in the barony of Fermoy, and county of Cork, by his wife Ellen Roche, daughter of William Roche, of Ballyhowly. Sylvanus died in 1638.

Lawrence Spenser, of Bandon, was the poet's second son. He died somewhere about 1654. He is not known to have married, or to have left descendants.

Peregrine Spenser, the poet's youngest son, was married, though we do not know to whom. It is

* *David Nagle.*—The mother of the statesman Edmund Burke, was a Nagle, the grand-niece of Sylvanus Spenser's wife. The orator may have been called *Edmund* after the poet. He passed a portion of his childhood in the parish of Monanimy.

stated that his eldest brother, Sylvanus, "in order to prefer him in marriage," made over on him the lands of Renny, near Kilcolman. He seems to have run through this estate. In a MS. in Trinity College, Dublin, he is described, on the 4th of May, 1641, as a protestant, resident in the barony of Fermoy, and " so impoverished by the troubles as to be unable to pay his debts." He left one son, Hugolin.

Catherine Spenser, the poet's daughter, is mentioned by Bentham, who places her between Sylvanus and Lawrence, and marries her to William Wiseman, of Bandon, but assigns her no descendants.

Edmund Spenser, the eldest son of Sylvanus, or the eldest son of the eldest son, (who, we conclude, was called after his grandfather, the poet,) had his estates erected into the manor of Kilcolman, by royal letters patent, on February 18, 1638. This was done to remedy defective titles. He died unmarried and without issue.

William Spenser, the second son of Sylvanus, became heir to his brother's estate, of which he was afterwards deprived. The following letter of Oliver Cromwell, respecting the restoration of the estate, and dated Whitehall, 27th of March, 1657, will be read with interest:—

"TO OUR RIGHT TRUSTY AND RIGHT WELL-BELOVED, OUR COUNCIL IN IRELAND:—

" A petition hath been exhibited unto us by William Spenser, setting forth that being but seven years old at the beginning of the rebellion in Ireland, [1641], he repaired with his mother (his father being then dead) to the city of Cork, and during the rebellion continued in the English quarters. That he never bore arms or acted against the Commonwealth of England. That his grandfather, Edmund Spenser, and his father, were both Protestants, from whom an estate of lands in the barony of Fermoy, in the county of Cork, descended on him, which, during the rebellion, yielded him little or nothing towards his relief. That the said estate hath been lately given out to the soldiers in satisfaction of their arrears, only upon the account of his professing the Popish religion, which, since his coming to years of discretion, he hath, as he professes, utterly renounced. That his grandfather was that Spenser, who, by his writings touching the reduction of the Irish to civility, brought on him the odium of that nation; and for these works, and his other good services, Queen Elizabeth conferred on him the estate which the said William Spenser now claims. We have also been informed that the gentleman is of civil conversation, and that the extremity his wants have brought him to have not prevailed over him to put him upon indirect or evil practices for a livelihood. And if, upon inquiry, you shall find his case to be such, we judge it just and reasonable, and do therefore desire and authorize you that he be forthwith restored to his estate, and that reprisal lands be given to the soldiers elsewhere; in the doing whereof our satisfaction will be greater by the continuation of that estate to the issue of his grandfather, for whose eminent deserts and services to the Commonwealth that estate was first given him.

" We rest your loving friend,

" OLIVER P."

The estate was restored, but not till after the restoration of the Stuarts. In July 31, 1678, he obtained a royal grant of other property, to the extent of nearly two thousand acres, in the counties Galway and Roscommon, among which was Ballinasloe, so famous for its fair. At the Revolution he joined King William, and it is stated in a representation of his claims, drawn up about 1700, that he had rendered important public services, by acting as a guide to General Ginckell, (afterwards Earl of Athlone) in his military operations in the South. For his zeal in this way he lost 300 herd of black cattle and 1,500 sheep, had his house plundered, and his only son wounded in twenty places "by the Irish army." In consideration of his services and sufferings, William III., in 1697, granted him the forfeited lands of Renny, which had belonged to his cousin Hugolin, who had taken the opposite side.* His title to these lands was disputed in 1700 by the Board of Trustees, appointed to determine the validity of all such grants. He went to England, to urge his suit, was introduced to the poet, Congreve, who introduced him to Montague, afterwards Earl of Halifax, then at the head of the Treasury, by whose means the grant was ratified.

This William Spenser (second son of Sylvanus) left, by his wife Barbara, a son, Nathaniel,† and a daughter, Susannah, of whom nothing is known, except that she is mentioned in her brother's will. We conclude that this Nathaniel was the son who received the twenty wounds from the Irish who made the raid on his father's sheep and black cattle. We find this son, in November, 1697, uniting with his father in executing a mortgage on their estates in Cork, Galway, and Roscommon, for £2100; and in February, 21, 1716, in selling the lands of Ballinasloe, to Frederick Trench, ancestor of the present possessor, the Earl of Clancarty.

This Nathaniel Spenser, son of William, son of Sylvanus, eldest son of the poet, or in other words Nathaniel, great-grandson of the poet, was styled

* *Opposite side*—Hugolin, united with his Catholic relatives the Nagles, who were the zealous supporters of James II.

† *Nathaniel Spenser.*—A third son of Sylvanus Spenser, and grandson of the poet, was so called. He was a clergyman of the Established Church. He married Margaret Deane, and died in 1669, intestate, and without issue, at Ballycannon, in the county Waterford.

Spenser of Renny, which appears to have been the only property that remained in the family. His wife bore the poetical name of Rosamond. He died in 1734, leaving four children, Edmund, Nathaniel, John, and Barbara.

Edmund, the eldest son, married Anne, the daughter of John Freeman, of Ballymague, in this county.

Of his brothers Nathaniel and John, or of his sister Barbara, we have no reliable information. It is probable they died unmarried, at the old family residence at Renny. Mr. O'Flanagan, in his " Guide to the Blackwater," says the last of the Spensers, of whom we have an authentic account, lived at Renny, or Rinny, and had contracted an intimacy with his housekeeper from which she inferred that he meant to marry her, and that this woman, who was also employed by her master as his barber, cut his throat while shaving him on the morning of the day on which he was to have been married to a lady in the neighbourhood. " In the small antique dwelling at Renny is pointed out the room in which she did the deed."

This would be a tragic winding up of the poet's immediate descendants, but there was a later than he, "*Edmund Spenser, of Mallow*," probably the nephew of the murdered man, and the son of Edmund Spenser who married Anne Freeman. He died in Mallow about 1790, leaving this sad epitaph for his tomb:—

" HERE LIES THE BODY OF EDMUND SPENSER,
GREAT-GREAT-GREAT GRANDSON OF THE POET SPENSER,
UNFORTUNATE FROM HIS CRADLE TO HIS GRAVE "

Hearing that he was buried in the graveyard of Mallow Church, I spent some time in seeking for a tomb-stone containing such an epitaph, but without success, although informed by two or three persons that they had seen the name of Spenser upon one of the stones. But very many of the inscriptions stand in need of the friendly chisel of some "*Old Mortality.*"

This must be the Spenser mentioned by a writer in the " Anthologia Hibernica," in 1793, as having resided a few years before in Mallow, and as having been "in possession of an original portrait of the poet, which he valued so highly as to refuse £500 which had been offered for it, with many curious records and papers concerning his venerable ancestor."

Doctor Todd speaks of a daughter of this Edmund Spenser of Mallow, as having married a Wm. Burns, who held some office in the English custom-house. She, too, was said to have had an original picture of the poet.

There can be no doubt that Mrs. Sherlock of Cork, now deceased, a descendant of the poet, had a picture of her illustrious ancestor, which she sent to her father, in London. Her daughter, who is still living, informed the writer that *she saw the picture.*

I lately visited Kilcolman Castle, the residence of the poet. It stands on the side of a small hill, about two miles from the town of Doneraile, and eight from Mallow. The castle is clothed with ivy to the top of the tower—the only tower which now stands, and which is about forty feet high. Among the ivy peeps out, here and there, the friendly looking little flower called the "forget-me not." Judging from the few names inscribed on the old stones, I should conclude the ruin is very seldom visited by strangers, or indeed by any one. The district around is greatly impoverished. Near the base of the castle is a stagnant lake, and on the margin of the lake stand a few desolate cabins. The people living on the estate and in the neighbourhood, appear never to have heard of the poet's name. An old shepherd, who was tending a flock of sheep within a few fields of the castle, told me that no one had lived in it "during duration." The poet who was once the Genius Loci of that part of the country, has not left behind even a "Nominis umbra." "Sic gloria mundi transit."

CHAPTER XVII.

THE EARL OF ESSEX—DEATH OF SIR THOMAS NORRIS—WARHAM
ST. LEGER AND HUGH MAGUIRE SLAIN—SIR GEORGE CAREW
AND JAMES FITZ-THOMAS.

A.D. 1599—1600.

ROBERT, Earl of Essex,[*] came to Ireland as Lord Deputy in April, 1599, with an army of twenty thousand foot and two thousand horse. So great an army, according to the Four Masters, had not visited Ireland since the time of Strongbow. He published a general amnesty, and promised to reinstate those who had been unjustly deprived of their property; but "not many of the Irish responded to those proclamations," they had, in fact, restored themselves. In the course of seventeen days, they left not within the length and breadth of the country of the Geraldines, a single son of a Saxon which they did not either kill or expel.

The deputy sent part of his army to garrison at Newry, Dundalk, Drogheda, and other towns, and marched with a force of about seven thousand to the South. He was attacked by O'More, and other Irish chieftains, in intricate ways and narrow passes. According to O'Sullivan Beare, five hundred of his best men fell in a defile called *Bearna na Cleti*, or the Gap of the Feathers, on account of the number of plumed hats or

[*] *Earl of Essex.*—His father, Walter Devereux, of whom we speak in chap. xii., p. 182, died in 1576, some said of poison. He died in Dublin, "before the end of a fortnight of a sudden fit of sickness. His shirt and heart were sent to his friends as tokens of his death."—*Four Masters*, A.D. 1576. His widow, Lettice Knolles, married Robert Dudley, Earl of Leicester.

helmets which strewed the ground. He pushed on, notwithstanding, into the Butler's country, where he was met by the Earl of Ormond. Sir Thomas Norris advanced from Cork to Kilmallock, hoping to overtake him before his arrival in Limerick. Thomas Burke, of Castleconnell, who was then in rebellion, met the president within two miles of Pallasgreen, in the county of Limerick. Sir Thomas fell mortally wounded "from the thrust of a pike, where the jaw-bone joins the upper part of the neck."

The Four Masters say he was carried from the field to Kilmallock, where he died in six weeks—O'Sullivan Beare says, to Mallow, where he died within fifteen days, and that he received his death-wound from the hand of John Burke, Nobilis Connachtus:—

"Aliquot inde mensibus Thomas Burkus Castelconelli Baronis frater qui ab Anglis desciuit receptis à Raymundo Barone, et eius fratre Guilielmo militibus in Muscria Kurkia* castella non satis munita expugnabat quæ circa loca Norris qui cum exercitu erat, cum equitibus amplius ducentis, & peditibus mille in Thoman ire contendit, illumque cum equitatu, & bombardarijs ad Killthiliam nanciscitur. Thomas, qui ducentos tantum perdites tunc habuit, loco cedere putauit. Earc non contentus Norris in eius ultimos ordines cum equitatu proruit : in cuius impetum Thomas sese conuertit, & Johannes Burkus Nobilis Connachtus Norrisem hasta per Galeam ferit in capite ferream hastæ cuspidem relinquens. Norris vulnere

---

* *Muscria Kurkia*, or Mucraighe Chuirch. "This was the ancient name of the barony of Clan-William, in the south-west of the county of Tipperary. The name Clan-William is derived from the clan or race of William Burke."—*Doctor O'Donovan.*

afflictus Moalam redit obi intra quindecim dies moritur."—*Hist. Cathol. Iber.*, &c., tom. 3, lib. 5, c. vi.

Sir Henry Norris,* whom the Four Masters style "a noble knight, of great name and honor," fell about the same time, at Bale-an-Eleteraigh, (now Finneterstown, in the parish of Adare, in the county Limerick) fighting by the side of Essex, with whom he came to Ireland. The following passage from the Four Masters is highly spiced with sarcasm:—

"The soldiers and warriors of the Earl of Desmond and the Geraldine host, showed them their faces. Fierce and morose was the salute and welcome which they gave to the representative of their sovereign, the Earl of Essex, on his first visit to them; for they discharged into their eyes the fire and smoke of their black powder, and showers of balls from straightly-aimed guns; and he heard the uproar, clamour, and exulting shouts of their champions and common soldiers, instead of the submission, honor, and mild and courteous words that should have been spoken to him." This rude reception caused Essex to leave Munster sooner than he had contemplated:—

"The Earl of Essex then proceeded to Kilmallock, and having remained three nights in that town, he directed his course southwards, towards Ceann-Feabhrath (a part) of the mountain of Caoin, the son of Dearg-dualach, with the intention of passing into Roche's country, and instead of proceeding to Cork, as it was thought he would have done, he directed his course across the ford at the Monastery of Fermoy,† and from thence (he marched with his

* *Sir Henry Norris.*—Henricus Norris eques Auratus Anglus Johannis & Thomæ frater in Catholicos equo vectus firmo bombardariorum agmine vallatus plumbea glande confossus egno corruit.—*Hist. Cathol. Iber. Comp.*, tom. 3, lib. 5, c. ix.

† *Monastery at Fermoy.*—An Abbey of Cistercian Monks was founded here in 1270 by Sir Richard de Rupella or de Rupe (now Roche) who was Lord Chief Justice of Ireland in 1261.

EARL OF ESSEX'S RETREAT. 319

forces) to Conachail,* Magh-Ile,,† and Lismore-Mochuda. During all this time the Geraldines continued to follow, pursue, and press upon them, to shoot at, wound, and slaughter them. When the earl had arrived in the Desies, the Geraldines returned in exultation and high spirits to their territories and houses. On the arrival of the same earl in Dungarvan, the Earl of Thomond parted from him there (and proceeded) along the seaside to Youghall, and from thence to Cork, and afterwards to Limerick. The Earl of Essex proceeded from Dungarvan to Waterford, thence into the country of the Butlers, and into Leinster. They marched not by a prosperous progress by the roads along which they passed from Waterford to Dublin, for the Irish of Leinster were following and pursuing, surrounding and environing them, so that they slew and slaughtered great numbers of them in every road and way by which they passed. The Gaels of Ireland were wont to say that it would have been better for him that he had not gone on this expedition from Dublin to Hy-Connell-Gaura, as he returned back after the first conflict that was maintained against him, without (having received) submission or respect from the Geraldines, and without having achieved in his progress any exploit worth boasting of, excepting only the taking of Cathair-Duine-Iasgaigh."

" After the killing of the president of the two provinces of Munster, and the governor of Connaught, ‡ as we have related in their proper places, the Earl of Essex and O'Neill (Hugh, the son of Fedorcha, son of Con Bacach) came to a conference in the first days of the month of September, and the end of their conference was that a peace was ratified between them till the end of two months, during which time each of

* *Conachail*, now Connough, a village in the barony of Kinataloon, in the east of the county Cork. Here are the ruins of a castle, built by Thomas, the father of the Sugan Earl.

† *Magh-Ile*, Moygeely.—*Four Masters, O'Donovan, A.D.* 1599, *p* 2119.

‡ *The Governor of Connaught*, Sir Conyers Clifford. O'Sullivan Beare says, he was pierced through with a pike. " He was left feebly stretched on the mountain," near Bealach Buidhe, in the townland of Garroo, in Connaught, when O'Rourke, who had joined O'Donnell's forces, came up, and ordered him to be beheaded.—See " A brief Relation of the Defeat in the Corleus, the 15th of August, 1599," edited for the Irish Archæological Society, by the Rev. Richard Butler, 1843.

them was to have his own part of the English and Irish. When the Earl of Essex had concluded a peace with O'Neill at this time, he proceeded to Dublin, and he remained not long there when he went to England, after having displayed a regal pomp the most splendid that any Englishman had ever exhibited in Ireland. He left Ireland without peace or tranquility, without Lord Justice, Governor, or President, excepting only that he delivered up the regal sword to the Lord Chancellor and to Sir Robert Gardiner. It was not known to any of the Irish at this time, whether the earl had gone to England to remain there, or return back again."

In the conference between O'Neill and Essex—which took place at Ballyclinch, now Anaghclart Bridge, on the river Lagan—the northern chieftain demanded that the Catholic religion should be tolerated, that the principle officers of state and the judges of the land should be Irishmen, and that he, O'Donnell, and Desmond, should enjoy the lands possessed by their ancestors. Essex had no authority to make such concession, so they parted after arranging an armistice of two months, of which the deputy took advantage to sail for England, about the first of November, 1599.

O'Neill opened the campaign in January, 1600, by marching into the South "to confirm his friendship with his allies in the war, and to wreak his vengeance upon his enemies." He was met and welcomed at the gates of Cashel by James Fitz-Thomas, the Sugan Earl of Desmond, now the arch-traitor of Munster. They proceeded westward through Clann-Gibbon, the Roche's country, and the territory of Barrymore. The Barry, at this time, was David, a loyal subject, so

O'Neill, who only preyed upon his enemies, or as he would say, his country's enemies, "traversed, plundered, burned, from one extremity to the other, both plain and wood, both level and rugged, so that no one hoped or expected that it could be inhabited for a long time afterwards." It was even a longer time before Barry forgave O'Neill or the Earl the injuries they did him.

Leaving Barrymore, write the Four Masters, "they crossed the Lee, and pitched their camps between the rivers Lee and Bandon, * on the confines of Muskerry and Carbery." "To this camp, came all the Mac Carthys, both southern and northern. Thither repaired two who were at strife with each other"—Florence Mac Carthy, who had married lady Ellen, the daughter of the late Earl of Clancare, and Donnell his "base-born" son.—The strife was to know which should be the Mac Carthy More. O'Neill and the assembled chieftains decided in favor of Florence, who was then and there installed. "Thither repaired the sons of the chiefs of Allow,"—the Mac Carthys of Dhuallow—thither repaired the O'Donohoes, O'Donovans, and O'Mahonys, and the greater number of the English and Irish of the two provinces of Munster," with the exception of David Barry, Cormac Mac Carthy, of Muskerry, and O'Sullivan Beare. Those who did not attend, sent presents and tokens of adhesion or submission.

It was during O'Neill's visit to the south that Warham St. Leger and Maguire encountered and slew

---

* *Between the rivers Lee and Bandon.*—We discover from a letter signed by Florence Mac Carthy, Owen Mac Eggan, and Donnell O'Donovan, that "O'Neale's campe" was "at Iniscare," now Inniscarra, in the barony of Barretts, about five miles south west of Cork.—Pacata Hibernia, book ii, ch. 6.

each other near the gates of Cork. This story is very differently told by the Four Masters and the author of the Pacata Hibernia. The former assert that Maguire went to scour the country in the vicinity of O'Neill's camp, of which St. Leger was advised, and went out, with a body of mail-clad horsemen, to meet him, as he marched through a narrow defile, by which he knew Maguire would pass; that he had not been long in ambush when Maguire came up. They met, hand to hand, and were both mortally wounded.

The following is from the Pacata Hibernia:—

"Sir Warham St. Leger and Sir Henry Power, riding out of the citie for recreation, to take the aire, accompanied with sundry captaines and gentlemen, with a few horse for their guard, not dreaming of an enemie neere at hande, carelessly riding every one as he thought good; within a mile of the towne, or little more, Sir Warham St. Leger and one of his servants, a little straggling from his companie, was in a narrow way suddenly charged by Macguire, who, with some horse (likewise dispersed) had spread a good circuit of ground, in hope either to get some bootie, or to have the killing of some subjects. They charged each other; Sir Warham discharged his pistoll and shot the traytor, and hee [St. Leger] was strucken with the other's [Maguire's] horseman's staffe in the head, of which wounds either [each] of them dyed, but none else on either side was slaine."

This Hugh Maguire was Lord of Fermanagh, and a commander of cavalry under Hugh O'Neill. Sir John Davies says,—"Hugh Macguire, that was slaine in Munster, was indeed a valiant rebel, and the stoutest that ever was of his name."

Some assert that O'Neill would not have returned to the north till May, if it had not been for the death of Maguire, which "caused a giddiness of spirits and a depression of mind in O'Neill, and the Irish chiefs in general." Maguire is styled the "bulwark of valor and prowess," a shield, a protector, a tower of strength, and pillar of hospitality.

O'Neill carried some of the Munster chieftains to the north as hostages, and others as prisoners, and committed Fitzgibbon, the White Knight—some of whose treacherous dealings had been exposed by the Sugan Earl of Desmond—to the keeping of Redmond Burke, who put him in hand-locks, and carried him through the country, making him lackie it by his horse's side, like a common horseboy. "After this," as the White Knight, who betrayed the Sugan Earl, said, "it might be well believed I had small cause to doe favours to James Fitz-Thomas."

A new Lord President came to Munster this year—the astute and Machiavellian Sir George Carew—who knew how to take advantage of these feuds among Irish lords and chieftains. We shall let this English knight speak for himself.

"Now the president discerning this war in Munster to be like a monster with many heads, or a servant that must obey divers masters, did think thus—that if the heads themselves might be set at variance, they would prove the most fit instruments to ruin one another. The two chief heads were the Sugan Earl (for so they called Desmond) commander of the provincials, and Dermond O'Connor, general of the bownoghs before mentioned. This Dermond O'Connor was a poor man in the beginning of his fortune, and not owner of two ploughlands in Connaught, his native country. His reputation grew partly by his wife, who was daughter to the old Earl of Desmond, and partly by his valour, being reputed one of the most valiant leaders and best commanders amongst the Irish rebels, by means whereof he had now the command of fourteen hundred men in his own bonnaght, and besides that, might strike a great stroke with the other, being (by Tyrone at his departure out of Munster) ordained chief commander of them all.

"This man did the president make to deal withal, for these reasons: First, because he knew the said Dermond, being a mere mercenary, and serving in Munster only for pay, might be induced, by large sums of money, to serve the queen as well as the rebels.

"Secondly, he had a very fit instrument whereby the more easily to work him to his will, namely, his wife, who being brought up some part of her time amongst the English, had not only learned the language, but stood reasonably well affected to the English government, and likely it was, she would use all her industry to advance the service, in hope that if it succeeded well, it would prove a good step or ladder to procure the liberty of her brother, James Fitzgerald, son and heir to Gerald, Earl of Desmond, slain, (now prisoner in the Tower,) and to raise his fortunes.

"Lastly it was publickly known that the Sugan Earl would never do service upon the bownoghs, except he might have both the title and possessions of the Earl of Desmond confirmed unto him, which her majesty would never condescend unto.

"Upon these grounds, in a very secret manner, he provided and sent a fit agent to sound the inclination of the Lady Margaret, for so was Dermond's wife named; and finding her fit to be wrought upon, the conditions should be propounded, viz:—that if her husband would take Desmond prisoner, and deliver him into the hands of the president, he should incontinently receive one thousand pounds sterling; and that he should have a company of men in pay from the queen, and other conditions of satisfaction to herself and her brother."

O'Conor, the general of the earl's mercenary forces, agrees to the terms, and prepares to carry the plan into execution, but he seeks some plausible pretence for arresting the earl, without publicly breaking with the party in rebellion. The pretence and proof are provided by the president. James Fitz-Thomas is to be accused of treachery, of having arranged with the president to deliver O'Conor into his hands. The president writes a letter, as if intended for the Sugan Earl, which is to fall into O'Conor's hands. Here is the letter, and it is as unknightly a production as was ever penned, although the editor of the *Pacata Hibernia*,* who thinks most highly of it, says "the contents thereof doe manifest the invention" of the president.

"*The* LORD PRESIDENT'S *letter to* JAMES FITZ-THOMAS.

"Sir, your last letter I have received, and am exceedingly glad to see your constant resolution of returning to subjection, and to leave the rebellious courses wherein you have long persevered. You may rest assured that promises shall be kept, and you shall no sooner bring Dermond O'Conner to me, alive or dead, and banish his bownoghs out of the country, but that you shall have your demand satisfied, which I thank God I am both able and willing to perform.

"Believe me, you have no better way to recover your desperate estate, than by this good service which you have proffered; and therefore I cannot but commend your judgment in choosing the

* *The editor of the Pacata Hibernia.*—The editor was Thomas Stafford, but there is little doubt the work was altogether indicted by Sir George Carew himself, the laudations of the president not excepted. It bears throughout the impress of his mind.

same, to redeem your former faults. And I do the rather believe the performance of it by your late action touching Loghguire, wherein your brother and yourself have well merited; and as I promised, you shall find me so just, as no creature living shall ever know that either did assent to the surrender of it. All your letters I have received, as also the joint letter from your brother and yourself; I pray lose no time, for delays in great actions are subject to many dangers.

"Now that the queen's army is in the field, you may work your determination with most security, being ready to relieve you upon a day's warning; so praying God to assist you in this meritorious enterprise, I do leave you to his protection, this twenty-ninth of May, 1600."

The remark, "touching Loughguire [Castle,]* wherein your brother and yourself have well merited," is a master-stroke, and sufficient of itself to damn the earl's character and reputation as an Irishman and a soldier with O'Neill, and every Irish chieftain in rebellion. The president, as we learn from his panygerist, got possession of this castle by bribing one Owen Grome, — to whom John Fitz-Thomas, the Earl's brother, had committed its care,—with "threescore pounds."

But let us see how O'Conor acts when he gets possession of the president's forged letter. He requests an interview with the earl, and when they meet, says, "My Lord, you are in hand"—arrested. "*In hand!* For whom, or for what?"—"You have combined with the English, and promised the president to deliver me, either alive or dead into his hands, and for proof behold these letters which were intercepted and brought to me."

* *Loughguire Castle*, now Lough Gur, in the Parish of Knockany, in the County Limerick, two miles and a half north of Bruff. The ruins of this castle remain to this day.

The earl is thunderstruck; O'Conor, who is cool and conscientious, must hold him in custody till he has consulted O'Neill, so he sends him to Castle Lyshin, to the care of his wife, Lady Margaret, and writes to the president, who was lying at Limerick, to come to Kilmallock, where Lady Margaret would deliver up the prisoner and receive the thousand pounds. The president comes in all haste, "the next morrow," (the twentieth of June,) " with a thousand foot and two hundred horse," but there is no Lady Margaret to meet him, and no James Fitz-Thomas, or Sugan Earl, to be had for a thousand pounds. The president is chap-fallen. O'Conor writes an awkward letter of apology, to say that Lyshin Castle was hardly beset. There is another explanation; Lady Margaret is first-cousin to the Sugan Earl, and he is "the handsomest man of his time." The president is beaten this time, but he will try again.

O'Conor, for whom Munster is too hot, gets a safe conduct to his own country, through the intervention of his wife, who does *not* accompany the traitor. He being now past Clanricard, and within seventeen or eighteen miles of Limerick, Theobald Burke of the Ships, with a company of a hundred foot in her majesty's pay, meets and assails him, notwithstanding his safe conduct. He flees for refuge to an old church. They set fire to the church, and kill forty of his men as they rush through the flames. He is taken alive, and beheaded the next day.

We said the president would try again. The name of *John Fitz-Thomas* is mentioned in the account of Loughguire Castle. He was brother to James Fitz-Thomas, a noble youth, who offered to take his brother's place as a prisoner in Shandon Castle. Sir George Carew, employed a person named John Nugent, to assassinate this young man. We must not be shocked into a disbelief of this. It was part of the president's policy. If the heads of the monster, which he styles REBELLION, cannot be set at variance, they must be cut off, and the more quietly it is done the better:

"At this time Nugent * came to make his submission to the president, and to desire pardon for his faults committed. Answer was made him, that, for so much as his crimes and offences had been extraordinary, he could not hope to be reconciled unto the state, except he would deserve it by extraordinary service, which, saith the president, if you shall perform, you may deserve not only pardon for your faults committed heretofore, but also some store of crowns to relieve your wants hereafter. He presently promised not to be wanting in anything that lay in the power of one man to accomplish, and in private, made offer to the president, that, if he might be well recompensed, he would *ruin* within a short time, either the Sugan Earl, or John Fitz-Thomas, his brother.

"And indeed very likely he was both to attempt and perform as much as he spake. To attempt, because he was so valiant and daring, as that he did not fear anything; and to execute, because by reason of his many outrages before committed, the chief rebels did repose great confidence in him. The president having contrived a plot for James Fitz-Thomas (as is before

---

* *Nugent.*—He is styled one John Nugent, sometimes servant to Sir Thomas Norris, late president of Munster.—Pacata Hibernia, vol. i., p. 67.

shewed) gave him in charge to undertake John, his brother."

But the matter must be arranged in this case—as well as in that of the elder brother—so as not to excite the suspicion of the party in rebellion. Here, again, the Lord President displays his genius. Nugent is to appear before the president and council in public, and ask for protection, and to be driven with obliquy and threats from their presence :—

" But because the matter might be without suspicion, upon the next morrow, the council being set, and a great concourse of people assembled, Nugent reneweth his suit for the continuance of his protection.

"But the president rehearsing in public audience, a catalogue of his mischievous outrages lately committed, told the council that having farther inquired, and better considered of man and matter, for his part he thought it an action of very ill example, to receive into mercy such a notorious malefactor. The council were all of the same opinion, who, reviling him with many biting and bitter speeches, and assuring him, that if it were not for a religious regard, that was holden of the queen's word, he should pay a dear price for his former misdemeanor, and so, with public disgrace, was he dismissed their presence."

He goes forth with all the prestige of this abuse to work his diabolical purpose. He finds his intended victim at Loughguire Castle. It is just before the place is betrayed. He also meets one John Coppinger there, to whom he reveals his object. Coppinger seems to approve. John Fitz-Thomas, John Coppinger, and John Nugent ride out together, leaving the castle in the care of Owen Grome. Nugent permitted the young nobleman "to ride a little before him, minding —his back being turned—to shoote him through with his pistoll; which for the purpose was well charged with two bullets. The opportunity offered, the pistoll bent, both heart and hand ready to do the deed," when Coppinger, whose eye was on him, snatched the weapon from his hand, and cried out "Treason!"—John Fitz-Thomas turned about to seize the traitor. Nugent rode a good horse and spurred it hard. The horse stumbled, he was taken, and the next day hanged. He confessed that it was his intention, after shooting the younger brother, to post to the camp, where the elder lay, call him aside, tell him of his brother's death, and "execute as much on him."

The president has failed again, but he will try a third time. He consoles himself, in the interim, thus, for he cannot believe he could make a mistake. "This plot though it attained not fully the desired success, yet it proved to be of great consequence, for now was John Fitz-Thomas possessed with such a jealous suspicion of every one, that he durst not remain long at Loughguire, for fear of some other like attempt that might be wrought against him, and therefore leaving the castle in the custody of the said Owen Grome (who, as before, kept it a very short time) departed suddenly unto his brother's camp."

The "president is now on horse-backe in the midst of his army," preying, destroying, and burning the property of all rebels or suspected persons. John Burke, the brother of Theobald who slew O'Conor, desires what was then styled "protection," but his conscience will not allow him to swear allegiance to the queen. Sir George moves forward with his army, seizes his corn, and fires one of his castles. It is enough. John and his brother come " creeping upon their knees by his horse's side." The president " seeing, would not see them, and hearkening to another would not attend to them," till some one said " the Burkes are here," when he turned about and reproved them, and then granted the protection they required.

Such tactics had the effect of deterring those who wished well to the rebellion from taking an active part in it. Among the most distinguished of these was Florence Mac Carthy, who had been so lately installed Mac Carthy More, by O'Neill, the arch-traitor of the North. For him to hold back at such a crisis looked like treachery to " the cause." The following are extracts from a letter, dated June, 1560:—

"*A letter from* JAMES FITZ-MAURICE *to* FLORENCE MAC CARTHY.

" Cousin, your letters of the fifth of this present I received the eight of the same, wherein you write of your sickness, and the impediments that causeth your soldiers to be slow in prosecuting our general action. In your former letters you write and vow that there hath been neither peace, truce, nor cessation confirmed between you and the president. I am informed by my particular friends, and also by a letter (intercepted) from the president to you, that some mitigation of time is limited betwixt you and them, whereupon they depend your assistance to be restrained from us. If this be thus, it is far contrary to that I hoped, and much beyond the confidence reposed by O'Neill and myself in your vowed fidelity and service to God and our action. I perceive Donell Mac Cartie is raising head in disquieting your country, the redress whereof consisted in your constant assistance to be bestowed."

He entreats him in the end, if his sickness be not extreme, to collect his forces and meet him, or he will be compelled to suspect he has "some inward meaning contrary to the general action." He speaks in this letter of Donell Mac Cartie disquieting his country, and reminds him that for the redress of such grievances he must aid the party who had made him, and not Donnell, the Mac Carthy More.

Florence was evidently playing a double game. He was grown "more wise than honest," and if we are to believe the Pacata Hibernia, "became an intercessor to the president with frequent letters and damnable oathes, that he was in heart and intentions sincerely devoted to her majesty's service." James Fitz-Thomas writes again:—

"*A letter from* JAMES FITZ-THOMAS *to* FLORENCE MAC CARTIE.

"My Lord, your letters I have received, and the present time of service is now at hand, which by letters, nor any excuse so effectual ought to be delayed; and whereas you write that you intend to confer with the president and the Earl of Thomond, I marvel that one of your lordship's acquaintance with their proceedings doth not yet know their enticing baits and humours to entrap us all within the nets of their policies. Your vow to God and this action for the maintenance of the Church and defence of our own right should not for any respect be unregarded. You know that of long time your lordship hath been suitor to the Queen and Council, and could not at any time prevail, nor get any likelihood of your settlement; and now being duly placed by the assent of the Church, and us, the nobility of this action, your lordship should work all means possible for to maintain the same.

"You know the ancient and general malice that heretofore they bear to all Irish birth, and much more they rue at this present, so as it is very bootless for any of us all to seek their favour or countenance, which are but a means to work our total subversion; write to me effectually your lordship's mind, and what resolution you purpose to follow, whereby I may proceed accordingly. This army is but very slender, for they are but six hundred foot and eighty horse; I am, myself and Fitz-Maurice, six hundred foot and some horse. We expect your lordship's assistance, which we heartily desire, and not any further to defer us with letters as you respect us and the service; and whereas you write you have no force, your own presence, and the bruit of your coming, will much further the service and dismay the enemy.—2 September, 1600.

"Your loving cousin,

"JAMES DESMOND."

Some means must be devised to put down this warlike earl. The president has no desire to meet him in the field. A new thought strikes him,—to bring over to Ireland James Fitzgerald, the Parliamentary Earl, who had been sixteen years a prisoner in England. As he was the only son of Garrett, the sixteenth earl, the president concluded that the followers of the *Sugan* Earl would at once desert him on the appearance of James in Ireland. The expected landing of the earl was therefore publicly announced and bruited abroad, but as his arrival was delayed longer than the president supposed, he resorted to the trick of dressing up a servant in the livery and armorial bearings of the family, and of sending him through the country to attract the gaze of the public and set them talking.

Elizabeth, the English queen, was slow in liberating any of her state prisoners, but when she consented she sent him with a safe keeper, though for such caution there was little need, as the young man was as docile, tractable, and harmless as one of those monkeys which Italian boys lead through the streets of London with a string, and looked, we have no doubt, withered and old before his time, although every care had been taken to adorn him with coat, cap, and feathers.

He arrived at Youghal on the fourteenth of October, where we find, from the chronicles of the day, " He had like to have been overthrown with the kisses of the old calleaks," or hags. From Youghal he proceeded directly to Mallow, where the president waited to receive him, for to him was committed the power of regulating all his movements, or, if need-be, of curtailing his liberty. In a letter from her majesty, Elizabeth R., to the lord president, signed by " *Ro. Cecil,*" we read these words : — " Know this from us, that we shall never disallow it, *if you, in your discretion, find it necessarie at any time that you doe abridge him of any libertie or any favour* now afforded him."

After remaining long enough in Mallow to learn his lesson from the president, he was forwarded, under the charge of the Archbishop of Cashel, to Kilmallock. Nothing could surpass the hearty welcome which the Irish — the tenants and followers of the old earl — gave the young man as he entered this fine old town. The windows and tops of the houses were crowded with spectators, who showered down corn and salt upon his head as a token of welcome and prosperity.

This state of feeling lasted just twenty-four hours, for the next day, when returning with the Archbishop of Cashel from the Protestant Church, both he and the archbishop were hooted, cursed, spit upon, and bespattered with mud. The editor of the Pacata Hibernia says, " the young earl came to Kilmallock upon a Saturday, in the evening, and by the way, and at their entry into the town, there was a mighty concourse of people, insomuch that all the streets, doores, and windowes, yea the very gutters and tops of the houses were so filled by them, as if they came to see him whom God had sent to bee that comfort and delight their souls and hearts most desired, and they welcomed him with all the expressions and signs of joy, every one throwing upon him wheat and salt, an ancient ceremony used in that province upon the election of their new majors and officers, as a prediction of future peace and plenty. The next day being Sunday, the earl went to church, and all the way the people used loud and rude exhortations to keepe him from church. After service, the earl coming forth, was railed at and spet upon."

'There could be no mistaking these signs of the times, or the meaning of the *vox populi;* so the president, without much delay, put the hood on this poor hawk and sent it back to the queen, who immured it a second time in the Tower, where it died in a few months—some say from poison—more likely from imprisonment.

The Sugan Earl is at length driven, like his uncle, to the shelter of the woods and wild glens. He is accompanied by a harper—Dermot O'Dugan, of Ballyduff—whose music cheers the solitude of the lonely caves to which he flees for shelter. The president offers a liberal reward to any one who will take him dead or alive. Lord Barry undertakes to run him down with a hundred soldiers. The earl and his friend are surprised in a wood and surrounded. The harper takes the earl's cloak, and, with the "lapwing's policie" breaks cover. A hundred soldiers, with a "Hark away!" are at his heels. He escapes into Fitzgibbon's or the White

Knight's country. Lord Barry, who hates the White Knight as the White Knight does the earl, charges him, in a letter to the Lord President, with harbouring the arch-traitor. A falser charge was never made. The White Knight could never forget it was Fitz-Thomas who exposed his double-dealing to O'Neill, who delivered him to Redmond Burke, from whom he had lately purchased his liberty. The president sends for Fitzgibbon, "and rebukes him with sharp words and bitter reprehensions" for his negligence in " so important a business." He returns home bemoaning his hard fate. One of his followers, who " loved him dearly," compassionating his perplexity, said, "Follow me and I will bring you to where he is." Fitzgibbon followed to the cave of the Grey Sheep, above the glen of Aherlow, in the mountains of Slievo Grot in Tipperary. " It had a narrow mouth, yet deepe in the ground."

Fitzgibbon, who was accompanied by Redmond Burke and six or seven of his own followers, advanced to the mouth of the cave and called out, "*James Fitz-Thomas, come out and render yourself a prisoner.*" The earl came to the mouth of the cave and called on Redmond Burke to seize Fitzgibbon ; but " the wheel of his fortune being turned," they pointed their swords on himself, and his only companion, a foster-brother. The earl was disarmed, bound, and carried prisoner to Kilmallock, from Kilmallock to Shandon Castle, Cork, where the president, Sir George Carew, resided, and from Cork to the Tower of London, where he died, and lies buried with his cousin the Parliamentary Earl.

CHAPTER XVIII.

FLORENCE MAC CARTHY—JOHN ANNIAS—SIR GEORGE CAREW.

A.D. 1600—1601.

THE Lord President found in Florence Mac Carthy—whom he called "a Michavellian ambodexter"—an* antagonist worthy of his genius in state craft. England, ever true to the *divide et impera* policy, had sent him back to Ireland, after detaining him in England for eleven years,* in order to pit him against Donnell, the illegitimate son of the late Mac Carthy More, † who had usurped the title and laid claim to the estates. Florence understood all this. The whole arrangement is thus simply stated:—"Thou mayest be pleased therefore to understand, gentle reader, that the rebels of Munster being grown to such an exceeding strength, as you have heard; and amongst these, Donnell Mac Carthy, Florence's base brother-in-law, one of the chief, her majesty thought good to diminish their forces with sparing as much blood, and expending as little treasure as conveniently might be, and, therefore, knowing that Florence Mac Cartie was better beloved in the country than Donnell, having made many solemn vows, and

* *Eleven years.*—Florence was arrested by Sir Thomas Norris, the 4th of June, 1588, and was dispatched into Ireland in the month of May, 1599. He spent three out of the eleven years in the Tower.—*Pac. Hib., p.* 303.

† *The late Mac Carthy More* died in 1596.

taken many voluntary oaths for his continued loyalty, was dispatched into Ireland in the month of May, 1599, and to the end he might be the more encouraged, and better enabled to do her highnesses service, it pleased her majesty to direct her favorable letters to Robert Earl of Essex, then Lord Lieutenant of Ireland, authorising him to give orders for letters patent to be made, containing an effectual grant to the said Florence Mac Cartie, and Ellen his wife, and to the heirs male of their bodies, lawfully begotten, of all the country of Desmond, and such other lands, whereof he had any estate of inheritance; *but withall authorising the said Lord Lieutenant and Council to stay those letters patent in the haniper,* or deliver them, according as they should see cause,* in the proof they should make of the behaviour of the said Florence."

Florence Mac Carthy remained some time in Cork after his return to Ireland, and here one John Annias was employed as a spy upon all his actions. It appears from his examination that he was introduced to Florence, in Cork, as an engineer. Let us turn to

" *The Examination of John Annias, taken before Sir Nicholas Walsh and Justice Comerford, the* 13*th of October,* 1600 *:—*

" He saith that in May last Florence Mac Cartie sent one Maur [More] to him, wishing him to repair to his lodgings at Cork, and that Florence was desirous to be acquainted with him ; whereupon he came to

---

* *Haniper*, or hanaper was originally a basket of "twyggys" for holding state papers or deeds of any kind. The Illustrated London News, for December 1, 1860, contains drawings of an ancient skippet, or turned box, used for this purpose in the reign of Edward III., and a hamper or hanaper of the succeeding reign, lately discovered at Westminster.

Florence, and in Florence's chamber, he the said Florence (and none other but they two being present) said that he understood that this examinate was an engineer, and one that had skill in devising and erecting of fortifications, and that he would willingly employ him in the like. Annias demanding of Florence what or where he would have his works raised? He answered at Dunkerran,* wherein he might upon any occasion of extremity defend himself and James Fitz-Thomas against the English, and also wherein he might give succour to such Spaniards as should come to their aid."

This John Annias, who had been living for some time in Spain, was arrested in 1594, along with Patrick Cullen, a fencer, on the grave charge of having come to England to murder the queen. Cullen was hanged, and Annias offered to expiate his faults by doing her majesty good service. The nature of the service we learn from a letter addressed by him, when in the Tower, to the Privy Council, bearing date 1594. We do not give the whole letter.

"*To the Lords of Her Majesty's Honorable Privy Council.*

"To make amends for my faults past, behold, my lords, I am content to venture my life to do God and her majesty great service, and worthy to be commended, which is to discover, plainly, all those in England which should take part with the Spanish king against her majesty, by these reasons following:—

"All the king's business, either secret or known, passes the secretary's hands; and for his discharge, as also the king to know how his money and business goes, all is registered in a book; a brief

---

* *Dunkerran.*—It should be Dunderrow. Dunderrow is a parish, partly in the county of the city of Cork and partly in the baronies of Kinsale and Kinnalea. The mound or fort where Mac Carthy proposed to erect " his works " is now nearly removed.

notation of all business, which book remains always in the office, called the scritoria, at the left-hand, going into the court of the secretary's house; another register book answerable to the same is at Madrid. The key of this office the under-secretary keeps at Brussels; he is called Diego Geffrey, a Spaniard, and one that I am very well acquainted with.

"All Englishmen in England, either nobleman or gentleman, whatsoever estate he may be, what number of men he is able to make use of, and what money he hath received, or bestowed either upon his children or kinsmen at Rome, Rheims, Douay, or Louvain, and of what place or province in England, or if he be alive or dead, or put to death for persecution, as they name it so, and all those who pay tribute to the queen, and what satisfaction the king makes them therefor, the day and year. Behold, my lords, all is noted in these register books.

"I have seen with my eyes Holt, and Gordon the Scot, very often after secret conferences with the secretary then confer in the scritoria office, with these register books, either to write down more names converted to them or cross out such as be dead or put to death. Seeing I know this to be true, and that I have been well acquainted with these offices, I shall undertake and venture my one life to make amends for my faults to win credit, I shall, by God's help, without fail, bring this book to your honors' hands with all diligence."

He then goes on to state how he will accomplish his object.

"I will make acquaintance with the scritoria office, and cast an eye where the register book lies, in what place; then I shall have a handful of dough about me, and clap the key of the office door fast in the dough, that the print remain still, and cause a key to be made of the same, taking leave of his excellency beforehand, and providing a rope, double the height of the wall, that I might draw the rope back again to myself.

"I will provide a supper for a dozen persons, gentlewomen, music, and this under-secretary invited beforehand; about seven o'clock I will open this office, with a black lantern under my cloak, and find out this register book, then come back to entertain the company, and after every man has gone to his rest and lodging I will take the ready way over the walls with the rope provided, and go all night either the way to Liege, to Flushing in Zealand, or to Calais. And thus I undertake to bring this book with me, and without doubt I shall bring it to pass.

He says in this letter that the cause of his faults was "a certain opinion of religion"—he had been a Catholic—"but having perused the bible now a year, he is fully satisfied and *reformed.*" In proof of his reformation and genius in picking locks and scaling walls, he adds "I have discovered to Mr. Lieutenant [of the Tower] how I might escape and go unknown to my keeper very easily." He complains of being a prisoner two years, of his great misery "noe clodes at all, excepte towe shurtes Mr. Lyftenant" gave him. Whether he was employed by the honorable privy council to go to Spain and steal the book in which the Spanish secretary kept the names of those who were disaffected to her majesty, we cannot say, but there can be no doubt that he got new clothes before he came to Munster, where we find him doing a stroke of business with Sir George Carew, knight, who sends him with a letter to Sir Robert Cecil, and speaks of him as Mr. Annias who is returning to England, to furnish himself with some necessaries:—

"1600, *April* 30. CAREW *to* CECIL.

"Sir, this bearer, Mr. Annias, is returned into England to furnish himself with some necessaries which he wants. I have conferred with him and do like his projects; he promises to return presently, which I beseech you to expedite. And so referring my larger discourses to the dispatch now I have in hand, I do humbly rest,

"Your honour's most bounden,

"Shandon Castle,   "GEORGE CAREWE.
"This 30 of April, 1600."

What the necessaries were for which he had to go to England we cannot say. Carew makes a mystery of it. Those who knew Carew, and his arrangements with Nugent to assassinate John Fitz-Thomas, might whisper *poison*. Something that would be slow and sure. There was no licensed apothecary in Cork, none, at least, that Carew would trust to poison his enemy. The president when sick, and in want of a doctor, writes to the queen, from Cork, Sept. 29, 1602, "Ireland is destitute of learned men of English birth; and with Irish physicians *—*knowing the good will they beare me*—if they were learned, I DARE NOT VENTURE."

The report was abroad, that Carew and Cecil had engaged John Annias to poison Florence. Cecil, of course, repudiates the charge, and writes to Carew to hang Annias at once. Dead men tell no tales. It would appear that "the wicked and horrible wretch, Annias, had given out the vile untruth" of both president and secretary:—

"1600, *Oct*. 15. CECIL *to* CAREW.

"It remaineth now that I may say something to you concerning Annias, who hath never deceived me, for I hold him a villian. First, the Lord God doth know it, my soul never had the thought to consent to the poisoning of a dog much less of a man. True it is, if to take a rebel alive, or to bring their head, I was contented to hear his promise, though for my own part I never believed him, I do therefore pray you, and conjure you, by all the love you bear me, to find the means to take him, and seeing he hath otherwise offended the law; be assured of this from me, that it must be his hanging and public confession must clear us from this odious im-

---

* *Irish physicians*.—There were the O'Cullinans, the hereditary physicians of the Kings of Desmond or Cork. It was a saying in Irish, when a person was despaired of, "an O'Cullinan could not cure him." Doctor Callanan, of Cork, is a descendant of these celebrated Irish physicians.

putation. Remember, sir, what I write, I pray you, and think of it, for there is no other way to clear it. And know this from me, that when you have him, if you keep him long alive, he will escape from you by one means or another; send him not out therefore, nor spare his life, for then it will be thought, whatsoever he sayeth to clear us, that it is to save his neck.

" London, 15 Oct., 1600."

The hanging of Annias, even with a "publique confessyon," could never "clere" such men as Cecil and Carew of the "odious ymputacon." It looks too like murdering a man whose evidence might be damaging. It has a dark and suspicious appearance, to say the least. Cecil writes again three weeks after :—

" 1600, *November* 8. CECIL *to* CAREW.

" I expect daily, to understand, what you have done with that wicked and horrible wretch Annias, who hath given out (as it seemeth) so vile an untruth of you and me concerning Florence, of which I protest to the Lord I never entertained the thought. I trust, therefore, you will come by him by one means or another, that he may pay the ransom of such a villainy."

The Lord President was as anxious to catch the traducer of his fair fame as the secretary. Annias was arrested two days before Cecil wrote his first letter, and, we conclude, saved his life by giving evidence against Florence Mac Carthy. Cecil's first letter is dated the 15th of October, 1600, and the examination of John Annias seems to have taken place before Sir Nicholas Walsh and Justice Comerford, and is dated the 13th of October, 1600.

After giving this evidence against Florence, he was, we conclude, cast off by both parties. He turns up after this in a most pitiable plight, " poorelie arraied and barefotted," wandering as a vagrant about Cork, when he is arrested by the mayor, who may have heard of the particular interest which Cecil took in him. The following is the mayor's letter:—

"1601, *March* 6. JOHN MEADE, *Mayor of Cork, to* CECIL.

"I am bold to advertise your honour, lately restrained in the Tower, was found upon the walls of this city, poorely arraied, barefotted, and altogether disguised from his wonted attire; who, being brought before me, I examined his name, and he said his name was John Magues; whom I did know by eyeing him narrowly, and committed him to the gaol, where he is to remain till he has his trial by law, and with whose apprehension I have acquainted the Lord President, for which he was very thankful. Your honour hath received notice, heretofore, of his behaviour since his last departure from thence, wherefore, I think it unnecessary to repeat the particulars.

How he escapes from the hands of both mayor and secretary on this occasion, without hanging, is a mystery; but escape he did. Perhaps he broke prison.* We find him in the June of 1602 writing to Father Dominick Collins respecting the defence of Donboy Castle, which was then besieged by Sir George Carew.

"*A letter from* JOHN ANNIAS *to* DOMINICK COLLINS, *Jesuit at Donboy.*

"Be careful of your fortifying, continually, with a most special care, raise in height the west side of your port, fill your chambers on the south and north sides with hides and earth, what battery is made suddenly repair it like valiant soldiers, make plain in the south side the remnant of the broken houses, make ways out of the hall to shower and cast stones upon the port, and if the enemy would attempt the like, dig deep that place we first began, and a trench above to defend the same, as I have said unto you. Although we expect speedy relief out of Spain, yet be you wise to preserve

* *Broke prison.*—To escape from Cork prisons was very common, as we may have occasion to shew by and bye.

the store of victuals discreetly. Devise yourselves all the invention possible to hold out this siege, which is the greatest honour in this kingdom. With the next I shall prepare shoes for you. Send me the cord or long line, and the rest of the saltpetre, with all the iron barriers, seven pieces in all. Salute in my name Richard Mac Gaghegane, praying God to have of his special grace that care of your success.

" From the camp, the — June, 1602.

"Your loving Cousin,
"JOHN ANNIAS.

" To Father Dominick,
" Beerhaven, these."

The following letter was written the night before his execution:—

"*A letter from* JOHN ANNIAS *to the* BARON OF LIXNAW, *a little before his execution.*

" In trust is treason. So Wingfield betrayed me. My death satisfies former suspicions, and gives occasion hereafter to remember me; and as ever I aspire to immortalize my name upon the earth so I would request you, by virtue of that ardent affection I had towards you in my life, you would honour my death, in making mention of my name in the register of your country. Let not my servant, Cormack, want, as a faithful servant unto me. Let my funeral, and the service of the Catholic Church be observed for the soul. Here I send you the pass and letter of that faithless Wingfield, having charged the bearer upon his duty to God to deliver this into your hands. O'Sullivan was strange to me, but inures himself to want me. Commend me to Captain Tirrell, O'Connor, your sister, and Gerode Oge. This the night before my execution, the eight day of November, 1602, and upon this sudden I cannot write largely.

"Your loving bed-fellow sometimes,
"ISMABITO."

He speaks in this letter of former suspicions. What were these? Had they reference to the report of his having been employed to poison Florence Mac Carthy? If so, he thinks his death should "satisfy" such suspicions, and cause him to be remembered. The style and tone of the letter is not that of a thoroughly debased and bad man. His desire to immortalise his name, and to have it mentioned in the registry of his country; his love for his friend, expressed in his dying hour; and his care of his faithful servant, are not the marks of one totally depraved. It is possible after all, perhaps probable, that he never contemplated the poisoning of Florence; but that his great enmity to Cecil and Carew caused him to give out (as yt semeth) "so vyle an untrewth." Let us be just and charitable to them all, to the secretary and president, as well as to Annias. Whatever was his crime, it did not justify Wingfield's entrapping him by a "false passe and letter." In those days there was too much truth in the words *"in trust is treason."*

That portion of Annias' examination before Sir Nicholas Walsh and Justice Comerford, which treats of Mac Carthy's proposed works at Dunderrow, near Kinsale, must have been very damaging to the newly liberated chieftain. Two of the principal charges brought against him by Sir Thomas Norris, when arresting him in 1588, was his love of Spaniards, and of the Old Head of Kinsale.

But he managed, notwithstanding what Annias said, and all that was suspected, to get back to Desmond, and was shortly after, as we have seen, installed as Mac Carthy More, not by the queen, or her lord deputy, but by O'Neill. On this occasion he was "sworne on a Masse booke, to be true to Tirone." This must have been wormwood and gall to the English ministers, an upsetting of their favorite maxim — "Sapens nisi serpentem comederit non sit draco,"—Unless the serpent eat the serpent, there can be no dragon. As they desired, Florence has destroyed Donnell, so they have "the great serpent," or dragon, but not a dragon to guard golden apples for the queen, but one prepared to raise his crest against her sacred majesty.

"Whereby the indifferent reader may perceive with what prepared hatred, and prepensed malice this gallant was affected, even in this first scene of his devillish tragedie; that there might bee no indecorum, his subsequent proceedings were in all poynts correspondent to these timely beginnings; for having now left Corke, and gotten footing in his (supposed) countrey of Desmond, hee wrote severall letters to the gentlemen neere adjoyning, namely the O Sulevan, Mac Finnin, the two Odonoghs, and others, to assemble at a time and place appoynted, to create him Mac Cartie More; and whosoever he was that refused to come, he persecuted as his mortall enemie."—*Pac. Hib.*

Some of his people attack and kill some of the queen's forces under the command of Captain Flower, a few miles from Cork. The president demands an explanation. He writes a letter "stuffed with damnable oaths and execrable blasphemies," in which he denies all knowledge of the slaughter. He has even the audacity to go to Cork and see the president, who gives him his confidence, and informs him he is starting on an expedition to the west, which Mac Carthy at once communicates to James Fitz-Thomas, who prepares to meet him. The president discovered this treachery by James Fitz-

Thomas' intercepted reply, which began thus : "My good lord and cousin, your letters of the 18th of May I received the 25th of the same, wherein you relate the manner of your proceedings with the president in Cork, and also his determination towards the west of my county. I, thank God, have prevented that which he expected."

Mac Carthy was generally very cautious in his mode of correspondence. We give the following letter as a specimen of the apparent dash united with great caution. He knew he was writing to a scoundrel. It is addressed to the White Knight, who betrayed the Earl of Desmond :—

"*A letter from* FLORENCE *to the* WHITE KNIGHT.

" Damnation, I cannot but commend me heartily unto you, *as bad as thou art*, and do also most heartily commend me to your two sons. I would be very glad to speak with you for your good; and because I cannot speak with you myself, yet I would have you in anywise credit your daughter, Mistress Mac Donough, concerning me, and to believe from me whom she sends, or what she sends you word of by a trusty messenger. I would have you to determine about Pierce Oge; and that I may speak with you, I mean about *Gortnetoberd* of *Tullylease*, send word to Pierce and Dermond of the day with him, and send me word and I will come without all fail. In the meantime I leave you to God. Palace, this seven and twentieth of August, 1600.

" Your assured loving Friend,

" FLORENCE MAC CARTIE."

This letter was shewn by the White Knight to the Lord President. Fitzgibbon explained that the message sent him through his daughter, Mac Donogh's wife, was *a reproof for his submission to the queen.* We are not surprised that the president, knowing all these things, was anxious that he should visit Cork again. He sends for him. Florence is within a few days to meet the Governor of Kerry. The Governor of Kerry, Sir Charles Wilmot, sends for him. Mac Carthy is "shortly to repair to the president; and so deluding both he would come to neither." To use his, Sir George's, own illustration, when trying to entrap the Earl of Desmond—this halyard or hawk was not to be taken by such lime-twigs. He was as cunning, and as much on his guard, and as hard to unearth as the oldest fox in Desmond; he therefore resolves to catch his cub.

"The president not holding himselfe sufficiently assured of Florence with his two pledges, his base brother and kinsman, still importuned the bringing of his eldest sonne, according to his promise upon his first protection; hee having no pretext for his longer stay, sent to Owen Mac Teg Mergagh in Desmond to carry his said sonne to Corke, there to bee left as a pledge for him; within a few dayes after this message sent, Florence receiving advertisement from Tyrone, of certaine Spaniards landed in the North, and hearing continuall rumors of Northern forces, to infest the province, dispatched a messenger to the said Owen Mac Teg Mergagh to make stay of his sonne for a longer time, viz.:—untill hee might perceive what would bee the issue of those preparations; but before the messenger could come, the said Owen was with the child upon his way, and come to Corke before the said messenger overtook him, but had not as yet delivered the child out of his owne custody; wherefore receiving this countermand, hee secretly conveyed the child out of the citie, and returned with him againe into Desmond, where he was kept as before, untill Florence had seene that there was neither Irish nor Spaniards appeared to his aide, succour and comfort." *Pac. Hib.*

There can be no doubt that Florence Mac Carthy was deeply compromised in the Spanish landing at Kinsale, although he was arrested and safely lodged in the tower before the arrival of Don Juan de Aquila.

They employed Donough Mac Cormac to write the following letter to Philip, King of Spain, not that he required an amanuensis,* but he remembered, written words remain. Donough Mac Cormac was under the same impression, for he got Thomas Shelton to copy what he indited for another. But notwithstanding all this caution, this, and other letters fell into the hands of Sir George Carew.

" *A letter from* Donoghe Mac Cormock, *in the name of* Florence, *to the* King of Spain.

" Having received direction from the Earl of Clan-Care,† I would not omit this opportunity; at the departure of the Archbishop of Dublin,‡ and Don Martin de La Cerda, to make knowen to your

* *Not that he required an amanuensis.*—Doctor O'Donovan, speaking of Florence Mac Carthy's letter on Irish antiquities, written in the Tower, says, " The letter throughout is distinct, without a blot, and exhibits only two erasures. What minute characters the hand of such a giant could form, and with what certainty and precision it could trace, line after line, in faultless parallels, and with intervals so minute that there seems upon the page but a sharp, slender thread of white around each word, may be judged from the fact, that three pages and twenty one lines of a sheet, foolscap size, sufficed to contain the whole of this long letter to the Earl of Thomond.—See Kilkenny Archæological Journal, new series, vol. i , p.p. 203-229

† *Earl of Clancare.*—This was false of Donough Mac Cormack. He concludes that the title of Earl of Clancare would sound better in the king's ears than that of Mac Carthy More.

‡ *The Archbishop of Dublin* had a hand in this letter, for Shelton writes to Florence " by direction of the Lord Archbishop of Dublin, and at the request of Mac Donogh, your agent here, I did write a letter, addressed to the King of Spain, subscribed by him."

majestie, how the said earle hath written to your majestie by two or three wayes; but understanding that these letters came not to your royall hands, hee hath now againe written by me to your majestie, making offer as well of his person and lands as of his vassals and subjects to your royall service; humbly beseeching your majestie to receiue favour, and aide him with your power and liberall hand, seeing there is no other that can and will assist us better against these heretikes in this holy enterprise. From Donegall, the fift of January, 1601.

" Your majesties loyal vassall to kisse your royall hands,

" DONOGHE CARTIE."

The next is a letter from the Archbishop to Mac Carthy :—

"*A letter from the* SPANISH ARCHBISHOP OF DUBLIN *to* FLORENCE MAC CARTIE.

" Right Honourable Lord, God is my witnesse, that after my arivall in Ireland, having knowledge of your lordships valour and learning, I had an extreame desire to see, communicate, and conferre with so principall a personage; but the danger of the way would not permitt mee. I am now departing into Spaine, with grief that I haue not visited those parts; but I hope shortly to returne into this kingdome, and into those parts to your satisfaction; and be assured, that I will performe with his majestie the office that a brother ought to doe, that he should send from Spaine. Because by letter I cannot speake any more, I leaue the rest untill sight. The Lord haue your lordship in his keeping according to my desire. From Donegall, the sixteenth of January, 1601.

" Yo MATEO ARÇOBISPO DE DUBLIN."

Hugh O'Donnell also writes Mac Carthy in his own dashing and soldier-like style—" Our commendations to you, Mac Cartie. We have received the letter you sent the 14th of October, and we swear by our word that you are no less grieved that you see us not, than we ourselves." He concludes, " you shall receive news of what Spaniards came to these parts by John Fitz-Thomas and Donogh Mac Cormack."

Florence was also in correspondence with Dermot Mac Carthy. Indeed, this Dermot, who was his kinsman, acted as a sort of agent, or ambassador in Spain, where he had resided some years. He writes to Florence in March, 1600, wishing him joy of his return to Cork, after his eleven years detention in England; he advises him to write to Philip, and say what force he will be able to raise in Ireland, what towns or castles he can place at his majesty's disposal; and to say if Cork could be surprised. He hopes the King of Spain will send an army to Ireland in spring. He tells Florence to send his letters through Don Diego Brochero, a great favourer of the Irish nation, and in great credit with the King.

O'Neill also writes to Florence, Feb. 6th., 1600, and exhorts him to serve valiantly against the Pagan beast. We cannot say whether Hugh intended this compliment for the queen or the English church.

We are told by Stafford—though we don't believe it—that Mac Carthy's wife told Sir Charles Wilmot, that "her husband's heart was malicious to the state; and that "Shilie," or Shelah, the wife of O'Sullivan More, and sister to Florence "exclaimed upon her brother as the cause of her husband's imprisonment." This was natural enough.

The president and secretary had no occasion to descend to such gossip in order to justify the arrest of Florence. Florence was a sincere rebel, who loved his country and religion and hated everything English, the Lord President, therefore, resolved to put him out of the way before the arrival of the Spaniards, so he sends a strong force to storm his stronghold at Pallis, and bring him a prisoner to Cork.

Here he is committed to the care of Sir Anthony Cooke, who carries him and James Fitz-Maurice—who are described as the two firebrands of Munster — to London. Arrived at London, they are brought before the council, who send them to the Tower. Here Florence lay till the 9th of July, 1614, when the Earls of Thomond and Clanricard, Sir Patrick Barnewell, Lord Delvin, Sir Randulph Mac Donnell, Sir Donnell O'Brien, Dermot MacCarthy, and David Condon united with him in a bond of £5,000 for permission to leave the Tower, but not to depart out of the realm of England, or to travel one day's journey from the city of London without license, under the hand of six of Her Majesty's Privy Council. How long he lived, or when he died, we as yet have no reliable data. A petition from his son, dated 1631, speaks of his father as still under restraint.

James Fitz-Thomas, the last Earl of Desmond, died in the Tower in 1603. His brother, John, went to Spain the same year, where he bore the title of Conde de Desmond. He died at Barcelona, leaving one son.

CHAPTER XIX.

THE SPANIARDS AT KINSALE.

A.D. 1601.

THE Lord President of Munster received the first official intimation of the sailing of the Spanish fleet, which arrived at Kinsale, by a letter from the secretary Cecil, dated from "the court at Windsore, this twelfth of August, 1601." It begins thus:—

"Sir George Carew, on Wednesday last, certain pinnaces of her majesties met with a fleete of Spaniards, to the number of fiftie saile, whereof seventeene are men of warre, the rest are transporting ships, as by this note inclosed doth appeare, which my intelligencer sent me at their going out. These ships cannot be but for Ireland, from which coast the storme kept them, unlesse it should be said that the king will land them in the Low Countries, which I will never beleeve hee durst adventure, knowing how long wee have expected them, and have fourtcene good ships out, which, if you compare with the note inclosed of his, you shall find that wee might be ashamed to suffer his fleete to land so quietly, and our fleete in the taile of them.

"But (which is more certaine) to confirme my opinion ever for Irelande, this proportion is fit for Ireland; there it may work mischief; and besides that they which met them, saw them set their course from the Sleeue (where they were on Wednesday) just for Ireland, and (as I verily thinke) they will fall for Limerick; for in Spaine it was advertised me, that their rendezvous was for the Blaskys, which you know is on that coast, about the Dingle or the Ventry."

The "note enclosed" from Cecil's private agent, or *Intelligencer*, is dated from Lisbon, the 25th of July, 1601, nearly a month before Cecil wrote Carew. It contains no name, but the agent is thoroughly acquainted with the subject on which he writes. John Annias could not be more definite:—

" Here at Lisbon, there are stayed about two hundred sailes of ships, out of which number *five and fortie onely* are selected for transportation of souldiers.

" The number of souldiers are sixe thousande,* whereof three thousand are kept aboard the ships, lest they should runne away, the other three thousand are a comming from Andaluzia and those parts, in a fleete of ships and gallies, under the conduct of the Adelantados sonne unto Lisbon.

" The ships which carie the souldiers are of the burthen of one hundred, one hundred and fiftie, and not above two hundred tons. The Spaniards doe refuse greater ships of the East Countries, which are stayed at Lisbon, and make choise of the smallest vessels they have for their purpose.

" Of their five and fortie sails of ships, seventeene saile onely are fitted for men of warre, whereof eleaven of them are but small ships, the other sixe are gallions, the Saint Paul, the Saint Peter, the Saint Andrew, and three smaller gallions of the king's, whose names I know not.

" For the manning of their ships, fifteene hundred sailors were sent hither out of Biskay.

" The Marquess of S.ta Croce goeth admirall in the Saint Paul, Sibiero, alias Seriago, vice-admirall, in the Saint Peter. They make account to bee ready by the last of July, and ride with their yards acrosse.

" The two ships of Dunkerke (which have remained long at Lisbon) doe make ready to come away with the fleete."

Cecil sends Carew a private note lest the provincials should betray him. There was no man in wide Munster

* *The number of souldiers are sixe thousand.*—Three thousand was about the number that came to Kinsale with Don Juan de Aquila. Another thousand may have landed at Baltimore and Castlehaven.

who more thoroughly appreciated the maxim, "*take care of yourself*," than Sir George. But we give the note ; for friendship and personal kindness among men in high places, are like green spots and sheltered nooks among the cliffs of high mountains, the heads of which are covered with snow.

"My deere George, now will I omit all the petty particulars of many things, because the great storme (which I presume is fallen upon Mounster) drownes all my petty cares, and wounds my soule for care of you, of whom I know not what to expect, but as a lost childe, for though I know you are not so mad as to runne to the enemies mouthes, with a dozen persons in comparison, yet I am desperately affraid that the provincials should betray you; even those I meane that must or will seeme to be principally about you, &c."

A Captain Love arrived in Cork harbour, and sent the president a letter, dated the 13th of September, stating that he had seen five-and-forty sail at sea, on the north of Cape Finesterre, bearing north, he therefore conjectured that Ireland was their destination. Every one was in daily expectation of the Spanish fleet, some fearing and more desiring it. When a strange sail appeared above the horizon,—"*It is a Spanish ship!*" If accompanied by a second,— "*It is the Spanish fleet!*"

But the real Spanish fleet came at last, on the 20th of September, "towards night." The sovereign of Kinsale sent a messenger to inform Sir Charles Wilmot, who was in Cork, that a fleet of five-and-forty ships were observed from the Old Head of Kinsale; that they had passed the mouth of the river, and were bearing up for Cork harbour. The information was correct; the Spaniards were preparing to enter the Cove, when the wind "suddanely scorted, whereupon they tacked about, and made for Kinsale."

There was no army in Kinsale able to oppose their landing;* the force consisted of fifty foot and forty horse, which departed for Cork, "the better sort of persons going with them, with all their goods."

The Spaniards marched with five-and-twenty colors towards the town. The gates were thrown open, and the sovereign, with his white rod, went about billeting them upon the inhabitants. Stafford says, the people were more ready to receive them "than if they had beene the queene's forces." To encourage them in such good conduct, to banish fear, and "win their love by gentle and mild usage," Don Juan de Aquila, the Spanish general, who appears to have been a man of singular politeness, made the following proclamation:—

"*A Proclamation made in Kinsale by* DON JUAN DE AQUILA, *to give contentment to the inhabitants of Kinsale.*

"We, Don Juan de Aquila, general of the armie to Philip, Kinge of Spaine, by these presents doe promise that all the inhabitants of the towne of Kinsale shall receive no injury by any of our retinew, but rather shall be used as our brethren and friends, and that it shall bee lawful for any of the inhabitants that list to transport, without any molestation in body or goods, and as much as shall remaine, likewise without any hurt.

"DON JUAN DE AQUILA."

The whole Spanish force consisted of about three thousand men, under the command of Don Juan de Aquila, Maestro del Campo General; Don Francisco

---

* *To oppose their landing.*—" Captain William Saxey's company lay then in garrison, but because the town was of small strength, unable to withstand so powerful an nemy, order was given to Sir Charles Wilmot, [by the Lord President, we conclude] that they should quit the same, and retreat to Cork."—*Pac. Hib.*, p. 337.

de Padilla, Maestro del Campo; Antonis Centono, Maestro del Campo, and forty-two Captaines, besides other officers.

Don Juan describes the town as a "place contayning not above two hundred houses, on the side of a river, invironed with hills, and without any kind of defence. There is in the middle of the haven a certain, almost an island, on the which it seemeth good to Don Juan to have a fort made." The "Old Fort," as it is styled, remains to the present day.

"As soon as Don Juan had lodged himself, he dispatched messengers to the Earles Tyrone and O'Donnell, advising them of his arrival. The naturals [natives] of the country report the forces of the earles* to be much less than was given out to us." The queen's people and forces had carried away all the cattle and corn of the district, and broken down the mills. All the Spaniards could get was "a few cowes from the poore peple, who are glad to sell." English troopers come every day to the walls, to see what the Spaniards are about. The Spaniards, having no cavalry, must submit to the indignity. A skirmish occurs near the castle of Rincurran, which is in the possession of the Spaniards; some were hurt, but none slain.

The new Lord Deputy Mountjoy, Sir George Carew, the Earl of Ormond, Sir Richard Wingfield (marshal of the army), and Sir Robert Gardiner (the Chief Justice) were in Kilkenny holding a council as to what they should do, *if* the Spaniards arrived, when Sir Charles Wilmot's letters announced the arrival. They

---

* *The earles.*—We conclude that O'Donnell, as well as Tyrone, was styled an earl.

are taken by surprise. Some propose they should hasten to Dublin to collect a sufficient force. The president, if we can believe Stafford, says to the deputy, "No, rather go to Cork or Kinsale with your page, than turn your back on the enemy." This looks more like Mountjoy than Carew. But let it be the latter. The deputy then asks, what about supplies? The president has provided the supplies. The deputy is so overjoyed that he rises from his chair and takes the president in his arms. That very day the Lord Deputy, the president, and Sir Robert Gardiner leave Kilkenny, for Cork. They stop the first night at Lord Dunboyne's, the next at Clonmel, the next with Lord Roche, and the following day they are in Cork.

And, "now are we come," exclaims Sir George, " to the siege of Kinsale, a place ordained, wherein the honor and safety of Queen Elizabeth, the reputation of the English nation, the cause of religion, and the crown of Ireland must be by arms disputed."

The Spaniards were in want of horses. They had brought sixteen hundred saddles, " hoping," as they had been promised, " to find horses in Ireland." The imprisonment of Florence Mac Carthy had disarranged everything, and struck terror into the hearts of most of the subordinate chieftains of Munster. In this emergency, Don Juan and Brother Matthew, the Spanish Archbishop of Dublin, write to Tyrone and O'Donnell to hasten their coming.

"*A letter from the* ARCHBISHOP *of* DUBLIN *unto* TYRONE *and* O'DONNELL.

" Pervenimus in Kinsale, cum classe & exercitu, Regis nostri Philippi; expectamus vestras excellentias qualibet hora, veniant

ergo quàm velociter potuerint, portantes equos, quibus maximé indigemus, & jam alia via scripsimus, non dico plura valete.
"FRATER MATHEUS ARCHIEPISCOPUS DUBLINENS."

The letter of Don Juan, in its noble brevity, is worthy of Julius Cæsar.

" A qui estamos guardando a veustras Senorias illustrissimus Como largamente otra via hemos escritos. A Dios 12. Oct. 1601.

"DON JUAN DE AQUILA.
" Excellentissimis Dominis
" Don O'Neale and O'Donnell."

Don Juan, " Commander in God's War," makes a proclamation to all the Irish Catholics in Kinsale, Cork, and other villages and cities, in which he explains that they owe no subjection to Queen Elizabeth, who has been deprived of her kingdom, and her subjects absolved from their fidelity, by the Pope. But this has not the desired effect, for Cormac Mac Carthy, Lord of Muskerry, and his people, unite with the deputy against the strangers. The Irish are marched up to the very trenches, that the Spaniards may see the side they have taken. They even come to blows with the foreigners, and are found to strike hard and home. The Spaniards make a foray on the " island, as it seemed,"— the tongue of land in the mouth of the harbour—and carry off three hundred cows and a number of sheep, which they bring to Castle Park. Captain Taaffe* pursues the party, and retakes a portion of the prey beneath the walls of Castle Park.

The castle of Rincurran, which lies outside the town, is in the hands of the Spaniards. It is besieged by the

* *Captain Taaffe* was the grandfather of Theobald, Lord Taaffe, the commander of the Irish army at the battle of Knockninoss.

Lord Deputy. Don Juan sends a party of five hundred men from the town to its relief. A sharp skirmish occurs, in which the Spaniards are beaten back and a commander taken prisoner; Lord Audley, Sir Oliver St. John,* and Sir Garrett Barry are wounded. The officer in command of the castle sounds a drum, and asks for permission to parley. It is granted by Carew. " There came with their drum an Irishman, borne in Corke, who prayed, in the name of the rest, that they might be permitted to leave the castle, arms, bag and baggage, and enter Kinsale." They are refused. They send a drum with a serjeant, and after the serjeant a commander, who insists on leaving the castle with their arms. They are refused, and the battery again begins to play with "furie," when another drum is sent, and the place delivered up. Dermot Mac Carthy, or Don Dermutio, the Spanish agent of Florence Mac Carthy, was the only Irishman taken prisoner on this occasion. The commander was allowed to wear his sword on leaving the castle, and to deliver it into the hand of the Lord President, which he did " upon his knees." The prisoners were brought into the English camp, and then sent on to Cork. Sir George received the following letter of thanks from the queen, the 31st of October, 1601 :—

"HER MAJESTY'S *letter unto the* LO. PRESIDENT.

" My faithfull George, if ever more service of worth were performed in shorter space than you have done wee are deceived; among many eye-witnesses wee have received the fruit thereof, and bid you faithfully credit, that what so witt, courage, or care may doe, wee truely finde they have beene all truely acted in all your

* *Oliver St. John,* who became Lord President of Munster, was the granduncle of the celebrated Lord Bolingbroke.

charge, and for the same beleeve that it shall neither bee unremembered nor unrewarded; and in the mean while beleeve my helpe nor prayers shall never faile you.

"Your soveraigne that best regards you,

"Eliz. R."

Intelligence was at this time communicated that O'Donnell was on his march to the relief of Kinsale. The Lord President is dispatched, much against his will, with a force of about three thousand men, two thirds of whom were Irish, to intercept the northern chieftain. O'Donnell managed to give the president the slip, near Holy Cross, in the county of Tipperary, although they lay one night within four miles of each other; but the country, as Stafford or Sir George says, "stood so partially effected to the traitors, as by no promise of reward or other satisfaction could they be induced to draw any drought upon them," or get any information of O'Donnell's movements from them.

It would appear from the examination of Dermot Mac Carthy, or Don Dermutio, who was made prisoner at the siege of Rincurran Castle, that the president was in danger of being arrested and delivered into the hands of Don Juan, by Cormac Mac Dermot, Lord of Muskerry, and his captains and followers, who composed a large portion of the army. Sir George says,— but it is *after* Don Dermutio's examination,—" I ate with him, and many times had private conference with him, not seeming to take notice of any of his treacherous ways." Sir George gave himself credit for great shrewdness and penetration. But it is quite possible that Florence's Spanish agent may have spread this report, in order to spite the Lord of Muskerry, who joined the queen's party.

O'Donnell, who made, without rest, "the greatest march with cariage that hath beene heard of"—above thirty-two Irish miles—passed through Muskerry to Castlehaven, where six Spanish vessels with troops and great store of ordnance and munition had arrived. O'Neill came to the south about the same time, and encamped at no great distance from the English lines. These arrivals gave great confidence to the Irish chieftains, the most of whom gave up their castles to be garrisoned by Spanish troops:

"Untill this time none of the provincials of Mounster, that had beene either protected or pardoned, relapsed; but now upon the comming of these seconds to Castlehaven, Sir Finnin O'Drischall and all the O'Drischalls, Sir Owen Mac Cartie's sonnes, and almost all the Carties in Carbrie, Donnell O'Sulevan Beare, O'Sulevans More's eldest son, Donnell Mac Cartie, the Earle of Clan-Care's base sonne, with all the Carties of Desmond, John O'Conner Kerry, the Knight of Kerry, all the protected and pardoned men in Kerry and Desmond, and all else from Kinsale and Limericke westwards, joyned with O'Donnell and the Spaniards; whereat little wonder is to bee made, considering what power religion and gold hath in the hearts of men, both which the Spaniards brought with them into Ireland. Donach O'Drischall delivered unto them his castle at Castlehaven, which commanded the harbour; Sir Finnin O'Drischall (who never in the course of his whole life had beene tainted with the least spot of disloyaltie) rendred unto them his castle of Donneshed at Baltimore, and his castle of Donnelong, in the island of Inisherkan, betwene which castles all entrances into that haven was debarred; and Donnell O'Sulevan surrendered unto them his strong castle of Dunboy, which absolutely commands Bearehaven; these three harbours being without all exception the best in the west of Mounster."

The royal appointments, pay, and presents of Philip, King of Spain, had a very powerful effect upon our Irish chieftains, and reminded them of their Spanish descent. "Blood is thicker than water." Let us hear O'Sullivan Beare on this subject:—

"*A letter from* DONNELL O'SULEVAN BEARE *unto the* KING OF SPAIN.

"It hath beene ever, most mighty and renowned prince, and most gracious Catholike king, from time to time, manifestly proved by daily experience among us, the Irish, that there is nothing worketh more forcibly in our hearts, to winne, and to draw our love and affection, than naturall inclination to our progeny and ofspring, and the memoriall of the friendship, which sticketh still in our minds; chiefely the same being renewed, cherished, and kept in us by mutuall affection, and by showing like friendship to us also; wee, the mere Irish, long sithence deriving our roote and originall from the famous and most noble race of the Spaniards, viz., from Milecius, sonne to Bile, sonne to Breogwin, and from Lwighe, sonne to Lythy, sonne to Breogwin, by the testimony of our old ancient bookes of antiquities, our petigrees, our histories, and our cronicles.

"Though there were no other matter, wee came not as naturall branches of the famous tree, whereof we grew, but beare a hearty love and a naturall affection, and intire inclination of our hearts and minds, to our ancient most loving kinsfolkes, and the most noble race whereof wee descended.

"Besides this, my soveraigne, such is the abundance of your goodnesse, and the bounty or greatnesse of your liberality, *now every way undeserved of our parts*, as tokens of love and affection by your majestie shewed unto us, that it is not fit nor seemely for us but to bestow our persons, our men, and our goods in the service of a prince that dealeth so gratiously with us, that sendeth forces of men, great treasure, victuals and munition for our aide, against our enemies, that seek to overwhelme and extinguish the Catholike faith diabolically, put to death our chieftaines tyrrannously, coveting our lands and livings unlawfully.

"For the foresaid considerations, and for many other commendable causes me moving, I bequeath, and offer in humblenesse of mind, and with all my heart, my owne person with all my forces, perpetually to serve your majestie, not only in Ireland, but in any other place where it shall please your highnesse; I commit also my wife, my children, my mannors, townes, countrey, and lands, and my haven of Dunboy, called Biara-haven (next under God) to the protection, keeping, and defence or commericke of your majestie, to be and remaine in your hands, and at your disposition.

" Also at your pleasure bee it (my liege Lord) to send defence and strong keeping of the haven of Dunboy, first for yourselfe (my soveraigne) to receive your ships, and for mee also as your loving servant, so that the Queene of England's ships may not possesse the same before you, while I follow the warres in your highnesse behalfe. I pray Almighty God to give your majestie long life, health of body and soule, with increase of grace and prosperity. So I betake you to the keeping of God.

" From the campe neere Kinsale, the nine and twentieth of December, 1601, Stilo Novo.

" Your most dutifull loving servant,
" DONNELL O'SULEVAN BEARE."

O'Neill showed himself on a hill about a mile and a half from the English camp, where he had "a fastness of wood and water." The English were now between two fires—the besiegers were besieged. During the day the Tyrone horse hovered round their camp; at night the Spaniards made sorties upon their entrenchments. Although their artillery played upon the town, they "had no meaning to make a breach." This was the state of things when Don Juan pressed the Irish general to attack the English camp, and throw provisions into Kinsale:—

" The Irish reduced the English to great straits, for they did not permit hay, corn, or water, straw or fuel, to be taken into the Lord Justice's camp. They remained thus for some time, watching each other, until Don Juan, the general of the Spaniards, sent a letter privately to the Irish, requesting them to attack a part of the Lord Justice's camp on a certain night, and (adding) that he himself would attack the other part of it on the same night; for they (the Spaniards) were reduced to great straits by the English, as the English were distressed by the Irish.

"The chiefs of the Kinel-Connell began to deliberate in council on this suggestion, and they were for some time dissentient on adopting this resolution, for it was O'Neill's advice not to attack them immediately by any means, but to keep them still in the strait in which they were, until they should perish of famine,* and the want of all the necessaries of which they stood in need, as some of their men and horses had already perished. O'Donnell, however, was oppressed at heart, and ashamed to hear the complaint and distress of the Spaniards without relieving them from the difficulty in which they were, even if his death or destruction, or the loss of his people, should result from it; so that the resolution they finally agreed to was, to attack the Lord Justice's camp, as they had been ordered."

It was finally decided to attack the English camp at night, or at least before break of day. The Irish might have succeeded in surprising the Lord Deputy, but there was a man in that camp that could not be surprised. He, or his panegyrist, gives all the credit of the information to a bottle of aqua-vitæ.

Tuesday, the 22nd of December, Brian Hugh Oge Mac Mahon, "a principal commander in the Irish army," whose eldest son had been a page to the Lord President, sent a boy to Captain Taaffe, praying the Lord President to let him have a bottle of aqua-vitæ. The president, "for old acquaintance," could not refuse this modest request.

The next night, the 23rd of December, the same messenger brought a letter, thanking Sir George for

---

* *Perish of famine.*—" If Tyrone had laine still, and not suffered himself to be drawn to the plaine ground by the Spaniards' importunity, all our horse must needs have been sent away or starved."—*Moryson's Hist. of Ireland,* Book ii., c. ii.

the whiskey, and telling him to stand on his guard; that he, Mac Mahon, was at the rebel council, where it was resolved the next night to attack the English camp, and that the Spaniards were also in readiness to sally from the town.

The Lord President posts off to the Lord Deputy and receives his instructions. We feel assured that Sir George slept none the next night. The night is far gone when a horseman rides up and says, "*My lord, its time to arm, the enemy is near the camp.*"

But Sir George does not arm; he has singular ability of keeping out of danger. He remains behind to watch the Spaniards. Mountjoy takes the field, and points to a piece of ground where the Irish must force a passage, saying to the marshal, "Here I am resolved to give the enemie battaile."

Tyrone approaches at the head of his troops, hoping to take the English by surprise, and finds them at the ford, prepared, in all the panoply of war, to dispute the passage. He retires before them, which is not his wont — the Four Masters say, in order to unite his forces with those of O'Donnell, whose troops had lost their way in the dark—the deputy gives the order to follow. The marshal, seeing the enemy in some disorder, asks permission to charge. The Irish horse, that are posted on the side of a bog, stand firm. The Earl of Clanricard and Sir Richard Greame advance and charge with a thousand foot, but cannot break the Irish ranks. Sir William Godolphin rides up with the Lord Deputy's horse, Captain Mynshall with the Lord President's horse, and Sir John Barkley with two or three companies of foot; they unite their forces, and again charge, and carry all before them. The Irish are broken, scattered, and slain.

Captain Tirrell, the friend of O'Neill, was in command of the seven hundred Spaniards that had landed at Castlehaven; this division of the enemy was also broken, slain, or taken prisoners. The Lord Deputy's soldiers pursued the skipping kerne and heavy-armed galloglasses for two miles, and returned to the camp when they were "tyred with killing." The Irish generals left twelve hundred dead on the field, besides eight hundred wounded, many of whom died that night.

If we can believe Stafford or Carew, and no one could be better informed than Sir George, there was no one slain on the English side but Sir Richard Greames' cornet. Sir Henry Davers was hurt with the sword slightly; Sir William Godolphin, a little razed on the thigh with a halbert; and Captain Crofts, the scout master, with a shot in the back. Not above five or six of the common soldiers hurt. The Earl of Clanricard had "many faire escapes, being shot through his garments; and no man did bloody his sword more than his lordship that day. He gave no quarter, and commanded his soldiers to kill the rebels." For these daring deeds he received, at the hands of the Lord Deputy Mountjoy, the order of knighthood "in the midst of the dead bodies," and there they gave God thanks for their victory, and discharged a volley of shot.

Don Juan, who is on the qui-vive, and the very tiptoe of expectation, hears the volley, and concluding it is the Irish marching victorious on Kinsale, dashes out to meet them. He sees the Spanish colors carried in triumph by English soldiers, and makes a hasty retreat into the town.

Stafford concludes his account by rehearsing a prophecy in which this battle was predicted. Lord Thomond had read it in an "olde Irish booke of prophesies," containing the Irish name, and date of the battle. "I deliver," says Stafford, "nothing but trueth," and as "one swallow makes no summer, so shall not *this one true prophesy* increase my credulitie in predictions of that kinde."

After this defeat Don Juan de Aquila was desperate, but this did not justify the black treachery with which he acted towards his Irish friends, who had lost all in their hasty and over-anxious zeal to relieve him.

One week after the battle, on the 31st of December, Don Juan sent a message to the deputy, and asked permission to parley. Like Sir George Carew, he could use his tongue and pen better than the sword. Sir William Godolphin is sent to his camp, whom he addresses in the following style:—

"I have found in your viceroy a sharp and powerful opponent, yet an honorable enemy; in the Irish, not only weak and barbarous, but (as I feared) perfidious friends. I am so far in my affection reconciled to the one and distasted to the other, that I invite you to an overture which will be profitable to the state of England, and little prejudicial to the crown of Spain."

The overture was, to deliver up Kinsale, and all other places—the very castles which the Irish chieftains had put into his hands—on condition of his being allowed to depart on honorable terms, with all the necessary appliances of transports for his army.

The deputy agrees, provided the Spanish general will leave his treasure, munition, and artillery behind, as an acknowledgment of his having been vanquished. Don Juan is most indignant; he refuses peremptorily; such a proposition touches his honor; not a hoof must be left behind in Kinsale; he would rather endure the utmost misery, than be guilty of so foul a treason against his prince, and so great a dishonor to his profession. Should such a thing be even mentioned again —let the deputy resume the sword.

After these heroics, the Don descends from his high horse, and reminds the viceroy that he gets Castlehaven, Bearehaven, and other places, "bettered by his art and industry, and provided with victuals, munition, and good artillery, all furnished by Spain." He thinks the deputy would get these things cheap, though he paid two hundred thousand ducats for them.

So thought the deputy, he therefore resolved, without further parley, to accept the conditions. The following is a copy of the article of composition:—

"The Articles of Composition betweene the LORD DEPUTIE and COUNCELL, and DON JUAN DE AQUILA.

MOUNTJOY.

"In the Towne of Kinsale, in the Kingdome of Ireland, (the second day of the moneth of January, 1602,) betweene the Noble Lords the Lord Mountjoy, Lord Deputie, and Generall in the Kingdome of Ireland, and Don Juan de Aquila, Captaine and

Camp-master General, and Governour of the Armie of his Majestie the King of Spaine, the said Lord Deputie being encamped, and besieging the said towne and the said Don Juan within it, for just respects, and to avoyd shedding of blood, these Conditions following were made betweene the said Lords Generalls, and their Campes, with the Articles that follow :—

" First—That the said Don Juan de Aquila shall quit the places which hee holds in this kingdome, as well of the Towne of Kinsale, as those which are held by the souldiers under his command, in Castlehaven, Baltimore, and the Castle of Beere-haven, and other parts, to the said Lord Deputie, or to whom he shall appoynt, giving him safe transportation (and sufficient) for the said people, of ships and victualls, with the which the said Don Juan with them may go for Spaine, if he can at one time, if not in two shippings.

" Item—That the souldiers at this present being under the command of Don Juan in this kingdome, shall not beare armes against her Majestie the Queene of England, wheresoever supplyes shall come from Spaine, till the said souldiers be unshipped in some of the Ports of Spaine, being dispatched (as soone as may be) by the Lord Deputy, as he promiseth upon his faith and honour.

" Item—For the accomplishing whereof, the Lord Deputie offereth to giue free passport to the said Don Juan and his army, as well Spaniards as other nations whatsoever, that are under his command, and that hee may depart with all the things hee hath, armes, munitions, money, ensignes displayed, artillery, and other whatsoever provisions* of warre, and any kind of stuffe, as well that which is in Castlehaven, as Kinsale and other parts.

"Item—That they shall haue ships and victuals, sufficient for their money, according and at the prices which here they use to giue, that all the people and the said things, may bee shipped (if it be possible) at one time, if not at two, and that to bee within the time aboue named.

"Item—That if by contrary winds, or by any other occasions, there shall arriue at any Port of these kingdomes of Ireland, or England, any ships of these (in which the said men goe) they bee intreated as friends, and may ride safely in the harbour, and bee victualled for their money, and haue moreover things which they shall need, to furnish them to their voyage.

"Item—During the time that they shall stay for shipping, victuals shall be given to Don Juan's people at just and reasonable rates.

"Item—That of both parts shall be cessation of armes, and security that no wrong be offered any one.

"Item—That the ships (in which they shall goe for Spaine) may passe safely, by any other ships whatsoever, of her Majesties the Queene of England; and so shall they of the said Queene, and her subjects by those that shall goe from hence, and the said ships being arrived in Spaine, shall returne assoone as they haue unshipped their men, without any impediment given them by his majestie, or any other person in his

---

* *Provisions.*—The following were the rations of each soldier:—Every week—four days flesh, three days fish. Every flesh day—bread, twenty-four ounces; beef, six ounces. Every fish day—bread, twenty-four ounces, and one ounce of butter. For every hundred men, one pipe of wine.—*Pacata Hibernia*, p. 443.

name, but rather they shall shew them favour, and helpe them (if they need anything;) and for security of this, they shall giue into the Lord Deputies hands, three captaines such as hee shall choose.

" For the securitie of the performance of the articles, Don Juan offereth that he will confirme, and sweare to accomplish this agreement: and likewise some of the captaines of his charge shall sweare and confirme the same in a severall writing.

" Item—That hee in person shall abide in this kingdome, where the Lord Deputie shall appoynt, (till the last shipping) upon his lordship's word: and if it happen that his people be shipped all at once, the said Don Juan shall goe in the same fleet, without any impediment given him: but rather the Lord Deputy shall giue a good ship, in which hee may goe; and if his said men be sent in two shippings, then he shall goe in the last.

" And in like sort the said Lord Deputie shall sweare and confirme, and giue his word in the behalfe of her Majestie the Queene and his owne, to keepe and accomplish this agreement, and joyntly the Lord President, the Lo. Marshall of the Campe, and the other of the Councell of State, and the Earles of Thomond and Clanricard, shall sweare and confirme the same in a severall writing.

" I doe promise and sweare to accomplish and keepe these articles of agreement, and promise the same likewise on the behalf of his Majestie Catholique, the King my Master.

" DON JUAN DE AQUILA.

This document is also signed by " GEORGE CAREW, THOMOND, CLANRICARD, RICHARD WINGFIELD, ROBERT GARDINER, GEORGE BOURCHIER, and RICHARD LEVISON."

These articles having been duly executed, the Spaniards were shipped off with despatch. " Haste was made for their embarking at two sundry times." There were shipped at Kinsale, under the care of Captain Francis Slingsbye, 2,070; at Baltimore and Castlehaven, under the care of Captain Harvey, 415; from other places, 540 —making a total of 3,025; " besides captains, inferior officers, priests, religious men, and a great company of Irish."

CHAPTER XX.

DON JUAN IN CORK.

A.D. 1602.

DON JUAN having made all the necessary arrangements for the embarkation of his troops, went with the Deputy and the Lord President to Cork. The Lord Deputy lodged in the Bishop of Cork's house,* Don Juan in the city, and the President at Shandon Castle.

It is the 10th of February. Don Juan is busy making preparations to embark, when the president hears that a Spanish pinnace has arrived in some western port, with letters from the King of Spain to the Spanish general. Sir George Carew posts off to the bishop's house to the deputy, and asks him if he has a desire to know the nature of the correspondence. It may be commanding Don Juan to remain. Mountjoy says his heart is itching to have the letters in his hands, and prays the Lord President to intercept them, if he can "*handsomely doe it.*"

It is just one of those things which Sir George *can* do handsomely. He sends for Captain Nuce, and tells him to select a few trusty men, to deck them out like

* *Bishop of Cork's house.*—William Lyon was at this time Bishop of Cork, Cloyne, and Ross. He was appointed in 1583.

bandits, and rob the messenger of letters, money, and even horses, and leave him and his guide bound in some wood. Captain Nuce meets the Spaniard within five miles of Cork, and does his business to perfection. He brought the packet to the president at Shandon Castle, the day Don Juan is dining there. The Spanish messenger, who has been unbound by some friendly hand, gains the city that evening, and tells Don Juan that he has been robbed of his despatches by soldiers in the guise of bandits. The Spanish general goes to the deputy, grievously complaining that his messenger has been robbed by soldiers. The deputy is very sorry; "debaucht souldiers" is a common thing in every army, but he suspects it was done by country thieves, that they might shew the letters to their friends in rebellion. Don Juan is by no means satisfied with this reply, and requests the deputy to inquire of Sir George, of whom he has "a vehement suspicion." The Lord Deputy answers,—"Upon his fayth, he was sure *the president had them not;* which hee might well doe, for they were in his owne possession." In order to satisfy the Don, Mountjoy published a proclamation, and offered a reward to any one who could discover the thieves, promising to *spare the lives of those who committed the theft*, on their coming forward, and making a full confession.

The letters were of so grave and important a character, and so explicit as it regarded Philip's determination to conquer Ireland, that we doubt, if Don Juan would have ventured to embark his forces in the face of them. The first is from the Duke of Lerma:—

"*A letter from the* DUKE OF LERMA *to* DON JUAN DE AQUILA.

"Not many dayes past I wrote unto you, and now I make answere to those which I received from you the thirteenth of the last October, assuring you, that his majesty puts great confidence in your care and valour. As touching the men, and other things which you demaund, there is dispatched a good quantitie, and more is in preparing, and make you no doubt, but still more shall bee in sending, as much as may bee: for his majestie hath it before his oyes, and I have taken in hand the solliciting thereof; wherefore you may bee assured, that you shall not want any thing which may bee sent that is needfull. There is now in readinesse 150 launces, which shall be presently embarqued, and more men are in levying with expedition, with whom money shall be sent. And so referring myselfe (for the rest) to his majesties dispatch, I will say no more, but to assure you, that in all things which may concerne you, esteeme mee ever to bee your sollicitor. God keepe you. Valladolid, the fourth of December, 1601.

"EL DUQUE DE LERMA, MARQUES DE DENIA."

The next letter is from Lerma to the Spanish Archbishop of Dublin, who had accompanied Don Juan to Kinsale:—

"*A letter from the* DUKE OF LERMA *to the* ARCHBISHOP OF DUBLIN.

"I have received your lordship's letters, giving thanks to God for the successe of your journey, for by it it appeares that there is a way and doore open for many good purposes for his service, and his majestie hath much confidence of the care and zeale which your lordship hath for the progression in the same. Now we send you a good body of men, with such things as is necessary, and more shall be prepared, and so continue sending as much as wee may, whereof you need not doubt; for his majestie (whom God preserve) holds it before his eyes, forasmuch as the most important thing (appertaining to this businesse) is the joyning of the earles with Don Juan de Aquila, his majestie commandeth your Lordship to doe in it your uttermost endevour, according to the confidence hee hath in your zeale. God preserve your lordship. From Valladolid, the fifth of December, 1601.

"EL DUQUE DE LERMA, MARQUES DE DENIA.

"Let not your lordship be wearied with your travells, I hope in God they will be full of good successes.

The next letter is from the Spanish secretary. It is full of promise, and one well calculated to spur the Spanish general to great things:—

"*A letter from the Secretary* YBARRA *to* DON JUAN DE AQUILA.

"By Captaine Albornoz I wrote unto your lordship, and I wish that this dispatch may overtake him (at the Groyne) according to the desire I hold, that it, and that which goes with it, were with your lordship, certifying you that as much is done (as may be) for your supply in all things. I wrote unto your lordship, that there were two companies of horse ready to be sent to you, *but now I say there is three*, and in them two hundred and twenty souldiers, well armed and horsed; and it please God they shall be all embarqued in this moneth. God in his divine mercy guid them.

"There is men levied in all Castile and Portugall, and shipping embarged to transport them, victuals, and other necessaries in providing; and now at this instant there is embarqued in Lisborne, in the Groyne, and Saint Andera more than sixe thousand hanegas of wheat, and three hundred pipes of wine, and some beanes and rice, and sixe hundred arrobas of oyle; and moreover, besides this which I say is embarqued, there are commissaries taking of more up, and no care shall bee wanting to hasten them away.

"I have spoken with Captaine Moreles, and of that which hee hath told mee of the seat of the place, and of the small number of men your lordship hath, I feele myselfe grieved; *but when I call to mind what a person Don Juan de Aquila is, the way is open unto me to expect great matters*, and I hope God will grant the same according to the worth of your lordship against your wicked enemies.

"Let your lordship hasten the joyning of the earles with you, for of all things that is most important, which being done, before the queene can reenforce her army, all is accomplished; I am desirous to heare that the excellent good horsemen were with your lordship, that with them your lordship may winne honour in the field, &c.

"From Valladolid this seventh of December, 1601.

"ESTEVAN DE YBARRA."

We conclude from the tone and style that the next letter was dictated by the king himself, and that the writer was the king's confidential secretary :—

"*A letter from the Secretary* FRANQUESA *to* DON JUAN DE AQUILA.

"His majestic is much satisfied for the good government (in those occasions) of your army, and I hope in God, that with the succours which now shall be sent unto you, it will be bettered, in such sort, that you will not onely bee able to defend yourselfe from the enemies, but also to chastise them, the meanes to effect the same, is for you to hold yourselfe as you are, untill the succours aforesaid doe come; in the meane time, the more you are pressed upon, the more will be your reward and recompence, which his majestie will conferre upon you, the which I will thrust on as occasion shall offer it selfe, and bee always vigilant in these things which shall concerne your lordship as I have beene. God preserve your lordship according to my desire.

"From Mansilla, the thirteenth of January, 1602."

The following letter was written *after* O'Donnell's arrival in Spain, telling of the signal defeat of the Irish before Kinsale. The king is by no means discouraged. If Don Juan had any of the old blue blood of Spain in his veins, the following letter was well calculated to send it in a warm current through his whole frame :—

"*A letter from the* DUKE OF LERMA *to* DON JUAN DE AQUILA.

"By that which Zubiare and Pedro Lopez de Soto hath written, and by the comming of the Earle O'Donnell, who is now in the Groyne, wee have understood of the overthrow of the earles, and from thence is gathered that all the forces are now bent against you, and that your onely valour and wisdome hath been able to resist them; and let the great estimation his majesty holdeth of you mitigate the care which this businesse may bring you.

His majestie hath commanded me speedily to prepare gallant succours, both by land and sea, which is done, and shall bee presently dispatched, and this ship is onely sent to advertise you thereof, to the end that you may with the more courage defend your selfe, and to bring a true report in what state you stand, which may more particularly appeare unto you by his majestie's letter, which with this you shall receive.

"Hee hath commanded me to add this, that hee hath in his favour made you one of his councellors, of his councell at warres, which I congratulate with you, assuring you on his part that, God willing, hee will conferre greater favours upon you; wherefore proceed cheerefully, as both now and heretofore (in the course of your life) you have done, taking every occasion to strengthen your selfe in this siege, and to endammage the enemy, that hee may not hinder you, and to assure the army no man living hath received greater rewards from his majestie then you shall; I take upon myselfe the care of it, and I pray you to write me such good newes as I desire, whereof I hope in God. In Mansilla, the thirteenth of January, 1602.

"EL DUQUE DE LERMA, MARQUES DE DENIA.

" God is my witnesse, I neither eate nor sleepe with lesse care then any one of them that are with you, and I would willingly be in the perill of every one of you, and if the shedding of my blood might be advantageous, I would readily giue it for you all that haue such need. Doe your endeavours, for presently succours shall be sent unto you.

" To Don Juan de Aquila, Master of
the Campe, Generall of the Men-
of-Warre in Ireland."

The last letter is subscribed YO EL REY "I, the king." Doctor Doran says, *Yo El Rey* has a thundering echo about it :—

"*A letter from the* KING OF SPAINE *to* DON JUAN DE AQUILA.
"EL REY.

" Don Juan de Aquila, Master of the Campe, Generall of my Army in Ireland; by that which Pedro de Zubiare, and Pedro

Lopez de Soto haue written unto me, I haue understood of the defeat of the Earles Oneale and Odonnell, and likewise I now see that all your hopes remaines in your valour and wisdome; wherein I haue such confidence, that I hope in the middest of so many dangers and labours (wherewith you are inuironed) that you will preserue the army untill more succours of shipping, men, armes, and munitions be sent unto you, which are with al possible expedition in preparing, and shall bee speedily dispatched; you may make use of them, and take reuenge of the enemy, and untill they come, which shall be (as I have said) with celerity, preserue yourselfe.

"I doe not advise you of any particulars, because I assure myselfe of your judgement and experience, that knowes how to make your advantage of such occasions as the enemy shall give, for the benefit of the siege. And your selfe and the army (which is with you) shall have good testimony of my bounty, thankfulnesse, and honour I will doe unto you all; and so much doe you signifie unto the army from me. The Duke of Lerma shall write more unto you. From Mansilla, the one-and-thirtie of January, 1602.

"Yo El Rey.

" To Don Juan de Aquila, Master
 of the Campe, Generall of our
 Army in Ireland.

" Don Pedro Franquesa."

Don Juan de Aquila remained in the most blissful ignorance of this correspondence. "All the while" Don Juan was at Cork, the president and he had familiar discourse together; but for the most part their passages of speech was between jest and earnest; somewhat sharp, and especially when they spoke of religion, and their sovereigns, or nations. But the Spaniard "carried a good respect of the president, as by writing and presents sent, which shall in its due place appear."

Neither deputy or president were at ease. Mountjoy, writing to the lords of the English council, from Cork, on the 15th of February, says, " it appeareth by some letters intercepted, that the king of Spain purposeth to send a larger supply with all expedition." Again, " that his heart is very much set upon the enterprise of Ireland." Don Juan will do his best to stay the new arrivals, and if he arrives in Spain before they start, has no doubt of succeeding; but Don Juan himself " stays, to goe the last." But one ship, containing a hundred and sixty Spaniards, has left Kinsale for Spain. There are vessels in the harbour, able to carry away fifteen hundred more, but the winds are contrary.

The wind changes on the 20th of February, and 1374 soldiers set sail from Kinsale to Spain. Don Juan embarked at Kinsale on the 8th of March, and sailed on the 16th. The lord deputy, writing to the English council, says, "Don Juan and all the rest of the Spaniards departed from Kinsale, on Tuesday, the 16th, and that the wind since hath served so well, as we assure ourselves, by this, they are near the coast of Spain." The following letter announces his arrival, and his high opinion of Carew, notwithstanding the theft of the dispatches:—

"*A letter from* DON JUAN DE AQUILA *to the* LORD PRESIDENT.

" Muy illustre sennor: to say the truth I am very glad that I am in Spaine, and that the passage was good which I was to make. I confesse unto your lordship, that I am so much obliged for the honourable and good termes, which the Lord Deputy and your Lordship vsed there in the service of your Prince, in all things which concerned me, that I desire some apt occasion to manifest my selfe to be a good paymaster (as I ought) for these courtesies, and for the assurance thereof, your lordship may send securely to me, to command any thing you please for your service; and that your ship and passeport shall bee friendly received; and for that in this countrey there is no fruit of more estimation than wines of Ripadavia, limmons and orenges—these few are sent to make a proofe thereof, and the willingnesse I haue to serue your lordship; whom I commend to God.

" From the Groyne, the second of Aprill, 1602."

Sir George Carew, who appears to have flattered the Spaniard to the top of his bent, replies — sending an ambling hackney — with this sly stroke of wit and humour:—

" I have received profit by the Book of Fortification which your lordship left me at your departure, and hold it as a relique in memory of you, and as a good scholler, I have put some things in practise, whereof your lordship, *at your returne hither againe,* (which I hope in God will be never) may be a witnesse whether I hâve committed any error in the art or no. My greatest defect hath beene the want of the helpe of so great a master as your lordship is, of whom I am desirous to learne, not onely that art, but in all else concerning military profession, in the which I do give your lordship the preheminence. To conclude, I rest in all I may (my dutie reserved to the queene, my mistresse,) affectionately ready at your lordship's service, and so kissing your hands. I beseech God to preserve you, with many happy yeares.

" From Corke, the seventeenth of September, 1602."

The Spanish general not only lost the favor of the king, but any reputation as a general he may have won. He was banished from the court, and confined to his own house, where he died soon after of chagrin.

Captain Walter Edney, who carried the present, was apprehended, and detained for nine months. The ambling hackney was " detayned " by Earl of Carazena, " to his own use."

CHAPTER XXI.

THE SIEGE OF DUNBOY CASTLE.

A.D. 1602.

THE indignation of Donnell O'Sullivan Beare was unbounded when he discovered that Don Juan had stipulated to deliver his castle of Dunboy into the hands of the lord president. Writing to Don Pedro Zubiaur, from Bearchaven, Feb. 20th, 1602, he says, "our state since your departing, notwithstanding many crosses, was reasonable well, until a bruite came to us, credibly, that Don Juan de Aquila, who did not only agree and compound to yield the town of Kinsale, but also other castles and havens delivered voluntarily by the others."

In another place, he says, "losing the same unexpectedly, and surrendered into the hands of most heretical enemies, I am not only disappointed of all power, but driven to run to the mountains, and there live like wolves, for the safety of my life, and leave to their merciless discretion all the poor men, women, and children, with in the length of twenty leagues containing."

In writing to King Philip, (Feb. 20th, 1602), he says, "I came to their presence, tendering my obeysance to them, in the name of your majesty, and being with four hundred at my own cost, towards your service I yielded out of my mere love and good will, without compulsion or composition, into their hands, in the name of your majesty, not only my castle and haven, called Bearehaven, but also my wife, my children, my country, lordships, and all my possessions, for ever to be disposed of at your pleasure.

"They received me in that manner, and promised (as from your highness) to keep and save the said castle and haven during the service of your grace. Notwithstanding, my gracious lord, conclusions of peace was assuredly agreed upon, betwixt Don Juan de Aquila and the English, a fact pitiful, and, (according to my judgment), against all right and human conscience. Among other places, whereof your greatness was dispossessed, in that manner which were neither yielded nor taken to the end they should be delivered to the English, Don Juan tied himself to deliver my castle and haven, the only key of mine inheritance, whereupon the living of many thousand persons doth rest, that live some twenty leagues upon the sea coast, into the hands of my cruel, cursed, misbelieving enemies, a thing, I fear, in respect of the execrableness, inhumanity, and ungratefulness of the fact, if it take effect, as it was plotted, that will give cause to other men, not to trust any Spaniard hereafter, with their bodies or goods upon those causes."

Captain Roger Harvey, and Captain Flower, had been commissioned, on the 10th of January, to take possession of Castlehaven, Donneshed, and Donnelong at Baltimore, and Dunboy at Bearehaven. Harvey was successful, but Flower failed "by reason of foul weather and contrary winds." Castlehaven was in charge of Pedro Lopez de Soto, the Veador. He received Captain Harvey, who brought letters from Don Juan, with great politeness, and entertained him with great humanity, and over their Spanish wine they spoke in this wise :—

Soto.—Is it not a miserable and lamentable thing, to any man's conscience, to see the daily effusion of blood, and infinite expense of treasure, which this war between Spain and England doth produce?

Harvey.—It is too high a mystery for me. Princes are God's ministers on earth, and what they do is beyond our ability to scan. He at the same time throws out the hint, that Philip must have a great deal of money to spare or he would not throw it away on Ireland.

Soto.—And you think gold is so abundant with us?

Harvey.—The Indian world, which you possess, makes us believe it.

Soto.— Be not deceived, but if it were so, the king's infinite number of garrisons would devour another Indies. Then his war in the Low Countries, for which he may thank the Queen of England. If she had not assisted those traitors he would never have molested either England or Ireland.

Harvey.—Then I see it is not religion or conscience that brought you here, but revenge.

Soto.—And did you think otherwise? I know you did not, and if you say so I know you dissemble, for the place where you have been brought up hath better discipline.

Harvey. —Why? Where have I been brought up?

Soto.—I heard that you were near in blood to the president, and that from a child you have followed him.

HARVEY.—I must thank you for your good opinion of me, but have you ever seen the face of the president?

SOTO.—I assure you no, for which I am very sorry, for I hear he is a worthy gentleman, and one of the wisest men in Ireland; and if I would take Irish opinion, *they confidently affirm that he hath a familiar.* They say he knows all things, and that nothing is hidden from him.

Whatever Sir George's knowledge may have been, there was one matter of which both Soto and Harvey were perfectly ignorant, namely, that the O'Driscolls had made themselves masters of the castle while they were discussing the conduct and character of princes and presidents over their wine; and if Harvey's two brothers had not sailed up within sight of the castle, with some heavy ordnance,—in the very nick of time— they might have had some trouble in regaining possession. The Spaniards were trying to get in again, by undermining, when the Harveys entered the haven. " Upon sight of the ships," the O'Driscolls—"by composition to depart in safety—rendered it to the Spaniards, who had lost two of their soldiers in the attempt."

Captain Roger Harvey and his friend, Soto the Veador, set sail, the 23rd of February, for Donnelong, Baltimore, where they were "feasted" by the Governor Andreas de Aervy. Here they shipped seven pieces of cannon. On the 26th, both the castles, Donnelong and Donneshed, were, with "Spanish gravitie" and Greek faith, delivered into the hands of the English.

The case was different with Dunboy Castle, Bearehaven, for which Captain George Flower shipped, in " a hoy, or vessel of a hundred and twenty tons," with two companies of soldiers; but do all he could, by reason of foul weather and contrary winds, he could not land, and was therefore compelled to return. He lost fifty of the soldiers and all of his crew — with the exception of seven — from some infection. Donnell O'Sullivan Beare took advantage of the delay to regain possession of Dunboy Castle.

Although the Spaniards were in possession of Dunboy, O'Sullivan Beare, who had voluntarily delivered it into their hands, resided there, when it suited his convenience. It was beneath its roof* he penned or indited his letter to Philip, King of Spain, and, we conclude, to the Earl of Carazena, and that to Don Pedro Zubiaur, in which he calls Don Juan " a brute." But he did not speak in this style to Francesco de Saavedra, the Spanish governor, in command.

It is the dead of night, the Spaniards are sleeping soundly, but the key of the castle is with Francesco. O'Sullivan has a mason or two among his Irish friends inside, who work a hole in the castle wall, through which eighty armed men enter; among whom we have Thomas Fitz-Maurice, Lord of Lixnaw, the descendent of Raymond le Gros, Donnell Mac Carthy, Captain Richard Tirrell, the friend of O'Neill, Captain William Burke, James Archer, the Jesuit, (who acted as a decoy duck in the hands of Owny O'More, in seizing the person of the Black Earl of Ormond), and another priest, Father Dominick Collins,† we conclude, to whom John Annias wrote about the saltpetre. A

* *Beneath its roof.*—" Dunboy, viz., Beare-haven, the twentieth day of February, 1602."--Pac. Hib., p. 487.

† *Father Dominick Collins* was born in Youghal. He " had been brought up in the wars of France, and there, under the league, had been a commander of horse in Brittany, called Captaine Le Branch."—*Pacata Hibernia*.

thousand wild kerne and stalwarth galloglasses are within gun shot outside.

The day begins to dawn as Archer—the mind of the party—taps at Francesco's door and requests his presence in "Osulevan's chambers." He comes, and is informed that the Irish are in possession of the castle; that they intend to guard it for the King of Spain, that a larger force is outside, "within harquebusse shott of the castle," that neither he nor his men shall receive hurt, but they must not resist. Francesco was thunderstruck, but made no resistance. Some of his men discharged a few muskets, and killed three Irishmen, but that was all. The Spaniards were then disarmed, and sent to Baltimore, to be shipped for Spain, with the exception of the captain, a few of the better sort, and three or four gunners, who might make themselves useful, should the castle be besieged.

When the report of the surprise of Dunboy Castle was made to Don Juan, who was then in Cork, he took it for a great affront; he feels his honor compromised; he must march the Spaniards from Kinsale who have not yet embarked, and retake the castle, and deliver it, according to the composition, into her majesty's hands. Mountjoy and Carew, "who were desirous to see his heels towards Ireland," requested him not to trouble himself, that it was no fault of his that the castle had been surprised; that when he was gone they would take order for reducing it. He is stayed by these words, but must write an account of the affair to the King of Spain, the Earl of Carazena, and Pedro de Zubaire. Here we take our leave of this Don Juan or Don Quixote, and turn to the siege of Dunboy.

The Lord President despatched the Earl of Thomond before him, to prepare provisions and munitions of war. In his instructions, dated the 9th of March, 1602, he says,—" When you are in Beare, if you may, without any apparent peril, take a view of the Castel of Dunboy." He directs him to leave no means unessayed to get Donnell O'Sullivan Beare into his hands. He had given him some private instructions on this subject:— " Give all the comfort you may to Owen O'Sullivan." Owen O'Sullivan laid claim to the Castle of Dunboy. " Have special care to prosecute and plague the O'Crowleys, who have assisted Dermot Moyle Mac Carthy. Sir Owen Mac Carthy's sons, if they be well handed, will prove the best instruments of doing so, as he stands between them and the lord of the country." How unlike a gallant soldier all this. What a developement it affords of the divide and conquer principle. Even the Deputy Mountjoy, who *was* a brave soldier, says, writing to the English council,—" As for Fineen O'Driscoll, O'Donovan, and the two sons of Sir Owen Mac Cartie, they and their fellows, since their coming in, are grown very odious to the rebels in these parts, *and are so well divided in factions amongst themselves, as they are fallen to preying and killing one another, which we conceive will much avail to the quieting of these parts.*" Stafford says,—" It was thought no ill policie to make the Irish draw bloud one upon another, whereby their private quarrels might advance the publike service."

Thomond did his best to follow his instructions, but was not able " to take a view of the Castle of Dunboy." He was stopped at the Ceim an Ghabhair,* or the Goat's

* *Ceim an Ghabhair*, now Keamagower, alias Cromwell's Bridge, parish of Kilcaskin.

Pass, in the mountains of Beare, by Captain Tirrell, who with O'Sullivan Beare, kept the field, leaving the care of the castle to his constable, Richard Mac Geoghegan. The Four Masters say the sons of Owen [O'Sullivan] were assisting the earl against O'Sullivan [Beare], because the O'Sullivan had taken Dun-Badi and Beare from their father, by the decision of Council beyond and here,* and was accustomed to say that he should, by right, receive the rents of Bantry." O'Donovan was also at strife with O'Sullivan Beare on this occasion, and had some fighting with him at this place. But Captain Tirrell had taken so strong a position in the mountains of Beare, that Thomond was compelled to turn back. He left part of his army on Whiddy Island, in Bantry Bay, a place " very convenient for the service," and returned with the rest of the forces to Cork, to report progress to the president, who prepares to take the field in person.

He left Cork, feeble and weak, much against the advice of his friends, on the 20th of April, 1602, and encamped that night at Owneboy—Awnbuidhe—near Kinsale, where Tyrone received the great overthrow; the 24th, he marched to Timoleague, where he executed three rebels; the 25th, to Rosscarbery; the 26th, over the Leap to Castlehaven; the 27th, to Baltimore; the 29th, they encamped on a mountain near " Kilcoa, being a castle wherein the rebel Conoghor, the eldest son of Sir Fineen O'Driscoll, knight, held a ward; the 30th, the army dislodged and drew to Carew Castle, built in ancient time by the Lord President's

* *The Council beyond and here.*—The English and Irish Council.

ancestors, and by the Irish called Downemarke, or the Marques his house, being two miles distant from the Abbey of Bantry, where wee sate downe, as well to give annoyance to the rebels as to tarry the coming of the shipping with victuals, munition, and ordnance; at which place Captaine George Flower with his garrison (left there by the Earle of Thomond) fell in unto us."

On the 1st of May Captain Taaffe made a foray, with a troop of horse from the camp, and brought in three hundred cows, a great number of sheep, and some horses. A foray was made on the 3rd, by the sons of Sir Owen O'Sullivan—" who was firm and deserved well of her majesty"—who brought in fifty cows and a number of sheep. On the 4th, a descendant of the famous Aenghus O'Daly,* the poet of Muintir-Beare, was arrested, and brought before Sir George. He was committed for trial at the next sessions, and not hanged or shot, there and then, because Sir George held him as a descendant of the hereditary bards or rhymers of his ancestors.

"This O'Daly's ancestor," writes Stafford, "had the country of Moynter-bary [Muintir Beare] given unto him by the Lord President's ancestor, many hundred yeares past, at which time Carew had to his inheritance the moiety of the whole kingdome of Corke, which was first given by King Henry the Second unto Robert Fitz-Stephen. The service which O'Daly and

---

* *Aenghus O'Daly.*—(See pages 66 to 68.)—" Several of the Dalys, or O'Daly's of Muintir, claim descent from him; namely, Daniel Daly of Ahakista, deceased, and several others; but the widow Connell, alias Mary Daly, now [1852] in the Bantry Workhouse, is believed to be the nearest akin to him."—*The Tribes of Ireland*, p. 14, edited by Doctor O'Donovan.

his progenie were to doe, for so large a proportion of lands, unto Carew and his successors, was, (according to the custome of that time) to bee their rimers, or chroniclers of their actions."

The following letter, dated from the "Campe, nere Bantrie, the seventh of May, 1602," was, we suspect, written at Carew Castle. It is unworthy of a soldier, though he speaks of the faith of a gentleman. Understanding, says Stafford, that the Spanish cannoniers were still in Dunboy, as well in regard they were strangers, but especially to deprive the enemy of their service, he wrote a letter in Spanish to them:—

"*A letter from the* LORD PRESIDENT *to the* SPANISH CANNONIERS *in Dunboy.*

" When Don Juan de Aquila (Generall for the Spanish Armie in Ireland) departed from the Citie of Corke, having a care of your safeties, requested mee to favour you, saying, That contrary to your willes the traytor Donnell O'Sullivan (by force) held you in his Castle of Dunboy, there to serve him as cannoniers. I now calling to mind his desire, (in the love I beare him, being so great a captaine, and so honourable a person as he is) and in consideration of the promise I made him, doe write this letter unto you, promising (for the reasons before mentioned) that when I shall sit downe (with my forces) before the castle (where you are) if then you will quitt the same and come unto mee, I will, *by the faith of a gentleman,* and a christian, make good my promise to Don Juan de Aquila; not onely to secure you in comming to me, and in the like safetie to bee with mee, but also to relieve and supply your wants, and likewise, at your pleasure, to accommodate you with a ship, and my passport, safely to passe into Spaine, in such manner as hath been already accomplished to the rest of the Spanyards that are returned to their countrey.

" This above written I am obliged by my promise to Don Juan to fulfill. But if you have a desire to finde or receive further favours at my hands, you may with facilitie deserve it, that is, when you leave the castle to cloy the ordnance, or mayme their carriages, that when they shall have need of them, they may proove usclesse, for the which I will forthwith liberally recompense you answerable to the qualitie of your merit.

" Lastly, if there bee in your companies any strangers, (English and Irish excepted) which are likewise by force held (as you are) these my letters shall be sufficient to secure their repaire to me, and also to depart, as hath beene before mentioned, conditionally, that you and they present your selves unto mee, before our ordnance shall begin to batter the Castle of Dunboy aforesayd. But if on your part default be made, I holde myselfe clearely acquitted of my promise made to Don Juan, and to bee free from breach of faith on my part, and you ever after incapable of this favour of my promised offer. Returne me your answer by this bearer in writing, or by some other in whom you have more confidence.

" From the Campe neere Bantrie, the seventh of May, 1602.

" To the Spanyards held by force
  in the Castle of Dunboy."

The letter to the Spanish cannoniers produced no effect, but the Lord President, nothing discouraged, will try again. On the first of June, the Earl of Ormond and Sir Charles Wilmot are instructed to land with their regiments on Beare Island; the president and Sir Richard Percy follow on the second. Here occurs a private meeting between Richard Mac Geoghegan, the constable of Dunboy, and Thomond, who tries to tempt him to betray his trust. In the map of the siege of Dunboy, we have a sketch of the two figures. The incorruptible Mac Geoghegan appears to be moving off with a flag of truce, and — the back of my hand to you, Thomond—while Thomond follows in a somewhat threatening attitude. " Whether Mac Geoghegan did intreat the earle that he might have a safe-conduct to speake with him, I am uncertaine, but of this *I am sure*, that the earle's meeting with him was not without the president's knowledge. All the eloquence and artifice which the earle could use avayled nothing, for Mac Geoghegan was resolved to persevere in his wayes; and in the great love which hee pretended to beare unto the earle, hee advised him not to hazard his life by landing upon the main land, where stood the castle. The interview, as we have stated, took place on Beare Island."

This interview occurred on the fifth of June, 1602. On the same day a Spanish ship sailed up the Kenmare river to Ardea Castle, where O'Sullivan kept war stores. This vessel was sent especially from Spain, to know the state of Dunboy Castle, King Philip's last stronghold in Ireland. There was a good supply of Spanish gold aboard — some said twelve thousand pounds.—Ellen Cartie, the wife of Owen O'Sullivan, then a prisoner with Donnell O'Sullivan in Ardea Castle, saw £3,710 distributed among fourteen persons. O'Sullivan Beare got £1500; Dermot Moyle Mac Carthy, Florence's brother, £300; Sir Fineen O'Driscoll and his son, Conor, £500 between them; O'Donovan, £200; John Fitz-Thomas, brother of the Sugan Earl, £200; Archer, the Jesuit, £150; Donough Moyle Mac Carthy, £160; Conor Kerry, the Knight of the Valley, Conor Mac Namara, and Richard Blake, £100 each; O'Donnell Mac Carthy, the Bast., £400. Capt. Tirrell, and his company of bonnoughs, must have received a large portion of the £12,000. We read also of four boats of wine, and munitions of war.

The money was committed to the care of Owen Mac Egan, who is styled in the Pacata Hibernia, "the

Pope's Bishop of Ross,* and Vicarius Apostolicus," and had a magical effect upon the beseiged. The letter is addressed to the constable of the castle, and is written in a pleasant cheerful style:—

"*A letter from* OWEN MAC EGAN *to* RICHARD MAC GOGHAGAN *at Dunboy.*

" Master Richard, I commend mee unto you, being very glad of the good report I heare of you, whereby I cannot but expect much (with God his assistance) in that lawfull and godly cause of you. I am sorry, but it was my lucke to conferre with you, and with the rest of your company, and informe you of all the state of the matters of Spaine; but upon my credit and conscience, there is no peece of service now in hand in all Christendome for the King of Spaine, then the same that yee have. How great it is to God, and necessary for our countrey affaires you know. Moreover, within few dayes you shall have releefe of men come to helpe you thither out of Spaine: the great army of fourteene thousand men are forth comming, you shall all be as well recompensed, both by God and by the Kings Majestie, as any ward that is in all the world againe; have me I pray commended to all, and especially to father Dominick, and bid him bee of good courage; there comes with the army a father of the company an Italian, for the Pope his Nuncius, in whose company I came from Rome to the Court of Spaine, and there hee expects the armies comming hither, hee shall give all a benediction, yea I hope within your castle there, spite of all the devils in hell.

" From the Catholike Campe, this present Wednesday, 1602.

" Your assured Friend,

" OWEN HEGAINE.

" In my sacrifice and other poore prayers I will not faile, but commend you and your good cause to God; our shippe did arrive three dayes agon, and our letters is come to the king by this time. *Nisi Dominus custodierit civitatem, &c.*"

The president drew his forces to the main land,

* *The Pope's Bishop of Ross.*—Dr. O'Hea, the present Catholic Bishop of Ross, informs the writer, that that Mac Egan was " Bishop elect of Ross;" but, it is supposed, he had never been consecrated."

within a mile of Dunboy, on the 7th of June, 1602. An arm of the sea, or haven, ran between the castle and the camp.

Sir George stole out of the camp, with Sir Charles Wilmot, and a hundred foot, to view the castle, and the adjoining ground. He finds "a faire place, of good ground, and of capacity sufficient to encamp in, within twelve score yards of the castle, and yet out of sight of it, by reason of a rising interjacent. And upon the top of a small ascent, in the midst of rocks, a faire green plot of ground, not a hundred and forty yards distant from the castle, like a natural platform sufficiently large for the artillery." Everything seems to favor Sir George. His party are seen reconnoitering, and some shots are fired. Sir Charles Wilmot's horse is hit on the foot. The president, if we may believe Stafford, was not deficient in personal courage:—

"The same day (June 15th) the President, the Earle of Thomond, and Sir Charles Wilmott, taking a guard of foot with them, rode (for recreation) out of the campe towards our last camping place, and riding softly by the sea side, (all three in ranke) having left their foot behinde them, they espied a gunner in the castle traversing a pecce of ordnance. This fellow (said the president) will make a shott at us: the word was no sooner spoken but fire was given. The president knowing that gunners doe evermore lay before a mooving marke, rayned his horse and stood firme; the Earle and Sir Charles started forward, and the bullet grazed even at their horse heeles, beating some of the earth upon them. The president glad to see them past danger, laughing, sayd, That if they had been as good mechanicall cannoniers, as they were commanders, they would have stood firme as hee did."

Dunboy Castle was of great height, with a turret on the south west, resting on a strongly arched floor. An iron falcon * was mounted on the turret. The outer wall or barbican was sixteen feet high, and four feet thick, faced with sods, intermingled with wood and faggots. This outer wall was defended by turrets and curtains.

The president's battery opened on the turret of the castle, at five o'clock in the morning, on the 17th of June, and continued to play upon it for five hours, till nine in the forenoon, when turret and falcon " tumbled downe." The cannon then opened on the west point of the castle itself, which fell at one o'clock. On its fall, a messenger was sent with a flag of truce, offering to surrender, if they got their lives. The messenger was executed. A breach is made, and the barbican mounted, and the English colors planted on one of the turrets; but the invading party fought for a full hour and a half before the eight feet of ground, that divided the barbican from the castle, could be crossed. All who entered this narrow passage were at once crushed with stones and shot from above. But the besieged did not perceive, till it was too late, that in filling up, or partially filling up, this passage, they were making a causeway for the enemy to pass. " The ruins, therefore, made a way that leads to a spike" or window, through which a sergeant enters and gains the top of the arch, upon which the castle turret stood. Where one enters, so may another. The besiegers, in their

---

* *Falcon*, a cannon, about seven feet long, diameter at the bore, five inches and a quarter.

turn, come down on the enemy, whose condition is desperate. About forty rush out, and make for the shore; all are slain, save eight, who take to the water; they are pursued, and their blood tinges the blue waves of the Atlantic. Three leap from the arched roof, one of them, a notable rebel, Melaghlin O'Moore, who had "plucked" the Earl of Ormond from his horse, when made prisoner by Owny Mac Rory O'Moore—and were slain by the soldiers. We shall conclude the description of the siege in the words of Thomas Stafford:—

"Then Mac Goghegan, chiefe commander of the place, being mortally wounded with divers shott in his body, the rest made choise of one Thomas Taylor, an Englishman's sonne, (the dearest and inwardest man with Tirrell, and married to his neece) to bee their chiefe, who, having nine barrels of powder, drew himselfe and it into the vault, and there sate downe by it, with a light match in his hand, vowing and protesting to set it on fire, and blow up the castle, himselfe, and all the reste, except they might have promise of life, which being by the Lord President refused, (for the safety of our men) his lordship gave direction for a new battery upon the vault, intending to bury them in the ruines thereof, and after a few times discharged, and the bullets entering amongst them into the cellar, the rest that were with Taylor, partly by intercession, but chiefly by compulsion, (threatening to deliver him up if hee were obstinate) about ten of the clock in the morning of the same day, constrained him to render himself simply, with eight and fortie more being ready to come forth.

" Sir George Thornton, the Serjeant-major, Captain Roger Harvie, Captain Power, and others, entering the vault to receive them, Captain Power found the said Richard Mac Goghegan lying there mortally wounded (as before) and perceiving Taylor and the rest ready to render themselves, raised himselfe from the ground, snatching a light candle, and staggering therewith to a barrell of powder (which for that purpose was unheaded) offering to cast it into the same, Captain Power took him, and held him in his armes, with intent to make him prisoner, untill he was by our men (who perceived his intent) instantly killed, and then Taylor and the rest were brought prisoners to the campe.

" The same day fiftie-eight were executed in the market-place, but the Fryer Taylor, and one Tirlagh Roe Mac Swiney, a follower unto Sir Tirlagh O'Brian, and twelve more of Tirrell's chiefe men, the Lord President reserved alive, to trie whether he could draw them to doe some more acceptable service than their lives were worth. The whole number of the ward consisted of one hundred and fortie-three selected fighting men, being the best choice of all their forces, of the which no one man escaped, but were either slaine, executed, or buried in the ruines, and so obstinate and resolved a defence had not bin seene within this kingdome.

" On our part we lost in the place Thomas Smith, Captaine, Francis Slingsbies, Lieutenant, and some others; and many of our men were burnt with powder and fireworks, which the enemie cast amongst them as they were in fight. Men of note hurt: Captaine Dodington shot with two bullets in the body, but not mortall; his Lieutenant, Francis Kirton, shot in the arme and thigh; divers Sergeants, and sixtie-two souldiers maimed and wounded, of which some are dead since, and others like to follow. And amongst the rest, Sir Anthony Cooke, Sir Garrett Harvie, Captaine Skipwith, and Captaine Roger Harvie, received severall bruises with stones and iron bullets flung upon them, but being well armed, they received no great hurt.

"In the castle we gayned ten peeces of ordnance, whereof fower were brasse, two of them being broken by our battery, and another piece of brasse was likewise broken by our ordnance, before any part of the castle fell, which the prisoners say is so deeply buried in the ruines, as the search of the metall is not worth the labour; all the carredges were, by the fall of the castle and by our artillery, so broken, as no one of them were left serviceable. Moreover, there was of powder nine barrels, some great shot, but their whole store, by reason of the ruines, wee could not well find. There was also in the castle some quantities of wine, vinegar, oyle, corne, beefe, and hides, which the souldiers made pillage of."

On the 22nd of June, 1602, the castle of Dunboy was blown into the air, and all its works and fortifications utterly destroyed.

Some of Captain Tirrell's men were among the prisoners. The president propounded a "stratagem" to the captain—some accomplished piece of devilment, no doubt—by the doing of which he and his men were to get their lives and liberties. He replied, "I will ransom my men with money, if that be accepted, but to be false to the King of Spain, my master, or to betray the Catholic cause, I will never." His men were accordingly executed.

Taylor, who was accused of being engaged in the murder of Captain George Bingham, at Sligo, was carried to Cork and executed. His body hung in chains, " not far from the North Gate."

Dominick Collins, the friar, "in whom no penitence appeared," and who would not " merit his life either by discovering the rebels' intention or by doing some service that might deserve favour," was hanged at Youghal, the town where he was born. James Archer, the Jesuit, and Conor O'Driscoll, the son of Sir Fineen O'Driscoll, escaped to Spain; O'Sullivan Beare and Captain Tirrell into Kerry.

CHAPTER XXII.

BLARNEY CASTLE AND CORMAC MAC DERMOT MAC CARTHY.

A.D. 1602.

THERE is one more castle in the county of Cork which the Lord President desires to see in the hands of the state before he can write the last page of his *Pacata Hibernia*. The name of the castle is BLARNEY, and it is in the possession of Cormac Mac Dermot Mac Carthy, the Lord of Muskerry, a nobleman, who has been long reconciled; who united his forces with those of the Lord Deputy Mountjoy, at the siege of Kinsale; who marched with the Lord President to Holycross, to meet O'Donnell, and bar his way to Munster; who ate and drank with the president, and for aught we know, was his " loving bed-fellow sometimes;" but now that Dunboy is taken, and his services are no longer required, Sir George is about rewarding him in the Cyclopean fashion of eating him last; but the affair is somewhat delicate and requires wise handling.

The Lord of Muskerry has a cousin called Teige Mac Cormac, son to that "well-deserving gentleman," Sir Cormac Teige Mac Carthy, " the rarest man of all the Irishry." This young gentleman was in the president's troop of horse, but stole away to the Spaniards. He now desires to be reconciled, and what is more fortunate, has some claims on Muskerry. He is encouraged to approach the president. He writes from his fairy castle of Carrig-a-pooka.* The letter is dated June, 1602 :—

"*A letter from* TEG MAC CORMOCK CARTIE *to the* LORD PRESIDENT, *entreating the remission of his offences.*

"Right Honourable, my dutie most humbly remembred; having long forborne, though thereby disquieted in mind, and ashamed of myselfe to send unto your honour: yet presuming upon her majesties mercie and your favour, I have made bold to become a petitioner to your honour, that it may please you to admit me thereunto, and to forgive and forget my faults, considering they were not malicious, but youthfull, and not of pretence to hurt her majestie or her subjects, but in hope to recover against my Cosen, Cormock Mac Dermody, some meanes to maintaine my decayed estate, and still likely to be suppressed by his greatnesse, who will by no meanes give me a portion of land to live upon, as was promised upon the delivery up of Kilcrey by your honour, wherein, as of the rest, I doe againe humbly beseech your favour, and so as with a repentant and penitent transgressor of the lawes, I doe humbly submit myselfe to her majesties grace, and will endeavour myselfe hereafter by my good deeds and services, to wipe out the memory of my former follies. Expecting your favourable answer, I most humbly take my leave.

"From Carrigifuky, this ninth of June, 1602.

"Your honour's most humble to command,

"TEG MAC CORMOCK CARTIE."

The president's displeasure is so deep that he cannot receive him into favour except he merits it "by some signal service." The young gentleman of Carrig-a-pooka knows that the service required will play the very mischief with the old gentleman at Blarney, but

* *Carrig-a-pooka.*—Carrickafouky, which means Fairy-rock Castle, built by the Mac Carthys of Drishane.—*Smith*, vol. 1, page 182. It is on the road from Macroom to Killarney. The Pooka or Puck, in Ireland, is a mischievous sprite, almost tantamount to the devil; very different from Shakspeare's "*Gentle Puck.*"

having some claim on Muskerry he does it with good will.

" He deposed first, that Dermot Mac Carthy had undertaken traffique with Don John de Aquila, letters ordinarily passing betweene him and the said Cormock, and in particular, hee averred, that hee saw Don John, himselfe, to deliver unto James Galde Butler, (Cormock's wife's brother) two letters, the one from the king and the other from the church; but from what particular church-man hee could not certainely affirme, but by all probability it should seeme to bee from the Pope; these two letters were by him sent to bee delivered to Cormock, aforesaid, together with his owne commendations in these words:—Commend me to your brother-in-law, Cormock, and deliver him these two letters, the one from the king and the other from the church --which were the same night delivered.

" Moreover, hee was deposed (by vertue of which oath he affirmed) that upon his knowledge Cormock had secret conference with Owen Mac Eggan, since his last arrivall out of Spaine, and that from him hee had received eight hundred duckets impresse, and thereupon had accorded to yeeld into the Spaniards hands (immediately upon their landing) his strong Castle of the Blarny, situate within two miles of Corke, which deposition was afterwards confirmed by the testimony and evidence of sundry other credible personages; these informations concurring with the examinations of Dermond Mac Cartie, by the Spaniard called Don Dermutio, (executed at Corke, of whom before you have heard) and also manyfold proofes, existing of his often combination with Tyrone, O'Donnell, Florence

Mac Cartie, and James Fitz-Thomas, with other triviall treasons ordinary amongst these Provincials, the president, with the advice of the Provinciall Councell, thought it a matter of very dangerous consequence to permit such grosse and palpable treasons to escape unpunished."

On these depositions it is privately resolved that the Lord of Muskerry be arrested, and that his strong castle of Blarney be seized. In order to avoid suspicion, the president takes a journey to Kinsale, to view Castle Park, which had been in the possession of the Spaniards, and gives instructions that Sir Charles Wilmot, Captain Roger Harvey, a serjeant, and four-and-twenty foot, "should make a shew of going to hunt a buck" in the neighbourhood of Blarney; and being hot and weary with the chase, call at the castle on their return, and ask for "wine and usquebagh, whereof Irish gentlemen are seldom disfurnished." The hunting party call. The dogs are baying, and the bugles sounding round the bawn, but whether it was that the dragoons did not manage their horses like huntsmen, or that they overdid the thing, the warders on the wall were suspicious, and refused to open the gates. Sir Charles Wilmot may ride round the moat, and admire the "maine rock"* on which the castle stands, and praise its exterior, as the fox did the shining feathers of the crow, and "much importune to see the romey within," but the warders shake their heads. Neither Sir Charles, nor one of his people,

---

* *Maine rock.*—"His castle of Blarney is one of the largest and strongest castles in the province of Munster, for its fower piles, joyned in one, seated upon a maine rock, so that it is free from myning; the wall eighteene foot thick, and well flanked at each corner to the best advantage."—*Pac. Hib.*, p. 598.

were permitted to enter the gates, or "hardly to look within the gate of the bawne." They must hunt the buck in some other way.

We are not informed in what way the Lord of Muskerry was arrested, but it was managed by the Chief Justice, Saxey, who committed the prisoner to the care of the "gentleman porter," Master Ralph Hammon, till the president's pleasure should be known, at his return from Kinsale. The president returns, and Mac Carthy complains of his apprehension. Sir George will call the Chief Justice before him, and take order that no unjust or sinister proceedings shall be taken against him; but, in the meantime, advises him to submit till the day of trial.

He is called before the president and council, at Shandon Castle, and solemnly denies all the charges, and especially all dealings or combinations with Owen Mac Eggan, or Mac Egan, the Pope's Apostolic Vicar. The president replied that this was the only matter of importance with which he could be arraigned, his pardon covering any former charges. He was therefore requested, as a proof of his loyal and guiltless heart, to deliver up his castle of Blarney, with the promise of having it restored, if the charge of his dealing and complicity with Owen Mac Egan, were not fully proved. To this he objected. An order was therefore issued to the gentleman porter, to keep him "*in yrons closer than before*, untill he should demean himself in more dutiful conformitie." Captain Taaffe, in whom Mac Carthy reposed much trust, was employed to persuade him to surrender the castle; undertaking—"upon his credit"—to preserve his goods from loss or danger. Mac Carthy, perceiving that "the president was resolved either to make him bend or breake," commanded his constable to deliver the castle into the hands of Captain Taaffe. Whether or not he stipulated for his liberty we cannot say, but he did not gain it.

This Lord of Muskerry was possessed of two other castles, which were deemed of "good importance to command the country, the castle of Kilcrea,* and the castle of Macroom." Kilcrea was rendered—we are not told how—to Captain Slingsby, whom the president sent there to take possession. The case was different with Macroom, seated in the heart of Muskerry, and environed about with woods and bogs. The president sent Captain Flower, and afterwards Sir Charles Wilmot, to lie before it, and gain it by sap or mine, or other stratagem. That which Sir Charles could not accomplish, was done by a very simple accident. The warders having killed a pig, and having "no water to scald the same, were constrained to singe her, as the manner of some countries is." The fire caught the thatch of a cabin, within the bawn, and then the castle. The guard rush out, when about fifty of them are slain, and the smouldering ruins possessed by the Lord President's troops, by whom it is furnished, victualled, and rendered tenable.

We have related, in a previous part of this history, how the Lord President sent to London for the son of the great outlawed Earl of Desmond, in order to pit

---

* *The Castle of Kilcrea.*—Mr. Windele calls it "a pile of considerable extent, though inferior in importance and size to that of Blarney. Its site is enclosed by a narrow moat, still filled with water. The castle itself is a square tower, seventy feet high."

him against the Sugan Earl, then in rebellion. The friends of Cormac Mac Dermot, Lord of Muskerry, resolve to copy the president in this instance, by having the young lord of Muskerry, who is at this time a student at the University of Oxford, privately conveyed into Ireland. John O'Healy, "one of Cormac's old theeves" is to be the messenger. He is aboard, in the hold of the vessel, with the necessary letters and credentials. The vessel is to sail from the port of Cork, by the next tide, when the president gets a whisper of the plot. John is caught, and searched, but manages to throw his letters and money into the sea, so nothing could be proved.

The president, who is doubly suspicious of Dermot Mac Carthy, sends for Master Ralph Hammon, the gentleman porter, and charges him, on his duty to the state, his allegiance to her majesty, and the love he bears himself, to be as careful of the Lord of Muskerry as of his own life. He also sends for the bishop of Cork, and requests him to warn Hammon to be vigilant. The bishop does so, "gravely and pathetically"—"Abundans coutela non nocet." Master Richard promises to be careful, but, at the same time, requests the president not to torment his mind with imaginary doubts.

Sir George Carew's conduct in this instance—if correctly reported—was well calculated to strengthen the suspicion that he had "*a familiar*."

Forty-eight hours have elapsed. The night is dark, as a woman passes beneath the iron-barred windows of Shandon Castle. She sees something white emerging rom one of the windows, and gives a scream. The guard are up. The Lord of Muskerry's chamber examined. His lordship escaped by the window, in his shirt.

He was assisted by his trusty servant, Mahon Oge O'Lynne. A number of gentlemen were waiting to receive him. Pursuit is made, but it fails. Mac Carthy gains the wilds of Muskerry, where he may snap his fingers at the president.

Donnell O'Sullivan of Dunboy, and his trusty friend, Captain Tirrell, who are still at the head of a considerable force among the mountains of Beare, hasten into Muskerry, and offer their assistance. Mac Carthy does not like to refuse, but fears to accept their services. His eldest son is a prisoner in England; his wife, younger son and daughter, in close custody in Cork; he therefore resolves to parley with the president. He writes to the Bishop of Cork, to the Chief Justice, and to Captain Taaffe, to intercede for him. The whole council judged "his suit reasonable"— they see Tirrell's soldiers in the background—the president, therefore, would not dissent from their "unanime opinion." He meets the president on the 21st of October, 1602, and "falling down on his knees" humbly beseeches her majesty's mercy. "The president and council beholding the man, and weighing the words which proceeded from him—not without evident testimony of inward grief and unfeigned sorrow — although, peradventure, arising, like Esau's tears, from the sense of his loss more than from conscience, or feeling of his folly—thought good to receive him into her majesty's grace."

For this act of grace two reasons are given by Stafford. The first is the apparent reason, the latter the real motive:—

"First, considering the insupportable losse which hee had sustained since his imprisonment, in the taking of two, and burning his third castle, wherein (as being the place of his most especiall abode) his best mooveables (whereof hee was very well furnished) were consumed and burnt; and that the harvest of his countrey, betweene her majesties forces, and the rebells, (for in the same they had made their abode for a whole moneth) was valued at five thousand pounds, which, as a just punishment, was fallen upon him.

"Secondly, it was *well weighed*, what a helpe and courage his combination would have afforded to the rebels, if hee had obstinately run a rebellious course, for hee was at that time the strongest man in followers of any one of the Irish in that province, and his countrey in strength and fastnesse equall with the worst part of the same; and that which required no lesse respect was the situation of his countrey, reaching even to the walls of Corke, whereby the greatest part of her majesties forces must, of necessity, have beene employed in Muskerry, which would have given great impediment to the prosecution of the service in other parts, whereas by receiving him the warre would bee removed farther off and the greatest tempest of disturbance avoyded.

"That hee was deepely infected, and fowly stained with manifold treasons was too manifest, yet this difference was made betweene him and others, that they were in publicke action professed traytors, and he a jugling traytor.

"Though hee had joined with a forraine enemy, yet not in so hainous a manner as some other, for they solicited strangers to invade the kingdome, but strangers having invaded the kingdome solicited him to partake with them.

" The three castles (before-mentioned) no doubt were great bridles upon him, and in time (no doubt) would have wrought the effects desired, which was to banish him out of his countrey. But considering the charge and incumbrance, subject to some losse, that would grow in victualling of them, and many lewde and unsettled persons ready to joyne with him (if they had perceived him inclinable to continue a rebell) which might have bred newe broyles, and protracted the warres of Mounster *in infinitum.*

" Againe the benefit, that by his prosecution and extirpation might have redounded to her Majesty, was that thereby his land should have excheated unto her, which in the opinion of all wise men would have proved too deare a purchase.

" Farther, besides his submission and his sonne that was a prisoner in England, his second son, also, and his castle of Blarney, were held as pledges upon him.

" And whereas the L. Deputie had devised the forme of an oath for the Northern Protectees, he was content to sweare and subscribe to the same oath; and lastly himselfe with foure of the best barons of parliament in Mounster, were bound in three thousand pounds for his future loyaltie and subjection, so that hee was bound in heaven and in earth, before God and before man, by law and by nature, and nothing but onely hell was remayning for his farther assurance."

But what of that most inveterate rebel, Captain Tirrell? Now or never, says the president, is the time to attack this daring freebooter. The moment he hears of Mac Carthy's submission, he is off among the mountains of Kerry. Sir Samuel Bagnall is ordered on his track, and if possible to intercept him, or take him by surprise. He finds Tirrell encamped in the midst of woods and bogs, on the western confines of Muskerry. One of the Mac Carthys of Muskerry, Owen Mac Teige, of Drishane, approaches his wild camp by night, and returns in safety, and informs Bagnall that the enemy is lying in three divisions, with a "strong wood" at their back; a bog, half an Irish mile wide, in their front; and "cragged and rocky mountains" on either side. The colonel resolves to attack the three divisions together. The night is pitch dark; the English steal along, within a furlong of the camp; they have no doubt of surprising it, for all seem sunk in sleep, when a soldier—an Irishman, we suspect—stumbles, and his gun goes off—those sort of *accidents* often occurred under similar circumstances. The alarm is given; Tirrell runs away in his shirt, his wife at his heels in no better plight. About eighty of his men are slain. Her majesty's troops not only took the usual spoil of cows, sheep, and horses, but "some remnants of velvet," gold and silver lace, English apparel in satin and velvet, and "a portmanteau," containing a quantity of Spanish coin. Captain Tirrell was as fond of "brave attire" as Sir Walter Raleigh. He was fearfully enraged at the loss of his portmanteau, and all the velvet, satin, gold and silver lace, and Spanish coin it contained, and wreaked his vengeance on some churls and poor people before he fled to the fastnesses of Desmond and Beare.

Three months after this he marched with his bonnoughts, or mercenary troops, out of Munster, though strongly entreated to stay by O'Sullivan Beare, from whom he had lately received a great impost of Spanish money.

William Burke took the command of O'Sullivan's troop in the place of Tirrell, but seeing a number falling away, "cursed and damned himself," for staying so long in Munster, and soon after followed Captain Tirrell into O'Carroll's country.

O'Sullivan Beare and O'Conor Kerry were now the principal leaders of the Irish. O'Conor Kerry was the intimate friend of the great O'Donnell, who wrote him the following letter from Spain :—

"*A letter from* O'DONNELL *to* O'CONNER KERRY.

"What newes are here, the Doctor and Dermond Odrischal may largely report unto you; but of this one thing you may bee fully assured; that the king will not omit the winning of Ireland, if it cost him the most part of Spaine. His Majestie doth send you money and munition. I pray let our enformation of you bee found true, and your service encourage our king to further merit you. I pray you send mee the relation of the newes of our countrey, in such sort, as if there be any bad, it be concealed from the Spaniards, and knowen to me; where the deputie with the queenes forces are occupied, or where they are in garrison.

"At the Groyne, the foure and twentieth of May, 1602.

" Your loving friend,

" HUGH O'DONNELL.

" To his loving friend O'Connor Kerry,
 these give in Ireland."

This noble Irish chieftain, whose letter to his friend is so full of hope and confidence, died of anguish of heart and sickness, within four months after penning this epistle. O'Donnell left Castlehaven for Spain on the 6th of January, 1602, and landed at Groyne, near Corunna,* on the 14th. He was nobly received by the Earl of Carazena, and invited to his house, which hospitality he declined, on account of indisposition resulting from sea-sickness; he was therefore lodged in a "faire house not farre" from the earl's. He left Groyne on the 27th, when the earl gave him "his right hand, which, within his government, he would not have done to the greatest duke in Spain;" and at his departure presented him with a thousand ducats. He was received with great honor and magnificence by the prelates of St. James of Compostella; and was visited at St. Martins by the Archbishop, from whose hands he received the sacrament, and a thousand ducats. He was received by the king at Zamna, in the province of Castile. He knelt down before Philip, and would not rise till the king had promised to grant three requests—first, to send a well equipped army with him to Ireland, as soon as possible; secondly, that when Philip had conquered the country, he would place no O'Donnell, above himself, Hugh; thirdly, that he would never deprive either him or his successors of any of the rights or privileges they derived from their ancestors. The king graciously promised all he required.

He returned to Corunna, where he waited till Au-

* *Corunna.*—" He walked through the town, and went to view *Breogan's Tower,*" from which the Milesians departed in sailing for Ireland.—*Four Masters,* A.D. 1602.

gust, consumed with anxiety. He can endure the delay no longer—he must see the king again. He arrives at Simancas, two leagues from Valladolid, where Philip held his court. Here the fever of his brain attains its climax; he sickens, and dies in seventeen days, on the 10th of September, 1602. His remains are conveyed to the palace of Valladolid in a hearse, surrounded by a countless number of the state officers, council, and guards. His body lies in the monastery of St. Francis, where he was interred. Luminous torches, bright flambeaux, and beautiful wax-lights are burning round him.

"Alas!" exclaim the Four Masters, recording his death, "the early eclipse of him who died here is mournful to many. He was the head of the conference and council. He was a mighty and bounteous lord, with the authority of a prince to enforce the law. A lion in strength and force of character; a dove in meekness and gentleness. He was a sweet-sounding trumpet, endowed with the gift of eloquence, and a look of amiability which captivated every one who beheld him."

O'Sullivan Beare and O'Conor Kerry had no longer hope of aid from Spain. If they stay longer in Munster they will be hunted down like famished wolves.

"O'Sullivan, after having been deprived of this castle [Dunboy], went with his cows, herds, and people, and all his moveables, behind his rugged-topped hills, into the wilds and recesses of his country. The Earl [of Thomond] and his army, and O'Sullivan and his forces, continued shooting and attacking each other until the Christmas time. The two armies were entrenched and encamped face to face in Gleann Garbh [Glengarriff], which glen was one of O'Sullivan's most impregnable retreats. His people now began to separate from O'Sullivan secretly without asking his leave. First of all Captain Tyrell went away from him, and he was obliged himself to depart in the Christmas holidays, without the knowledge of, and unperceived by the earl."

They travelled the first night from Glengarriff to Ballyvourney, in West Muskerry; the second night to the barony of Duhallow; the third night to Ardpatrick, in the county of Limerick, and so on to the Shannon, but not without fighting their way, and the loss of a few men.

"As they passed the skirts of Muskerry, they were skirmished withall by the sonnes of Teg Mac Owen Cartie, where they lost some of their men, and most of their carriage. In passing by Liscarcell, John Barry, brother to the Viscount, with eight horsemen and fourty foote, charged their reare, at the ford of Bellaghan, where he slew and hurt many of them, and of his part one horseman was slaine."

They crossed the Shannon in boats made from the hides of their horses.* They were assailed on the opposite bank of the river by the Sheriff of Tipperary; and further north by Sir Thomas Burke, (brother to the Earl of Clanricard) and Captain Henry Malby, the latter of whom they slew, and passed without further impediment into O'Rourke's country, or the county Leitrim.

* *The hides of horses.* " They killed many of their horses, and made shift with their hides to make certaine little boats, called by the Irish nevogs, [naebhog] in the which they transported their men and baggage."—*Pac. Hib.*, p. 658.

"Neverthelesse before all were past the river the sherife of the county of Typperarie, fell upon their reare and slew many of them. Being in Connaught they passed safely through the county of Galway, untill they came into the Kellies countrey, where they were fought withall by Sir Thomas Burke, the Earle of Clanriccard's brother, and Captain Henry Malby, who were more in number then the rebels. Neverthelesse when they saw that either they must make their way by the sword or perish, they gave a brave charge upon our men, in the which Captaine Malby was slaine, upon whose fall Sir Thomas and his troopes fainting, with the losse of many men, studied their safeties by flight, and the rebels with little harme marched into Orwyke's country."

When Sir Charles Wilmot entered the camp which O'Sullivan had deserted in Beare, "he found nothing but hurt and sick men, *whose paines and lives, by the soldiers, were both terminated.* Hereupon Sir Charles, with the English regiments, overran all Beare and Bantry, destroying all that they could find meet for the relief of man, so that the country was wholly wasted." They were themselves the first to suffer for this inhuman barbarity. "The sharpnesse of this winter journey did exceedingly weaken our companies; for the mountains of Beare being at that time quite covered with snow, tested the strong bodies, whereby many returned sicke, and some, unable to endure the extreamity, dyed standing centinnell."

We shall conclude the account of this most unhappy and terrific civil and religious war, with a scene in Carbery, where the Catholic bishop of Ross was slain:

"Understanding that the sonnes of Sir Owen Mac Cartie, and Donnogh Keugh, brother to Florence Mac Cartie, were retyred with their creates and followers into the strengths of Carbery, his lordship commanded Captaine Taaffe, (with the said risings out) fourtie of Sir Edward Wingsfield's company, and his owne troop of horse, to draw into those parts, and to endeavour the best service hee could upon them. Whilest the rest were busied by the Governour of Kerry in Desmond, as aforesaid, wherein it pleased God to give him good successe, for on the fifth of January, his foote entering their fastnesse, took a prey of two or three hundred cowes and garrans; the rebels in pursuit of their cattle gave them so brave a charge, as they were disordered, whereby some of them were slaine, which Captaine Taaffe perceiving, being in the head of his horse troope in the skirt of the fastnesse, and espying some of their horsemen to doe much hurt upon our foote, charged them into the wood, slew foure of their horsemen, and put all the rest to route, wherewith our men being encouraged, pursued them.

" Owen Mac Egan, the Pope's Apostolike Vicar, so often before mentioned, to put fresh heart into his company, with his sword drawne in one hand, and his portius and beades in the other, with one hundred men led by himselfe, came boldly up to the sword, and mainetayned a hot skirmish, until hee was slaine with a shot, whereupon his men (together with a fresh charge of our horse) were so amazed and terrified, partly by his death, and partly by their owne danger, that they brake instantly, and for better expedition throwing away their armes, leaped into the river Bandon, hoping by that meanes to escape, but that little availed them, for they all for the most part were either killed or drowned in the river.

"There were slaine in this service (besides Owen Mac Egan, who was of more worth then all the rest) above one hundred and twenty rebels, and of the provinciall rising out of our part a good number lost their lives, and many of Captain Taaffe's horses hurt. Wee got the armes of a hundred and fourtie, and all their horses, cowes, sheepe and garranes that were in the countrey neere adjoyning. There was also taken a Papist Priest, being as it seemed a Chaplaine to Mac Egan, whom the president (shortly after) caused to be executed in Corke."

This most inexorable president, upon his return to Cork, employed messengers to seize Mac Egan's papers, which Stafford says, "fell to my share." They consisted for the most part, of books of school divinity and a bull of Pope Clement VIII., "*Dat' Romæ, apud Sanctum Petrum anno Incarnationis Domini* 1595." Mac Egan must have been invested with the authority described in the bull for seven years before his death.

Stafford paints the character of this bishop in the darkest colors:—

"A principall meanes of this suddaine and universall reduction, was the death of that traitorly priest, Owen Mac Egan, which doubtlesse was more beneficiall to the state then to have gotten the head of the most capitall rebell in Mounster, for the respect that was borne unto him (by reason of his authority from the Pope and the credit which hee had obtained in Spaine) was so great, as his power was in a manner absolute over them all, and he onely was the meanes of their obdurate obstinacie; his dignity in being the Pope's Vicarius Apostolicus, did hold them in vassalage unto him, and the livings given him in Munster by the Pope's grant were to be valued (if hee might quietly have enjoyed them) at three thousand pounds per annum.

" And farther to engage the Popish clergy of Ireland unto him, hee had power to dispose at his pleasure of all the spirituall livings in the province of Mounster, by which authority, together with the credit he had gotten with the King of Spaine (well testified by the trust committed to him in transporting and disposing the Spanish money, last brought into Ireland) he had obtayned in a manner all power, both over the temporality and spirituality of Mounster, and to depaint him in his true colours, a more malitious traytor against the State and Crowne of England, never breathed, which well appeared by the barbarous tyranny hee exercised upon his owne countriemen; for as soone as any prisoners were taken, though of his owne countrey, birth, and religion, yet if they had served the queene, he caused them first, in piety, as he pretended, to bee confessed and absolved, and instantly, in his owne sight, would hee cause them to bee murdered, which religious tyranny in him was held for sanctity."

The author or editor of the Pacata Hibernia has given no data to substantiate these charges of cruelty. Mac Egan's letter to Master Richard Mac Geoghegan,*

* *Mac Geoghegan* and Mac Egan were originally the same name. Master Richard may have been a relative of the churchman.

the constable of Dunboy, is not only genial, kind, and cheerful—and these are not the traits of a cruel man —but sincerely pious, "I cannot but expect much, with God's assistance, in that lawful and godly cause." Then the conclusion, "In my sacrifice, and other poor prayers, I will not fail to commend you *and your good cause* to God;" and his "Nisi Dominus custodierit civitatem"—*Except the Lord keep the city*—and then his death! It is only to be regretted that men like Owen Mac Egan should persevere, when all reasonable hopes of success have departed. Both the English and Irish Armada had failed. Every stronghold in Munster was in the hands of the Irish government. A rising in Carbery, under such circumstances, was simple madness. All was irretrievably gone. Perhaps Owen Mac Egan *felt* that it was so, and did not care to outlive it; that, like some brave captain, he resolved to go down with the ship he commanded. Those days produced men of desperate courage. But many an honest man would prefer sinking with Mac Egan, to swimming with Sir George Carew, knight, Lord President of Munster.

Sir George is now prepared to write his Pacata Hibernia. He may write it in blood as far as Munster is concerned, for it lies as still as dead men can make it. But the contrary of all this was reported, to Carew's very great annoyance. "About this time it was vulgarly reported in England, by some who had their tongues pointed with slander, and their hearts stuffed with malice, that Munster was newly burning with fresh flames of rebellion; that the Viscount Roch, the Lord of Cahyr, and Cormock Mac Dermond, had entered into open hostility, and that Tirrell was come again into the province, and had taken the prey of Mallow from the garrison at noon day. Although the world may be satisfied concerning these slanderous reports, by that which hath been already delivered, yet to give more particular satisfaction to all, or to any that should make question hereof, the Lord Roch was never touched with the least spot of disloyalty against her majesty; yea, such loyal constancy did he always embrace and practise, that in the universal inundation of treasons, when all the province in general, and his father in particular, did combine against their anointed sovereign, at that time and ever since, did he continue himself within the lists of an obedient subject."

The statement concerning my Lord Cahir was equally false. As for Cormac Mac Dermot of Blarney, he had lost thirty of his best men in her majesty's service. Sir George may therefore take his departure with a quiet conscience, for a dog would scarcely venture to bark in this wide province.

And never sea-sick mariner, in a tempestuous storm, more desired his wished-for harbour, nor virgin bride, her nuptial morn, than Sir George to see the queen, and "kiss the shadowes of her royal feet." He knows not that these royal feet are on the very borders of the *Land of the shadow of Death*. But he delays in order to appoint Sir Charles Wilmot and Sir George Thornton joint Commissioners for the government of the province. He left Cork in February, 1603, remained about three weeks in Dublin, and on the 20th of March sailed for Beaumaris. He arrived in Chester in time to hear the first report of the queen's death. But he cheers up by the time he gets to Litchfield, where he assists the mayor in proclaiming King James, "which gave him new life." Sir George had learned to worship the rising as well as the setting sun. We do not know—nor do we care to inquire, for we are only too happy to drop his acquaintance— how many years he served for his new title of Lord Totnes. So cool and cruel, so cunning and unknightly a ruler never came to Ireland. We have his effigy in the *Pacata Hibernia*—a book written by a man who worshipped him as his Magnus Apollo—and a more sinister countenance we never beheld. We have no objection to adopt the former part of the circumscription—for the words go round the picture—"*Talis erat vultu, sed lingua, mente, manu!*"

END OF VOL. I.

www.ingramcontent.com/pod-product-compliance
Lightning Source LLC
Chambersburg PA
CBHW020540300426
44111CB00008B/737